SPEED SHOPS
Racing EQUIPMENT
GOODIES SPEED SHOPS

OTIE'S AUTOMOTIVE SPECIALTIES
SPEED-POWER & CUSTOM EQUIPMENT
ROAD • TRACK • DRAGS
MACHINE SHOP Service
Custom ENGINES
LERS
DUALS
EQUIPT.
AND
CAMS
J.E. RACING PISTONS
SPEED EQUIPMENT
PERFORMANCE
HI PERFORMANCE CAR SALES

Rod Tyler FORD CO.
MUSTANG CORRAL
Ford
STAMPEDE
ELECTRONIC IGN.
FORD

LA
P
H
DEIST
RADER WHEELS
-AMERICAN PRODUCTS Ltd.
GOODYEAR
GOODYEAR

Bob McClurg

The American SPEED SHOP

Birth and Evolution of Hot Rodding

CarTech®

CarTech®

CarTech®, Inc.
838 Lake Street South
Forest Lake, MN 55025
Phone: 651-277-1200 or 800-551-4754
Fax: 651-277-1203
www.cartechbooks.com

Edit by Bob Wilson
Layout by Chris Fayers

ISBN 978-1-61325-334-2
Item No. CT595

Library of Congress Cataloging-in-Publication Data Available

Written, edited, and designed in the U.S.A.
Printed in China
10 9 8 7 6 5 4 3 2 1

CarTech books may be purchased at a discounted rate in bulk for resale, events, corporate gifts, or educational purposes. Special editions may also be created to specification. For details, contact Special Sales at 838 Lake Street S., Forest Lake, MN 55025 or by email at sales@cartechbooks.com.

All photo restoration by Donny Sarian of Computer Graphics & Photo Restoration in Burbank, California.

DISTRIBUTION BY:

Europe
PGUK
63 Hatton Garden
London EC1N 8LE, England
Phone: 020 7061 1980 • Fax: 020 7242 3725
www.pguk.co.uk

Australia
Renniks Publications Ltd.
3/37-39 Green Street
Banksmeadow, NSW 2109, Australia
Phone: 2 9695 7055 • Fax: 2 9695 7355
www.renniks.com

Canada
Login Canada
300 Saulteaux Crescent
Winnipeg, MB, R3J 3T2 Canada
Phone: 800 665 1148 • Fax: 800 665 0103
www.lb.ca

TABLE OF CONTENTS

DEDICATION

This book is dedicated to the memory of automotive journalist Tom Madigan; to Jack Hart, who took the time to explain to an inquisitive lad of 8 years old (me) what hot rodding actually was all about; Town Barber Shop's Ralph Cornejo, who provided me with all the *Hot Rod* magazines I could possibly read; Marjorie and Victor McClurg, who gave me my first 35-mm camera; Villa Park High School journalism instructor John R. Osborn, who encouraged me to pursue a career in photojournalism; and Lee R. Kelley, my former boss at Petersen Publishing Company who mentored me throughout the years.

Above all, this book is dedicated to the memory of my father, Robert H. S. McClurg, and mother, Gladys L. McClurg, who gave me life and let me live it as I saw fit.

FOREWORD by TOM MADIGAN

Author Bob McClurg and I have been friends for many years. We have both spent most of our adult lives immersed in the world of high performance as journalists, working with various enthusiast magazines, and later as authors producing books.

Although my age shows that I started the journey a few years before Bob, when he asked me to offer the foreword to this book, I was delighted and honored. Once I became involved, I recalled the places and characters I met through the years to try and get a true picture on the subject of speed shops. It seems that I have taken the existence of speed shops always being around for granted.

However, as I began my quest, it was quickly apparent that I was wrong. So, like any investigative reporter, I did some research and uncovered a very interesting history. I then asked Bob if he would consider allowing me to make a few comments on what I had discovered. He not only agreed but also took things one step further. Bob opened the door and suggested that I could put my findings into quotations when appropriate. I therefore unabashedly took advantage of the opportunity to be part of this historic project.

Much of the beginnings of the hot rod and performance scenario had its birth in California. To some, this may not be a reasonable assumption. However, there is more than a grain of truth in my reasoning.

To be fair, history shows that there is another argument as to the beginnings of speed shops: that the need for parts and pieces required by the dirt track and board track racers of the Midwest and East created the concept of a location that would gather racing parts for sale. This is a true and legitimate statement.

From the very beginning, there has always been a gap between the highly specialized technology found at Indianapolis and on European Formula 1 circuits and the budget-constrained, blue-collar racers of the dirt tracks, bull rings, and county fair circuits of Middle America. The common denominator was the unfettered freedom of going as fast as possible.

Even before World War II, the racers on the lake beds were constantly experimenting with new ideas and concepts, which resulted in handmade inventions that helped produce more horsepower. Over time, the number of parts that were developed grew, and as in any consumer-driven business, the demand for those parts spread, which was driven by the needs of those not able to create parts on their own.

Historical accounts provide a rudimentary movement toward business ventures in which custom or handmade parts became available—even if buyers were subjected to finding these creations in the back room of established automotive locations and machine shops where quantities were limited to one or two units at a time. Mainly, the situation became a session of friends from clubs or groups who developed new ideas among themselves. Consequently, developments pretty much stayed secret or at least hidden from view so that others could not copy them. However, that all changed as more and more hot rodders came to the lakes to race.

A romp through history is a good starting point. California, especially Southern California, has always been blessed with a near-perfect climate when it comes to the automotive enthusiasts. The story unfolded during the 1920s as the automobile became more popular with the youth of the country. In those days, when a car was modified, it was not called a hot rod. That term didn't enter the vernacular until after World War II. In the early days, stripped-down Ford Model Ts, Model As, and Chevy 4-bangers were known as jalopies, or go jobs, and oftentimes were named for the class of machine they raced on the lakes: Lakester, Belly Tank, or Modified.

As for the dry lakes used by the racers, there were three major lakes that played a role in our story: Harper, El Mirage, and Muroc (the largest of the three). Muroc was named after the family that established the nearby town. When the Corum family founded the lake, its name was reversed as a namesake for the area. Muroc dry lake had one other significant footnote in history. The lake was raced on from the 1920s until World War II. In 1942, the military took over the lake, forced the racers out (some say by gunpoint), and converted the lake to Edwards Air Force Base, which was home to some of America's greatest aviation accomplishments.

The lakes, as they were known at the time, took up

thousands of square miles of the Mojave Desert in the Antelope Valley and were considered by the racers to be a gift of nature. The beds were formed through the process of winter rains flowing down from the mountains onto miles of hard sand. Then, the natural strong winds that blew in the desert swept the water over the sand at a high pressure and polished the surface into a perfect race course.

Ask any of the old timers what it was like, and they will tell the same story. Racing the lakes gave you the feeling of total freedom and unrestricted space to race as fast as you could without limitations. Aside from freedom, the dry lakes allowed racers to enjoy nearly year-round access [to test and tune]. The more time spent racing, the more innovations and development of new ideas materialized. Slowly, as new parts and pieces were discovered, racers realized that making parts could offer the opportunity to make money by selling to those who didn't have the ability or the conditions to make their own pieces. Could this trend catch on and become a form of commerce?

This story offers the answer. Right or wrong, it was our beginning. Problems that severely restricted the sport's growth in the early days included the long drive to Bonneville, El Mirage, Muroc, and Rosemond dry lakes (which were all far removed from civilization) and only being able to run once or twice a year.

Our nation's streets, boulevards, highways, and byways provided the ideal venue for hot rodders to flex their muscles, albeit illegal in most respects. Like early motorcycling, early hot rodding became an outlaw pastime and would have remained as such had it not been for forward thinkers, such as Wally Parks, C. J. "Pappy" Hart, Ak Miller, Mickey Thompson, Lou Senter, Lou Baney, and countless others.

The arrival of the sport's earliest drag strips (old Santa Ana, Madera, Old Dominion, Inyokern, Presque Isle, etc.) coincided with the publication of the sport's earliest enthusiast magazines (*Hot Rod*, *Car Craft*, and *Rod & Custom* were all founded from 1948 to 1953). The sport of hot rodding became legitimate, and we all know that with the legitimization of any American pastime, big business soon follows.

But, we may be getting ahead of ourselves here. Bob McClurg has spent over three-and-a-half years interviewing subjects, gathering hard-to-find photos, and digging up lesser-known facts to bring you this story, and in some instances, it hasn't always been easy.

— *Tom Madigan*
March 25, 2019 (R.I.P)

ACKNOWLEDGMENTS

Ben Akamine, Alabama Auto Racing Pioneers Hall of Fame; Bob Aubertin, director, Canadian Drag Racing Hall of Fame; Jim Aust; Sam Auxier Jr.; Jacob Bagnell; Cub Barnett; Brandon, Ashley and Frankie Bregel; Andy Brizio; G. K. Callaway; Richard and Joe Campos; Terry Capp; Jesus Christ our Lord and Savior; Jeg Coughlin Jr. and Sr.; Gary Victor Dubin, CEO, Dubin Law Offices, Inc., Honolulu, Hawaii; Denny Duquette; Steve Call, Edelbrock Corporation; David Forseberg; Leon and Darlene Fitzgerald; Denny Forsberg ; Bob Frey; Don and Paul Gallant; Donna Garlits, Don Garlits Museum of Drag Racing/International Drag Racing Hall of Fame; Eric Geisert; Red Greth; Vicki and Michael Hamilton; Chuck Hanson; Drew Hardin; Roger Harrell; Donnie Havers; Joe Hilger; Roy Hill; Guy and Karen Hislop; Ron Hodgson; Bill Holland; Brad Houston; Charles Howard and "Big John" Moore; Jim Inglese; Dave, Brandt, and Bonni Inglis; "TV Tommy" Ivo; "Top Hat John" Jendza; Bob Joenck; Eddie Justice Jr.; Lee and Judy Kelley; D. H. "Dave" Kerr; Jim Kelso; Chico Kodama; Calvin Koga; Rick and Koleen Kopec; Don Krenzer; Jim Lattin; Vincent Liska; Tom and Darlene Madigan; Mike Mantune; Jim McCraw; Jim McFarland; Dave McGaffee; Dave McClelland; J. B. and Brayden Meyer; Don Montgomery; Ron Mosher; Bruce Meyer, photos; Charlie and Liz Overfelt; Cody Parr; Brian Pain; David Paine; Richard Parks; Jerry Pierce; Ed Pink; Don Prieto; Steve, Bethany and Emily Reyes; Dave Rockwell; Dick Roseberry; "Gentleman Joe" and GiGi Carlson-Schubeck; Greg Sharp, curator, Wally Parks NHRA Motorsports Museum; Martyn L. Schorr; Cheri Sealock; Sandy Sloper; Jim Smith; Fred Van Senus; Pete Van Iderstine; Linda Vaughn; Tom and Deb Vogele; Brad Wallace; Dave Wallace Jr.; Rich Welch; Ed Weichsler; Wayne Wolfe; Bruce and Koleen Wheeler; and Alex Xydias.

CHAPTER 1

BIRTH OF A SEEDLING INDUSTRY

Automotive industrialist Henry Ford said that auto racing began 5 minutes after the second car was built. Early on, Ford proved his point numerous times not only in competition with his fellow auto manufacturers but also against the clock. Against Alexander Winton, Ford recorded 72 mph with his 538-ci twin-cylinder race car known as *Sweepstakes* on October 10, 1901, at the Detroit Driving Club course in Grosse Point, Michigan. Against the clock, Ford produced a chilling solo run of 91.37 mph in the *999* race car on October 12, 1904, in Lake St. Clair, Michigan. Motor racing indeed sold product and, more importantly, attracted publicity and investors.

Of course, racing was nothing new. Its roots trace back as far as 27 B.C. and the days of the Roman gladiators and their chariots. After centuries of relying on genuine horse power, the 19th-century invention known as the internal combustion engine universally unseated the horse as mankind's primary mode of transportation and power.

The first domestically promoted automobile race on record was the *Chicago Times-Herald* race won by Frank F. Duryea on November 28, 1895. However, the sport of motor racing (if you could call it that in those halcyon days) didn't find its legs until the dawn of the 20th century with events that include the Vanderbilt Cup in 1904, the New York-to-Paris enduro in 1908, and, of course, the granddaddy of all domestic automobile events, the inaugural Indianapolis 500 in 1911. These events were primarily for the wealthy, which left the common man standing at the rail (many of auto racing's earliest venues were converted horse tracks), choking in a cloud of dust and oil smoke. The earliest race cars were either hand built in well-equipped machine shops or they were blueprinted versions of big, expensive, and powerful production cars from Mercedes, Daimler, Rolls-Royce, Packard, Marmon, and Thomas, which all plied for the attention of the country's emerging motoring elite.

Had it not been for Ford's introduction of his beloved Model T on October 1, 1908, auto racing in its various

To celebrate Ford Motor Company's 100th anniversary, this photo of founder Henry Ford racing Alexander Winton on October 10, 1901, at Grosse Point, Michigan, was widely circulated. Ford's 538-ci 2-cylinder monster named Sweepstakes *produced a top-end speed of 72 mph.*

forms may have remained a sport of the affluent forever. Priced at an af-*Ford*-able $850 and powered by a 77-ci flathead four with 4:1 compression, Ford's Model T was rated at 20 hp and registered 83 ft-lbs of torque. The Model T, also known as a Tin Lizzie, weighed a mere 1,450 pounds in its first year and was capable of a top speed of 45 mph.

Lithe and quick, Ford's universal car was also as durable as an anvil with its vanadium steel ladder type of chassis and buggy spring suspension, but we doubt that it was ever intended to be a race car—or was it? Once the Ford Model T was stripped down, it became America's first hot rod. For example, from June 1 to June 23, 1908, Bert Scott and C. J. Smith won the New York-to-Seattle race in a stripped-down 1908 Model T (undoubtedly one of the first if not the first Model T speedster on record), but they were later disqualified for changing a broken axle. Nonetheless, Henry Ford was there at the finish to congratulate them.

In 1908, Henry Ford's little Model T established itself as a cross-country endurance racer when it competed in and won the New York-to-Seattle race carrying drivers Bert Scott and C. J. Smith across the finish line to victory. Unfortunately, the team was disqualified because they stopped to replace a broken axle. Henry Ford nonetheless thought well enough of their effort to be there to congratulate them. (Photo Courtesy Henry Ford Collection, Ford Motor Company)

Model T Mayhem

The timeworn credo that the Model T was "the car that put America on wheels" is a given, but Henry's Flivver also spurred a whole new automotive accessory industry. This new industry was lucrative enough for large-volume retailers like Sears-Roebuck & Company and Montgomery Ward to catalog Model T items by the hundreds, including side curtains, mud flaps, rear window defoggers, Boyce MottoMeters, dress-up kits, accessory pickup truck beds, camping tents, luggage racks, brake upgrade kits, Paragon disc wheels, Ruckstell 2-speed rear axles, Pullford tractor conversions, and snow plows. You name it, somebody was producing it for the Ford Model T. That especially rang true when it came to engine accessories, which had a two-fold development and purpose.

First, cars were becoming faster, more sophisticated, and more expensive. So, to keep up with the Joneses, the Ford Model T naturally availed itself to modification by corner garages, backyard tinkerers and shade-tree mechanics who looked to add a little oomph to their antiquated T or TT 4-banger engines without having to sell the farm to do so.

Second, With the cessation of World War I, circle track racing became popular again. Being that Model Ts were cheap and plentiful (15 million were produced), racing one was economically feasible for the aspiring American hot rodder. Highly modified versions of Henry's beloved T could be found setting records at dirt and board tracks all across the country.

Weekly features took place at venues such as Indianapolis, Indiana; Chicago, Illinois; Winchester, Indiana; Toledo, Ohio; Franklin, Nebraska; Detroit, Michigan; Hammond, Indiana; Milwaukee, Wisconsin; St. Paul, Minnesota; Cedar Rapids, Iowa; Louisville, Kentucky; Uniontown, Pennsylvania; Ventura, California; Corona, California; Los Angeles, California; Phoenix, Arizona; and Saskatoon, Alberta, Canada.

In some cases, all-Ford features occurred, where round track stars, such as Wilbur Shaw, Dick Calhoun, George Davidson, Ralph Ormsby, Les Allen, Noel Bullock, Dutch Baumann, Frank Kulick, L. L. Corum, and Fred Frame,

With the October 1, 1908, birth of the Ford Model T, garages like this (many of which had previously been blacksmith shops engaged in the carriage trade) sprang up all across the nation. To establish themselves in this new era, these dealerships sold and installed a myriad of aftermarket products that were specifically designed for the Ford Model T.

won races and set records. Not only was this the birth of affordable racing in this country but it was also the birth of the speed equipment industry, which is equally (if not more) important.

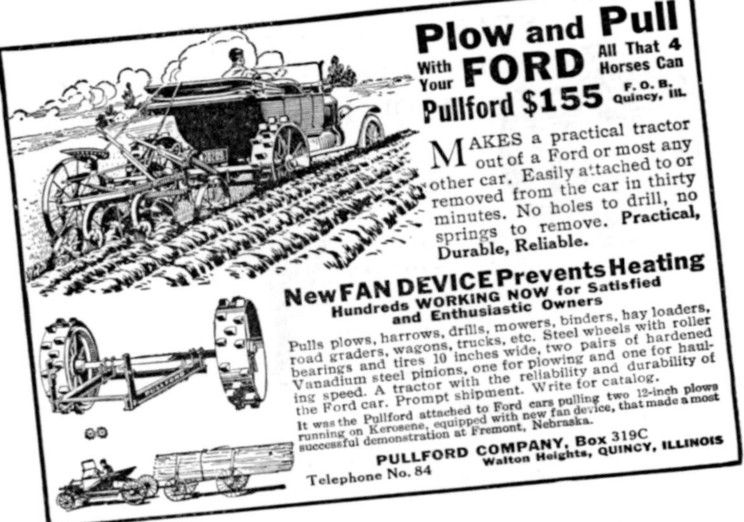

Many aftermarket products were available. For example, the Pullford tractor conversions produced in Quincy, Illinois, allowed Model T owners to convert their Flivvers into farm tractors in short order. When Henry Ford debuted his Fordson tractor in 1917, the Pullford was put out to pasture with all the other obsolete farm equipment.

Holley and Winfield

George M. Holley of Holley Motorette fame—a future carburetor king and former motorized bicycle racer (1901) and horseless carriage manufacturer (1902 to 1906)—was one of the first automotive aftermarket manufacturers to patent a carburetor application for the Model T at Henry Ford's behest in 1908 and 1911.

In 1914, the Holley Brothers Company (George and his brother Earl), also known as the Holley Carburetor Company, introduced its Holley Manifold Replacement for the Ford Model T. According to a Holley sales brochure, the manifold was designed to enhance vaporization of the low-grade gasolines of the era and provide more power, smoother operation, and a "quicker get-away."

Self-taught mechanical genius Ed Winfield, also known as the Father of Hot Rodding, had a long and storied history with the Ford Model T. It began for Winfield at age 11 in 1912, when he stripped the body off the family's 2-year-old Model T (while his mother was away visiting friends) and was able to achieve a top speed 65 mph!

In 1919, Winfield hand built his first carburetor and ground his first camshaft for the Ford Model T. In 1924, he set the record for the World's Fastest Ford while driving the *Kant-Shore Piston Special* equipped with his infamous "two up, two down" Winfield-equipped Model T Ford engine. That same year, Ed and his younger brother Bud founded the Winfield Carburetor Company, and its official slogan was "Winner of the Field."

Throughout the mid-1920s and early 1930s, the Winfields made numerous carburetor models for specific applications. There was the H&V series (horizontal and vertical), the updraft M series, and the downdraft S and SR series. Best suited for the Model T was the Winfield M201A updraft carburetor for 1909 to 1927 T and TT engines. When mated to a Winfield Accessory Intake Manifold, it made a great aftermarket induction system for Henry's beloved Flivver.

Model T Cylinder Head Improvements

Of course, next to tweaking a T's induction system, improving on the original L-head (flathead) cylinder head proved to be the most advantageous. This was done by milling the OEM cylinder head, which lowered combustion chamber volume yet simultaneously increased the compression ratio and produced more power.

For example, take a stock 1908 to 1910 Model T cylinder head. Its combustion chamber volume measures 262 cc (16.0 ci per cylinder) with a corrected number of 14.0 ci at 4.2 pounds of compression. By milling that same cylinder head 0.125 inch, chamber volume is reduced to 257 cc

ADVANTAGES
OF THE
New York
VIBRATOR-LES
Coil Ignition

THE PRESENT TIMER, and half the wiring is eliminated.

STARTING IS CERTAIN and astonishingly easy even in the coldest of weather.

IT ENABLES CAR to be driven through dense traffic at a snail's pace and instantly accelerate with a smoothness and power that you never believed possible.

ENTIRE ABSENCE of sticking contact points, vibrator adjustments, coil replacements, and all ignition trouble.

THE DEVICE is throughly heat and waterproof, and is sold with a money back guarantee by a firm building ignition apparatus for the past fifteen years.

PRICE COMPLETE AS DESCRIBED **$20.00**

NEW YORK COIL COMPANY
338-340 PEARL STREET, NEW YORK

Mid-West Distributors
GRAY-HEATH CO., 1440 Michigan Ave., Chicago

NEW YORK
Vibrator-Les Coil
IGNITION FOR FORDS

The New York Vibrator-Less Coil Ignition for Fords allowed the owner/installer to discard the OEM Model T Ford coil and box and replace it with four self-adjusting vibrating coils, which also eliminated the need for an ignition timer. This setup guaranteed an easy start-up and operation in all types of weather, was 100 percent heat and waterproof, and retailed for $20.

The Ustus Limousette for Fords was offered for Model T touring car owners and roadster owners alike. Easy to install, Ustus Limousette side curtains provided safety and comfort for Ford Owners at $49.75 for touring and $33.25 for the roadster.

At Last!
A GASOLINE GAUGE
for the
FORD INSTRUMENT BOARD

$3.75
Complete

The Mark Anton Manufacturing Company, Inc. of Bellville, New Jersey, took the guesswork out of wondering if the Model T owner had sufficient fuel on hand with its gasoline gauge for the Ford instrument board. This easy-to-install gauge retailed for $3.75, was simple to install, and was even simpler to read with its glass-faced cross-section gauge.

The Uni-Coil Ignition System on Model T Ford Cars eliminated the need for that pesky original ignition system. It was easy to install using the easy-to-read directions.

DIRECTIONS FOR INSTALLING AND USING THE
Uni-Coil Ignition System
ON MODEL "T" FORD CARS

First disconnect the spark plug cables and remove spark plug No. 1 (by No. 1 we mean the plug next to radiator). Lay it on the engine with the cable connected to the coil and have spark lever on steering post all the way forward or in the retarded position. Turn engine carefully until spark takes place at No. 1 plug. Be very careful to stop engine the instant the coil begins to vibrate. This method is a simple way of ascertaining the proper firing position for those not skilled in timing the motor.

The timer is next removed and by taking off the nut and prying off the small collar, a pin will be found which is pushed or driven out and then by means of a screw driver, the part carrying roller and spring of your timer can be pried off the shaft. The loose gear accompanying our bracket is slipped on time shaft, the same pin and collar being used to fasten the gear to shaft. The nut should be tightened securely.

The bolt located directly under oil filler, which holds end plate to crank case is removed, as is likewise the bolt on opposite side. Our bracket is then placed in position having first loosened up bolt that tightens the fan belt. See that the bracket fits inside central turned out surface of end plate, and by means of two longer bolts we furnish secure

In 1914, the Holley Carburetor Company published this leaflet touting the Holley manifold replacement for the Ford Model T, which enhanced fuel vaporization and was one of the automotive aftermarket's first power enhancers.

Mechanical genius Ed Winfield and his brother Bud released a series of aftermarket carburetors and camshafts for vintage Fords. This photo shows Winfield behind the wheel of his "two up, two down" Model T–based Kant-Shore Piston Special *race car that was billed as the* World's Fastest Ford. *(Author Collection)*

(13.6 ci per cylinder), yielding a corrected compression ratio of 4.6 psi. The result is a slight improvement in performance for increased workloads and day-to-day driving. However, when it came to measurable performance gains, bolting on an aftermarket Model T cylinder head provided the desired increase in usable hp.

Waukesha-Ricardo

British engineer Sir Harry Ralph Ricardo is credited as being the father of the Waukesha-Ricardo Model T cylinder head, which was patented on November 11, 1923, by the Waukesha Motor Company based in Waukesha, Wisconsin. Variants include the Hein-Werner-Ricardo T-Head.

Sir Harry was one of the movers and shakers behind establishing octane ratings for fuels. He was also the co-designer of the sleeve-valve engine, which was popularized in America by Charles Knight from Willys-Knight motorcar fame.

Ricardo is also touted for his swirl chamber combustion design research for diesel engines. The Waukesha Motor Company–licensed Ricardo (W-R) head featured a 272-cc combustion chamber and a corrected cylinder head volume of 14.6 ci. It also boasted significant power increases of roughly 12 to 20 percent over a stock Model T 4-banger with improved torque at only a small increase in compression (a 4.0 to 4.2 ratio stock and 4.3 to 4.5 modified). These factors made the W-R an attractive purchase for those looking to increase power in their Model Ts.

Model T aftermarket cylinder heads that were similar to the W-R included Haibe, H-Power, Green Engineering, Reeder, Giant Power, Sherman Super Fire, and Simmons Super Power.

D. R. Noonan OHV Cylinder Head

When it comes to improving on the conventional Ford L-head 4-cylinder design, overhead valve (OHV) designs, such as D. R. Noonan, Craig-Hunt, Roof, Rajo, Frontenac, and others, were considered to be state of the art for their time and vaulted the Model T to the head of the pack when it came to performance. One of the earliest yet least known of the Model T OHV cylinder heads was created by D. R. Noonan of Paris, Illinois, who was a Model T cam grinder. In 1917, he advertised an 8-valve OHV cylinder head for the Model T.

The D. R. Noonan OHV cylinder head was developed at Noonan's well-established automotive machine shop that not only produced camshafts for Model T but also specialized in block preparation and rotating assemblies. However, due to the intensive machining process in the building of a Noonan head, it's doubtful that many of these 8-valve OHV heads were ever really sold to the general public.

Nonetheless, Noonan practiced what he preached, fielding the *Noonan Overland Special* dirt track racer (car #10) driven to victory by Benny Shoaff, Glen Fites, and Doc Roberts at venues located around the Midwest.

W. L. Hunt/Craig-Hunt

The W. L. Hunt/Craig-Hunt single overhead cam (SOHC) 16-valve cylinder heads (there were three) for the Ford Model T were advertised as "Making the Ford Fleet Footed—100 Miles per Hour in a Ford!"

First was the W. L. Hunt-16, a 16-valve, twin-plug, SOHC cylinder head that came out in February 1916. Introduced as "a Peugeot Racing type head for Fords," the timed cam lobes manually pinned to the camshaft were fully exposed and archaically hand lubricated. This camshaft rode on conventional shell-type bearings and was driven by a roller chain extending from the cam sprocket to the crankshaft. Intake and exhaust valves measured 1.5 inches in diameter and were set at 20 degrees. The recommended compression ratio for the W. L. Hunt-16 Model T cylinder head was 5:1.

The second variant of this design was known as the Craig-Hunt SOHC cylinder head, which featured a fully assembled camshaft that rode on ball bearings. Lubrication was handled by a cam-driven oil pump that sent a constant supply of oil to the cam lobes. A three-piece-aluminum rocker cover kept the system fully contained.

The third Craig-Hunt OHV cammer head variant

featured the same mechanical attributes as its predecessors but employed vertical shaft drive with beveled gears. Upgrades also included a gear-driven centrifugal water pump and an Eisemann magneto.

In closing, note that by 1919 to 1920, Craig-Hunt SOHC cylinder heads for the Model T 4-banger were sold exclusively by Speedway Engineering Company (not to be confused with Speedway Motors, the current speed equipment retailer in Lincoln, Nebraska) at 910 N. Illinois St., Indianapolis, Indiana, which arguably may have been the first speed shop on record. Although, the term *speed shop* was light years away from being coined.

Roof 16 Cylinder Head

In 1917, automotive engineer and race car driver Robert M. Roof had a chance meeting with Henry Ford at a race in Michigan. Roof came away with the inspiration to build the Roof 16-valve (Type A) cylinder head for Model T racing cars.

A Roof advertisement stated, "With a gain of (up to) 75 to 85 mph, Fords go like a shot out of a gun when equipped with Roof's Peugeot-type cylinder heads!" Roof's Type A head was offered for $95 as a bolt-on kit that included the cylinder head, rocker-arm assemblies, pushrods, 1.5-inch-diameter intake and exhaust valves, spacers, and gaskets. The head produced an advertised 36 to 42 hp depending on the compression ratio and camshaft. It should be noted that Roof's early-production Type A cylinder heads succumbed to rocker-arm failure and exhibited a propensity to leak. However, with the teething problems ultimately fixed, the Roof Type A OHV Model T cylinder head became wildly popular.

Later that year, Roof released the Type B general purpose (16-valve) OHV head with 1.25-inch-diameter intake and exhaust valves and an improved rocker-arm design. When used with a Ford Model T camshaft and Ford's standard 4:1 compression ratio, the Type B head produced 32 hp. The Type B head was followed by the Roof Type C 16-valve cylinder head in 1923, which was essentially an improved version of the Type B head. At the 1926 Indianapolis 500, Frank Lockhart drove a Roof-equipped Ford to victory.

But why the inference to Peugeot? A good guess is that manufacturers W. L. Hunt and Roof were paying homage to Peugeot, the European patented holder of the first four-valve OHV cylinder head design that made headlines worldwide when it set a world record at 170 kph at Brooklands April 1913. Buick Motors held the US patent rights on the OHV design stateside, so it was quite possible that this was done to avoid potential patent infringement litigation by either or both parties.

Rajo

In 1919, retired circle track racer Joe Jagersberger doubled the performance of the Model T 4-banger with the release of three application-specific Rajo cylinder heads through his firm, Rajo Manufacturing. In the name *Rajo*, the letters *Ra* stood for Racine, Wisconsin, and *jo* stood for the first two letters of the first name of its creator. Trindl Sales Corporation at 61 E. 24th St., Chicago, Illinois, was the exclusive distributor.

First was the Rajo eight-valve Model 30-4 OHV street head that featured four exhaust ports and one intake port on the right-hand side of the head. This particular head sold for a whopping $57.75.

Next was the 1920 release of the improved Model 31-2 Rajo head, which retailed for $78.75 and again featured four exhaust ports on the left and one intake port on the right. This particular head design won the famed AAA-sanctioned 1922 Pikes Peak Hill Climb with driver Noel F. Bullock and his Rajo-Ford-powered *Junkyard Special*.

The last head was released in 1924. The Rajo Model 35-C (also known as the improved Rajo valve-in-head and later as the Model C) featured two intake ports and three exhaust ports on the right side of the head. It was during this time that future Ford flathead speed equipment designer Eddie Meyer raced a Rajo-equipped Ford Model T with great success. Also in 1924, Jagersberger and com-

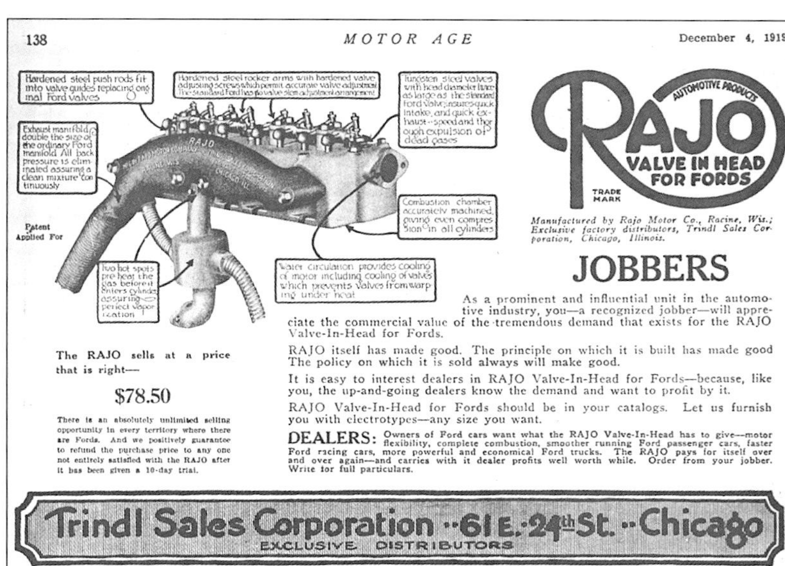

The interesting thing about this Rajo Motor Company advertisement (Motor Age, December 1919) advertising its valve-in-head, or overhead valve, aftermarket conversion for Model T Fords is that it advertises for jobbers and dealers. Trindl Sales Corporation of Chicago, Illinois, was the exclusive warehouse distributor (WD) for the product. (The WD network is covered in chapter 4.)

pany also produced a Rajo dual overhead cam (DOHC) cylinder head for Model T and TT. However, the design was sold to Jack Gallivan shortly after its public debut. Gallivan marketed the product as the Gallivan DOHC, and he experienced a reasonable degree of success with this head, building up a $3\frac{7}{8}$-inch bore x $2\frac{1}{8}$-inch stroke, 200-ci Model T 4-banger that was dyno tested at 175 hp.

In 1926, Rajo Joe redesigned this head and called it the DOHC Rajo, and circle track racer Russell Trudell raced one with reasonable success.

Frontenac

Frontenac OHV cylinder heads for the Ford Model S and Model T were undoubtedly the most popular OHV Model T cylinder heads. They were designed by engineer C. W. Van Ranst for the Chevrolet brothers (Louis, Arthur, and Gaston) between 1920 and 1921. According to a February 1927 Chevrolet Brothers Manufacturing Company sales brochure, three OHV Frontenac Model T cylinder heads were readily available:

• Model T Frontenac cylinder head for Ford commercial and pleasure cars
• Model R: 8-plug, single-carbureted; for racing cars only ($100)
• Model S-R: 16-spark plug, twin Zenith-carbureted, SOHC; for racing cars only ($130 to $215)

Distinguishing differences between the first two models were intake and exhaust valve sizes, port volume, and compression ratio. When it came to the Model S-R, the obvious difference was the SOHC design and the number of spark plugs. Optional equipment available for Fronty Fords included aluminum pistons, twin American-Zenith carburetors, and specially designed intake and exhaust manifolds. The Street (S) head was $98.75, the Model R head was $100, and the Model S-R head ranged from $130 to $215 based on the options ordered.

Creditable test data from back in the day was about as rare as hen's teeth. However, the Chevrolet brothers dyno tested a stock Model T 4-banger engine at the Purdue University engineering labs and realized 17 hp. Using the same Model T engine, they installed a 6:1-compression Frontenac Model T Street head and realized a 90-percent increase in power (33 hp) while reducing engine vibration with noticeably cooler operating temperatures. When it came to touting Frontenac's Model Rs and Model S-Rs in competition, the Chevrolet brothers favored actual trackside performance data to lab-test data.

Between September 1921 and October 1923, Model R Fronty Fords set world speed records and race averages at Warren, Indiana; Indianapolis, Indiana; and Uniontown, Pennsylvania. Furthermore, in July 1923, Model S-R Frontys set track records at both the Indianapolis Hoo-sier Speedway and Ventura Speedway half-mile tracks. Of all the Fronty Fords that set records and won races (and there were many), one of the most noteworthy was the Model S-R that Gaston Chevrolet drove to win the 1920 Indianapolis 500 with a trophy-winning speed of 88.618 mph. Another glowing Fronty Ford endorsement from the era, although it was unofficial, occurred on May 30, 1923, when Henry Ford posed behind the wheel of the Barbour-Warnock Fronty Ford Model S-R racer at the Indianapolis 500. The car qualified fifth at 86.92 mph and finished in fifth place, which was ahead of the factory Mercedes and Bugatti drivers, who recorded an average lap time of 82.58 mph.

Fronty Model D-O

Considered to be a forerunner to the famed Offenhauser Indianapolis 500 champion car engine, the Frontenac D-O dual overhead cam (DOHC) 16-valve cylinder head of 1923 was built to satisfy the ever-increasing need for speed on the circle track racing circuit. Manufactured from gray iron and fully machined, the water-jacketed cylinder head featured valves that measured $1\frac{9}{16}$ x $3\frac{1}{4}$ inches and were set into the cylinder head at 30 degrees with removable valve stem guides.

The D-O also utilized specially wound valve springs and custom seats and keepers. Tappets were held in place with lock nuts. Two force-fed lubricated mechanical camshafts were timed by a silent chain that was $1\frac{1}{4}$-inches wide and kept proper tension via a patented idler. The oil-fed cams and valvetrain were housed in twin-hump

Gaston Chevrolet proudly poses behind the wheel of his Fronty Ford-engine racer that had just captured the trophy at the 1920 Indianapolis 500 and registered a lap average at 88.618 mph. (Photo Courtesy Indianapolis Motor Speedway Archives)

After its fifth place finish at the 1923 Indianapolis 500, the Chevrolet Brothers from Indianapolis, Indiana, took out advertisements touting the Power, Speed, Flexibility, and Economy of their OHV Frontenac cylinder head for Fords.

closest in one of their late 1920s-era catalogs by using the label *speed specialties*.

From all indications, the speed equipment industry, which in its infancy seemed to be solely relegated to the wholesale manufacturing of Ford-related drivetrain parts, appeared to be here to stay. Some may ask, "With approximately 35 domestic auto manufactures in the US by 1925, why not make speed equipment for other makes of engines?" Due to less popularity and affordability, any speed equipment manufactured outside of the Ford realm was generally limited production or handmade in onesie or twosie fashion. The exception was early Chevrolet 4-banger products. It wasn't until the late 1940s

In 1928, the Chevrolet brothers got the closest to using the term speed equipment *when publishing their February 1927 catalog using the words* speed specialties *to describe their Model T Ford–based race car product line.*

aluminum cam covers. The 16 spark plugs were located at TDC. Intake and exhaust ports measured $1^5/_8$ inches in diameter. Measured compression was 12:1.

These cylinder heads were quite pricey when compared to the Frontenac S, R, and S-R models, listing for $500 without the exhaust manifold, intake manifold, and Zenith carburetor. With those speed parts included, the price was $600. However, they more than made up for the cost with performance, as a Fronty D-O was capable of 110-mph terminal speeds. A. Davidson's Model D-O Fronty Ford won the National Ford Championship on October 21, 1923, at Chicago Speedway.

Inching Closer to Retail

The Chevrolet brothers, Hunt/Speedway, Root, Rajo, and others offered everything from singular components to complete Model T–based race cars, but they weren't referred to as *speed shops*. The Chevrolet brothers got the

Henry Ford was so pleased with the performance of the fifth-place-finishing Barbour-Warnock Fronty Ford race car that he posed behind the wheel for this post-race publicity photo. (Photo Courtesy Indianapolis Motor Speedway Archives)

that speed equipment manufacturers designed, manufactured, and mass marketed speed equipment for other popular engine makes on a large scale.

"A" Certainly a Good Place to Begin Again

Alphabetically speaking, Ford repeated history with its October 28, 1927, introduction of the 1928 Model A. In reality, the Model A was more Edsel Ford's baby than it was Henry's. History cites that the elder Ford would have stubbornly gone on manufacturing the Model T indefinitely had it not been for Edsel. Ford may have dominated the automotive sales market from the get-go, but by the mid-1920s, Chevrolet, Hudson, Buick, Dodge, and other nameplates were seriously encroaching on the outskirts of what had previously been taken for granted as Ford Country.

The Ford Model A was referred to by many as a *Baby Lincoln* because styling cues were taken from 1928 Lincoln production cars. The new Model A recaptured the hearts of the American motorist and was available in more than 25 bodystyles. Moreover, it featured three pedal driving controls, which had become a standard in the industry, a non-synchromesh toploader 3-speed manual transmission, an electric starter, a cowl-mounted gravity-flow fuel tank that did not require a fuel pump and was also deemed far safer than one hanging over the back wheels, and front windshield safety glass.

The Model A's valve-in-block 201-ci 4-cylinder engine (3.875-inch bore x 4.250-inch stroke) produced 40 hp at 2,400 rpm, which was twice as much as that of the Model T. It also delivered a whopping 128 ft-lbs of torque, which was 45 more than its predecessor, and was capable of terminal speeds up to 65 mph. The Model A's L cylinder head (part number A60508A) came with a wedge-shape combustion chamber that was between 142 and 148 cc's and sported a published compression ratio of 4.22:1.

The Model AA came with a higher-compression-version L head (5.5:1) for handling extreme payloads; it weighed 65 pounds. In 1931, Ford released its Police Head (part number A-6050-B), which featured a heart-shaped combustion chamber between 178 and 184 cc and had a published compression ratio of 5.22:1. The Model A induction system consisted of a single-barrel Zenith updraft Ford carburetor that was good enough for the average motorist but not for the aspiring hot rodder especially because Chevrolet, Chrysler, and other competing brands hit the ground running with larger-displacement 4-cylinder and 6-cylinder L head and OHV engines.

Model A Speed Equipment

Like the Ford Model T, performance enthusiasts were (for a brief moment in time) content to mill down a stock Model A cylinder head 0.100 to 0.125 inch to obtain a little more compression, while others bolted on the 1931 Model A Police head, 1932 Model B head, or 1933 Model C head. However, all three of those upgrades made use of stock Ford parts, and we're talking about speed equipment here.

Winfield: Yellow and Red

One of the first aftermarket cylinder heads for the Model A bore the highly respected Winfield name and was sold directly through Winfield's Glendale, California, shop or through a small network of Winfield retailers. A number of Winfield cylinder-head configurations were manufactured for the Model A, and two of the most popular were the Yellow head and the Red head.

The Yellow, or #6, cylinder head featured a 6:1–compression, crowfoot combustion chamber and utilized an 18-mm spark plug. This head was primarily used in street applications, and when it was combined with a Winfield cam, carburetor, and aftermarket intake, the hp doubled and made the A Bone run like Jack the bear.

The Red, or #7, cylinder head featured the same crowfoot combustion chamber design (albeit at 7:1 compression) and also utilized an 18-mm spark plug. When partnered with a set of flat-top pistons, a hot Winfield cam,

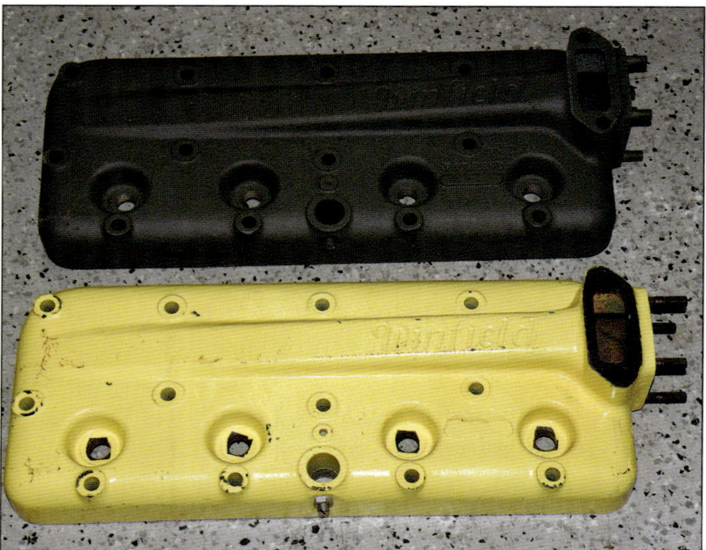

When it came to revving up the Ford Model A, Ed Winfield, came out swinging with his 6:1-compression Yellow and 7:1-compression Red cylinder heads. In this photo, the Red cylinder head is painted Model A green, which transformed Henry's Lady into an absolute brawler when partnered up with a Winfield-grind camshaft.

a Winfield- or Stromberg-carbureted single or dual after-market intake, and custom exhaust, a Winfield-equipped A banger was capable of close to 100-plus hp, which at the time was nothing to sneeze at.

Miller-Schofield and Friends

Famed Indianapolis 500 winner Harry A. Miller was a pioneer of early Ford speed equipment. Miller, together with financier George L. Schofield and engineer/designer Leo Gossen, designed a trio of aftermarket cylinder heads for the Ford Model A and Model B. These included a 6:1–compression flathead design that enjoyed moderate success, a 6.5:1 high-compression OHV design known as the Miller-Schofield OHV that enjoyed immense popularity and sales, and the extremely rare and costly Miller-Schofield DOHC cylinder head design that performed exceptionally well. However, with only three Miller-Schofield DOHC cylinder heads built, it was more of an engineering prototype than anything else.

Act I: Miller-Schofield OHV Simplicity in design and adaptability were the Miller-Schofield OHV's chief calling cards. With intake and exhaust valves at 1.92 inches (as opposed to 1.50 inches) relocated from the engine block to the cylinder head and actuated by a set of Buick rocker arms, airflow was freer and more direct to the 6.5:1–compression combustion chambers. The Model A and Model B engine was capable of 86 hp at 3,200 rpm when using a set of flat-top pistons, an aftermarket intake manifold (Winfield or Bell), and fueled by a Winfield or Stromberg 1-barrel carburetor. Unfortunately, product introduction was poorly timed, as the Great Depression caused the company to shutter its doors. However, that is not the end of this story.

Act II: Cragar OHV In mid-1930, well-known board track racer Harlan Fengler teamed with financier/publishing company magnate Crane Garts of Crane Publishing Company, purchased Miller-Schofield's assets, and began producing the Miller-Schofield OHV cylinder head. The company was renamed *Cragar* by borrowing the first three letters of Crane's first and last name. All of the original M-S patterns and tooling were used, and the newly christened Cragar OHV looked good on paper. However, the Great Depression once again forced the short-lived enterprise into bankruptcy in 1932.

Act III: The Wight Knight Comes to the Rescue In spite of the Great Depression, George Wight's Bell Auto Parts remained a solvent and growing business. The company sold remanufactured Model T parts to the racing establishment, which was not an easy thing to do, while methodically adding products of its own manufacture under the Bell Auto Parts brand, including intake and exhaust manifolds, valve covers, side plates, and ignition system components.

With the folding of F & G, Wight purchased the company's assets lock, stock, and barrel in 1933 and brought the Cragar name under the Bell Auto Parts corporate umbrella. This was the first instance of a speed shop manufacturing and retailing its own in-house product line (or lines) of speed equipment from valve cover to oil pan dedicated to a specific make. Under the guidance of Wight's successor Roy Richter, the Cragar name went on to become a corporate entity in its own right and it continues to be a major player in the automotive aftermarket to this very day.

George Wight stands in front of the newly lettered "CRAGAR" front window at Bell Auto Parts. Wight saved the Cragar OHV conversion for the Ford Model A when he purchased the manufacturing and distribution rights from Crane Garts, who had previously purchased manufacturing rights from original manufacturer Miller-Schofield. (Photo Courtesy Greg Sharp Collection)

This is a surviving example of a Cragar OHV–equipped 1930 Model A Ford engine equipped with a four-tube header and Winfield S-R carburetor.

Rajo for the Model A

Upon the Model A's release, Joe Jagersberger refined his OHV Model T setup and made adaptable improvements to the Model A. The most notable improvement was the inclusion of a *RAJO*-script, cast-aluminum valve cover and felt valve cover gasket that effectively addressed the T-banger's most glaring complaint: oil leakage.

Other key players in the Model A Ford speed equipment segment included Riley and Roof as well as lesser-known brands, such as Cook, Christie, Duray, Evans, Fargo, Miller, Rutherford, Schebler, Simmons, Sparks, Wheeler, and Weiand. To find pristine examples of any Model A Ford speed parts today is akin to finding the Holy Grail. It all depends on how badly you want them and how much time and money with which you're willing to part.

Rajo's valve-in-head setup for the Model A Ford mirrored the company's Model T version albeit upgraded with an aluminum valve cover to prevent oil spillage.

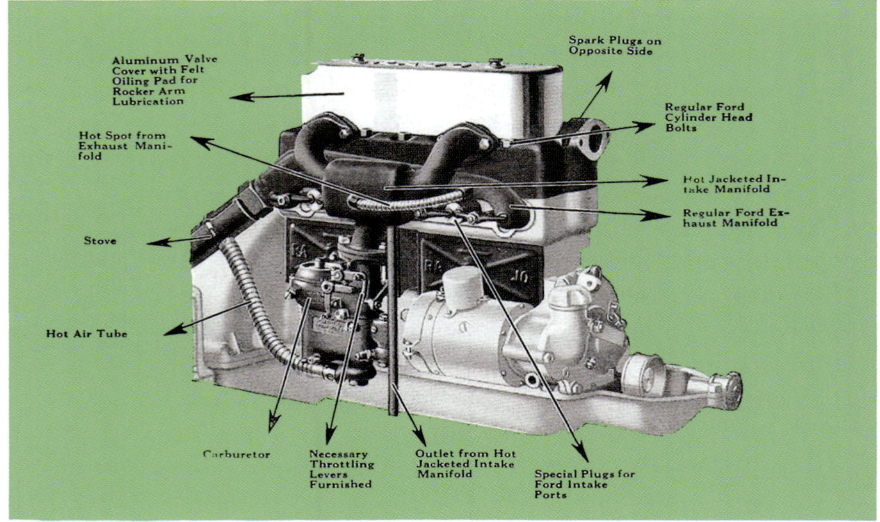

The Improved Model A Rajo Valve-in-Head
Improved Power, Flexibility and Speed

The Wizard of Model A Speed Equipment

Ron Mosher, a Model A hard-core parts collector from Newhall, California, is known as the "Wizard of Model A Speed Equipment" for good reason.

"I've been playing with Model As and cars in general ever since I was 14 years old," Ron said. "I've drag raced them. I've hill climbed them. I've toured them and raced them at the Bonneville Salt Flats. Throughout the course of this, I've belonged to a number of clubs, including the San Fernando Valley Model A Club, the Model A Ford Club of America, the Super Ford Club, which is one of the Southern California Timing Association (SCTA) clubs [membership is required to run at both Bonneville and El Mirage], and I also belong to the Four Ever Four Cylinder club [established in 1954], which is actively involved in racing of all kinds."

After moving West in 1960 to beautiful downtown Burbank, California, Ron was immediately immersed in the hot rod culture and did a lot of street racing and drag racing at the early drag strips, including Lions and San Fernando.

"When it comes to Model As, I've always worked on original cars, including the blue-ribbon cars, where every nut and bolt in a restoration is technically correct," he said. "In fact, I ran the Judging Standards Committee for the

Model A and Model B Ford expert Ron Mosher stands outside his shop located in Newhall, California. If you're into hard-core Model A and Model B speed equipment, this is the place to go.

Model A Ford Club of America for six years. Our committee revised and updated the standards that are used for the judging of all Model A Ford show cars."

For 13 years, Ron and his wife, Carol, also managed, edited, and published Ford A Speed Technology (F.A.S.T.)

Ron's shop is Model A and Model B speed equipment heaven. He has virtually every brand-name manufacturer of vintage and reproduction Model A Ford L-head and OHV cylinder heads in stock. Ron also stocks a limited supply of Model T speed parts; and yes, they are for sale.

This Evans Model A cylinder head was also on the shelf, sitting alongside examples of Winfield Red, and Winfield Yellow Ford Model A cylinder heads.

Ron shows us a Hi-Turb (high turbulence) cylinder head for the Ford Model A.

Ron also stocks this Simmons Super Power Head for the Ford Model A.

magazine, which is devoted to Model A and Model B Ford technology and anything before 1934 US 4-cylinder production.

With a background like that, Ron is knee deep in Model A and B (and Model T to some extent) speed parts.

"I was at an event in Reno, Nevada, and was on a tour when I got passed by a Model A Tudor sedan," he said. "The car had a slopeside Miller head, and it belonged to Jim Brierley, who is considered sort of the unofficial godfather of 4-cylinder Ford stuff. I got hooked up with him to the point where not only did I join all the clubs but we also became racing partners and set a trio of land speed records with a Model B engine belly tank.

"We were also involved in putting on the Antique Nationals, which has been at many of the old/new drag strips in Southern California. This event began in the early 1970s and is going strong 50 years later."

With Ron's indoctrination to the world of fast 4-bangers,

Over in the OHV section, there are examples of Rucker, McKee, Murphy, Rutherford, McDowell, etc. cylinder heads that are ready and waiting on the shelf.

he shifted his focus when it comes to Model A Ford restoration.

"These days I only build tour cars, meaning that you can make modifications to them where they can run 65 to 70 mph," he said.

And why would you want to do that?

"Namely because of safety concerns, while having fun

Looking for Model A and Model B intake manifolds? Ron has a few.

This trio of Winfield M carburetors shows the difference in size.

Ron holds extremely rare 2-Flynn sidedraft carburetors that fit on a Riley four-port cylinder head.

Ron is a Model A carburetor expert and has rebuilt hundreds of them.

Is this guy a hard-core Model A enthusiast or what? This is an example of the front section of a 1928–1929 Model A Ford converted to an air compressor. Two cylinders fire while two cylinders pump air.

This particular A Bone features a Mosher-built Model B block with a George Butler reproduction Riley 3-valve aluminum cylinder head, Red's header, and two English Stromberg 97s.

Ron's 1929 woody wagon is powered by a 1933 Ford Model B block at 7.0:1 compression. It has a counterweighted crankshaft, mild street cam, reproduction Miller-Schofield OHV cylinder head manufactured by Steve Serr (complete with Chevrolet valves and roller rocker arms), Volkswagen-specification Weber carburetor, and Red's header. At 1,800 rpm, this engine will cruise at 65 mph all day long. Parked next to it is Ron's 1929 Lo Boy roadster, which is powered by an original Cragar OHVHD with three Stromberg carburetors (two 97s and an 81). (Photos Courtesy Ron Mosher and Author)

as the ulterior objective," Ron said. "Have you ever tried to get on the freeway with a stock Model A? It can be really scary."

Ron explained that the tour-car movement has revitalized the Model A speed equipment segment of the hobby to the point where speed equipment has become a whole new cottage industry. New speed equipment, cylinder heads, overdrives, and the like have become a lucrative business for Ron—not to mention that it also created an awareness among old-time hot rodders. Somewhere out there, original Model A and Model B speed equipment still exists and has value.

Among all of that hallowed hot rod hardware is the aftermarket Model A cylinder head, old and new.

"Right now, I know of four new Model A cylinder heads that are in process," Ron said. "But when it comes to the original stuff, there are at least 120 different name brands and/or types of Model A and Model B cylinder heads."

When it comes to Model A and Model B intake manifolds, it's the same story. Ron has at least 100 different makes and styles hanging from his rafters. And what about carburetors?

"There are some carburetors that were built specifically for Model As, but Model A performance enthusiasts would also take anything from Chevrolet 1-barrel carburetors to Webers, all kinds of Winfield carburetors, and Holleys and make them work," Ron said. "With the right kind of intake manifold, just about any carburetor will fit. Some Model A intake manifolds are homemade, while others were manufactured in small-job shops like the second Hilborn Model A fuel injection manifold that I happen to have. They would make one up as the need arose. Some would work, and some wouldn't."

Ron has examples of fully synchronized Model A transmissions that use late-model Ford gearsets, Model A overdrives, and even how to adapt a Ford F-100 steering box to the Model A's antiquated single-leaf, drag link, straight-axle front suspension. According to Ron, any all of these additions make a much more civilized and drivable Model A.

"I've been all over the world with my Model As," he said. "My 1929 Model A station wagon, or "woody," has 80,000 miles on it. It's been to Europe, Alaska, Nova Scotia, and New Zealand. We ship them over in containers, go out in groups of 50 cars, and stay out for as long as a month at a time. It's all about the people you meet and the places you go. I would have never seen the world as I have seen it had it not been for these road trips.

"One interesting thing (and it always happens), you can be in the middle of nowhere and pull in for the night, and if there's a car guy within 10 miles, he'll find you."

CHAPTER 2

FLATHEAD FEVER

Ford's 221-ci monobloc-design flathead V-8 Model 18 made its debut on March 9, 1932, in the equally revolutionary 1932 Ford V-8, or Deuce, as hot rodders fondly call it. This engine was the kissing cousin of the same-year-release Lincoln 90-degree flathead V-12.

Henry Ford wanted to develop the new flathead V-8 project in total secrecy. Instead of using the first-class Ford engineering facilities in Dearborn, Michigan, between 1926 and 1932, he sequestered a few of his most-trusted engineers (Carl Schultz, Ray Laird, Don Sullivan, Laurence Sheldrake, and Emil Zoerlein) at Thomas Edison's workshop at the yet-to-be-completed Greenfield Village complex, which was a stone's throw away from the River Rouge. The reason behind the secrecy is not known, but it was the automotive pioneer's last central engineering contribution to the products bearing his name, and it was undoubtedly one of his finest. In fact, in future years, the Ford flathead V-8 was listed by Ward's Auto World as one of the 10 Best Engines of the 20th Century. Let's take a closer look.

The term *monobloc* was used to describe an engine block that featured the crankcase and cylinder banks incorporated into one singularly cast component. These days, the monobloc V-8 engine is taken for granted, and the design concept dates back to 1902–1904. Many of the more-expensive, hand built, or limited-production luxury cars from that era, such as the 1914 Cadillac, featured a monobloc V-8.

However, Ford's new V-8 was the first mass-produced cast-iron monobloc engine in the industry, and Ford owed much of its initial manufacturing success to longtime FoMoCo foundry wizard Charles E. "Cast-Iron Charlie" Sorensen, who pioneered techniques in workflows, materials handling, and advancements in mass-production castings. The result was a relatively strong but light three-main cylinder block that featured a spur-gear activated camshaft that was driven off of the front of the crankshaft. Intake and exhaust valves for each cylinder bank were mounted inside the V, while the intake manifold fed the intake ports that were likewise located at the top of the V block. Full-length water jackets enhanced

Henry Ford tinkers with Ford Motor Company's latest engineering marvel, the 221-ci 1932 Model 18 flathead V-8 engine. The engine was designed and developed in secrecy between 1926 and 1932 by Ford engineers. At 5.5:1 compression, Henry's new V-8 produced 65 hp. (Photo Courtesy Ford Motor Company)

piston cooling. However, the routing of the exhaust valves through the water jacket areas put a heavy load on a pair of archaic belt-driven mechanical water pumps, which was not one of Ford's better ideas. This led to overheating and even engine failure—a problem that Ford would address and readdress throughout the flathead's 22-year (US and Canada combined) production run.

Another engineering first was that Ford developed and patented new heat-treating and materials-handling processes. These processes allowed the forging of cast-iron crankshafts that proved just as strong as the customary forged steel and were considerably less expensive to produce. Flathead engines built from 1932 to 1935 featured poured Babbit main and connecting-rod bearings that required skill and sophisticated machining to

This 1933 Ford V-8 kicks up some dirt negotiating a turn during the 1933 Elgin Road Races. The new Fords were powered by the greatly improved Model 40 Ford flathead V-8 engines that had 75 hp and a 6.33:1 compression ratio.

install. Midway through 1935 and onward, Henry simplified the process by substituting more reliable shell-type cadmium-silver alloy rod and main bearings.

The original 221-ci flathead V-8 of 1932 featured 5.5:1–compression cast-aluminum pistons (bore 3.0625 inches) that swung on 3.750-inch H-beam connecting rods (initially with Babbit bearings) with two rod ends mounted per single rod journal. As previously mentioned, the flathead's solid-lifter, three-bearing camshaft also featured an extra lobe at the rear to power its mechanical fuel pump. The spur timing gears were manufactured using an experimental plastic that Ford was developing at the time called Bakelite. A cast-iron timing gear cover served as the mounting platform for the flattie's gear-driven, single-point ignition system.

The Ford flathead's Achilles heel was inadequate engine cooling, but Ford more than made up for it when it came to engine lubrication. The high-pressure lubrication system on the main bearings and connecting rods kept the flathead's critical components well oiled regardless of the engine's operating level. The pump was driven using a drive gear at the back of the camshaft while an analog oil pressure gauge kept the driver informed of what the lubrication system was doing.

Over the years, there has been discussion regarding optimal oil pressure readings for flatheads. Opinions vary. However, a good rule of thumb is to check the viscosity of the oil that is being called for by the factory, and it should help provide an idea of the optimum PSI.

Henry cast his 21-stud, water-jacketed cylinder heads in steel (in 1932) and then aluminum (from 1933 to 1938). Passenger-car cylinder heads accommodated a set of 18-mm spark plugs and featured 45- to 50-mm combustion chambers. Note that combustion chamber size and compression ratios changed in the ensuing years along with a myriad of other physical improvements.

The flathead engine's induction was handled by an aluminum intake manifold that was fed by a Detroit Lubricator 1-barrel carburetor in 1932 and early 1933. Ensuing years saw the use of a 2-barrel venturi-style carburetor. Air filtration was handled by an oil-bath air cleaner.

As the years progressed, Ford addressed inherent design problems (such as engine cooling and the porosity of castings, etc.), and the flathead went through a number of incarnations. Ford debuted the 221-ci Model 18 in 1932, the Model 40 in 1933, the Model 40a in 1934, the Model 48 in 1935, the Model 68 in 1936, the 136-ci Model 74 (also known as the V-8 60 or 17-Stud) flathead engine in 1937, the Model 82A in 1938, the Model 922A in 1939, the Model 022A in 1940, the 239-ci Ford Model 8a in 1949, the Model 0A in 1950, the Model 1A in 1951, the Model BA in 1952, and the Model BF in 1953.

Mercury debuted the V-8 60 flathead 99A in 1939, 09A in 1940, 19A in 1941, and 29A in 1942. Curiously, V-8-660s were not available for the 1941 and 1942 models. The 8CM was used on 1946 to 1954 Mercurys, and Mercury released the 255-ci Model BG, which was only available in Mercury cars, plus Ford (US) and Canadian Mercury trucks. Lastly, there was the 337-ci Model 337 used across the board for large-truck service.

Early Ford V-8s Dominate

The famed AAA-sanctioned Elgin Road Races in Illinois began in 1910 and ended in 1920. However, a brief

Event-winner Fred Frame poses in this post-event picture with his Cote Motor Company–sponsored car No. 10.

Michigan, office on April 13, 1934. In the letter, the Ford V-8 was praised as the couple's favorite getaway car. The letter is on display at the Henry Ford Museum (also known as the Edison Institute) at Greenfield Village in Dearborn for public viewing. It reads:

Tulsa, Oklahoma
10 April
Mr. Henry Ford
Detroit, Michigan

Dear Sir,
While I still have got breath in my lungs, I will tell you what a dandy car you make. I have drove Fords exclusively when I could get away with one. For sustained speed and freedom from trouble, the Ford has got ever other car skinned, and even if my business hasn't been strictly legal, it don't hurt anything to tell you what a fine car you got in the Ford V-8.
Yours Truly,
Clyde Champion Barrow

revival in 1933 provided the perfect opportunity for Ford dealers to show off their newly improved, 75-hp, 6.33:1-compression-ratio 1933 Ford flathead V-8s.

The event featured 11 of the new Fords, and they dominated the Stock car class. On the measured 8½-mile route with a total racing distance of 213 miles, contestants raced north up Lark Avenue to McLean Boulevard, west to Highland Avenue, south onto Combs Road, and then east onto Galena Road (Illinois State Highway 20), where they eventually returned to Elgin's Lark Avenue in front of packed grandstands.

Exactly 2 hours, 32 minutes, and 6.01 seconds after the green flag dropped, Fred Frame and his Cote Motor Company Ford V-8 roadster crossed the finish line first to claim the checkered flag with an average speed of 80.22 mph. Frame and second-place finisher Lou Moore (Shanesy Motor Co.), a fellow Ford driver, were clocked as fastest in class, registering up to 100 mph on the straightaways.

Praise from Bonnie and Clyde

Bonnie Parker and Clyde Barrow's bank-robbing exploits and subsequent crime spree across the Southwest from 1932 to 1934 have been documented in books and romanticized on the silver screen. While many of the so-called facts about this lawless couple have taken on fictional properties, there is one document that remains the undisputed truth, and that is an April 10, 1934 letter written by Clyde Barrow to Henry Ford.

The letter was logged as received at Ford's Dearborn,

1935 Miller-Ford V-8 Issues at Indy

In 1935, famed Indianapolis 500 race car constructor Harry Miller entered into an agreement with the Ford Motor Company to build 10 Miller-Ford V-8 Specials for competition in the upcoming 1935 Indianapolis 500. These unique, low-slung design, front-wheel-drive Miller-Ford V-8 racers were produced in Dearborn, Michigan, at Miller-Tucker Inc. That's the same Tucker of Tucker Torpedo fame. The cars were powered by rearward-facing Sullivan-Stromberg 97 quad-carbureted, 21-stud, 221-ci, Ford flathead V-8 engines that were mated to 2-speed Miller transaxles.

Unfortunately, there wasn't enough time to iron out all the bugs before race day. The four Miller-Ford V-8s that qualified suffered from steering box failures because the steering boxes were located too close to the flathead exhaust manifolds, which caused the fluid inside to percolate. With no lubricant, the steering gears got hot, expanded and locked up. What a ride that must have been! Suffice to say, the 1935 Miller-Ford Indy project was

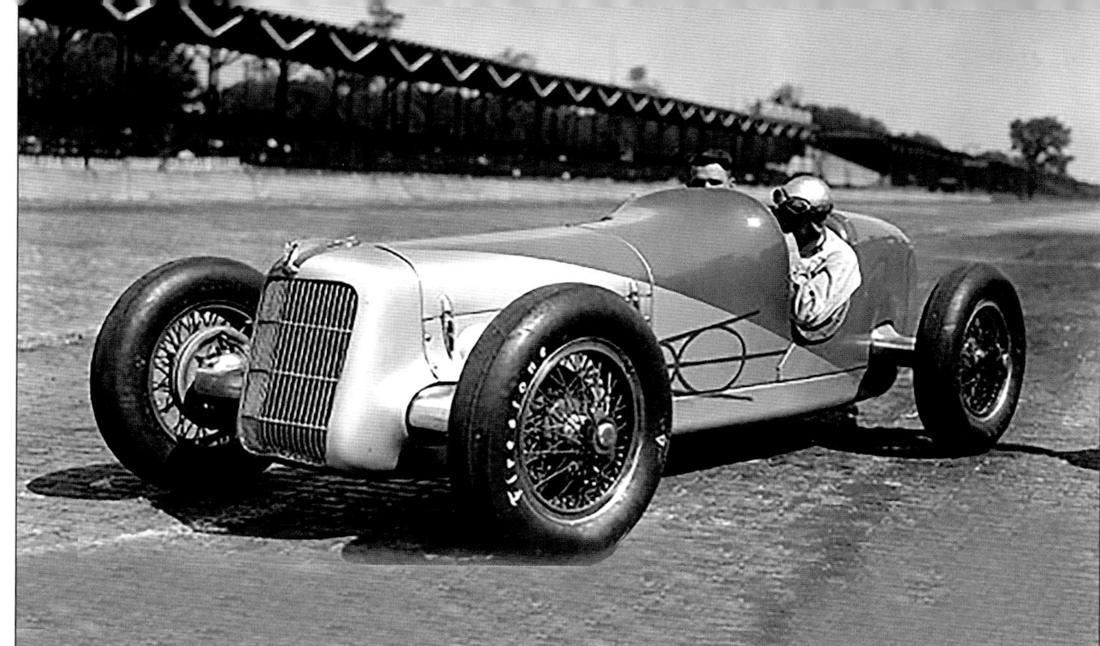

This is an example of a front-wheel-drive 1935 Miller V-8 Special complete with a reverse-mounted, Sullivan-Stromberg-equipped, 221-ci Ford flathead V-8 engine. Too bad there wasn't enough time to properly shake these cars down before race day because the overheating steering box problem could have most likely been easily remedied.

a total failure. Henry Ford was so furious that he ordered for the cars to be dismantled. So, any 1935 Miller-Ford Indy V-8 race car that you see today has been assembled with parts from the original 10 cars. Ironically, the best performance for the ill-fated 1935 Miller-Ford V-8 Indy car team effort was a 29th-place finish with car number 35 driven by George Bailey at 113.432 mph.

Popular Flathead Engine Modifications and Components

The most obvious high-performance power-adders for the Ford flathead V-8 engine family were carbureted intakes and cylinder heads because those not only increased performance but also provided the all-important wow factor when the hood was lifted. When it comes to the subject of intakes, who did what first has always been the subject of controversy.

The late Tom Madigan, an automotive author, believed that in the late 1930s, Wayne Morrison built the first commercially sold intake for the flathead V-8. However, Madigan said it was a mere twin-carb Y extension that bolted to the factory intake pedestal, which was a popular early flat motor modification. Or, was it a complete intake?

In 1937, industry pioneers Phil and Joan Weiand introduced the Hi Weiand dual-quad intake manifold for the Ford flathead V-8 60 engine and made the Southern California–based manufacturer one of the first, if not *the* first, in the speed equipment industry to do so.

Others believe that it was Robert M. Roof of Anderson, Indiana, who bears that distinction. When it came to building a better engine, Roof didn't discriminate. He created speed parts for Cord, Chevrolet, Dodge, Studebaker, and even Ferguson tractor through his association with several different companies. The Roof 2x4 intake for the Ford flathead and Roof two-piece spark plug cylinder heads for the Ford flathead V-8 60 are highly sought-after, and even more so are the extremely rare and seldom-seen Roof DOHC setup for flatheads.

Back in the late 1930s, mechanical geniuses Tommy Thickstun and Frank Baron were likewise caught up in the race to develop a complete line of Ford flathead speed equipment. Thickstun Development Company based in Inglewood, California, is credited with manufacturing an assortment of pre-war 2, 3 and 4 single- and 2-barrel venturi carburetor flathead intakes as well as the first pop-up piston for flatheads.

When World War II came along, Thickstun earned a job as an aviation engineer in the US Army Air Corps. Post–World War II efforts included Thickstun high-compression flat motor cylinder heads that he marketed as "dealer options," as speed shops were few and far between in those days. One of Thickstun's best customers was the Los Angeles Police Department (LAPD).

Sadly, Tommy Thickstun died of a heart attack in 1946 at age 34. One can only wonder what marvelous automotive inventions he took with him to his grave. Soon thereafter, dry lakes and dirt track racer Bob Tattersfield purchased Thickstun's equipment, patterns, inventory, and manufacturing rights from Tommy's estate. Together with engineer Frank Baron, Tattersfield continued manufacturing high-quality flathead induction system components into the mid-1950s under the Tattersfield brand name.

The story goes that in the mid-1930s, Vic Edelbrock Sr. had an automotive repair shop in Los Angeles, California. In 1938, Edelbrock bought a 1932 Ford flathead V-8 roadster and immediately began to hop up the car. Edelbrock collaborated with Tommy Thickstun on one of Tommy's first flathead intakes and used his beloved Deuce as the test bed.

Feeling that he could do better, Edelbrock designed his own intake known as the Slingshot and was literally off to the races. From 1938 to 1941, Vic drove his Deuce up to the dry lakes, removed the fenders, running boards, and top, and ran the black roadster, which was clocked at 112 mph at El Mirage and ultimately 121 mph at Harper Dry Lakes. When it came to manufacturing those finned-aluminum cylinder heads that so famously bear his name, Vic Sr. felt that he could do better.

Upon hearing stories from his fellow dry lakes and stock car racing cronies about Ford's 81AS Rocky Mountain High Altitude/Natural Gas/Police Pursuit cylinder heads, Edelbrock bought a set. These cylinder heads featured a smaller combustion chamber than stock and when milled a bit did extremely well in competition.

After a few tweaks and twists, Vic Sr. came up with a working prototype, and it was off to the foundry. Edelbrock sold a ton of these cylinder heads and didn't discriminate. In the late 1940s and early 1950s, he shipped product to moonshine runners in the Deep South—it's no small wonder why to this day you see the name Edelbrock prominently placed on the front fenders of every NASCAR Monster Energy, Xfinity, and Gander Outdoors Series race car—and also shipped product to South America.

Vic Sr. was also well-known in California Racing Association (CRA) circles for his Bobby Meeks–engine, methanol-burning, flathead V-8 60 midget, and was a strong supporter of early NHRA drag racing. Early successes in dirt track, dry lakes, drags racing, etc. combined with other Edelbrock engineering firsts laid the foundation for Edelbrock Equipment Company of Torrance, California, which to this day remains a key player in the speed equipment industry.

In 1919, dirt track and boat racer Eddie Meyer, brother of three-time Indy 500 winner Lou Meyer, went into business repairing Model T Fords at his shop in Redlands, California, and also became a successful dirt track racer in 1923 and 1924 driving a Rajo-engine Ford Model T track car.

In 1928, Bud Meyer (Eddie's brother), Eddie's son, and his father co-founded Eddie Meyer Engineering in West Hollywood, California, and produced superior-quality flathead speed equipment from the late 1930s to early 1950s. In today's collector market, Eddie Meyer flathead parts are highly prized and command what collector's call *stupid money*.

Between late 1930 and early 1950, Eddie Meyer Engineering's clientele list included the likes of Clark Gable, who drove a mean Eddie Meyer–equipped dark blue 1950 Ford Club Coupe. Meyer also produced some of the industry's most-gifted talent with an employee roster that read something like a virtual who's who of hot rodding, with alumni including Ray "Racer" Brown, Ed Pink, Phil Remington, Louis Senter, and Tom Sparks.

Vic Edelbrock Sr., a hot rod industry pioneer, proudly stands with the 1932 Ford roadster that he acquired in 1938. Vic would drive his Deuce up to the dry lakes, remove the top, fenders, and running boards and test the latest flathead equipment that he had been working on. Ultimately Vic's Deuce reached a top speed of 121 mph at Harper Dry Lakes. Today, this car is fully restored and on display at Edelbrock's museum in Torrance, California. (Photo Courtesy Edelbrock)

All smiles, Vic Edelbrock Sr. poses with a fresh run of Edelbrock Equipment Company flathead cylinder heads fresh from the machine shop. (Photo Courtesy Edelbrock)

Testing of all Edelbrock flathead products was carried out using the speed equipment manufacturer's trusty Heenon-Froude dynamometer. (Photo Courtesy Edelbrock)

Here's a shot of the Edelbrock Equipment Company when it was located in Hollywood, California. Edelbrock's California Racing Association (CRA) midget and its methanol-burning Bobby Meeks V-8 60 engine is being serviced. (Photo Courtesy Edelbrock)

An early rolling test bed of the Edelbrock Equipment Company was Jim "Jazzy" Nelson's 1948 Fiat Topolino altered with a 315-ci Mercury flathead engine that ran strong loads of nitromethane. Times were in the low 9s at 132-plus mph. (Photo Courtesy Greg Sharp Collection)

Eddie Meyer stands in front of his shop, Eddie Meyer Engineering, with an employee in West Hollywood, California. (Photo Courtesy Greg Sharp Collection)

Eddie Meyer and his brother, Bud, confer over a flathead engine set up for a Meyer-equipped offshore powerboat. (Photo Courtesy Greg Sharp Collection)

This is a Ford flathead V-8 engine equipped with an Edelbrock intake and heads that is on display at the Eastern Museum of Motor Racing in York Springs, Pennsylvania.

This 1932 Ford highboy, which is a work in progress, sports a set of Barney Navarro cylinder heads and Fenton Headers, and the two-pot intake manifold is an Edelbrock product.

Barney wrings out his 27-T at the dry lakes, posting the last civilian pre-war clocking at Lake Muroc on November 16, 1941, at 107 mph.

In 1932 Jim White, also known as Jim Harrell, opened Jim White's Speed Shop in a small building on the front lot of a piece of property where Jim lived at San Pedro and 99th streets in Los Angeles, California. A year later, White relocated the business to a more suitable location, 10924 S. Main St. at the corner of Main and 109th Place in Los Angeles, where he and his brother Nick Harrell remained until Jim's passing in June 1976. It was there that they not only built racing engines (Harrell Racing Engines) but also manufactured their own brand of cylinder heads and intakes for the Ford flathead under the Jim's Speed Shop brand. Also doing business under the same roof was Jim's Auto Parts, lending credence to the phrase, "Busy hands are happy hands!"

With the beginning of World War II looming on the horizon, Barney Navarro took a brand-new 1939 Ford flathead V-8 and went 107 mph on November 16, 1941, to set the last known speed record for a civilian at Lake Muroc. The car was fitted with a set of his own-design cylinder heads and a modified Hi Weiand intake. To pay for the intake that Phil Weiand had so generously loaned him, Barney went to work for Phil machining parts.

Barney served in the US Army Air Corps, and after the war, he opened up his own shop. Navarro Engineering was established in Glendale, California, in 1947, and the company began to design revised-internal-geometry Ford flathead intake manifolds and high-compression cylinder heads bearing his name. When the flathead aftermarket flat-lined in the mid-1950s, Barney became involved in boat racing. Barney's boss, steel magnate Henry J. Kaiser, was so impressed with Navarro that he brought him in as a consultant on numerous projects. The most noteworthy project was the Kaiser Medical Heart Pump. Barney's interests were widespread. He also designed and patented a concrete cutting saw. To his dying day Barney often said, "There's nothing more fun than learning."

By the dawn of the 1950s, it seemed that everyone was in the flathead equipment manufacturing business. Other names included Colonel Alexander, Ed Almquist (one of the nation's first mail-order retailers), Eddie Edmunds/Aaron Fenton (the latter of Fenton shifter and aluminum wheel fame), Owen Bentry, Burns, Cyclone, Jack Davies, D&S, Earl Evans, Granatelli-Grancor of Indianapolis 500 and STP fame, Jim Harrell of Jim Harrell Racing Engines fame, Jack Henry, Don Sullivan of Hexagon Tool Company, Smith-Jones, Kelly Brothers, Wayne Morrison, Offenhauser, Mal Ord, Jack Raddke, Al Sharp, and a guy named George Harvey, who advertised a homemade Stromberg 97 carbureted intake in an early 1950s issue of *Hot Rod* magazine for a whopping $40! As was stated earlier, it seemed that everyone was in the flathead speed equipment manufacturing business.

But seriously folks, how many carburetors does one really need? It all depends on the specific use and application. In racer's jargon, there were two-pot, three-pot, four-pot and—believe it or not—six-pot flathead carburetor applications. These intakes routinely called for the hottest single-barrel and 2-barrel venture-style carburetors of the day, such as those from Stromberg, Carter, or Winfield.

Prevailing wisdom indicated that more carburetors made more power, but it also meant more headaches, as I can readily attest. While functioning as photo editor for *Hot Rod* magazine from 1976–1979, I had to "fall under" the hood of my Edelbrock/Stromberg tri-carburetor-equipped 0A flathead engine 1950 Ford F1 panel truck on numerous occasions during evening rush-hour traffic on the Hollywood Freeway. It got to where I could fix the floats on the center carburetor—it had progressive linkage—as fast as any NASCAR crewman. What was the lesson? Sometimes less is more. I eventually relented and switched to a 390-cfm Vega-Holley and Sharp 4V intake, but prior to making the switch, I always

Ford flathead expert D. H. Dave Kerr's 1950 Ford Club Coupe with a Stromberg 97 Tri-Power 0A flathead engine can be seen around his home base in Fort Smith, Arkansas. As a former counterperson at Cutter Ford in North Hollywood, California, "Dirty Dave" can practically recite FoMoCo part numbers in his sleep.

carried a couple of Stromberg 97 carburetor rebuild kits with me in my tool box.

For those daring enough and with deep-enough pockets, machining material from the top of a flathead block (decking) and between the valves and the cylinders (relieving) helps increase power. Increasing the size of the intake and exhaust passages by porting and polishing also increases air intake and fuel flow. Increasing compression can be achieved by milling the heads, whether they are stock or aftermarket.

Other surefire ways to increase power include changing the camshaft to a product from Winfield, Clay Smith, Harmon-Collins, etc. and installing oversize pistons from Thickstun, Eddie Meyer, Jahns, etc. Because of its interchangeability, a Mercury crankshaft is a popular upgrade for the 239-ci Ford flathead V-8 engine. You can always go the Ardun or Roof OHV route. However, in that case, this question must be asked: How deep are your pockets?

Dry Lakes Racing and the SCTA

Since the November 29, 1937, incorporation of the Southern California Timing Association, hot rodders have found the dry lakes of the Mojave Desert to be the ideal location to test their mettle. In 1937, seven members of the Road Runners Car Club (Wally Parks, Ak Miller, Eldon Snapp, Jack Henry, Henry Cameron, John Riley, and Jack Shadford) met in a Huntington Park, California, garage and formulated the idea of creating an official sanctioning body to act as the voice of dry lakes racers. Up to that point, dry lakes racing activities were sanctioned by individual car clubs and/or the Muroc Racing Association with events principally taking place at Muroc Dry Lake.

The scope of the SCTA, however, would be on a much-broader scale, as events were sanctioned at Muroc, Cotati, Rosamond, Harper, and El Mirage Dry Lakes. The SCTA was comprised of seven founding clubs and had its first officially sanctioned event on May 16, 1938, at Muroc Dry Lake. The beauty of dry lakes racing was that the racer was at liberty to run a myriad of different engine combinations. It seemed as though there was a class for anything and everything from Roof Super Giant Power–equipped Chevrolet 4-cylinders, Frontenac or Rajo Model T 4-banger conversions, 2- and 4-port Rileys or Model As with Winfield or Roof L-heads, 4-port Riley A-Bones, and Cragar OHVs to more sophisticated powerplants like Studebaker, Miller, Duesenberg, Packard, etc.

However, since the day when the first Ford V-8 broke the stillness of the Mojave Desert, Henry's little side-valve V-8 became *the* choice of dry lakes racers and set countless land speed records. No other engine (short of the immortal Chevrolet small-block) has witnessed such a high degree of popularity throughout the 1940s, 1950s, 1960s, and 1970s.

Let's backtrack somewhat. Prior to World War II, SCTA members bombarded the record books and took home SCTA Championships: Ernie McAfee in 1938, George Harvey in 1939, Bob Ruffi in 1940, and Vic Edelbrock Sr. in 1941.

On June 1, 1942, all racing in the US was suspended by official government decree, and if the racers didn't leave the dry lakes voluntarily, they were forcibly removed. Gasoline, oil, and rubber was in short supply, and scrap metal at a premium. Most (if not all) SCTA members went off to war.

The dry lakes were silenced, but the unbridled passion of those involved was not. During downtime, GIs talked about or showed treasured pictures of two things: women and the hot rods they had waiting for them back home. In the meantime, Wally Parks—ever the dedicated hot rod journalist—and others exchanged mail with Veda Orr of the Karl and Veda Orr Speed Shop in Culver City, California. Veda co-edited the SCTA newsletter and mailed thousands of copies to club members stationed overseas in the military. During the war years, this prompted hot rod pioneer Tom "Stroker McGurk" Medley to say, "Veda was the glue that held hot rodding together."

At the war's end in 1945, 70,000 troops per month were discharged, and it wasn't long before the familiar cackle of an uncorked Ford flathead V-8 broke through the still air at the dry lakes. On September 7, 1945, the SCTA was reorganized. Wally Parks was president; Randy Shinn, secretary; and Mel Leighton, treasurer.

The first post-war lakes meet was in April 1946 at El Mirage, and events coverage was in the December 1946 issue of *CT News*. Dry lakes racing continued in popularity. Ak Miller was elected as SCTA president in 1947 with Wally Parks as secretary. Parks's duties were two-fold because he was also in the process of putting together the first issue of *Hot Rod* magazine (January 1948) along with *Hot Rod* founder Robert E. Petersen. That same year, the SCTA joined the National Safety Council in an attempt to curb illegal racing activities.

As legitimate drag strips (such as Santa Ana, Inyokern, Famoso, and others) sprang up, dry lakes activities began to diminish, which prompted Parks to write an editorial for *Hot Rod* where he stated that due to poor course conditions from overuse, dry lakes racing may have to be abandoned in favor of other venues, such as abandoned airport runways, where America's youth could legally let it all hang without fear of consequence. And so, drag racing was born, and with proper organization, it was here to stay.

As drag racing's popularity grew, Ford flatheads (such as those belonging to Calvin Rice, Art Chrisman, the Bean Bandits, and countless others) dominated the early drag racing classes. This sent a tidal wave of American youth running off into the night, seeking to purchase speed equipment, and with it, the American speed shop was born!

Even today, Ford flatheads hold numerous land speed records. For example, Ron Main and his Dick Landy–engine *FlatFire* streamliner achieved 700 hp and 302.674 mph to set a new world record in the XF/BXF class at the Bonneville Salt Flats in 2003. Old Henry would have been proud!

The Saga of the Smith-Jiggler Ford V-8 60: The Little Engine That Could
Vintage photos courtesy Bill Jones and Greg Sharp

In a bygone era filled with known speed equipment manufacturers (such as Navarro, Winfield, Thickstun, Edelbrock, Gran-Cor, Sharp, Evans, and Weiand) that specialized in Ford flathead engine parts, the somewhat-uncommon, albeit unique-name Smith-Jiggler seems completely foreign to many.

"In the pre–World War II days, the 'Poor Man's Offy' was the 136-ci Ford V-8 60 [manufactured from 1937 to 1940], and there were dirt tracks everywhere you looked around San Antonio," said retired racer Drew Williams. "It seemed like there was a midget parked in front of every corner gas station."

Local San Antonio, Texas, businessman T. Noah "Tiny" Smith Jr. had owned a number of top-ranked cars, including the famed Pop Dryer–constructed Checkerboard championship-winning midget purchased in 1939 and piloted by a number of highly respected drivers from that era. Like most of the local dirt track racers, Smith's midgets were generally powered by modified versions of the 136-ci Ford flathead V-8 60 engine. However, the race-prepared Ford V-8 60s exhibited a rather nasty habit of transforming themselves into scalding tea kettles!

Smith's answer to the problem was fairly simple and somewhat inspired. He took the heat out of the engine by welding up the exhaust passages on the Ford V-8 60 cast-iron engine block while leaving the intake valve inside the block to do its job. Accordingly, Smith funded the design

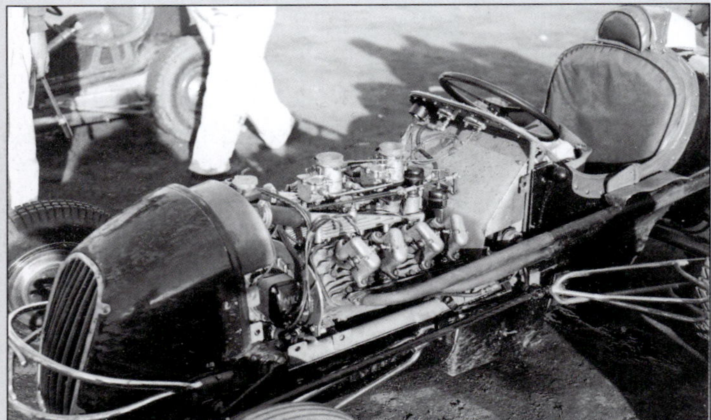

The 134-ci Smith-Jiggler semi-OHV V-8 60 engine was the creation of one T. Noah "Tiny" Smith and aircraft engineer Pete Leonard. The Smith-Jiggler V-8 60 made a great methanol-burning midget engine. The racing version of the Smith-Jiggler V-8 60 retailed for $1,050. A detuned street version was also available for $750, and "do-it-yourself kit" was also made available. (Photo Courtesy Greg Sharp Collection)

This is the actual Smith-Jiggler V-8 60 display engine that the late Bill Jones, a racing legend, assembled out of parts gathered from across the country to honor T. Noah "Tiny" Smith at the 1989 Oval Track Racer's Reunion, bringing tears to Smith's eyes.

The Smith-Jiggler V-8 60s were machined at the Smith family business Luling Oil and Gas in San Antonio, Texas, and were assembled at 514 6th St. in San Antonio, Texas. (Tiny Smith Photo/Courtesy Bill Jones Collection)

This side view not only shows the massive F-head exhaust ports but it also shows evidence of where the original flathead V-8 60 exhaust ports were welded. Note the sizeable exhaust port/combustion chamber used on these engines. This was serious stuff here, folks!

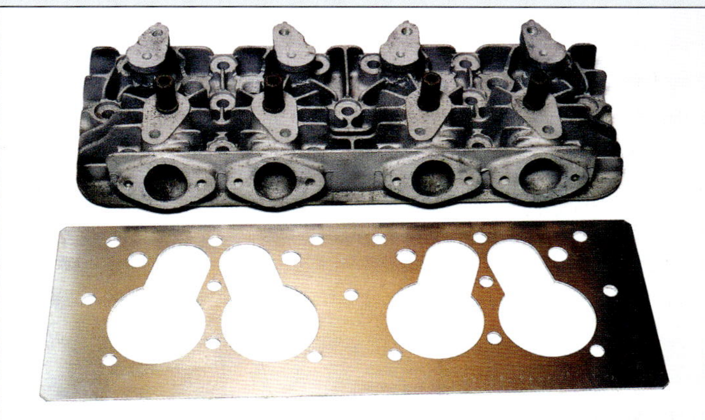

All Smith-Jiggler V-8 60s used wafer-thin aluminum head gaskets with either the finned-aluminum race head or the cast-steel street version.

of an all-new air-cooled finned F cylinder head (US patent number 200000248916) with the exhaust valve located inside the head. Smith hired aircraft engineer Pete Leonard to produce the blueprints and had machinist Eddie Anderson, who worked at the family business Luling Oil and Gas, perform the prototype work. These pieces were foundered locally, and Luling's Jessie Garcia, Greg McMillan, and Bob Miller performed the final machine work and assembly.

One of the key ingredients to the success of this new type of F cylinder head was a very short exhaust passage that not only eliminated the overheating problem but also relieved excessive back pressure in the cylinder. To accomplish this, it was necessary to devise a special 15-degree pedestal mount/oil cup reservoir and pushrod-actuated rocker-arm assembly. The Smith-Jiggler V-8 60 engines (named so by racers because of the jiggling OHV rocker-arm setup) also featured a special semi-OHV-grind Winfield R4 camshaft, a set of Eddie Meyer forged-aluminum pistons, a Barker magneto, special Smith-Jiggler water jacket runners, and a Smith-Jiggler/Eddie Meyer 2x2 intake manifold that was outfitted with a pair of Stromberg 91 carburetors.

Smith-Jiggler V-8 60 Specs
Bore: 2.6 inches
Stroke: 3.2 inches
Displacement: 136 ci
Pushrod length: 13.8 inches
Compression ratio: 11.1:1
Horsepower: 115 at 6,500 rpm
Price: $1,050

Race versions of the Smith-Jiggler V-8 60 were available in two configurations: with the stock bellhousing left on the block for use with conventional Ford or LaSalle 3-speed

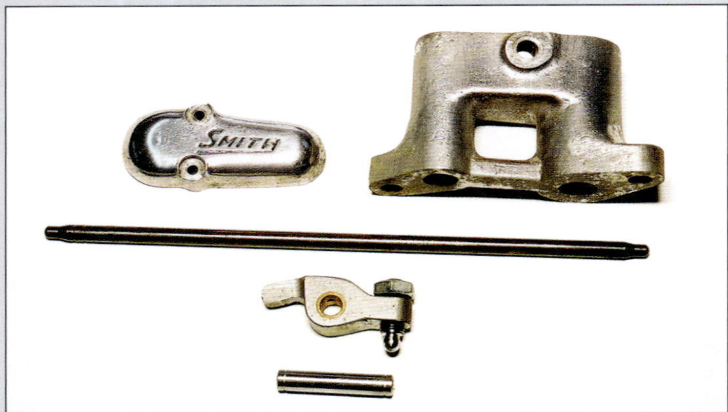

This is the somewhat-unique pedestal rocker box and rocker-arm setup, which is complete with 13.8-inch-long pushrod and cup.

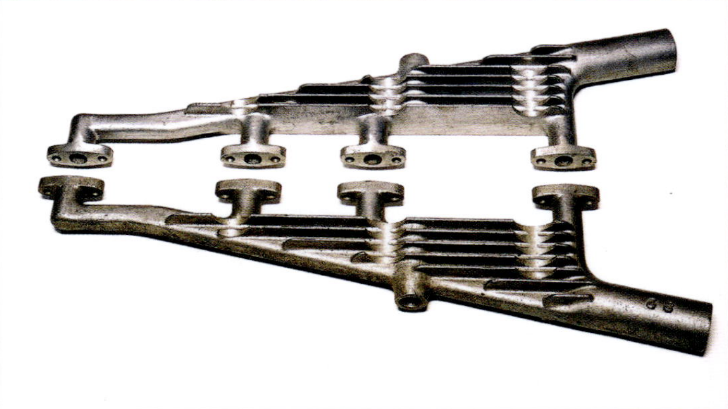

These are the cast-aluminum water jacket runners used on the Smith-Jiggler V-8 60 engine. Note the use of exterior cooling fins on all of these components.

The cast-aluminum front cover and filler necks on the Smith-Jiggler V-8 60 engine are similar to Eddie Meyer flathead components.

Early Smith-Jiggler V-8 60s initially made use of Barker magnetos, which were ultimately replaced by a more available and better-quality Harmon-Collins-manufactured unit.

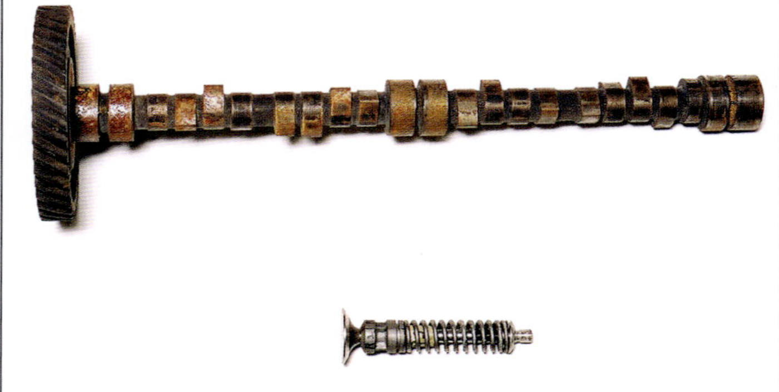

The very-early Smith-Jiggler V-8 60s used Winfield R4 cams. Later versions employed a Harmon-Collins cam.

After initially suffering from oil starvation problems and inferior rocker-arm castings, the Smith-Jiggler V-8 60 went on to become quite popular in Southwest midget racing circles, often beating King Offy at its own game. In fact, Tiny Smith's little engine (which sounded like no other Ford V-8 60 flathead engine around—especially on methanol) became so popular that some racing associations would not allow it to compete against King Offy.

There was, however, another side to the Smith-Jiggler V-8 60 story that began around 1952. That was the same year that second-generation MG TD sports cars were introduced in the US. Another family enterprise, Smith Import Motors specialized in the sales and service of MG, Jaguar, and Rolls-Royce cars.

However, like the stock Ford flathead V-8 60, the 4-cylinder MG was notorious for overheating, especially in hotter climates like that of Texas. Tiny Smith came up with a 9.0:1–compression, de-tuned version of his famous Smith-Jiggler V-8 60 and dropped it between the frame rails of his daughter Sugar's MG. It was a full decade before another Texan

transmissions or as a trimmed version for competition use with an in-and-out gearbox. They could be obtained by contacting Tiny Smith at the 2300 Alamo National Building in San Antonio, Texas, by visiting his manufacturing facilities at 514 6th St. in San Antonio, Texas, or by calling Fannin-8961.

by the name of Carroll Shelby came up with the inspired notion to drop a lightweight American V-8 engine into a medium-priced, English-built sports car.

Tiny Smith offered engine conversions through his San Antonio, Texas, distributorship in kit form for $450 and as a turn-key feature for $750. With an ever-watchful eye on the up-and-coming South Texas SCCA amateur sports car scene, Smith also offered a sleeved 1.9L, 119.36-ci competition version of the Smith-Jiggler V-8 60 complete with a Harmon & Collins cam for $1,050.

All told, Tiny Smith only manufactured about 30 Smith-Jiggler V-8 60 engines and about 20 V-8 60 engine conversion kits, which is a modest output by today's standards, so they're pretty rare.

Check out the exhaust ports and valve pockets on those 11.1:1–compression S-J aluminum cylinder heads.

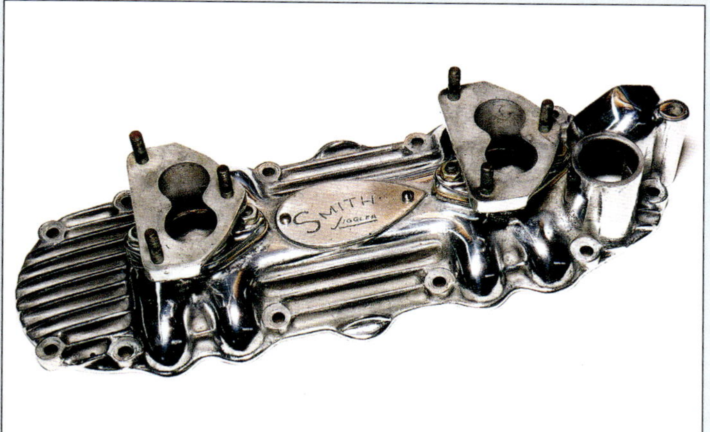

The Smith-Jiggler V-8 60s also use a modified Eddie Meyer 2x2 intake manifold with the Smith-Jiggler nameplate attached.

On the top is a Smith-Jiggler V-8 60 aluminum race head with 11.1:1 compression. On the bottom is a Smith-Jiggler steel street head with 9.0:1 compression.

The Smith-Jiggler V-8 60s also used a set of Eddie Meyer connecting rods and pistons.

CHAPTER 3

THE OHV WARS: THE KING IS DEAD; LONG LIVE THE KING

Historically speaking, Ford Motor Company's venerable flathead V-8 engine enjoyed a long and colorful life. Manufactured from 1932 to 1953 (1932 to 1954 in Canada), the "flat motor," in its various incarnations, powered everything from production cars, trucks, and tractors to Indy racers, powerboats, moonshine runners, land speed record holders, drag racing cars, and, of course, hot rods. Moreover, until 1961, the Flattie forged on as the engine of choice in Brazilian, Chilean, Spanish, Australian, and the Netherlands-manufactured SIMCA automobiles and was used in certain German-built Ford trucks until the early 1970s. Talk about staying power!

However, nothing lasts forever. By the late 1940s, became increasingly clear to Detroit's Big Three that the overhead valve (OHV) engine design, which had proven itself for decades in straight-6 and straight-8 OHV applications) was far superior in smoothness, reliability, and performance. Suffice to say, the OHV "wars" were officially on.

Cadillac OHV

Cadillac and Oldsmobile introduced their new OHVs at about the same time, but since Cadillac was GM's premiere nameplate, it is covered here first.

In 1933, Ed Cole went to work at GM straight out of General Motors Institute of Technology (GMIT) and quickly earned a reputation as a person who gets things done. GM immediately assigned Cole to the M41 Walker Bulldog Tank program (at the time part of the Cadillac Motor Division) to groom him for bigger and better things. In 1939, he became president of Cadillac Motor Division.

In 1946, Cole and GM engineers Harry Barr and Jack Gordon resurrected a pre–World War II OHV design that they had been toying with during hunting excursions to Michigan's Upper Peninsula (UP), and the 7.25:1-compression, 331-ci Cadillac OHV passenger-car V-8 engine was the result.

Cadillac Motor Division's 90-degree OHV engine (at 7.25:1 compression and 331 ci) was designed in 1946 by GM engineers Harry Barr and Jack Gordon and debuted in the 1949 models. Initially rated at 160 hp at 3,750 rpm and 312 ft-lbs of torque at 1,800 rpm, once mated to GM's Hydra-matic transmission, the Cadillac OHV proved to be a powerful and reliable luxury performance package. With each ensuing year, Cadillac grew in size. For example, a 1955 Coupe DeVille had a gross vehicle weight (GVR) of 4,610 pounds; therefore, a bigger and more powerful engine became a necessity.

Cadillac's new five-main 90-degree OHV featured a 3.81-inch bore and 3.65-inch stroke at 331 ci. The new Caddy's oversquare, friction-reducing, cast-iron V-8 block (as opposed to being undersquare, which creates more friction and wear) featured a 268.2-mm deck height, 4.625-inch bore spacing, a forged-steel crankshaft and connecting rods, cast-aluminum pistons, a hydraulic camshaft, and a 5-quart-capacity (6 quarts with the filter) wet-sump oiling system.

Weighing 50 pounds per cylinder head, Cadillac's new V-8 featured wedge-shaped combustion chambers with 1.25-inch-diameter intake valves and 1.18-inch-diameter exhaust valves activated by hydraulic lifters and oil feed shaft rocker arms that were held in place with by a series of four bolts. Exhaust scavenging was handled by a pair of cast-iron exhaust manifolds.

Cadillac's induction system for 1949 featured a cast-iron low-rise, dual-plane intake manifold; Carter WCD 722-S 2-barrel carburetor; and oil-bath air cleaner. Cadillac's single-point ACDelco distributor fired a series of eight ACDelco spark plugs through ACDelco spark plug wires. Dyno tests produced 160 hp at 3,750 rpm and 312 ft-lbs of torque at 1,800 rpm. Once mated to GM's Hydra-matic transmission, the Cadillac V-8 proved to be a powerful and reliable luxury performance package.

Cadillac led the way in the performance race, but it was more out of necessity than a competitive desire because Cadillacs grew bigger and heavier each year to the degree that mid-1950s and early 1960s Cadillacs were tagged as "chrome-laden barges." Still, Caddys became the No. 1 choice of movie stars, well-candied corporate executives and the nouveau riche. So, if you could afford to own one, you loved them.

The 1950 Cadillac 331-ci, 7.5:1–compression engine was equipped with a Carter WCD 845-S 2-barrel carburetor and oil-bath air cleaner. Dyno tests produced 158 hp at 4,000 rpm and 312 ft-lbs of torque at 1,800 rpm.

Cadillac's 8.25:1–compression OHV for 1951 featured an oil-bath air cleaner and Rochester 7001200 2-barrel carburetor, which produced 210 hp at 4,500 rpm and 330 ft-lbs of toque at 1,800 rpm.

The 1952 Cadillac 331-ci OHV featured 9.0:1 compression, an oil-bath Rochester 7001200 2V carburetor and produced 250 hp at 4,600 rpm and 345 ft-lbs of torque at 2,800 rpm.

Cadillac would have to continue without input from its illustrious corporate father Ed Cole, who was appointed to be chief engineer at Chevrolet Motor Division in 1952, and we all know how well that turned out.

Cadillac's Rochester-carbureted 331-ci engine for 1953 featured 10.01:1 compression and produced 300 hp at 4,600 rpm and 345 ft-lbs of torque at 2,800 rpm.

In 1955, Cadillac Motor Division achieved a degree of notoriety that other corporately funded advertising programs could only dream of, with Chuck Berry's unforgettable chartbuster titled "Maybellene" from Chess Records.

The Cadillac V-8 experienced a growth spurt in 1956 and saw a growth in displacement to 365 ci.

In 1959, Cadillac again grew in size—this time to 390 ci. However, by 1963 the new 390-ci engine used the same exterior architecture as the original engine from 1949 but was redesigned from the inside out.

The year 1968 marked the last of the original OHV Cadillac V-8 engine design from 1949. In its final year of production, the powerplant had swelled to 429 ci. Of course, all of this displacement and hp gluttony was carried over to the Gen II Cadillac big-block engines of later years. Cadillac Motor Division also immersed itself in a small-block Cadillac engine program using an assortment of different design applications that eventually included the small-block Chevrolet 350, but this is where we step off.

Cadillac on the Road and Track

Cadillac owners at the time were credited for making record-breaking (albeit questionably legal) cross-country jaunts of one kind or another. For example, some owners would drive from Los Angeles, California, to Las Vegas, Nevada, in three hours or less. It was no problem, or as one Cadillac owner succulently put it, "It passed everything on the open road except the gas pumps."

Many racers held genuine Cadillac power in high regard, and the late Sir Sidney Allard was one of them. Allard's Cadillac-engine roadsters, or Cad-Allards as they were known, were the scourge of Great Britain's early 1950s sports car trials.

In 1950, Californian Briggs Cunningham's infamous Cadillac-engine *Le Monstre* race car set the European endurance racing establishment on its collective ears at the 24 Hours of Le Mans, placing 11th overall. Cunningham continued to visit the Sarthe Circuit throughout the early 1950s, bringing with him a series of limited-edition Cadillac- and Chrysler-engine Cunningham hybrids.

Another specialty car manufacturer to rely on genuine Cadillac power was Kurtis Kraft, which was founded by Frank Kurtis. In the early to mid-1950s, Kurtis Kraft built a total of 30 Cadillac-engine 500S roadsters. Briggs Cunningham, Frank McGurk, and Mickey Thompson each drove one. In addition, Jack Ensley of Edinburgh,

Indiana, drove his Kurtis Kraft 500S to the 1954 SCCA B/Modified Production Championship.

Cadillac engine transplants of a more bizarre nature include the Bill Frick Speed Shop (Rockville Center, Long Island, New York), Frick-Tappet Fordillac, and Studillac engine conversions from the early 1950s.

Meanwhile, drag racers, such as "Ohio George" Montgomery and Oklahoman Cody Parr, experimented with Cadillac power in their race cars. Montgomery's 1933 Willys gasser won the Autolite-sponsored Little Eliminator class and the award, which was a 1960 Ford Falcon Ranchero, at the 1960 NHRA Nationals with one while Cody Parr's 1923 Model T roadster won class during the 1956 NHRA Nationals at Oklahoma City. However, due to the fact that the majority of the hot rod parts on these cars and others like them were handmade, very little if any vintage Cadillac OHV speed equipment remains.

Oldsmobile Rocket 88

In September 1948, the Oldsmobile Division of General Motors released its new-for-1949 303-ci OHV V-8 Rocket engine. It was born during a United Auto Workers strike that shut down GM production from November 1945 to March 1946. Oldsmobile Motor Group draftsman Gilbert Burrell, who also contributed to the Cadillac V-8 engine project, privately worked on the new Oldsmobile V-8 in a non-official capacity for his own interest and amusement while studying concepts for new GM cars and new GM engines.

Six weeks after the strike ended, Burrell showed his designs to Oldsmobile Chief Engineer Jack Wolfram and Oldsmobile General Manager Sherwood Skinner. Realizing that Burrell's designs showed great promise, Wolfram and Skinner organized a new Advance Design group to develop a new OHV-8 engine, and Burrell was promoted to chief engineer. Code named the *SB 49* and based on the high-compression studies of GM's Charles Kettering, the first 287-ci Oldsmobile prototypes ran in November 1946 and were dubbed the *Futuramic 98*. However, with the coming of higher-octane fuels from 1950 onward, the production-version Oldsmobile V-8 (code 890) was renamed *Rocket 88* and initially expanded to 303.7 ci.

Oldsmobile's Lansing, Michigan, foundry produced the 90-degree cast-iron engine blocks (3.4375-inch bore and 3.43-inch stroke), which hosted a five-main forged-steel crankshaft, eight forged-steel connecting rods, and 7.25:1–compression cast-aluminum "slipper" pistons.

Oldsmobile's wedge-shaped 60-cc-combustion-chamber cylinder heads featured 1.75-inch-diameter intake valves and 1.4375-inch-diameter exhaust

Oldsmobile played heavily on the nation's fixation with rockets and space travel and named its new OHV the Rocket 88. Originally conceptualized by Oldsmobile Motor Group draftsman Gilbert Burrell during a United Auto Workers (UAW) strike, Oldsmobile's 7.25:1 compression ratio, 303.7-ci OHV was dyno tested at 135 hp at 3,000 rpm and registered 263 ft-lbs of torque at 1,800 rpm. It was backed by a Kettering-designed Oldsmobile Hydra-matic transmission.

valves, while later engines (1956 and onward) featured 1.75-inch-diameter intake valves and 1.5625-inch-diameter exhaust valves. Valvetrain hardware consisted of a hydraulic cam, lifters, and pushrods working in conjunction with oil-fed shaft-mount rocker arms. Induction came in the form of a cast-iron dual-plane intake topped with a Carter WGD 714-S 2V carburetor. Lubrication came from a wet-sump oil pump and 5-quart pan (6 quarts with the paper-element filter). Ignition duties were handled by an ACDelco single-point distributor, ACDelco spark plugs and ACDelco spark plug wires.

Dyno tested at 135 hp at 3,000 rpm and 263 ft-lbs of torque at 1,800 rpm and backed up to a Kettering-designed Oldsmobile Hydra-matic transmission, an Oldsmobile Rocket 88 was capable of 0 to 60 mph in a little over 12 seconds and a top speed of 97 mph. It was once said that an Oldsmobile Rocket 88 could suck the chrome off the side of a Ford (unless the Ford owner had made a substantial investment in aftermarket speed parts). That saying was proven repeatedly on the budding NASCAR Grand National circuit, where drivers Curtis Turner, Fireball Roberts, and Dick Linder won 5 of 8 Grand National races driving Oldsmobiles.

By 1952, Oldsmobile Rocket 88s and Super 88s used Carter 4V carburetors, which increased the numbers to 160 hp and 260 ft-lbs of torque.

The 1953 Oldsmobile V-8s saw a jump in compression from 7.5:1 to 8.0:1 and a bump to 165 hp and 275 ft-lbs of torque.

In 1954, Oldsmobile's inner dimensions increased to 324 ci, or 3.875 inches, while the stroke remained at 3.4375 inches. Oldsmobile 88 and Super 88s operated at 8.25:1 compression at 170 and 185 hp while respectively registering 295 ft-lbs and 300 ft-lbs of torque.

In 1955, compression climbed to 8.5:1 with 185 hp and 320 ft-lbs of torque in the Oldsmobile 88 and 202 hp at 332 ft-lbs of torque in the Super 88 and 98 cars. Of particular interest is how drag racing pioneer Arnie "the Farmer" Beswick's Oldsmobile 88s produced back-to-back class wins at the 1955 and 1956 NHRA Nationals in Great Bend, Kansas, and Kansas City, Missouri, respectively.

The last year of the Oldsmobile 324 was 1956. Once again, compression was on the rise at 9.0:1, and performance numbers were 230 hp and 340 ft-lbs of torque in the Oldsmobile 88 and 240 hp and 350 ft-lbs of torque in the Super 88 and 98 cars.

In 1957, Oldsmobile introduced its 9.25:1–compression 371, which featured a 4.0-inch bore and 3.6875-inch stroke.

In 1958, Olds 371 engines were rated at 10.0:1 compression, came with a Carter 4V carburetor, and produced 277 hp and 400 ft-lbs of torque for the 88s and 305 hp and 410 ft-lbs of torque for the Super 88 and 98 packages. Even bigger news for 1958 and 1959 was the release of Oldsmobile's limited-production 371-ci J-2 Golden Rocket high-performance OHV engine option, which featured 10.0:1 compression, 312 hp at 4,600 rpm, and 415 ft-lbs of torque at 2,800 rpm with Tri-Power. Oldsmobile Motor Division essentially built these engines for race-only purposes and charged $83 for the 3-speed manual transmission J-2 and $314 for the Hydra-matic version. However, due to continual tuning problems and the fact that the J-2 was expensive to produce, the J-2 engine option was short-lived. Oldsmobile also produced a 371 2V that year that produced 265 hp and 390 ft-lbs of torque but was not without some well-publicized valvetrain problems.

In 1959, Oldsmobile performance took a marked downturn thanks to the Automobile Manufacturer's Association (AMA) ban on factory-sponsored racing that lasted into 1961. The last of the original Rocket V-8 engine series was the 394 that was produced from 1959 to 1964 and was available in both 394 Rocket and Sky Rocket trim. Spec-ing in at 9.75:1 compression and featuring a 4.125-inch bore and 3.6875-inch stroke, standard 394 Oldsmobile Rocket V-8s used 2V carburetors and produced 315 hp.

Drag racing legend Gene Adams (lower left), who had been racing Oldsmobiles since 1949, poses with several team members: the late Leonard Harris (standing and holding his helmet) and partner Ronnie Scrima (kneeling right) along with Culver City, California, sponsor Albertson Oldsmobile CEO Lou Albertson (standing right) and sales manager Phil McNab. (Photo Courtesy Greg Sharp Collection)

However, the 1961 through 1963 Sky Rocket and 1964 Oldsmobile Rocket 4-barrel V-8s were high compression at 10.0:1. The 10.0:1–compression Sky Rocket produced 325 hp and 435 ft-lbs of torque. The 1962–1964 10.25:1–compression Rocket model increased power to 330 hp at 440 ft-lbs of torque. Lastly, a 10.5:1 version of the Rocket with 345 hp was also produced in 1963.

Drag racing owes a considerable debt of gratitude to Oldsmobile, and Oldsmobile owes a considerable debt of gratitude to drag racing.

In the early 1960s, Oldsmobile big-blocks became the preferred choice of the NHRA/AHRA blown gasser and street roadster classes. The reasons were simple. These engines were cheap and plentiful. They produced gobs of torque and horsepower. They were easy to service, and

The Southern California gasser team of (Fred) Stone, (Tim) Woods & (Doug "Cookie") Cook first burst onto the scene in 1962 with the Swindler II, an Oldsmobile-engine 1941 Willys coupe that competed in both the A and B/Gas Supercharged classes. For the next five years, Stone, Woods, & Cook traded records back and forth with the likes of Junior Thompson, K. S. Pittman (who also ran Oldsmobile-powered 1941 Willys coupes), and "Big John" Mazmanian's Chrysler, while running in the mid-to-low 9s. Today, Swindler II sits quietly in the Price Automobilia Collection in Long Beach, California.

In February 1970, stocker star Gene Berg and his 1950 Oldsmobile 88 V/Stocker squared off against Ford star Richard Charbonneau and his 1967 427 Fairlane station wagon for the trophy in the NHRA Winternationals Stock Eliminator runoff. Charbonneau just barely nipped Berg in the lights for the win.

they could (for the most part) keep up with the Chrysler Hemis, which were more expensive to build, tune, and maintain.

Oldsmobile maven Gene Adams virtually cut his teeth on Oldsmobile power. He drove his step-father's 1949 Oldsmobile in the Stock classes at old Santa Ana from 1952 to 1953 prior to moving the car into the B/Gas class and ultimately into the B/Gas Supercharged class running a GMC supercharged 370-ci Oldsmobile engine. Of course, Adams and blown Oldsmobiles go hand in hand, competing in the altered and early dragster classes and partnering with the likes of car builder Ronnie Scrima and team driver the late Leonard Harris (Century Oldsmobile) and later with replacement driver the late Tom "Mongoose" McEwen driving Adams's famed Oldsmobile-engine Shark car.

Who can forget the immortal Willys gasser team of Stone, Woods, & Cook, or gasser greats K. S. Pittman, Junior Thompson, and street roadster pilot Hugh Tucker, who were all proponents of big-block Oldsmobile power? More importantly, there were unsung heroes, those behind-the-scenes people who made Oldsmobiles tick, including cylinder head guru Joe Mondello, fuel injection specialist Stuart Hilborn, B&M Hydro Stick kingpins Don and Bob Spar, and cam-grinding icon Jack Engle. Without their mechanical engineering savvy, the Oldsmobile Rocket OHV speed equipment saga may have fizzled on its launching pad at least from a drag racing perspective.

Hemi 331-ci V-8: 1951–1955

Up next was the original Chrysler Corporation's revolutionary 331-ci Fire Power hemispherical-head OHV engine that made its debut in 1951 Chryslers. The intake and exhaust valves oppose each other or are splayed in a hemispherical or bowl-shaped combustion chamber with the spark plug located in the dead center between the two to create a more-even burn while optimizing intake and exhaust duties.

In reality, Chrysler Corporation was experimenting with hemispherical cylinder head technology as far back as 1939 on its V-12 and V-16 Patton M47 tank and Republic P47 Thunderbolt engine projects. However, short of overall applied theory, using the hemispherical combustion chamber principle, the cam-in-block, 90-degree Chrysler Fire Power *Hemi* V-8 passenger-car engine (or *Type I*, which was designed under the guise of Chrysler Project Engineering Vice President James Zeder) was an extremely different animal.

The 331's cast-iron block featured a bore size of 3.8125 inches and a stroke of 3.625 inches, which by today's standards is considered a relatively normal-size small-block V-8. However, in 1951, it was considered quite huge and visually quite impressive especially with a set of cross-flow hemispherical combustion chamber cylinder heads bolted on. The Type I Hemi featured a cast-iron crank, 2.50-inch mains, 6.625-inch I-beam connecting rods, and forged-aluminum pistons. The Type I's cylinder heads were equipped with 1.806-inch-diameter intake valves and 1.50-inch-diameter exhaust valves set at 53 degrees. They had massive intake and exhaust ports and some fairly complex 3.370-inch-length intake and 4.6250-inch-length exhaust double rocker-arm shafts.

Due to this sophisticated valvetrain, the new Hemi head featured less quench than rival wedge head designs. The Type I's superior volumetric efficiency made it extremely sensitive to compression and fuel octane ratings, and the engine performed like gangbusters at high RPM levels, delivering a hefty 330 ft-lbs of torque at 2,600 rpm. Most Hemi cars built in 1951 featured a Carter 2V carburetor that produced 180 bhp. Toward the end of the 331's production run in 1955, Chrysler released the

In 1951, Chrysler Corporation unveiled its 331-ci Chrysler Fire Power hemispherical combustion chamber (Hemi) V-8 engine. Six years later, Chrysler's 392 Hemi became the granddaddy of all the hemis and a favorite choice of drag racers from all classes. Surprisingly, here is one 392 Hemi (a 10.0:1–compression ratio, twin Carter WCFB bullet that produced 370 to 380 hp) in its natural habitat.

high-performance Chrysler 300-C. The name echoes how the Hemi engine produced 300 hp at 4,400 rpm, which made it the most powerful 331 of them all. The engine was fueled by a pair of Carter wrought cast 4-barrel (WCFB) carburetors.

Chrysler 354-ci Hemi: 1956–1959

The 2x4 Carter WCFB-equipped 354-ci Chrysler Hemi from 1956 was the first engine of its type to be rated at 1 hp per cubic inch with an actual SAE rating at 355 bhp. The bore size that year increased to 3.9375 inches, and stroke increased to 3.625 inches. Valve size increased to 1.94-inch-diameter intake and 1.75-inch-diameter exhaust. The remainder of the 354's valvetrain geometry remained the same as the 331. Chrysler also offered a single-carbureted 280-hp version of the 354 Hemi, which saw duty in the Chrysler New Yorker and Imperial Custom and Crown models. From 1957 to 1959, the 354 Hemi was also adapted for heavy-duty use and became known as the Power Giant V-8. Chrysler's Marine Division also marketed the 354 Hemi from 1956 to 1958 for use in small powerboat applications, using varying compression ratios and a hydraulic valvetrain.

Chrysler Fire Power 392 Hemi V-8: 1957–1958

Known as the granddaddy of the Top Fuel motors, a new raised-deck, 392-ci Chrysler Hemi block made its debut in 1957. At 10.87 inches of deck height, this new block was 0.5 inch taller than the 331 and 354 Hemis and featured a 4-inch bore and 3.906-inch stroke, using a 3.69-inch-diameter cast-iron crankshaft and 6.957-inch I-beam connecting rods. Because of its taller deck height, the 392's cylinder heads were cast a bit wider so that early Hemi intake manifolds (primarily the 2x4 Carter intakes) could be used with these new Hemi cylinder heads along with the new tall-deck block. The 392s had 2-inch-diameter intake valves and 1.750-inch-diameter exhaust valves, again using the Hemi's tried-and-true double rocker-arm system. By 1958, the final year of the series, the 392 Hemi was available in three power packages.

Advertised as America's Most Powerful Car, *Motor Life* magazine tested the top-of-the-line Chrysler 300-C convertible in its August 1958 issue. The car was equipped with a 10.0:1–compression 392 Hemi and twin Carter WCFBs. Power was rated between 375 and 380 hp, and Chrysler's Hemi ragtop boasted a power-to-weight ratio of 12.52:1. It produced 0-to-60 terminal speeds (using the Daytona Beach Acceleration Contest as a basis) in 9.1 seconds, which is hauling gas, especially for a 4,908-pound luxury car. Chrysler also offered a 10.0:1–compression

*It didn't take drag racers long to nestle Hemis of all sizes between the frame rails of some of the sport's most popular cars such as the Tucson, Arizona–based Speed Sport roadster (also known as **Old Noisy**) that made use of a Stromberg 97–carbureted Offenhauser log intake manifold and direct drive.*

Most people would throw this old boat anchor away, but this is what many big-name 1950s, 1960s, and 1970s drag racers started out with. (Photos Courtesy Don Prieto and Bob McClurg)

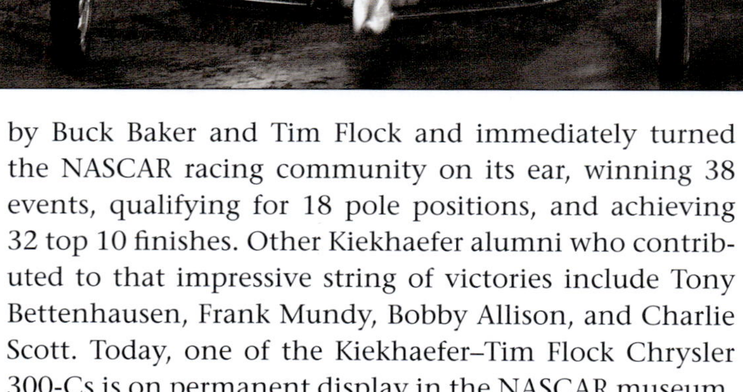

Model 392 Hemi rated at 345 hp as well as a 9.25:1–compression 392 Hemi rated at 325 hp. Both were equipped with a single Carter WCFB.

Note that the Hemi was also offered in a number of smaller-displacement packages in the Type II 1952 to 1958 276- to 345-ci De Soto Fire Dome V-8s and Type II 241- to 325-ci Dodge Red Ram Hemi V-8s. Although these Hemis were not initially known as performance engines, further development in later years by dry lakes and drag racers unveiled their true high-performance potential.

Trackside, the Chrysler Hemi established itself as a true performer. In 1955, Mercury Marine CEO Karl Kiekhaefer pulled into Daytona Beach with a pair of Mercury Marine–sponsored Chrysler 300-Cs driven by Buck Baker and Tim Flock and immediately turned the NASCAR racing community on its ear, winning 38 events, qualifying for 18 pole positions, and achieving 32 top 10 finishes. Other Kiekhaefer alumni who contributed to that impressive string of victories include Tony Bettenhausen, Frank Mundy, Bobby Allison, and Charlie Scott. Today, one of the Kiekhaefer–Tim Flock Chrysler 300-Cs is on permanent display in the NASCAR museum.

Like the Ford flathead that preceded it, the automotive aftermarket cranked out high-performance parts for the Chrysler Hemi like cordwood—as "Big Daddy" Don Garlits attests.

"My first Hemi came out of a wrecked 1954 Chrysler New Yorker," Garlits said. "I used a set of Jahns pistons,

"Big Daddy" Don Garlits retrieved his first Hemi out of a wrecked Chrysler New Yorker and paid a whopping $400 for it, which was a lot of money in early-1950s America. Shown in this picture with Garlits's third Swamp Rat dragster are (from left to right) Garlits, his wife, Pat; brother Ed Garlits; and crewman Ed Pantley. (Photo Courtesy Donna Garlits)

an Isky cam, a Weiand log manifold [Phil Weiand also cast the first top-mount GMC supercharger manifold for the early Hemi], six Stromberg 97 carburetors, a set of Champion spark plugs, a Vertex magneto, and a Schiefer clutch. What acceleration that thing had. It just kept pulling and pulling."

"The main thing with the Chrysler Hemi was of course its cylinder heads," added the late professional drag racer Tom "Mongoose" McEwen. "Those round combustion chambers with the intake and exhaust valve on both sides and the spark plug located in the middle—I mean, the breathing was so good with those engines. From the very beginning, the Chrysler Hemi was pretty much the king!"

The late Tom "Mongoose" McEwen poses alongside his Tirend Activity Booster 400-plus-inch early Hemi the day before OCIR's $14,000 Winner Take All Drag Race won by Oklahoma Hemi racer Bennie "Wizard" Osborn.

Buick's Nailhead OHV

Founded in 1897, Buick is one of the nation's oldest and most popular automotive nameplates. In the fall of 1953, Buick Division of General Motors (under the auspices of Buick Chief Engineer Verner P. Mathews and Special Projects Staff Engineer Joe D. Turlay) unveiled a replacement for GM's tried-and-true 320-ci

In 1953, Buick broke away from its "grandpa car" image with the release of the 264-ci Fireball (Nailhead) OHV V-8. A number of different-compression-ratio Buicks were released that year from 7.0:1 to 8.5:1.

straight-8 OHV engine that had been in use since 1931. Buick's 264-ci Fireball 90-degree V-8 engine was named after the 1930s show car property, being that it was Buick Motor Division's 50th anniversary and nostalgia was in style, and the engine became an immediate sensation. It was new from the ground up, compact, and low profile. However, Buick's new V-8, which was designed to fit in the engine bays of Buick's newer, sleeker, and lower-profile B-body cars, wasn't born with the familiar *Nailhead* moniker; instead, that was earned.

Buick's 90-degree cast-iron V-8 engine block featured 4.75-inch bore spacing, a counterweighted cast-iron five-main crankshaft, forged-steel connecting rods, and domed cast-aluminum pistons. The baseline 2V 264-ci Fireball V-8 engine used in the Buick Specials featured a 3.625-inch bore and 3.20-inch stroke at 7.0:1 compression, whereas its upscale brother, the 4V 322-ci Fireball V-8 used in the Buick Roadmasters, featured a 4.00-inch bore and 3.20-inch stroke at 8.5:1 compression.

Now, that's all well and good, but what about those uniquely designed pent-roof combustion chamber cylinder heads? Buick designed its "Valve-In-Head" (in GM terminology) cylinder heads (both the right side and the left side are interchangeable) so that the relationship between the combustion chamber, exhaust port, and pushrod angle would allow a more streamlined port alignment, albeit somewhat restrictive at higher RPM levels. Buick countered this by using a more-aggressive camshaft that provided more bottom-end torque and a noticeable lope.

Buick's intake and exhaust valves were laid out in a vertical row, actually resembled nails (hence the nickname *Nailhead*), and measured 1.75 inches in diameter for the intake and 1.25 inches in diameter for the exhaust. These valves used long-reach pressed-steel shaft rocker arms, while later-year Buick engines used cast-aluminum shaft rocker arms. Buick's humpback valve covers nostalgically resembled (for lack of a better description) an elongated version of a Hostess Twinkie.

Gen II Buick Nailhead

Gen II Buick Nailheads were produced from 1957 to 1966 and shared the same bore spacing as their older brothers albeit with larger bore sizes. For example, Buick's 364-ci Nailhead manufactured from 1957 to 1961 with a 9.5:1 compression ratio featured a bore size of 4.125 inches and a stroke of 3.40 inches.

Buick's 401-ci Nailhead V-8 engines from 1959 to 1966 again featured 9.5:1 compression. The bore size was 4.1875 inches and the stroke was 3.64 inches. Lastly, Buick's 1963 to 1966 425-ci Nailhead V-8s featured a 4.3125-inch bore and 3.64-inch stroke.

Juice Feeding the Buick Nailhead

When it came to intake manifolds, late 1950s and early 1960s Buick Nailheads could be ordered with an optional 2x4 Carter aluminum 4-barrel (AFB) carburetor setup that was capable of producing 360 hp at 4,400 rpm. Buick also offered a single Rochester Quadrajet setup, but that was eventually discontinued. While many parts are not interchangeable between Gen I and Gen II Nailheads, Buick's ACDelco-manufactured distributors will interchange with Gen I, Gen II, and Buick's aluminum small-block, which is sometimes referred to as the Gen III. The same thing goes for oil pans, timing chain covers, valve covers, and exhaust manifolds.

This is only a primer on the Buick Nailhead engine family. Due to a number of running production changes, speed building one of these engines is considerably more expensive and infinitely more complicated than building a small-block Chevrolet or Ford OHV. Fortunately, the internet is rife with Buick experts ready to point the would-be Nailhead builder in the right direction. In addition, CarTech Books recently published *Buick Nailhead 1953–1966: How to Rebuild and Modify* by Gary Weldon.

Stardom & Cardom

Television fans who grew up in the late 1950s will remember the show, *Highway Patrol* that aired from 1955 to 1959 and starred actor Broderick Crawford. Buick cop cars played a key role in the early days of that show—real Buick cop cars, not glamorized street cars.

In late 1954, the California Highway Patrol (CHP) contacted six domestic automobile manufacturers to advise them that the CHP was looking to replace its existing fleet of aging police cars. Buick Division responded with its Model 68, which was specially built and based on a Buick Special chassis that featured a Century two-door sedan body using Buick Special front sheet metal. It was powered by a 322-ci Fireball V-8 that had a 9.1:1 compression ratio and was rated at 236 bhp.

Buick won the CHP contract based on performance and price ($2,490.00 per unit), and 268 cars were ordered. The first CHP Buick Highway Patrol car was completed and delivered March 22, 1955. With a 50/50 ratio of manual 3-speed transmission cars to Dynaflow automatic transmission cars, the CHP Buicks were largely popular and highly respected. That is, unless you were being pulled over by one.

In spite of restrictive breathing on the exhaust ports, Buick Nailhead V-8s made great racing engines. Famed road racer and Hollywood Motors President Max Balchowsky of *Old Yeller* fame and "TV Tommy" Ivo are synonymous with Buick performance, and not too surprisingly,

In late 1954, the California Highway Patrol queried a number of Detroit's finest to produce a new Police Pursuit Package cop car. Buick rose to the occasion and built sort of a hybrid called the Model 68 using a combination of Buick Century and Buick Special chassis and sheet metal components. It was powered by a 9.1:1–compression ratio, 322-ci Fireball V-8 that was rated at 236 hp. Buick ultimately won the contract, and the State of California bought 268 of them.

Whenever people speak of Buicks, the name "TV Tommy" Ivo immediately comes to mind. In 1961, Ivo built his four-engine Buick Showboat exhibition car. Ivo said, "When Hot Rod magazine did a center spread on my twin-engine car, that was quite a feather in my cap, so when I was getting ready to build my four-engine Showboat, I walked right into Buick Division in Detroit with magazine center spread hot in hand and told them that I needed some motors. You should have seen the look on the face of Glendale, California's Barnett Buick service manager when all of those engines started showing up!" (Photo Courtesy Tommy Ivo)

their careers intertwined. In 1953, Ivo was making movies in Hollywood, while Balchowsky, who helped GM co-develop the 322-ci Buick Nailhead V-8 as a race engine, was building his Buick engine *Old Yeller II*. Tommy often hung out there between shoots. There's little wonder why Ivo's first hot rod, a 1923 Model T roadster pickup, was Buick powered.

Tommy continued drag racing Buicks throughout the 1960s using a single-engine gas dragster, a side-by-side twin gas engine dragster, two gasoline-burning Buick engines in tandem, and then his four-engine Buick *Showboat*, which is one of the most famous exhibition cars in all of drag racing. In addition, drag racers Gas Ronda, Ed Garlits, and Tony "Loner" Nancy launched their drag racing careers driving Buicks.

When it comes to designing speed equipment for any type of American V-8 engine, hot rodders largely drive the market, and it was no different with Buicks. Cam grinders such as Chet Herbert and Ed Iskenderian came up with numerous cam profiles for the Buick Nailhead V-8s. When it came to Buick induction systems, pioneers such as Fred Offenhauser, Vic Edelbrock Sr., and Stuart Hilborn immediately come to mind. For pistons and piston rings, Jahns and Grant led the way. Vertex built magnetos. Offenhauser and Eelco built engine dress-up kits for the Buick Nailhead, and the list goes on and on.

Ford Y-Block

In 1954, Ford introduced its 239-ci deep-skirt 90-degree Y-block V-8 engine, which, like the flathead that preceded it, initially displaced 239 ci. At the time, the shared-design Ford and Lincoln-Mercury Y-block was considered very rigid and as tough as an anvil. It was built to function in an across-the-board capacity when installed beneath the hoods of light-duty cars, such as the newly introduced Ford personal car (the Thunderbird), all the way through Ford's heavy-duty truck and industrial equipment lines.

Internally, the Ford Y-block's nickel-iron cylinder block featured a 3.5-inch bore and 3.1-inch stroke and was outfitted with a cast-alloy-iron five-bolt main crankshaft, a set of forged-steel connecting rods and three-ring-fitted flat-top aluminum pistons at 7.2:1 compression. Wedge-design cylinder heads featured vertically stacked high-turbulence intake ports with side-by-side 1.64-inch-diameter intake valves and 1.51-inch-diameter exhaust valves actuated by adjustable shaft-mounted rocker arms. Although not known for its breathing characteristics, a 2V-equipped 239-ci Y-block V-8 was capable of producing 130 hp at 4,200 rpm and 196 ft-lbs of torque at 2,000 rpm.

In 1955, Ford increased Y-block displacement to 272 ci for passenger cars and also introduced its 292-ci, 8.5:1–compression, 3.75-inch bore Thunderbird Special V-8 engine. The standard 272 featured a 2V Holley carburetor and was rated at 162 hp at 4,400 rpm and 258 ft-lbs of torque at 2,400 rpm. The M-Code Power Pack Thunderbird Special V-8 Engine Option utilized a Holley "Toilet Bowl" 4V carburetor and was rated at 182 hp at 4,400 rpm. The Thunderbird Special V-8 Engine Option was across the board on all Ford V-8 cars and denoted by a small chrome *Thunderbird Engine Option* script affixed to the front fender flanks.

In 1956, the standard 2V U-Code Ford Y-block produced 173 hp at 4,400 rpm and 260 ft-lbs of torque at 2,400 rpm with a manual 3-speed overdrive transmission, and 176 hp at 4,400 rpm and 264 ft-lbs of torque at 2,400 rpm when equipped with the Ford-O-Matic transmission. The Thunderbird Special V-8 grew to 312 ci and featured a 3.80-inch bore and 3.44-inch stroke at 9.0:1 compression and was rated at 225 hp (automatic) and 215 hp (manual).

The big news for 1957 was the release of Thunderbird's 312-ci V-8 engine that had 9.7:1 compression, a 3.80-inch bore, and a 3.44-inch stroke. The 312 was available with a single 2-barrel or 4-barrel Holley carburetor (rated at 245 hp and 245 ft-lbs of torque), the E-Code 2x4 Holley package (rated at 300 hp), or an optional 325-hp McCulloch VR-57 supercharger system. Thunderbirds with this option were affectionately referred to as *Blower Birds*. Due to size limitations, the Ford Y-block was replaced in 1958 with the introduction of the Ford-Edsel (FE) big-block engines.

Pontiac Strato-Streak V-8

It is somewhat ironic that Pontiac Motor Division (PMD) spent more time and money to develop a marketable OHV V-8 engine than any of its GM counterparts yet it took the longest to bring one to market. In the fall of 1954, the 287-ci Strato-Streak V-8 was released, and it debuted in PMD's all-new 1955 model lineup. The reason for this was a fairly conservative managerial infrastructure at Pontiac that felt that the existing OHV straight-8 powerplant was more than sufficient. However, that did not mean that PMD was not experimenting with the V-8 engine concept.

As far back as 1932, while still going by the name *Oakland*, the division briefly offered a 251-ci flathead V-8. In 1945, PMD designed a 269-ci flathead V-8 that was similar to Cadillac's 346-ci production V-8, but due to an impend-

In 1955, Pontiac came out with a whole new line of Tin Indians, and the upscale models, such as Catalina, were powered by PMD's new-from-the-ground-up 239-ci Strato-Streak V-8.

The Pontiac Strato-Streak OHV took a radical departure from using a shaft rocker-arm system like Cadillac, Oldsmobile, and Buick, sharing an engineering innovation, namely, self-adjusting, fulcrum-mounted individual rocker arms. This system was originally designed in 1948 by General Motors Engineer Clayton Leach and tried for the first time on both Pontiacs and Chevrolets.

ing industry-wide shift to OHV V-8 engines, the project was abandoned. However, that wasn't the end of it.

In 1949, Pontiac built its first experimental 8-cylinder OHV based on the 90-degree Oldsmobile Rocket V-8 engine block, but again, the project was stillborn. Had it not been for General Manager Robert M. Critchfield, who in 1952 was appointed to pull PMD out of a major sales slump, development of a Pontiac-branded V-8 may have gone on indefinitely. Critchfield pushed PMD to develop an affordable V-8 to compete in the midrange market against Oldsmobile, Buick, and (in due course) Chevrolet.

The result was Pontiac Motor Division's new Strato-Streak V-8, which featured a cast-iron 90-degree block with 2.5-inch-diameter main journals, a cast-iron four-bolt main crankshaft, forged-steel connecting rods, and cast-aluminum pistons. Bore size was 3.75 inches with a 3.25-inch stroke at 287.2 ci. Pontiac's wedge-shaped combustion chamber cylinder heads featured 1.781-inch-diameter intake valves and 1.50-inch-diameter exhaust valves. Rather than employing shaft-mounted rocker arms like Cadillac, Oldsmobile, and Buick, Pontiac's Strato-Streak V-8 featured self-adjusting, fulcrum-mounted individual rocker arms that pivoted on pressed-in rocker-arm studs like the 1955 Chevrolet. This system was originally designed in 1948 by GM engineer Clayton Leach and implemented for the first time on 1955 Pontiac and 1955 Chevrolet production-line V-8 engines.

Pontiac's Strato-Streak V-8 could be ordered in three versions: a Rochester 2V model with 7.4:1 compression that had 173 hp at 4,200 rpm and 256 ft-lbs of torque at 2,200 rpm and was backed by a 3-speed manual transmission; a dual-range Hydra-matic transmission model with a Rochester 2V at 8.0:1 compression that was rated at 180 hp at 4,600 rpm and 264 ft-lbs of torque at 2,400 rpm; or an optional 8.0:1–compression Rochester 4V, dual-range Hydra-matic-only version that produced 200 hp at 4,600 rpm and 278 ft-lbs of torque at 2,800 rpm.

Pontiac's new Strato-Streak V-8 engine was well received with the American motoring public, as the pre-1955 Pontiacs were largely viewed as rehashes of pre–World War II technology. *Motor Trend* magazine tested three 1955 Pontiacs early in the season: a 180-hp Pontiac Star Chief sedan, a 200-hp, 4V Star Chief Catalina Custom, and a 180-hp Pontiac Safari station wagon.

The Star Chief sedan recorded a 0 to 60 mph time of 13.6 seconds and recorded a top speed of 100.3 mph. Obviously, with an additional 20 hp on board, the Catalina Custom was quicker and faster, reaching 0 to 60 mph in just 12.7 seconds. Conversely, the 180-hp Pontiac Safari station wagon was road tested a total of 2,600 miles, and

when it came to fuel economy (pretty important stuff when you're on the open road), the Safari recorded an average 16.6 miles per gallon.

1956, You Ain't Seen Nothin' Yet!

Not one to rest on its laurels, PMD upped its game in 1956 with the release of its 8.0:1–compression ratio, 316.6-ci V-8 rated at 205 hp (or 215 hp with optional dual exhaust). Next was an 8.9:1–compression ratio, 316.6-ci 4V version that was found under the hood of the Pontiac Star Chief at 240 hp. Horsepower increased to 270 with optional dual exhaust.

Regarding the latter, *Motor Trend* magazine tested a fully loaded Star Chief four-door sedan without air-conditioning and recorded 0 to 60 mph numbers at 11.1 seconds and 50 to 80 mph times in the low-13-second range while recording a terminal speed of 106.1 mph. Lastly, the Tin Indian tribe offered a 7.9:1–compression 2V economy V-8 that posted an unspecified horsepower rating but was assumed to be no less than that from the previous year.

Now here's where things start to get interesting. In January 1956, PMD announced the availability of an optional 10.0:1–compression, 316.6-ci V-8 engine equipped with a hotter cam, stiffer-rate valve springs, a dual-point mechanical distributor, twin Rochester WCFB 4V carburetors, and dual exhaust. Rated at 285 hp, PMD's "Extra Horsepower" V-8 engine option was squarely aimed at the high-performance market, NASCAR, and (to a lesser extent) NHRA's emerging Championship Drag Racing Series, which in the mid-1950s was just beginning to find its legs.

However, that wasn't the really big news. Instead, it was the appointment of Semon E. "Bunkie" Knudsen as general manager of PMD. Knudsen came from an automotive family steeped in tradition. His father, three-star US Amy General (ret.) William "Big Bill" Knudsen had been one of Henry Ford's right-hand men during Ford's formative years. Then, in 1922, Big Bill departed from Ford to work for General Motors, first with Chevrolet Division and then with Pontiac, where he was appointed general manager. Finally, Big Bill ascended to the presidency at General Motors from 1937 to 1940.

Bunkie Knudsen's rise to fame began after receiving an engineering degree from the Massachusetts Institute of Technology (MIT) in 1936, after which he went straight to work at PMD in 1939 and remained there throughout the war years. In 1955, Knudsen ascended to the general manager position at Detroit Diesel. In July 1956 (less than a year and a half later), he was appointed to be the general manager at PMD.

Knudsen brought along with him Pete Estes from Oldsmobile and John DeLorean from Packard. With this trio of gearheads at the helm, it came as no surprise that eight new high-performance versions of the 1957 Pontiac Strato-Streak V-8 (with 3.50-inch bore and 3/16-inch stroke at 347 cubic inches) roared to the market. Boasting a higher-nickel-content steel block, 2.62-inch-diameter main bearings and main bearing caps, vented valve guides, and an improved lubrication system, the new 347 was big news.

Leading off was an 8.5:1–compression ratio 2V economy 347 V-8 that produced 227 hp at 4,600 rpm and 333 ft-lbs of torque at 2,300 rpm. Next in PMD's engine arsenal was the 10.0:1–compression ratio 2V 247 that produced 252 hp at 4,500 rpm and 354 ft-lbs of torque at 2,400 rpm.

PMD's first Rochester 4V Pontiac engine package had an 8.5:1 compression ratio and produced 244 hp at 4,800 rpm and registered 360 ft-lbs of torque at 2,600 rpm. Next was the 10.0:1 High Compression 4V that produced 270 hp at 4,600 rpm with 350 ft-lbs of torque at 2,800 rpm, which was followed by PMD's 10.25:1 Ultra High Compression 347 V-8 that produced 314 hp at 4,800 rpm and 375 ft-lbs of torque at 2,800 rpm.

In 1957, Pontiac produced two entirely new induction systems. The first was the 10.0:1–compression ratio, Hydra-matic-only Strato-Flite version, which had a trio of 2-barrel Rochester carburetors, or *Tri-Power*, as it so famously came to be known. This setup was capable of producing 290 hp at 5,000 rpm with 375 ft-lbs of torque at 2,800 rpm. Tri-Power also saw the light of day on the 10.0:1–compression ratio, flat-tappet cam NASCAR V-8 rated at 317 hp at 5,200 rpm and 375 ft-lbs of torque at 2,800 rpm. Also in PMD's induction systems arsenal for 1957 was the adaptation of GM's Corvette-inspired Rochester Mechanical Fuel Injection system. When bolted to a 10.0:1–compression ratio 347 Pontiac V-8, it produced 315 hp at 5,000 rpm and registered 375 ft-lbs of torque at 2,800 rpm. In 1957, PMD produced a total of 630 fuel injected Pontiac Bonnevilles, which more than 60 years later have become some of the most collectible Pontiacs of all time.

Engine displacement changed again in 1958 (this time to 370 ci) when Pontiac increased bore size to 4.06 inches while retaining the same stroke. The result was the new Tempest V-8. Although it replaced the Strato-Streak name that was used since 1955, it was in the same engine family. In 1958, Pontiac offered a number of different Tempest engine packages. There was the 285-hp Special Equipment engine that featured stiffer valve springs for sustained high-speed use, the 10.5:1–compression ratio Tri-Power engine that was rated at 300 hp, the 310-hp Rochester Mechanical Fuel Injection engine, and two 395 ft-lb 395-PK single 4-barrel

and 395A Tempest engines with Tri-Power.

The years 1959 and 1960 signaled the arrival of the new Wide-Track Pontiacs, which were essentially new from the ground up. New under the hood was a stroked-out 370, which now displaced 389 ci. Although it was still from the same engine family, the 389 featured 3-inch-diameter main bearings as opposed to the 370's $2^5/_8$-inch main-bearing diameter. For whatever reason, the new 389 Pontiac carried the *420* designation. There was the 215-hp Tempest 420E economy V-8. Then, there were the 330-hp 4V Tempest 420A and 345-hp Tri-Power high-performance engines. The year 1960 saw no major changes to the 389 V-8, although there were several new variants. Standard in the Bonneville with a manual transmission was a 235-hp version, while a 281-hp 389 was available with a heavy-duty (NASCAR and drag racing) manual transmission.

Mickey Thompson, Heap Big Chief in the Tin Indian Tribe

Perhaps the biggest news from PMD in 1959 was the alliance between General Manager Bunkie Knudsen and Long Beach, California, speed king Marion Lee "Mickey" Thompson. Backtracking to 1958, Mickey Thompson and Chief Mechanic Fritz Voigt built a full-body, twin-engine Chrysler dragster that was originally slated to compete at

In 1959, speed king Mickey Thompson struck a deal with Pontiac Motor Division of General Motors to provide four 389-ci powerplants for the Challenger I*. Initially, Thompson tried to run the Ponchos injected but fell short of producing the desired hp needed to break 400 mph. Undaunted, Thompson and Chief Mechanic Fritz Voigt redesigned the* Challenger I*, outfitting it with four GMC superchargers, and on September 9, 1960, Thompson drove the* Challenger I *into the record books at 406.60 mph.*

the upcoming US Nationals in Oklahoma City. However, the duo decided to stop at the Bonneville Salt Flats en route and make a "tune-up" run at 294.117 mph, and the rest was history.

Heartened by the results, Thompson and Voigt set about designing a four-engine, all-wheel-drive streamliner that was capable of breaking Englishman John Cobb's existing record of 402 mph, but what would they use to power it? Thompson initially pitched Chrysler Corporation, but since it was no longer manufacturing the 392 Hemi, the proposal fell on deaf ears.

That's when Thompson contacted lifelong friend Bunkie Knudsen, who was more than happy to ship Thompson four 389 Pontiac V-8 test engines. Suffice it to say that once Thompson perfected the basic body and chassis design of *Challenger I*, PMD was all in as a sponsor. Other sponsors included Mobil Oil, Goodyear Tire & Rubber Company, and Champion spark plugs. Thompson initially intended to run the Pontiacs in *Challenger 1* fuel injected, which he did. However, early testing at Edwards Air Force Base revealed that Mickey Thompson was about 300 to 400 hp shy of producing the desired power to eclipse Cobb's record.

That winter, Mickey Thompson Enterprises and the newly established Mickey Thompson Equipment Company threw all their collective efforts into reengineering the *Challenger I*. Four GMC 6.71 superchargers were mounted atop Mickey Thompson Equipment Company–foundered Pontiac supercharger intake manifolds. The internals of each engine were stuffed with the finest speed equipment available, including four sets of Mickey Thompson Equipment Company forged-aluminum connecting rods and four sets of Mickey Thompson Equipment Company forged-aluminum pistons.

The bodywork on *Challenger I* was reconfigured to accept a series of two humongous air intake scoops to cover the four GMC blowers. This time around, aluminum wheel fairings sealed off the front wheels. Thompson even repainted the *Challenger I* in a brilliant blue so that no one would mistake it for the "old" *Challenger I*. Nothing was left to chance.

In spite of losing power in one engine, Thompson set the one-way record at 406.60 mph at the Bonneville Salt Flats on September 9, 1960. Had he been able to successfully achieve a two-way average, that number no doubt would have been even faster, but he did nonetheless reset the record. Mickey Thompson and Pontiac were synonymous with each other throughout the first half of the 1960s or, more specifically, up until Bunkie Knudsen's departure from General Motors. That alliance was rekindled with Knudsen's late 1960s arrival at Ford, but that's another story for another time.

In 1963, PMD released a fleet of 14 lightweight 421 Catalinas dubbed Swiss Cheese Pontiacs. *With Pontiac's best driving them, such "Akron Arlen" Vanke (pictured) and others, the Swiss Cheese Pontiacs ran 12.30s at 118.00 mph in the quarter-mile. (Photo Courtesy Arlen Vanke)*

421 Super Duty

In 1962, PMD created its immortal 421 Super Duty V-8. PMD used the same casting as the 389 cylinder block but bored it an additional 1/32 inch and stroked it an additional 1/4 inch to bring displacement to 421 ci. Main bearing size was also increased from 3 inches to 3.25 inches in diameter. Dual Carter AFB (aluminum 4-barrel) carburetion produced 405 hp at 5,600 rpm.

However, NASCAR rules only allowed a single 4V to compete in its Grand National Series, so horsepower was dialed back slightly to 390. Nonetheless, 421 Pontiacs had a field day. Fireball Roberts, Smokey Yunick, Cotton Owens, Junior Johnson, Ray Nichols, and Joe Weatherly (winner of the 1962 NASCAR Championship with nine wins) did so with "Pure Pontiac Power."

In 1963, PMD produced a run of 14 lightweight 421 Pontiac Catalinas. Weighing 3,308 pounds (400 pounds less than stock), these cars were dubbed *Swiss Cheese Pontiacs* because approximately 120 to 130 holes were drilled in their chassis to reduce weight. Additional weight savings was achieved by using an aluminum hood, fenders, and doors. Even the 13.0:1–compression ratio 421 Super Duty V-8 engines (420 hp at 5,000 rpm) were put on a diet, using an aluminum 2x4 Carter AFB intake and cast-aluminum exhaust manifolds. Once placed in the hands of racers Arnie "the Farmer" Beswick, Don Gay, Howard Maselles, Jess Tyree, "Akron" Arlen Vanke, etc. quarter-mile times routinely ran in the 12.30-second zone at 118 mph.

The good news is that these 14 Pontiac Catalina

Big news for 1962 was the release of PMD's 421 Super Duty V-8 engine. When equipped with dual Carter AFB 4V carburetors, these engines produced 405 hp at 5,600 rpm. When outfitted with Tri-Power, 425 hp was immediately realized.

lightweights squeaked through production before GM's infamous moratorium on racing went into effect January 21, 1963, and they became some of the most collectible Pontiacs of all time. The bad news is also that these 14 Pontiac Catalina lightweights squeaked through production before GM's infamous moratorium on racing because these museum pieces never had the chance to reach their true performance potential.

The Chev-Ro-Lution

The 90-degree, 265-ci 1955 Chevrolet Turbo-Fire V-8 (produced from 1955 to 2003) was the last entry into Detroit's OHV engine wars and was (and still is) by far the best.

Designing the small-block Chevrolet V-8 began as early as 1952, when Ed Cole became chief engineer at Chevrolet Division and surrounded himself with the brightest engineers available, most notably including Harry Barr, who came from Cadillac. Chevrolet's lightweight, thin-wall casting (5/32 inch) 265-ci small-block V-8 went from the drawing board to production in about 15 weeks. It was introduced in the fall of 1954 to rave reviews in the new-from-the-ground-up 1955 Chevrolet Bel Air and third-year-production Chevrolet Corvette automobiles.

Cast at GM's Flint, Michigan, foundry using newly developed green core sand casting and manufacturing technology, exterior dimensions were 20.19 x 26.50 inches. With a bore of 3¾ inches and a stroke of 3 inches, GM's new offering used 8.5:1 compression, Autothermic three-ring (a top ring, expander ring, and single oil ring)

cast-aluminum pistons pressed onto 5.700-inch H-beam connecting rods with floating wrist pins. Rather than use the traditional cast-iron crankshaft, the 265 Chevrolet used a high-tech pressed forged-steel crank that rode on five main bearings equipped with an oscillating floating rubber damper.

The 265 Chevrolet engine made use of a solid-lifter camshaft and self-lubricating mechanical lifters with manual transmissions and hydraulic-lifter camshaft and hydraulic lifters when equipped with GM's Powerglide transmission. Lubrication was handled by a gear-driven mechanical oil pump that drew oil from a 4-quart oil pan and operated at 35 psi. The cylinder heads for each bank were interchangeable. There were no separate valve guides, and the valves (1.720-inch-diameter intake and 1.459-inch-diameter exhaust) ran directly through the cylinder heads. Huge intake and exhaust ports ensured optimum breathing and exhaust scavenging.

In 1955, Chevrolet broke with tradition and elimi-

In 1955, Chevrolet Motor Division hit the ground running with the release of the all-new Chevrolets. Styling was of course a key ingredient to generating sales, but engineering aspects were a close second. Chevy's new 265 OHV could be ordered in a number of trim levels beginning with a 2-barrel downdraft Rochester carburetor rated at 162 hp. Next was a Carter 4-barrel-carburetor version rated at 180 hp (or 195 hp when equipped with a solid-lifter cam). Partner that with dual exhaust and a manual transmission, and you were going places. (Photo Courtesy General Motors Media Archives)

Former Hot Rod *magazine journalist-turned-cam grinder Racer Brown was one of the first aftermarket cam grinders to grind high performance cam profiles for the small-block Chevrolet V-8 engine and was on the ground floor of the cam wars when he attempted to go head to head for cam supremacy with the great Ed Iskenderian. (Photo Courtesy Greg Sharp Collection)*

nated rocker-arm shafts. In their place it substituted lightweight stamped-steel individual rocker arms that oscillated on steel-on-steel ball joints that were supported by press-in rocker-arm studs. The fulcrum ball was held on the stud by an adjustable nut and locking screw. Valve lash was simply set by turning the adjustment nut to the desired setting. One-piece, *Chevrolet*-script, stamped-steel valve covers were held in place using a cork valve cover gasket with four 1/4-inch bolts.

The 265 Chevrolet's one-piece intake manifold eliminated the use of a separate cover over the lifter valley. Chevy's new small-block could be purchased with the 2-barrel downdraft Rochester carburetor rated at 162 hp at 4,400 rpm and 257 ft-lbs of torque at 2,200 rpm, the Carter 4-barrel carburetor rated at 180 hp at 4,600 rpm and 260 ft-lbs of torque at 2,800 rpm, or at 195 hp at 5,000 rpm and 260 ft-lbs of torque at 3,000 rpm when equipped with a Carter 4-barrel carburetor and solid-lifter cam. Exhaust duties were handled by a pair of log-type cast-iron exhaust manifolds that dumped

into a single-crossover muffler. That was a basic 265 Chevrolet small-block for 1955. When tested by *Auto Age* magazine, a 265 engine, Powerglide-equipped Chevrolet Bel Air four-door sedan went from 0 to 60 mph in 13.8 seconds and recorded a terminal speed of 101 mph. Separate tests also produced quarter-mile times for the same combination at 17.2 to 17.4 seconds.

That was Chevrolet for 1955, and from that time onward, the sky was the limit. Over the engine's 48-year history, displacement increased to 283 in 1957, 327 from 1962 to 1972, 302 for the special 1967 to 1969 Z28 Camaro performance models, 350 from 1967 to 2003, and 400 from 1970 to 1980. Other less-popular "low performance" small-block Chevy displacements included the 262, 305, and 307. All told, Chevrolet Division of General Motors estimated that more than 100 million small-block Chevrolet V-8 engines have been built since their late 1954 introduction. It's no small wonder that the performance aftermarket regards the small-block Chevrolet as the cornerstone of the industry.

"Parts Is Parts" and Chevrolet's Aftermarket Has Plenty of Them

With the release of the 265-ci Chevrolet pushrod V-8 engine, the performance aftermarket exploded practically overnight with new products: valve covers, carburetors, intakes, gaskets, fuel injection, camshaft and valvetrain components, connecting rods, pistons, stroker crankshafts, exhaust systems, aftermarket cylinder heads (which came later in the game), and more. Racer Brown was one of the first to grind cams for the 265 Chevy, and Ed Iskenderian, Clay Smith, Chet Herbert, and other big-name cam grinders weren't far behind.

In 1955, Vic Edelbrock Sr. made the cover of *Hot Rod* magazine when he wrung 375 hp out of one of these little engines, and Phil Weiand and other induction systems specialists conducted similar experiments. Rochester, Carter, and Holley all jumped on the 4-barrel-carburetor bandwagon. Chuck Potvin and Dean Moon adapted a crank-driven GMC supercharger to the front snout of GM's little Mouse Motor, Cragar designed a blower drive for the GMC 4.71/6/71 blowers, and Phil Weiand came up with the intake manifold to convert these engines to top-mount superchargers. Exhaust-system gurus Bob Hedman, Jerry Jardine, Jere Stahl, Doug Thorley, and others cobbled together thin-wall, mandrel-bent tubing (headers) to maximize peak horsepower. The bottom line here is that with the release of 1955's 265-ci Chevrolet small-block V-8 engine, the speed equipment industry practically became instantly revitalized.

The SBC Hot Rodding Legacy

The late Don Yenko, a specialty car builder and road racer, is photographed while racing his 283-ci small-block 1957 Corvette B/Modified car (one of many Corvettes that Yenko drove) at an undisclosed race track.

Throughout 1968 and 1969, car owner Roger Penske and the late Mark Donohue and their small-block Chevrolet Z28 Trans Am Camaros virtually dominated SCCA racing, winning the 1969 Trans Am Racing Championship.

Arguably the most famous Top Gas Dragsters of all time were the Peters & Frank Freight Train AA/GDs driven by a virtual who's who of drag racing talent, including the likes of Bob Muravez (known by his pseudonym Floyd Lippencott Jr.), Goob Tuller, Sam Davis, Billy Scott, "Wild Bill" Alexander, Mickey Thompson, Craig Breedlove, Tom "Mongoose" McEwen, and Leonard Harris. Prior to switching to twin Chryslers, the 'Train was powered by a pair of blown 380-ci Chevrolet small-blocks.

Small-block Chevrolets held their own in the AA/Fuel Altered ranks. In this photo taken August 5, 1967, the late Dale "the Snail" Emery lays rubber to virgin asphalt, driving Rich Guasco's infamous Pure Hell 1932 Austin Bantam during opening day at Orange County International Raceway.

The late Bill "Grumpy" Jenkins was the king of carbureted gasoline-burning small-block Chevrolet engines. This photo taken at the 1972 NHRA Winternationals in Pomona, California, has historical significance in that it was the very first run Jenkins put on his new Vega Pro Stocker in open competition against Melvin Yow. Jenkins won that event.

Throughout 1968 and 1969, Jenkins's racing partner, the late Dave Strickler, held the NHRA national record in SS/J throughout driving a pair of 302-ci Camaro Z28s.

It could be safely argued that when it comes to NHRA/IHRA drag racing, Stock Eliminator is where the small-block Chevrolet engine undisputedly rule the roost.

CHAPTER 4

THE BOOM YEARS: 1940–1970

Who opened the nation's first speed shop? That's been a decades-old question and the subject of discussion with hot rodders and car buffs wherever they meet. Arguably, Bell Auto Parts is the oldest speed shop on record.

Bell Auto Parts
Bell, California

Established in 1923, the business was located at 3633 Gage Ave., Bell, California, and founded by George Wight (pronounced *White*). Wight catered to Southern California's emerging elite on both board and dirt track circuits

The Bell Auto Parts satellite store known as the Palm Tree Oasis was first set up in 1949 on the dry lakes at Bonneville and served the racers' needs under the guidance of Bell Auto Parts employee "Roscoe" Turner, also known as the Mayor of the (Bonneville) Salt Flats. (Photo Courtesy Greg Sharp Collection)

and participated in some of the earliest land speed record contests conducted at Muroc, El Mirage, and Rosamond dry lakes prior to his passing in 1943.

In 1945, Roy Richter, who worked for Wight, assumed ownership of the business from George's widow and guided the company to new heights becoming an industry front-runner in both sales and manufacturing (i.e., Cragar Equipment Company, Bell Helmets, and Bell Safety Equipment).

Looks like a pretty busy place, eh? Bell Auto Parts was home to some of the most serious hot rodders operating out of the Los Angeles County Basin. (Photo Courtesy Greg Sharp Collection)

Under the ownership of Roy Richter (pictured), Bell Auto Parts developed everything from dropped front axles for early Fords to helmets and fire suits. To this day, Bell is a highly respected name in the safety equipment industry. (Photo Courtesy Greg Sharp Collection)

Lee's Speed Shop
Oakland, California

According to the majority opinion, Lee Chapel began selling race-prepared Ford Model T parts to dry lakes and dirt track racers at about the same time as Bell Auto Parts from a small shop on the property of a wrecking yard called Broken Drum Salvage at 3263 San Fernando Rd., San Fernando, California.

In 1933, Chapel moved the operation to 4557 Alhambra Ave., Alhambra, California, but closed the business in 1937 to be able to go midget racing. In 1939, Chapel moved north to Oakland, California, and reopened what was then known as Lee's Speed Shop, which was located at 1143 E. 14th St. Of particular interest is the fact that in later years, Chapel successfully marketed the Tornado OHV conversion for the Ford flathead V-8 engine and continued in the speed shop business until the mid-1950s.

Jim's Speed Shop/Harrell Racing Engines
Los Angeles, California

In 1932, Jim White, also known as Jim Harrell, opened Jim White's Speed Shop in a small building located on the front lot of a piece of property on San Pedro and 99th streets where Jim lived in Los Angeles, California.

A year later, White relocated the business to a more suitable location at 10924 S. Main at the corner of Main and 109th Pl. in Los Angeles, where he and his brother Nick Harrell remained until Jim's passing in June 1976. At one time or another, Jim's Auto Parts/Jim's Speed Shop and Harrell Racing Engines all lived under the same roof.

Pictured is a Harrell Engines dual-carburetor Ford flathead intake. Keep in mind that these intakes were manufactured in the early 1950s, but you wouldn't know it with all the fancy, CNC-like machine work. (Photo Courtesy Roger Harrell)

Harrell also produced these finned aluminum late-model flathead cylinder heads that were branded "Harrell Los Angeles" and sold through parent company Jim's Speed Shop. Speccing in with 64- to 67-cc combustion chambers, they breathed and performed rather well. (Photo Courtesy Roger Harrell)

White/Harrell also manufactured their own line of Ford flathead speed equipment, cylinder heads, and intakes.

Red Vogt's Garage
Atlanta, Georgia

Although not officially listed as a speed shop, Red Vogt's Garage (which called the corner of 565 North Avenue and Spring Street, Atlanta, Georgia, home) certainly qualifies as one.

Remember the fictitious Kogan's Speed Shop that waged war on the local moonshine-running establishment in United Artist's 1958 Robert Mitchum cult classic *Thunder Road* costarring Gene Barry, songstress Keely Smith, and Jacques Aubuchon? The mobster hangout in the movie was patterned (with great liberties taken of course) on Red Vogt's Garage.

Although the actual opening date is uncertain, many folks agree that Tom "Little Red" Vogt swung open his doors in the early-to-mid 1930s and gained notoriety by building moonshine runners and custom cars. Vogt's shop was frequented by an unlikely combination of affluent, excitement-seeking Georgia Tech engineering students as well as aspiring backwoods racers such as Lloyd Seay, who won the first official stock car race on record in 1938 at Lakewood Speedway in Lakewood, Georgia, with a 1934 Ford built by Vogt.

Another frequent visitor to Red Vogt's Garage was a man named Bill France Sr. Nine years later, Vogt assisted France in formulating the rules and suggested a name for the new automotive sanctioning body that France had in the works known as the National Association for Stock Car Auto Racing (NASCAR). The rest is history!

In 2002, Vogt was inducted into the Georgia Racing Hall of Fame in Dawsonville, Georgia, along with fellow inductees Lloyd Seay and Roy Hall.

Karl Orr Speed Shop
Culver City, California

The husband-and-wife team of Karl and Veda Orr were (to use the modern-day vernacular) early hot rodding's first super couple.

The irascible Karl Orr began dirt track racing Model Ts around Kingston, Missouri, in 1921 and moved in 1923 to Los Angeles, where he immediately became immersed in the LA car culture, which included dry lakes racing. In 1935, Orr earned a spot in the El Mirage 90 MPH Club with his 1932 Ford roadster. Then, he was crowned 1942's SCTA champ, a title that Orr continued to hold and improve upon until 1947.

History is unclear exactly how Karl and Veda met, but it was sometime in the early 1930s, as she would often accompany him to the races. The couple married

Karl and Veda Orr were hot rodding's first super couple. This is Karl's 1932 highboy roadster parked in front of the Karl Orr Speed Shop where the Orrs served the hot rodding community from 1940 to 1950. (Photo Courtesy Greg Sharp Collection)

Veda published Veda Orr's Dry Lakes Pictorial (shown is Vic Edelbrock Sr.'s personal copy) and Veda Orr's Hot Rod Pictorial. Both carried artwork by future AMC Chief of Styling Richard "Dick" Teague.

in 1936. In those pre–SCTA years, Veda went from spectator to participant. In 1937, she raced a full-fendered 1932 Ford at Muroc and recorded a top speed of 104.40 mph. She also raced under Russetta Timing Association sanctions and piloted the Taylor-Blair modified roadster to a record of 131 mph. Undoubtedly, Veda's greatest achievement was her May 26, 1947, SCTA record of 121.62 mph at El Mirage Dry Lakes with her 1932 highboy, which was a first for a woman in a previously male-dominated pastime.

In 1940, Karl and Veda opened the Karl Orr Speed Shop at 11140 Washington Pl., Culver City, California. Often, Veda ran the front counter while Karl was either chasing parts or working in the shop. During the war years (1943 to 1945), Karl worked at Northrop Aviation while Veda ran the shop almost exclusively and produced the California Timing (CT) newsletter that she mailed to hundreds of GIs stationed overseas.

In 1950, Karl accepted a permanent position at Douglass Aircraft in Santa Monica, California, and regrettably closed the doors to the Karl Orr Speed Shop. However, that's far from being the final act in this play. Karl and Veda Orr not only continued to race dirt track and dry lakes cars but Veda also published *Veda Orr's Dry Lakes Pictorial* and *Veda Orr's Hot Rod Pictorial* from 1946 to

When it came to racing the dry lakes, the boys had nothin' on Veda. She was one fast woman driving various cars, including her and her husband's 1932 Ford highboy roadster that was clocked at 121.62 mph at El Mirage Dry Lakes. However, Veda's all-time best was 131 mph at El Mirage in the Taylor-Blair modified roadster. (Photo Courtesy Greg Sharp Collection)

1953. Heading into their twilight years (the late 1960s), the Orrs opened a small speed shop on Sierra Highway at Mint Canyon in Newhall, California. Karl and Veda Orr passed away in 1988 and 1989, respectively.

Tom Madigan Weighs In

"Many of your World War II GIs dreamed of resuming their careers in the hot rod business, and many came home and used their military pay as a starting point. For example, legendary racer and innovator Akton "Ak" Miller was a real combat hero who came home and built a business in high performance (Ak Miller's Garage in Pico Riviera, California) and eventually became a part-time consultant for Ford-Autolite.

Bob Joenck came home to a two-pump gas station and a small garage in Santa Barbara, California, and turned it into one of the most respectable speed shops from 1948 to 1949 in the Golden State. Joenck used to tell stories about driving down to LA to stop at places like Edelbrock Equipment Company, fill up the trunk of his car with speed equipment, and drive back home again.

Q&A with So-Cal Speed Shop Founder Alex Xydias

Alex Xydias was another World War II veteran who dreamed about starting a speed shop and used his muster-out pay to make it happen. The following is a question-and-answer session with Xydias and author Bob McClurg.

Author: Ninety-eight years young, eh, Alex? You've seen a lot in those years. Where did it all begin?

Alex: I was kind of a hot rod kid. I went to Hollywood's Fairfax High School, and as it turned out, Jimmy Summers's custom shop was right across the street on Melrose and Fairfax avenues. Jimmy was an early custom builder, and he did some remarkable things. He was an absolute genius at chopping 1936 Ford coupes and Model A 5-window coupes, and they all came out perfect. I would go over to his shop after school and watch him working on these cars. The more I went, the more I became interested in hot rods.

Author: Watching was free?

Alex: Yes. I was young, and we had just gotten over the Depression. I graduated from Fairfax High School in 1940 and couldn't afford to own a car of my own, but I could afford to stand there and watch. Eventually, I did pick a little full-fendered 1929 Model A Ford roadster that I bought off a used car lot in Hollywood. I think I paid $65 for it. However, I had to have my mother drive it home for me because I still hadn't gotten my driver's license yet.

Author: So that's how it all began?

Alex: My buddies and I would drive out to the dry lakes on the weekends and watch Vic Edelbrock Sr. and those other guys run. Then, World War II came along. During the war, I would show pictures of my car and other friends' cars to my fellow soldiers in the US Army Air Corps. To this day, I don't know how I ever mustered up the courage, but I opened up So-Cal Speed Shop the day I got out of the service, which made a lot of people wonder.

In those days, the discharge center was located in Long Beach, California. Everybody had to go down there to get their discharge. With hundreds of thousands of us getting out of the service pretty much at the same time, they were so backed up that I would be sent home and told to come back again. Then, I would go back down there on the next day, and I would get sent back again! Well, I had time on my hands. I already rented a little store on Olive Avenue in Burbank. I already built the shelves and had done all the heavy lifting, so by the time I finally got discharged from the service on March 3, 1946, I was ready to open.

Author: But why beautiful downtown Burbank and not Hollywood?

Alex: Somehow in my mind, Hollywood didn't seem like the right place to have a speed shop. It didn't seem like a hot rod place even though Porter Muffler and Eddie

Alex Xydias proudly stands behind the Bobby Meeks–Edelbrock Mercury flathead-engine So-Cal Speed Shop streamliner that ran over 208.927 mph in 1950 at the Bonneville Salt Flats. (Photo Courtesy Bruce Meyer Collection)

Meyer were there and a lot of other well-known car people, so I drove out to Burbank and found this little building with a storefront on the end of it, and I instinctively knew that it was the right place.

At first, I was a little shocked that the owner would rent a brand-new building to someone who was going to open a speed shop, but his son (who was a barber) had just gotten out of the service too. He had a 1932 Ford roadster, so he may have talked his father into it, but everything just worked out. I remember the rent was $100 a month. To tell you the truth, I was a nobody in the car world. Sure, I'd been to the lakes a bunch, but I was just one of many who did. How I even got the courage to open up that shop I'll never know, but I did!

In those days, the US government offered a 50/20 deal for the regular guys who had just gotten out of the service. That was $20 a week for 50 weeks. On average, it came to $100 a month. I would drive to the Hollywood Social Security Office and turn in my weekly receipts, and if I didn't make $100, they would give me a check for the difference. At the start, nobody was coming in the door, so I had to drive down there several times. Gradually, people drove down Olive Avenue and saw the speed shop sign, and they started coming in.

Author: What kind of inventory did you carry?

Alex: I didn't have any money, so stocking cylinder heads and intake manifolds, which were both quite expensive, was a bit of a luxury. I had a lot of chrome-plated acorn nuts and chrome carburetor stacks and other nickel-and-dime stuff.

Both the So-Cal Speed Shop belly tank and a So-Cal 27-T street rod participate in what is believed to be the annual Burbank on Parade event held in April. (Photo Courtesy Bruce Meyer Collection)

The car that put So-Cal Speed Shop on the map was its famed flathead engine belly tank built by Xydias, Dean Bachelor, and Bill Burke. This car set a series of records in 1947 and 1948 at 145.395, 181.085, and 195.77 mph using various-displacement Ford flathead V-8 engines. Today, this car has been restored and is part of the Bruce Meyer collection.

Then all of a sudden, the guys started converting their cars over from Kelsey-Hayes wire wheels to steel wheels. Well, I had made friends with all the Ford parts countermen at dealerships around the San Fernando Valley. So, whenever a dealer would get in a shipment of steel Ford wheels I would buy every one they had and stock pile them in my shop. That's the kind of "speed equipment" I was selling in the early days, but that helped me make enough money to pay the rent and eventually grow the business.

I got to know all these guys in the San Fernando Valley who were the movers and shakers in the hot rod movement. One of them was Dean Bachelor, who became my partner in the streamliner. He came to the shop the second day I was open for business. Anyhow, I was selling all this little-guy stuff. There was this oil that was good for racing named *Sta Lube*, and I'm selling tons of it and anything else that I could do to make a buck. At the time Vic [Edelbrock Sr.] was over on [1200] North Highland Avenue in Hollywood in a little gas station, so I literally could drive right over the hill on Barham Avenue and pick up a set of heads or a flathead intake manifold and bring them back.

Author: How did you come up with the name So-Cal Speed Shop?

Alex: I'm not sure how I came up with that. It was just one of those things, and it ended up being perfect. After being in business for a year, I had built it up to the point that I wanted to get away from just being a speed shop and get into a place where I could work on some cars and maybe build a lakester of my own.

In 1947, I rented a lot over in Burbank at 1204 S. Victory Blvd. and ordered a Sears prefab two-car garage. By then, I had made friends with so many hot rod guys in the valley who were building homes either professionally or for themselves, so I had plasterers and construction guys, electricians—you name it—I had it as customers. I put the building right in the middle of the lot, and we put the whole thing up in about two days. Had I put it on the street, I wouldn't have had room to build a storefront, which I did. In 1948, I moved over from the original location, and it was business as usual. Eventually, I built another building out back that had stalls where you could work on cars, so business was okay.

Author: When did you build the So-Cal Speed Shop belly tank [car]?

Alex: Things were beginning to happen, so in the summer of 1948, we [Dean Bachelor, Bill Burke, and Xydias] built the So-Cal belly tank. The scallop color scheme on that car

Alex Xydias poses with a copy of the first-ever So-Cal Speed Shop catalog signed by industry pioneers Don Francisco, Wally Parks, Bill Burke, Tom Medley, and Stuart Hilborn. (Photo Courtesy Alex Xydias)

was distinctive, and it made it immediately recognizable. Neil Avery from Valley Custom built the headrest for me. I had a lot of pride in that car and the business in general, so everything we did on the car was first class. We started having measurable success at the lakes, breaking a total of five records at 145.395, 181.085, and 195.77 mph using three different-displacement unblown Ford flathead V-8 engines. When *Hot Rod* magazine came and put the car on the cover [January 1949], everyone in the world knew who we were. That was really a turning point for So-Cal Speed Shop.

Author: Any interesting stories?

Alex: One day in 1948, this Ford coupe pulled up in front of the shop. I'm looking out through the front window and I see Sandy Belond get out of the car. He was just starting out in the business making muffler systems and headers and stuff. Anyhow, he had come up with this new idea he called the Belond Equa-flow exhaust system that included the headers, the pipes, the mufflers and tailpipes. He claimed that it not only increased horsepower but it also increased mileage. It was the first effort by a hot rod parts manufacturer to build a product that you could install on your Ford street car and make it run better and have more power. I could see that this was not only a potential area of growth in the hot rod market but also in the mainstream automotive marketplace as well.

Pretty soon, I started calling the business So-Cal Speed & Power, and we're getting engineers from Lockheed coming in and cartoonists from Disney Studios coming over and bringing in their station wagons looking for more power to tow their boats and stuff, so the Belond thing came along at the right time. I rented the vacant lot next door, paved and put in an installation rack to handle the business.

Author: So, what was the next big growth spurt?

Alex: I was always looking for something new and exciting to sell. Now, those are actually not your typical So-Cal Speed Shop kind of part, but this so-called speed emporium began selling bolt-on continental kits. I don't remember who manufactured them. It wasn't Cal Custom, but we all started buying them; you could bolt one on the back of your 1950 Ford. They looked good and fit good. That was kind of the So-Cal Speed Shop story.

Author: Alex, you're being modest.

Alex: As soon as the article in *Hot Rod* magazine came out, it turned the So-Cal Speed Shop logo into something recognizable on a national scale. Trying to get on the cover of *Hot Rod* magazine was a dream for most people, and here we get on the cover a total of five times with the streamliner and the coupe. Talk about being blessed!

Popular Mechanics Weighs In

In 1960, *Popular Mechanics* magazine technical writer George Hill authored *Hot Rod Handbook and Directory of America's Finest Speed Shops*, a 145-page paperback book that covered the popular subject. Below is a breakdown of the chapter titles:

- Chapter 1: Why Do We Hop Up Stock Engines?
- Chapter 2: How to Hop Up Production Engines
- Chapter 3: Hot Rod Chassis Designs
- Chapter 4: Organized Hot Rodding Today
- Chapter 5: Bonneville National Speed Trials
- Chapter 6: The AAA's Speed Week
- Chapter 7: The 200-MPH Club
- Chapter 8: Speed Shops of The Nation
- Chapter 9: A Manufacturers' Directory
- Chapter 10: The Sports Car Association

Chapters 8 and 9 of the *Hot Rod Handbook* still have some relevance 60 years later and, if nothing else, provide

In 1960, Popular Mechanics writer George Hill wrote the Hot Rod Handbook and Directory of America's Finest Speed Shops, which provided an insider's look at the world of hot rodding. Out of print for 60-plus years, this book is treasured by vintage hot rod lifestyle literature collectors everywhere.

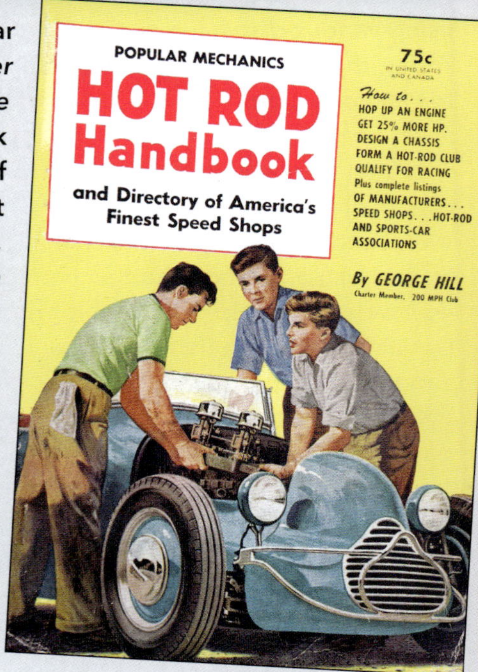

a historical window into the who's who of the 1960s American speed shop industry. In those two chapters, Hill alphabetically covered all 48 states as well as the territories of Alaska and Hawaii. Would you believe that a total of 617 participating companies were tallied, with 42 of them being cross-referenced in the Power and Speed Equipment subdirectory, with an additional 22 being cross-referenced in the Miscellaneous Manufacturers subdirectory? Not surprisingly, the state of California had the most entries at 140, and you might be surprised at just how many of those companies from all 48 states and the two territories surveyed are still doing business.

Although *Hot Rod Handbook and Directory of America's Finest Speed Shops* has been out of print for several decades, every once in a while, you can find a copy for sale on the internet or through antique automobile literature dealers. It will cost you a heck of a lot more than the original newsstand retail price of 75 cents, but it'll be well worth it!

Ansen Automotive
Gardena, California

An alumnus from the Class of 1946 was the late Louis "Louie" Senter of Ansen Automotive, who once said, "Cars are in my blood," and he wasn't just whistling Dixie.

Senter's love affair with the automobile began at age 12, when he won his class at the Gilmore Oil Company–sponsored soap box derby. Like many budding gearheads, Louis wasn't much for schooling—that is, until he enrolled in a vocational machine-shop class while in high school. Senter impressed both his instructor and, more importantly, his parents to the extent that ole mom and dad saw fit to buy him his first lathe, drill press, and welder as graduation presents.

In 1939, Louis went to work as a machinist and tool and die maker's apprentice for Byron Jackson Oil Tool Company (a division of BorgWarner) in Long Beach, California, for a whopping 40 cents an hour. When World War II broke out, Senter turned down a possible deferment to join the US Navy as a machinist mate.

Upon the war's end, Louis signed on with Eddie Meyer Engineering (EME) in Hollywood, California. In those days, EME was *the* place to be if you were into the local hot rodding culture. However, Senter decided that it was high time that he had a place of his own and opened up a machine shop with his brother Sol.

The business was located on Crocker Street in downtown Los Angeles, and in no time at all, the place was buzzing with local hot rodders. When Senter and his brother moved the business to Jefferson Boulevard in 1947, they took on noted engine builder Jack Andrews as partner and changed the name of the business to Ansen (for *An*drews and *Sen*ter) Automotive Engineering.

Louie later said, "We opened one of the first true speed shops in the city."

Ansen wasted no time developing product, including motor-mount kits, pressure pumps, steering wheels, manifold adaptors, etc. for Ford Model T, Model A, and flathead V-8s. Kits were devised to convert mechanical brakes from rods to hydraulic for early Fords. Dropped

Pictured in 1950 at 6317 Normandie Ave. in Los Angeles, this was Ansen Automotive Engineering's third location. Pictured (from left to right) are Lou Baney, George Cline, Louie Senter, Bill Childers, and Jim Kavanaugh. (Photo Courtesy Greg Sharp Collection)

Ansen Automotive Engineering was one of the first companies in the industry to offer a yearly catalog, the first of which sold for 25 cents. The 1951 catalog and a later 1970s-edition catalog are shown.

front axles were developed for Model As as well as 1932-and-onward Ford V-8s. Ansen had been in the mail-order business since 1945, but it greatly expanded the program and even produced its first catalog that sold for a whopping 25 cents.

Throughout 1949 and 1950, Ansen Automotive

One of Ansen's more-successful projects was its 4-banger Chevy II top-end engine package that transformed GM's docile little 4-banger into an all-out racing engine that was ideal for use in everything from dirt track cars to boats.

A staunch Ansen supporter was the late Tom Sturm, a Chevrolet racer who raced a series of Just for Chevy Lovers exhibition match race stockers in the mid-1960s under the Ansen Automotive Engineering banner.

Ansen aggressively advertised its products exploring all avenues of communication from serious to funny. Anything was game just as long as the ad in question got the point across and sold product. (Photo Courtesy Greg Sharp Collection)

Engineering built a number of race cars, including a roadster that went 151 mph at El Mirage Dry Lakes. In 1954, the company built the *Ansen Belmont Special*, a 1954 Studebaker that went 247 mph at the Bonneville Salt Flats. Louie also built an Offenhauser-eating Ford V-8 60-engine midget that raced on the board track at the LA Coliseum and the Pasadena Rose Bowl. The company participated in drag racing events held at the Old Santa Ana and Saugus drag strips. Senter's involvement at Indianapolis began with an IndyCar building project for racer Lou Bromme. The company also worked on an IndyCar project for 500 winner Jim Hurtubise. In those halcyon days, it seemed as though Ansen Automotive Engineering's corporate fingers were in every pie.

When it came to hard parts, the company manufactured high-tech Ford flathead crankshaft kits, and in the 1950s, it sold complete engines, shipping many to a number of top-flite NASCAR teams.

"We started getting lots of engine orders from the South, but we didn't know who these people were at the time," Senter said. "Turns out they were bootleggers who were outrunning the police. Then, we started receiving orders from police departments for engines so that they could catch the bootleggers!"

In 1950, Senter bought out his partners in Ansen Automotive Engineering, and the business finally became

At Ansen, anything was fair game, including this 374-ci Packard-powered dragster engineered by Ansen in 1961 and owned and driven by Don Duncan. (Photo Courtesy Greg Sharp Collection)

Undoubtedly one of Louis Senter's finest moments came when his Ansen Sprint aluminum wheels were chosen as rolling stock for the Jim Hurtubise–driven Frito Lay Special IndyCar No. 56. *(Photo Courtesy Greg Sharp Collection)*

100-percent family owned. That same year, the company moved to its new headquarters on Normandie Avenue in Los Angeles. The move was an expensive one, and Senter looked for ways to shore up that all-important bottom line.

"We were one of the first shops to sell used speed equipment along with our new inventory," he said. "During this period, we raced dragsters, sprint cars, midgets, and boats. We worked six days a week and we had all the bases covered."

Ansen also worked with George Barris on various car-building projects, including the coffin car for *The Munsters* TV show. Around that same time frame, the company developed the Posi-Shift, the first kit to move a column shift to the floor.

In the early 1960s, Ansen Automotive Engineering moved operations to Western Avenue in Gardena, California. By then, its catalog had grown to 100 pages filled with everything from pistons, connecting rods, and safety bell housings to the latest in Ansen T-shirts. The early 1960s was also the beginning of the custom-wheel era. While Halibrand and American Racing were busy shoeing the racers, companies like Appliance, Fenton, Mickey Thompson, Cragar, and Ansen outfitted the street crowd. Ansen's Sprint one-piece aluminum wheel took the industry by storm, and the company sold tons of them.

In 1969, Louis Senter sold Ansen to the Whittaker Corporation but remained as a consultant until 1974. In 1978, Louis was inducted into the SEMA Hall of Fame, and he was inducted into the *Hot Rod* magazine Hall of Fame in 1997. He received the 1998 Western Racing Association award for his 50-year contribution to racing and was inducted into the 1997 Dry Lakes Hall of Fame. On May 28, 2016, Louis Senter crossed the finish line for the last time. He was 95 years young.

Blair's Speed Shop
Pasadena, California

Born September 3, 1921, in Highland Park, California, dry lakes pioneer and hot rod industry mover and shaker Don Blair attended Lincoln High School in South Pasadena, California, prior to taking automotive classes at Frank Wiggins Trade School in Los Angeles, California.

Before striking out on his own, Blair learned the ins and outs of the auto parts business by working in early-1940s-era parts houses and machine shops around the Greater LA Basin. In 1945 (when Don was 25), his grandfather died and left him a modest inheritance, and Don bought a lot on Arroyo Parkway and founded Blair's Speed Shop. Don's brother Bruce came along with the deal and was responsible for engine building and chassis fabrication.

In the late 1940s, Blair erected a small building on Foothill Boulevard in Pasadena and hired his first employee, Tim Timmerman, only to outgrow the location a few years later. In the early 1950s, Blair purchased the former Thornton and Carlson Candies building, which had a showroom and was half a block down the street at 2772 E. Foothill Blvd. and Daisy Avenue, and called it home.

However, the responsibilities of the new shop didn't deter Blair from his racing activities. In 1945, as a member of the Pasadena Roadster Club, Don was the first to adapt a Roots-type supercharger that was cannibalized from a Mercedes-Benz and used on a Ford flathead V-8 engine. This setup powered his modified roadster, also known as *the Goat*, to a top speed of 141 mph with a

The black and white photo of Blair's Speed Shop was taken in the mid-1950s and shows a vintage sprint car parked alongside a Chrysler-engine dragster. The other photo shows Blair's Speed Shop in 2017. Very little has changed.

Today, Blair's is owned by Gas Supercharged and Altered racer Phil Lukens, who proudly carries the Blair's name into battle on the side of his Fiat AA/A. (Photo Courtesy Blair's Speed Shop)

Check out all the cool stuff inside Blair's showroom. It's sensory overload for gearheads.

In the late 1950s and early 1960s, Blair's set the standard for Tri-Five Chevrolet straight-axle conversions. Check out this immaculate 1955 Chevrolet D/Gasser.

two-way average of 130.27 at El Mirage Dry Lakes.

Throughout the 1950s, Blair's Speed Shop was well-known for its dropped front axles for early Fords and its expert chassis preparation. From the late 1950s to early 1960s, Blair's set the standard for Tri-Five Chevrolet straight-front-axle conversions, and everyone else followed. With Irwindale Raceway (established in 1965) just a stone's throw away, Blair's Speed Shop became the racer's one-stop shop on race weekends for spark plugs, oil, gaskets, race gas, nitro methane, alcohol, etc. Suffice it to say, Blair's sponsored many race cars that competed at Irwindale, including those that belonged to Robbie Robertson, Don and Betty Walker, Ruel Nicol, Don Lindford, and countless others.

However, the most notable cars of the Blair's Speed Shop–sponsored entourage were those belonging to the late Steve Bovan. In the early 1960s, Blair's Speed Shop sponsored the Bovan and Castro 1961 Corvette, which was followed with the sponsorship of Bovan's 1964 Plym-

The late Steve Bovan ran a series of hot Chevrolets under the Blair's Speed Shop banner. His most famous car was this 1965 Chevy Nova, the first of its kind to run a blown, nitro, 396-ci big-block Chevy engine in competition.

outh 426 Wedge match racer. In 1965, Bovan, Indy 500 great Sam Hanks, and Blair's made national headlines with the sponsorship of Bovan's blown, nitro-gulping, 427-ci 1965 Chevy II match racer. Bovan's follow-up act was the Blair's Speed Shop flip-top 1968 Chevrolet Camaro Funny Car. Both the Chevy II and Camaro were built in-house by Blair's chassis-meister Mike Hoag.

In 1974 after 25 years of ownership, Don Blair sold the business to gasser racer/employee Phil Lukens. In 1985, Don started Blair's High Performance, an engine-building facility that specialized in sprint car engines at 142 S. Glendora Ave., Glendora, California. Don Blair died September 29, 2011 at age 90.

Catalogues, Car Magazines, and Decals

At age 9, my parents gave me a subscription to *Hot Rod* magazine. As a youngster, I used to pore through each and every issue looking for speed equipment manufacturers that offered catalogs and decals (stickers) that I could buy with my hard-earned money that I earned from throwing papers on the week days and shining shoes on the weekends. That was my world! Although the likelihood of ever buying anything from one of the many catalogs that I sent away for was slim to none, I regarded them as an extension of my induction into the world of hot rodding, as they were informative reading.

When it came to collecting racing decals, Ed Iskenderian was my all-time favorite decal guy. Ed gave you real value for your money, which was pretty important to a 9-year-old kid. Isky would send you an assortment of decals for 25 to 50 cents. Remember the Iskenderian 5 Cycle Cams clown? I clearly was what you would call a decal junkie, and I got really good at writing letters to manufacturers begging for free decals.

I drove my parents and teachers nuts with racing decals stuck on my lunch box, schoolbooks, locker, bike—yes, it was "Moon Equipped"—on the headboard of my bed, and on the back of my bedroom door. I even

Collecting racing stickers is addicting. This photo was taken of the author and drag racing great Bob Muravez, also known as Floyd Lippencott Jr., standing in front of the door of his toy shop based in Hilo, Hawaii. (Photo Courtesy Sharon Muravez)

stuck them on the roof of my kid sister's playhouse. Now you can get as psychological as you want about this, but in my mind, there were (and are) a lot of people who have addictions that are worse.

Catalog Confessions
By Donna Leal

When my husband, Butch Leal (also known as the California Flash), was at Bill Thomas Race Cars in Anaheim, California, building his 1970 Camaro Pro Stock car, I helped out a little, but I was basically kind of bored.

Bill Thomas immediately noticed that and inquired, "You want to do some work? I'll be happy to pay you!"

My job was to open up the mail for the catalogs. He ran a little ad in *Hot Rod* magazine, advertising his latest catalog for $1, and I was amazed at the amount of response and the amount of money—all these $1 bills falling out of the envelopes! It was a real neat experience, and my eyes were opened to the volume and how powerful mail order was at that time."

Speedway Motors
Lincoln, Nebraska

Speedway Motors was founded in 1952 by D. William "Speedy Bill" Smith.

Born June 22, 1929, Smith was indoctrinated into the world of wheels at a young age by a neighborhood tinkerer named Milo Caslasky. At age 12, Smith built a go-kart using a mishmash of parts taken from a washing machine and a baby buggy. At age 14, Bill purchased his first real car, a Model T Ford, and he began fixing up and selling other Tin Lizzies to earn pocket money.

Ever since the night that Bill's father took him to midget races at Landis Field, he was forever hooked. After briefly racing dirt-track motorcycles, Smith graduated to dirt-track roadsters in 1949, but after driving through a fence during a race in Hastings, Nebraska, Smith hung up his helmet and driving gloves for good. After that, all of the cars Bill Smith built were driven by hired drivers, including the Tiny Lund–driven, Speedway Motors–sponsored 1956 Pontiac in NASCAR competition.

Bill Smith was a car guy from the get-go. Bill is shown sitting behind the wheel of the last race car he ever drove. After crashing through a retaining wall at a 1949 race at Hastings, Nebraska, Smith left the driving chores to other drivers. (Photo Courtesy Speedway Motors Archives)

Digressing somewhat, Bill's family lived on O Street, the main drag in Lincoln, Nebraska, where he witnessed the local hot rodding scene unfolding firsthand. It seemed as though all the local car guys hung out at Elmer's Conoco Station, so that was as good of a place as any to start exchanging ideas and bonding with other like-minded gearheads from the neighborhood, Smith said.

"It was amazing the lengths we'd go to get something we wanted for our car," he said. "For example, one day I heard a set of Smitty's mufflers, and I was absolutely enthralled. What was that sound? It was fantastic! Of course, I wanted a set for my 1940 Ford coupe. Unfortunately, the nearest set I could find was in Denver, Colorado. No problem. I simply drove from Lincoln,

After graduating from Nebraska Wesleyan University with a degree in industrial education, Bill Smith borrowed $300 from his fiancé (and future wife) Joyce Uphoff to open Speedway Motors in 1952. (Photo Courtesy Speedway Motors Archives)

Nebraska, to Denver, Colorado, [approximately 500 miles each way] just to buy a set. Back in those days, you did what you had to do."

Incidents like this likely planted the seed in Bill's mind to undertake his greatest endeavor, launching his own mail-order speed equipment business. In 1952, Bill was faced with a conundrum. Having just graduated with a degree in industrial education from Nebraska Wesleyan University, he was offered the security of a full-time teaching job at one of the local high schools for a whopping $2,750 per year. Conversely, Bill's racing endeavors were usually somewhat profitable, having grossed $4,500 the previous summer racing sprint cars. Smith was also making money hopping up cars for his buddies on the side and was likewise making a profit buying and selling fixer-uppers. Most importantly, Bill was engaged to his future wife, Joyce Uphoff.

At age 23, life seemed far too exciting to surrender to the mundane. Smith decided to roll the dice and give the dream of owning his own speed shop a chance. He borrowed $300 from his fiancé and opened Speedway Motors in a 300-square-foot building at 2232 O St. in downtown Lincoln.

In those early years, Smith did anything and everything he could just to keep the doors open, and that included selling snow chains during the winter. In the interim, Smith worked hard to establish himself and his fledgling enterprise with the major players in the speed equipment industry. Early on, Smith showed uncanny marketing acumen. For example, whenever he would receive a high-performance part, he would prominently display the part in his showroom window and put the empty box up on his shelf. That way it looked to the customer like there were two parts in stock instead of one!

Within two years (1954), Speedway Motors had grown to the point where Smith was able to move into a larger 5,000-square-foot, full-service facility at 1719 N St. in Lincoln. Simultaneously, Smith's racing endeavors were also beginning to pay dividends. The Speedway Motors *4x* sprinter driven by Lloyd Beckman was the local dirt-track killer, and we've already covered Speedy Bill's exploits in NASCAR racing. Both endeavors, and others like them, kept the name Speedway at the forefront of the industry, and the sales inquiries and parts orders started rolling in.

In early 1960, Bill and his wife, Joyce, launched the first Speedway Motors catalog. Smith was also advertising in *Hot Rod* and *Car Craft* magazines, and the orders started flooding in. However, there was a downside to Smith's success, and that was shipping. At the time, there was no United Parcel Service (UPS) depot in Lincoln, and USPS Parcel Post wasn't very dependable. Shipping by

This was a typical Saturday or "Sale Day" in the mid-1960s at Speedway Motors with Bill and Joyce right in the thick of things. (Photo Courtesy Speedway Motors Archives)

Bill Smith's dedication to American speed began in the 1960s when he began to collect old race cars and speed equipment. This resulted in the Bill Smith Collection of American Speed at 599 Park Creek Dr., Lincoln, Nebraska. Shown in this picture taken on dedication day are Bill and Joyce along with sons Carson, Craig, Clay, and Jason. (Photo Courtesy Speedway Motors Archives)

Greyhound or Continental Trailways overnight service (guaranteed within a 500-mile radius) seemed to somewhat alleviate the problem; although, it did not do so entirely.

In 1962, Speedway Motors opened its own fiberglass facility and began manufacturing plastic street rod bodies like 1923 Model Ts, Model A Fords, and 1932 Deuces. The company also opened a metal fabrication shop that manufactured chassis and suspension components. Voilà: the affordably priced Speedway Motors T-Bucket, the Speedway Motors Track-T, and the Speedway Motors 1932 Lo-Boy roadsters. The success of Speedway Motors in racing grew exponentially in United States Auto Club (USAC) Sprint cars and Outlaw dirt-track cars with memorable victories at the 1976 Hulman Classic with driver Jan Opperman and the 1978 Knoxville Nationals with the immortal Doug "Wolfie" Wolfgang at the wheel.

In 1989, Smith's sons Carson and Jason teamed up to win the American Indy Car Championship with their Bobby Unser–driven Lola Chevrolet. In a totally different kind of racing, the Speedway Motors–sponsored streamliner of John MacKichen with Tim Schultz as driver set the record for its class at the Bonneville Salt Flats in 1990 at 326.17 mph.

With their corporate hands in virtually every automotive pie, Speedway Motors again moved to a larger 500,000-square-foot facility in 2000 and opened its new 135,000-square-foot corporate offices that same year.

Throughout it all, Smith followed his passion of collecting vintage race cars, racing engines, and anything else that involves American speed. He also opened the 135,000-square-foot, tri-level Bill Smith Collection of American Speed at 599 Oak Creek Dr. in Lincoln, Nebraska.

Sadly, Bill Smith passed away in May 2014. Joyce followed in August 2014. Today, sons Carson, Craig, Clay, and Jason Smith guide the destiny of the 68-year-old, mail-order, speed equipment powerhouse.

Gratiot Auto Supply
Detroit, Michigan

In 1945, Bill Toia opened Gratiot Auto Supply on the northeast side of the Motor City at 9146 Gratiot Ave. Although small in size, Gratiot gained a huge reputation for having the right automotive replacement parts at the

Speedway Motors has always maintained a strong presence in mail-order and catalog sales. Here is an example of an advertisement that was printed in the April 1992 issue of Street Rodder magazine.

right time and providing fast and courteous customer service.

Upon his discharge from the US Army in 1957, Angelo Giampetroni, who had done odd jobs at the original store throughout his early teens, joined the business full time. Giampetroni, also known as Junior, was an absolute wizard at marketing. In no time at all, the name Gratiot Auto Supply was on everybody's lips. Giampetroni expanded the operation, which included eight stores in the Greater Detroit area, to become the largest speed shop in the state of Michigan. In the process, Gratiot Auto Supply sponsored a number of top-ranked drag racing cars that belonged to the likes of Al Bergler, Ron Mancini, Maynard Rupp, Pancho Rendon, the Ramchargers, and many others.

The company also published a new catalog every year. In the mid-1970s, it hired the First Lady of Drag Racing, Linda Vaughn, also known as Miss Hurst Golden Shifter, as spokeswoman for the company. Vaughn appeared on the cover of several Gratiot Auto Supply catalogs and in its print ads. Moreover, the blond bombshell from Georgia starred in Gratiot Auto Supply TV commercials that aired throughout the Greater Detroit Metroplex.

Gratiot had several marketing successes with the most noteworthy being the Gratiot Track-T roadster, which was available in kit form and aggressively promoted by *Hot Rod* magazine. However, by the early 1980s, the bubble burst due to the effects of the oil crisis, an ailing economy, a severely weakened domestic automobile industry that had seen the death of the muscle car and rise of the foreign import car, and high interest rates. The end came when foreign investors suddenly called in Gratiot's inventory loan. After 52 years in business, Gratiot Auto Supply was sadly no more.

This vintage Gratiot Auto Supply advertisement from the mid-1950s is fairly clever with its flathead-engine pony declaring, "We sell horsepower." (Photo Courtesy Gratiot Auto Supply Archives)

Linda Vaughn did a series of catalog covers as well as many promotional appearances for Gratiot Auto Supply and was extremely popular with GAS customers. One of Gratiot's more-successful promotions was its Gratiot Track-T street rod/kit car program, which made the cover of Hot Rod magazine. Vaughn reflects back on the moment.

Memories of Gratiot Auto Supply

This following is a compilation of quotes from prominent figures in the automotive industry who reminisce about their experience with Gratiot Auto Supply.

Al Bergler

Metalsmith, Funny Car Driver, 2004 NHRA Hot Rod Reunion Lifetime Achievement Award Winner

"We lived pretty close to Gratiot Avenue, which in those days [the early 1950s] was the used-car capitol of the world. At about age 14, Angelo Giampetroni used to ride his Whizzer bicycle to Gratiot Auto Supply. He did odd jobs there for founder Bill Toia like sweeping up and stocking the pop machine. When Angelo came out of the [US] Army, he went to work at Gratiot Auto Supply full time. At the time, I worked about a mile away at Matt's Collision, which is how I met Angelo. By then, Gratiot Auto Supply had become one of the biggest speed shops in the state of Michigan.

"I was running my Comp Coupe and somehow got

Upon inception, Gratiot Auto Supply (or GAS, as it was referred to by the locals) was engaged in the sale of stock replacement auto parts. That all changed when young Angelo Giampetroni (center) joined the organization fresh out of Uncle Sam's service in 1957. A dyed-in-the-wool hot rodder, Giampetroni gradually eased the company into the high-performance parts business, transforming it into the largest speed shop in the state of Michigan and the entire Midwest. (Photo Courtesy Gratiot Auto Supply Archives)

Gratiot Auto Supply's Angelo Giampetroni (bottom row, far left) accepts his Sponsor of the Year Ollie as part of the 1968 Car Craft magazine All-Star Drag Racing Team Awards. Other luminaries include (in no particular order) Doug Thorley, "Dyno Don" Nicholson, Keith Black, Jack Chrisman, Buddy Martin, "Dandy Dick" Landy, "Big John" Mazmanian, Bill "Grumpy" Jenkins, "Big Daddy" Don Garlits, Ed Iskenderian, Roland Leong, "Wild Willie" Borsch, "Ohio George" Montgomery, Gordon Collet, and others.

Al Bergler's Aggravation series of competition coupes and roadsters featured some of the first pro class drag cars that Gratiot Auto Supply ever sponsored. (Photo Courtesy Al Bergler)

From 1968 to 1976, Ron Mancini campaigned a series of 1968½ Hurst Hemi Dart Super Stocker's in the SS and Modified Production classes. Shown in action is one of his more successful entries, the candy red and black, Gratiot Auto Supply–sponsored Zoom-O 426 Hemi Dart, competing in NHRA Super Stock A/Automatic.

hooked up with Gratiot as a sponsor. Actually, I didn't get any money from them, but I got lot of free stuff [hard parts] through them. They also ordered my first dragster chassis straight from Scotty Fenn's Chassis Research."

Ed Weichsler
Former Holley Sales Representative

"While working for Holley, I called on Angelo at Detroit High Performance, Gratiot Auto Supply's warehouse. What a place! The amount of Holley product sold via their mail-order program and through their stores filled quite a few 50-footers.

"Angelo was a Holley fan, and Holley had a profound presence in all Gratiot Auto Supply stores. I remember opening the Ford Road store. That was the ultimate high-performance experience: a parking lot full of hot rods with all the tech reps there, parts flying off the shelves, and dear sweet Linda [Vaughn] gracing the room. She's not only gorgeous but she also knows how to sell her product line [Hurst Performance] inside and out. Just ask her."

Linda Vaughn
Miss Hurst Golden Shifter

"It was great working with Angelo and his wife, Kathleen. At the time, we were doing a series of TV commercials for Gratiot Auto Supply that aired around the Greater Detroit area. Angelo acted just like a director. He wanted things done his way, and only his way. After a while, we started calling him 'Angelo B. DeMille' [a play on the name of filmmaker Cecil B. DeMille]; it was great fun.

"Of course, Gratiot Auto Supply was one of our [Hurst Performance's] biggest dealers, and these commercials really became popular. One time, when I flew in for the Detroit Auto Show, Kathleen picked me up at the airport and said, 'Girl, you are a star!' I said, 'What are you talking about?' She went on to tell me that the local TV stations were running Gratiot commercials three times a day for the past month.

"When I got to the show, I got absolutely mobbed by these teenage boys and their daddies! It was absolutely

In 2018, Gratiot Auto Supply's Angelo Giampetroni was caught off guard when former GAS Flint, Michigan, store employee Jim Hanley presented him with a mint-condition 1970s-era Gratiot Auto Supply jacket and banner. (Photo Courtesy Jim Hanley)

great! They loved Gratiot Auto Supply. I remember my tagline on the commercial was, 'If you dig your car, truck, or van, man, come on down to Gratiot Auto Supply and tell them Linda sent you,' and all these people would come into their stores and say, 'Linda sent me! Linda sent me!'

"We also did a whole series of Gratiot Auto Supply catalogs as well and special programs like the Gratiot Auto Supply Street-T project, which made the cover of *Hot Rod* magazine. We also played the Gratiot commercials in the Hurst Performance booth at SEMA, so the whole thing went hand in hand."

Jon Lundberg
The Voice of Drag Racing

"Gratiot Auto Supply. Wow, what memories! I lived some 100 miles away in the state capitol of Lansing, Michigan. In the late 1950s, a group of us would pool our change for a tank of gas and would drive down to Gratiot Auto Supply just to look at all the cool speed equipment they had on display there. Bill Toia, Gratiot Auto Supply's founder, had every name brand of speed equipment stocked and ready to take home. It was like losing cats in a seafood store! Those experiences welded me to drag racing and hot rodding forever."

"Big Daddy" Goes Retail

Donald G. Garlits isn't called "Big Daddy" for nothing. The 91-year-old drag racing legend remains the undisputed king of the dragsters, having built and campaigned more than 34 Top Fuel cars that captured a total of 144 eliminator titles, including 17 World Championships.

During his formable years, Garlits operated a series of speed shops beginning in 1956 with the acquisition of an old dirt-floor gas station, also known as Don's Garage. It was at 12828 Nebraska Ave. in Tampa, Florida, and was where Garlits and his brother Ed built and campaigned the earliest of the *Swamp Rat*–series dragsters.

In 1960, Garlits and his wife, Pat, purchased an acreage six blocks south on Nebraska Avenue and built Don's Speed Shop (later was known as Garlits Automotive Parts and Machine), which was a state-of-the-art facility with the speed shop up front and the machine shop and fabrication shop in the rear. It was there that Garlits and the late Connie Swingle built everything from bare dragster chassis to turnkey race cars.

In 1964, acting on the advice of a number of corporate sponsors, Garlits pulled up stakes and moved from

This is "Big Daddy" Don Garlits's first speed shop at 12828 Nebraska Ave., Tampa, Florida. (Photo Courtesy Donna Garlits)

Don, his wife, Pat, and brother Ed Garlits pose with crew member Bobby Philips (far left) with the first Swamp Rat *dragster built at the aforementioned Nebraska Avenue location. (Photo Courtesy Donna Garlits)*

Tampa, Florida, to Troy, Michigan. There, he opened Don Garlits Incorporated at 85 Minnesota Ave., Troy, Michigan, with a focus on both mail-order parts and expanding the dragster-chassis-building business. Unfortunately, the move proved to be problematic on both business and personal fronts. With a growing number of employees to manage and an increased touring schedule that demanded more and more time, combined with the cold winters and that he and Pat's youngest daughter,

In 1960, Don and Pat purchased property six blocks south of the original shop and opened Don's Speed Shop, which was later known as Don Garlits Automotive Parts and Machine. (Photo Courtesy Donna Garlits)

Acting on advice from his sponsors, Garlits moved to Troy, Michigan, in 1964 and opened Don Garlits Incorporated. Shown in this photo are Don, Pat, Donna, Gay Lynn, and Miss Hurst Golden Shifter Linda Vaughn during the ribbon-cutting ceremony. (Photo Courtesy Donna Garlits)

In 1969, Garlits opened Don Garlits Hi-Performance World at 3420 W. Main St., Tampa, Florida. (Photo Courtesy Donna Garlits)

Gay Lynn, was starting school, Don and Pat decided to return to the Sunshine State. They built a beautiful new home with a shop attached at 812 Hwy. 574 and picked up where they had left off.

The year 1969 marked the opening of Don Garlits Hi-Performance World at 3420 W. Main St., Tampa, Florida, and a new building was later added to house the race car operations. Business boomed until the gasoline crisis of 1974 forced its closure.

With an ever-watchful eye toward the future, Don and Pat founded the Museum of Drag Racing, a nonprofit corporation, in 1974. After several years of hard work on the part of Don, Pat, the late Herb Parks, and Tommy "T. C." Lemons, along with craftsman Willie Wilde, the interactive Don Garlits Museum of Drag Racing opened in March 1984 at 13700 SW 16th Ave., Ocala, Florida, 34473, just off Interstate 75. This 24-acre facility features plenty of room for RV parking and is registered under the name *Garlits Attractions*. The site currently includes the Museum of Drag Racing and gift shop, Don's mechanical and restoration shops, an Antique Car Museum, and Don's private residence.

This was the speed shop that Don and Pat had always dreamed about. Unfortunately, Garlits had to close the doors in 1974 when the gasoline crisis hit. Far from being down and out, Don and Pat made plans to open the Don Garlits Museum of Drag Racing, which was officially dedicated in 1984 at 13700 W. 16th Ave., Ocala, Florida. (Photo Courtesy Donna Garlits)

Moon Equipment Company
Santa Fe Springs, California

Dean Moon, who lived from May 1, 1927, to June 4, 1987, grew up in the Southern California hot rod car culture. His father owned a local Norwalk, California, eatery called the Moon Café, where Dean worked as a bus boy and fry cook. The café was located on a lot that was big enough for Dean to build a makeshift go-kart track in the back that he referred to as *Moonza*, a tongue-in-cheek jab at the famed Italian race course in Monza, Italy.

Dean's first car was a 1932 Ford sedan, but it wasn't fast enough, so he swapped it for a flathead-engine 1927 Model T roadster that he raced at both El Mirage Dry Lakes and the Bonneville Salt Flats. Moon was as much into innovating as he was into racing. In 1950, he started his company at 10935 S. Bloomfield Ave., Santa Fe Springs, California, and began designing and manufacturing hot rod parts, such as multi-carburetor fuel blocks, Moon foot pedals, Moon wheel discs and Moon fuel tanks. He did so out of a garage behind his father's café, and everything was branded under the Moon Automotive Equipment Company name.

Hot Rod Industry News publisher Alex Xydias once commented that Dean, who photographed and wrote his own press releases, was so prolific that *Hot Rod Industry News* could count on having a Moon Automotive Equipment Company new product release published in each and every issue.

Regarding the company's world-famous Mooneyes logo, Moon received the inspiration from the slanted *00* lettering on the side of Creighton Hunter's *Slice of Pie* flathead-engine dragster, which resembled a pair of bugged-out eyeballs. In 1957, Moon's frantic eyeballs were reimagined by a professional artist from the Walt Disney Studios, and the rest is history. Today, the Moon Equipped logo is one of the most famous corporate logos in all of motorsports.

Moon Equipment Company was known for a number of firsts. In 1960, Moon purchased the designs, patterns, assets, and equipment from ignition, camshaft, and blower drive specialist Chuck Potvin. Moon reengineered

The home of many hot rodding firsts, Moon Equipment Company was where Carroll Shelby's original 260-ci Ford small-block engine Cobra roadster was born. (Photos Courtesy Rick Kopec and Shelby American Automobile Club)

For 2½ decades, Moon Equipment Company operated out of this spacious and highly identifiable facility at 10820 S. Norwalk Blvd., Santa Fe Springs, California.

Today, the company is owned by Shige Suganuma and Chico Kodama (pictured) and continues to produce Moon Discs, the product that put Moon Equipment Company on the map.

Mooneyes also produces varying sizes of Moon's famous spun-aluminum fuel tanks.

Mooneyes also replicated Dean's original Dragmaster chassis, Potvin-supercharged, Chevrolet-engine gas dragster known as Mooneyes (shown at the 2017 California Hot Rod Reunion in Bakersfield, California). The original is on permanent display in Don Garlits's museum.

Potvin's crank-driven small-block Chevrolet blower system, installed a test engine in his Dragmaster Chassis *Mooneyes* dragster and won class at the 1961 NHRA Nationals.

In 1962, after moving to its permanent address at 10820 S. Norwalk Blvd. Santa Fe Springs, California, Moon collaborated with Carroll Shelby on the aluminum-body, Ford small-block 260 V-8 engine CSX 2000 (also known as the Cobra). That same year, Moon worked with George Barris to reengineer the original Batmobile with a Moon-equipped drivetrain.

In 1963, Moon was the first drag car racer to ever travel outside the continental United States, when *Mooneyes* made exhibition runs in Monza, Italy. Then, in 1964, Moon was part of the United States Drag Racing Team that toured Great Britain and parts of Europe and Australia. That same year, Dean's Chevrolet-engine, Devin-fiberglass-body kit car *Moonbeam* set a record at the Bonneville Salt Flats at 206 mph and won the Brighton Speed Trials in England.

Here's a humorous Dean Moon story. Sitting prominently on display in the corner of Dean's showroom was a Moon-equipped, Fred Larsen–assembled big-block Chevrolet engine on an engine stand. Unbeknownst to those who stopped to admire it, Moon had the starter wired up to a remote switch behind his sales counter. Whenever an unsuspecting crowd of admirers would gather around the engine, Moon would hit the starter button!

After Dean died, Moon Equipment Company lapsed into the doldrums, and a year after Dean's wife, Shirley, passed away, the business closed

Here is a copy of one of Dean's earliest catalogs. It features 32 pages of hard-core hot rod hardware. At the time, the company was located at 10935 S. Bloomfield Ave., Santa Fe Springs, California.

entirely. In the early 1990s, Shige Suganuma, a longtime Mooneyes dealer in Japan relaunched Moon Equipment Company with business partner Chico Kodama as manager. Today, Mooneyes USA is back in business and is as strong as ever. In 2017, Dean Moon was posthumously inducted into the Don Garlits International Drag Racing Hall of Fame in Ocala, Florida.

Reath Automotive
Long Beach, California

Alabama-born Joe Reath spent his early years living with his grandparents Frank and Emma Reath in Tehachapi, California. After Joe's grandfather died, Emma Reath moved in with Joe's mother, Elaine, and his stepfather, Dr. Charles Ulrich, in San Pedro, California. Reath attended San Pedro High School and graduated in 1943.

After spending two years as a private in Uncle Sam's infantry, Joe was released from the US Army in 1945 and went to work porting flathead engine blocks for pattern maker/machinist/speed equipment manufacturer/dry lakes racer Earl Evans. At the time, Evans was widely recognized as the flathead king, and Joe received an excellent education working there.

In 1947, Joe switched gears and took a job in the punch-press department at Douglas Aircraft, where he ultimately became a foreman. He spent his days learning the ins and outs of metal fabrication and metallurgy from the finest craftsman in the business while spending his nights building engines for hot rodders and dry lakes racers.

As a member of the Road Runner's Car Club, Joe built engines and/or worked on cars owned by future *Hot Rod*

Here's an early-1970s photo of Joe Reath posing alongside his big-block Chevrolet-engine 1957 Ford Thunderbird taken at nearby Long Beach Harbor. Note the HMS Queen Mary *in the background.*

magazine publisher/creator Robert E. "Bob" Petersen, NHRA founder Wally Parks (*Hot Rod*'s first editor), Vic Edelbrock Sr., Ray Brown, Ak Miller, and others. Not satisfied with membership in just one car club, Reath jointly held membership in both the Arabs Car Club and the Lancers Car Club of Long Beach.

In 1953, Reath teamed up with old army buddy Harvey Haller on a flathead-engine belly tank. Unfortunately, Haller was killed while driving a DeSoto-engine Modified Model A roadster on October 3, 1953, at El Mirage Dry Lakes. At this juncture, Reath purchased all of Heller's equipment from his estate and began making plans to own his own speed shop. But first . . .

Oklahoma-born Delma "Dellie" Raymer graduated from Compton High School in June 1955, and she first met Joe at a local drive-in at Long Beach, California, in 1956.

"I was with some of my girlfriends, and he [Reath] was with some of his car buddies," Dellie said.

In no time and all, Reath had his new girlfriend attending the local drag races at Santa Ana Airport with him, and he even persuaded her to accompany him to El Mirage Dry Lakes to see what he actually did for a living.

"We spent a lot of time sitting in the push truck," Dellie said.

In October 1957, Joe and Dellie were married.

Backtracking slightly, Reath Automotive opened its doors in January 1957 at 10th Street and Cherry Avenue in Long Beach. An American success story based on the rewards gleaned from long hours and hard work, Dellie ran the front office while Joe was in the back, keeping

This employee photo was taken at Joe and Dellie's first Reath Automotive location at 10th Street and Cherry Avenue in Long Beach, California. (Photo Courtesy Greg Sharp Collection)

things humming along in the machine shop—and when we say *humming*, we really mean it!

When it came to race-preparing crankshafts, engine blocks and cylinder heads, Reath Automotive was the class of the field. Of course, having Lions Drag Strip only a half dozen exits north off the 405 Freeway certainly didn't hurt, especially on race weekends, making Reath Automotive *the* one-stop shop for racers.

By 1965, Reath Automotive had outgrown its original location and moved up the street to 33rd and Cherry avenues. In the process, Joe and Dellie employed some of the best racers, machinists, and salespeople in the business, including crankshaft wizard Henry Velasco and machinists Neil Loeffler and Jerry Ballard to name a few. Reath understandably sponsored a number of big-name dry lakes and drag racers, including Top Gas Dragster great George Bolthoff; Fuel racers Ratican, Jackson, and Stearns; and header king Doug Thorley, who won the first Funny Car Eliminator title at the 1967 NHRA US Nationals; Texas Fuel racers Vance and Hunt; Joe Malliard (Reath & Malliard AA/FD); Top Gas racer Gordon "Collecting" Collet; Tom "Mongoose" McEwen; and La Mirada, California, fireman-turned-professional Top Fuel and Funny Car racer "Big Jim" Dunn, from Dunn and Reath fame.

Knowing that the walk-in trade was truly where he and Dellie's bread was buttered, Joe made it a point to service not only the seasoned professional but also the up-and-coming racer or man on the street, offering sizeable discounts and long deals on parts and services.

However, with the dawn of the mass marketers and

Throughout the late 1960s and early 1970s, Joe and "Big Jim" Dunn campaigned a series of Dunn and Reath Top Fuel Dragsters and AA/Fuel Funny cars with notable success. (Photo Courtesy G.K. Callaway)

the loss of many of the state of California's famed drag strips to real estate speculators (Lions was the first to go), Joe and Dellie could see the writing on the wall. Reath Automotive officially closed in 2006.

After years of declining health, Joe Reath passed away on January 4, 2013, but not before becoming an honoree at the 1995 edition of the Southern California Automobile Club–sponsored, Wally Parks/NHRA Automotive Museum of Drag Racing–hosted California Hot Rod Reunion at Bakersfield, California, and the 1996 Lions Drag Strip Reunion. Furthermore, Joe had been posthumously inducted into the 2015 Dry Lakes Racing Hall of Fame, and both he and Dellie were inducted into the 2017 Don Garlits Museum of Drag Racing/International Drag Racing Hall of Fame.

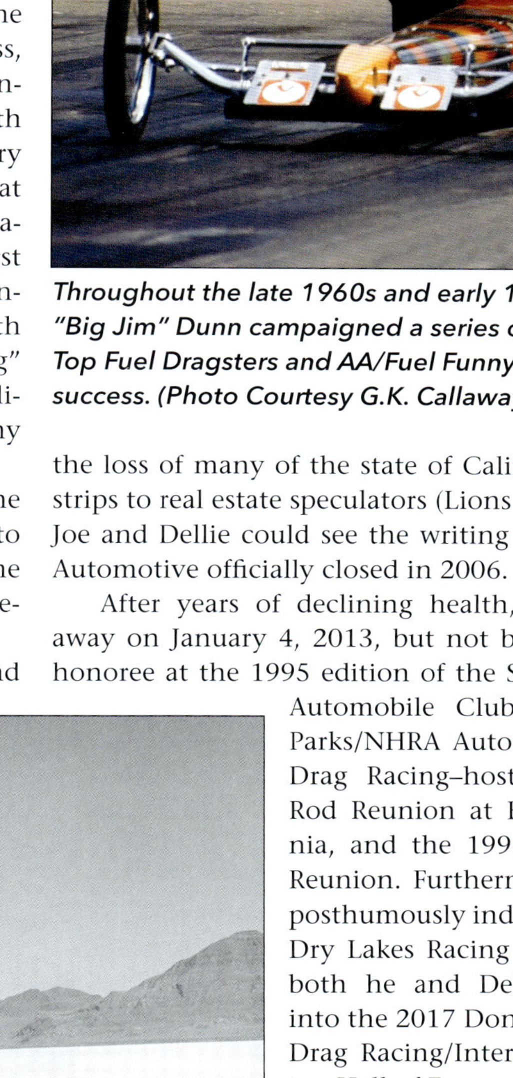

Reath Automotive was proactive in all kinds of racing. The Reath-sponsored, land speed record-holding Burke & Chastain Modified sports car was just one of many land speed record cars flying the Reath Automotive banner. (Photo Courtesy Greg Sharp Collection)

CHAPTER 5

SEMA AND THE SEMA SHOW

In 1963, Revell models of Venice, California, was developing a series of 1/25-scale plastic model-car kits based on real-life examples of nationally prominent drag racing cars that were campaigned by the likes of Stone, Woods, & Cook; "TV Tommy" Ivo; Mickey Thompson; Dean Moon; and Tony Nancy. At that time, the company's legal department attempted to fill a gap in the industry by addressing a potential trade regulation problem regarding the replication of corporate logos carried on the sides and being used by the subjects in question. One didn't have to be a nuclear physicist to see a potential legal problem on the horizon.

Trade regulation laws are those that are enacted by federal and state governments to promote unrestrained competition among businesses. Trade regulations extend into many categories of law, such as antitrust law, which prohibits anticompetitive acts like price fixing, monopolistic conduct, and deceptive practices. Consumer protection law, advertising law, trademark law, and franchise law also fall under the umbrella of trade regulations.

Obviously, Revell could and would not release any model car kit to the general public unless the product was 100-percent legally unencumbered. A call went out to industry insiders, such as Louis Senter (Ansen), Bob Spar (B&M), Roy Richter (Cragar), Els Lohn (Eelco), Ed Iskenderian (Iskenderian Cams), Vic Edelbrock Jr. (Edelbrock), John Bartlett (Grant Industries), Don Alderson (Milodon Engineering), Dean Moon (Moon Equipment Company) Paul Schiefer (Schiefer Manufacturing), Willie Garner (Trans-Dapt), Phil Weiand Jr. (Weiand Equipment Co.), Bob Hedman (Hedman Headers), Dempsey Wilson (Dempsey Wilson Racing Cams), Harry Weber (Weber Cams), and Robert E. Wyman advising them of a foreseeable legal problem having to do with advertising and trademark law, which fell under the umbrella of trade regulation laws. The result was the creation of the Speed Equipment Manufacturing Association (SEMA) with the above names listed as protectorates (founding members). Ed Iskenderian was appointed as SEMA's first president.

So, what else did the newly formed SEMA do? Aside

The first SEMA Show was held beneath the bleachers at Chavez Ravine's Los Angeles Dodger Stadium in January 1967 with 98 participating manufacturer member companies and approximately 3,000 attendees. (Photo Courtesy Don Prieto)

from protecting legally registered corporate trademarks, SEMA's mission was (and still is) to develop uniform standards for certain products used in motorsports competition. For example, the non-profit SFI Foundation Inc., which SEMA founded in 1978 but is now a separate entity unto itself, was to issue and administer quality-assurance standards of specialty performance and racing equipment by developing and administering certification and testing criteria for use in motorsports. Today, the SEMA/SFI stamp can be found on everything, including dragster and Funny Car chassis, safety harnesses, driver's suits, wheels, clutches, safety bellhousings, etc.

Other SEMA objectives were (and are) to promote the industry as a supplier to consumers involved in constructive activities of recreational and hobbyist value, to develop programs to encourage improved business practices among member companies, and to hold regular meetings to achieve unity as a business organization.

In addition, to the pursuit of new markets and helping to cultivate them, SEMA's vigilant and relentless role as an industry watchdog has (through its maintaining of a government affairs office in Washington, D.C., and key locations worldwide) averted ill-conceived legislation that could have, if passed, reaped disastrous repercussions to the industry and motorsports as a whole. To quote then–SEMA President and CEO Chris J. Kersting:

"Working together as a coalition, members of SEMA have the benefit of proficient legal representation," he said. "It would at least border on being prohibitively expensive for a company to individually tackle the problems involved with legislation and regulation by government agencies, in particular those that cause hardship among small- to medium-size business entities. More than ever, SEMA membership carries with it a benefit that far outweighs the annual fee paid by a company to be an active member."

Part of that membership includes receiving SEMA's official house organ, *SEMA News*, which keeps its membership informed of potentially ill-advised legislation and what's being done about it. Throughout its 57-year history, SEMA has segmented itself to address a broader membership mix. For example, old car scrappage programs have been an ongoing concern to hobbyists. The Automotive Restoration Market Organization (ARMO) section of SEMA has been at the forefront of efforts to assist states and municipalities with the design of acceptable collector and recycling programs. Instead of scrappage programs, SEMA stresses the merits of inspection and maintenance programs, which is important not only to ARMO but also the general automotive parts and service sectors.

The list of SEMA's involvement goes on and on (visit sema.org), but one program well worth mentioning is the SEMA Memorial Scholarship Fund, which is dedicated to fostering the next generation of automotive aftermarket industry leaders and innovators. Assistance is available for career paths in the automotive industry in accounting, engineering, as a race car driver or crew member, in administrative information technology, sales and marketing, advertising, business, manufacturing, as a technician, design and graphics, photography and

A young Joe Hrudka stands (second from left) in the Mr. Gasket booth many years ago. (Photo Courtesy Don Prieto)

Bob Hedman, founder of Hedman Hedders (left), was one of the original founding members of SEMA and a strong supporter of the first SEMA Show. (Photo Courtesy Don Prieto)

journalism, and transportation. A minimum 2.5 GPA is required as well. For scholarship information, visit sema.org/scholarships.

In 1963, SEMA's founders could not have imagined the eventual scope of the association as a guardian and leader in motorsports industry affairs. The yearly SEMA Show (occasionally referred to as the Academy Awards of the Automotive Aftermarket) at the Las Vegas Convention Center in the first week in November is open to qualified member applicants (speed shop owners) and validates SEMA's dedication and resolve to the automotive aftermarket.

The first SEMA Show was described as a card table and folding chairs affair, as the late Jim Deist, Deist Safety Company founder and president, attests. (Photo Courtesy Don Prieto)

Iskenderian Cams employee Ted Frye strikes a pose for Don Prieto's camera prior to the opening of the show. (Photo Courtesy Don Prieto)

Show History

In 1965, noted automotive journalist and *Speed Equipment Directory* magazine publisher Noel Carpenter organized the Speed and Custom Equipment Dealer Association trade show (SCEDA), which was the first of its kind and offered an insider's-only viewing of what the speed equipment industry offered. Based on that initial success, Carpenter produced the second-annual SCEDA trade show in 1966. However, this time SEMA lent its name and promotional prowess. Although not officially considered a SEMA event, the association received a share of the profits for the use of its name. Now, here's where the plot thickens.

Robert E. Petersen of Petersen Publishing Company fame (a direct competitor of Carpenter) had simultaneously started his own speed equipment expo and promoted the event through PPC's trade publication *Hot Rod Industry News* with Alex Xydias as editor and Dick Wells

Vic Edelbrock Jr. was another original founding member of SEMA. That Edelbrock Equipment Company display pales in comparison to the huge displays that the Edelbrock Corporation of today shows annually. (Photo Courtesy Don Prieto)

Bob Spar, co-founder of B&M Automotive Products, extols the performance virtues of the latest and greatest items B&M had to offer. (Photo Courtesy Don Prieto)

from Petersen's Special Events Division acting as show producer. Petersen out-horsepowered Carpenter and ultimately won SEMA's backing. The first official SEMA Show was in January 1967 under the bleachers at Chavez Ravine's Dodger Stadium. Although the show was quite small (98 manufacturer members and 3,000 attendees) compared to the mega shows of today (2,400 booth spaces and 160,000-plus attendees), it was nonetheless a start. At the inaugural SEMA Show, booth space was $375 each, and highlights included a Ford GT40 on display in

That flimsy card table looks like it's about to buckle from all the weight of those cast-iron cylinder heads, which are proudly displayed by a very young Larry Ofria from Valley Head Service. (Photo Courtesy Don Prieto)

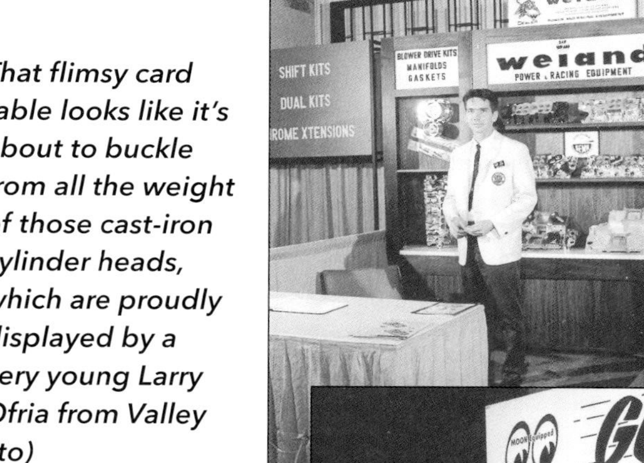

Phil Weiand Jr. mans the booth at the Weiand Equipment Company. (Photo Courtesy Don Prieto)

Believe it or not, this was SEMA's first corporate display. That's original SEMA employee Burk Le Sage standing in the center. (Photo Courtesy Don Prieto)

Dean Moon, one of the founding members of SEMA is accompanied by Melba, also known as Miss Moon Equipment Company, at the first SEMA Show held at Chavez Ravine's Dodger Stadium in Los Angeles, California. (Photo Courtesy Don Prieto)

The late Bill Simpson (left) of Simpson Safety Equipment fame was another early SEMA exhibitor and made great strides in the racing vehicle safety industry. (Photo Courtesy Don Prieto)

"Wild Bill" Shrewsbury's appropriately named L.A. Dart exhibition wheel stander was one of four vehicles displayed at the first-annual SEMA Show. Today's events attract display vehicles in the hundreds. (Photo Courtesy Don Prieto)

the Shelby American booth and "Wild Bill" Shrewsbury's *L.A. Dart* exhibition wheel stander.

The Acronym Redefined

In 1970, Corporate Council Earl Kitner convinced SEMA's Board of Directors that, with the changing times, the word *speed* might carry antisocial connotations when dealing with sensitive governmental issues, and the orga-

Shelby American displayed an early-production-run Ford GT 40 along with a complete line of Shelby American and Ford Racing go-fast goodies. (Photo Courtesy Don Prieto)

At Anaheim, corporate displays took on an openness that had not been previously enjoyed at the original venue; the Fenton Manufacturing Company custom wheel display was one such example.

SEMA's 1974 move to the Anaheim Convention Center not only signified growth but also increased interest from SEMA members in the industry.

NASCAR great Richard Petty signs autographs in the Wix Filters booth at the 1975 SEMA Show.

nization changed its name to the Specialty Equipment Market Association.

In 1974, the SEMA Show moved to the newly completed Anaheim Convention Center directly across the street from Disneyland. Aside from providing the much-needed exhibit space, which helped sales and attendance figures increase dramatically, the show's close proximity to the Magic Kingdom afforded the opportunity for many members to turn an otherwise run-of-the-mill business trip into a family outing. In its new venue, the SEMA Show continued in popularity and catered to the needs of industry representatives rather than consumers and developed a reputation as a place where serious business deals were written.

SEMA also took on the trappings of a social event with must-attend functions like the *Drag News* cocktail mixer and SEMA Awards Banquet, where big-name entertainers, such as ATCO recording artists April Stevens and Nino Tempo of the song "Deep Purple" fame, rubbed elbows with SEMA attendees.

The last year that the SEMA Show called the Anaheim Convention Center home was 1976. The show had been a runaway success that year with 570 booths filling virtually every square inch of space of the Anaheim Convention Center. However, more space was needed.

In 1977, SEMA moved to the Las Vegas Convention Center, where space (if only momentarily) didn't seem to be a problem. The SEMA Show continued to grow, and

Hank Monroe from the Monroe Shock Absorber Company and Miss Monroe Shocks exhibited the company's wares at SEMA in Anaheim. In the background is Mickey Thompson's Mach 1 Mustang AA/FC, which was Monroe sponsored.

Provocatively attired young ladies (like this woman shown in the U.S. Mags booth) became all the rage at SEMA Shows throughout the 1970s.

After three years at the Anaheim Convention Center, SEMA experienced growing pains and had to move on. In 1977, SEMA moved to the Las Vegas Convention Center, and it's been there ever since.

In 2018, Ford Racing displayed one of the cars that started it all, including Henry Ford's 2-cylinder Sweepstakes race car that defeated Alexander Winton in a race at Grosse Pointe, Michigan, October 10, 1901.

Car manufacturers, such as Ford Motor Company, identify heavily with SEMA and rely on it for customer feedback and input. Shown are Ford's new GTs on display at the 2018 event.

Chrysler Corporation is another believer in SEMA. Its huge corporate display annually takes center stage in the lower level of the south hall that was completed in 2002.

During SEMA Week, the front parking lot of the Las Vegas Convention Center becomes the SEMA proving ground, where manufacturers provide hands-on thrills.

This overhead view taken at the 2018 SEMA Show clearly illustrates the high degree of member participation and member attendance. A virtual sea of chrome and color, the event has often described as a land of toys for big boys.

so did the size of the Las Vegas Convention Center. For a number of years, construction crews and SEMA conventioneers coexisted with every square inch of newly constructed space being gobbled up by SEMA exhibitors.

In 1980, the Innovations Day seminar program debuted and was a smashing success with Lee Iacocca as the featured speaker. Willie Nelson headlined the entertainment at the SEMA Awards banquet.

In 1982, SEMA assumed full control of the show from Petersen Publishing Company's Special Events Division. From that point onward, actual management of the show was handled by outside contractors.

In 1983, an import parts segment was added to the show under the auspices of the Automotive International Association, hence the name change to the SEMA/AIA Show. The name of the show changed again in 1984 with the inclusion of Automotive Parts and Accessories (APAA) to the roster. That year, the SEMA/AIA/APAA Show banquet was a genuine barn burner with the Platters as headliners and comedian Gallagher filling the marquee.

In 1986, comedian and gearhead Jay Leno made his first of a number of appearances at SEMA as guest emcee at the awards banquet. In 2017, Leno filmed a *Jay Leno's Garage* segment at the SEMA Show and officiated the 2019 SEMA New Products Awards breakfast.

In 1988, the idea of sectionalization, where exhibitors were grouped according to specialties, forever changed and improved the way that all future SEMA Shows would be held. Since 2003, the entire show has been sectionalized into specific market niches, which made negotiating the show much easier.

In 1990, all SEMA exhibitors became eligible to submit an entry into the SEMA New Products Showcase at no additional fee. The really big news came in 1992, when SEMA/AIA, the Automotive Service Industry, Motor Equipment Manufacturer's Association, and Auto-

Clevelander Al Nosse's blown 426 Hemi/ZF 5-speed 1933 Willys street machine is graced by Miss Mother's Wax at the 2016 SEMA rendition.

SEMA annually showcases some of the most beautifully unique street rods, customs, street machines, 4x4s, and race cars in the realm. Shown in these two photos are Russ and Lora Freund's pearl purple, flathead-engine Ford Model T roadster named Take Out-T.

motive Parts and Accessories Association (ASIA/MEMA/APAA) came together to form the Automotive Aftermarket Industry Week (AAIW), a weeklong extravaganza that not only took up the entire Las Vegas Convention Center but also the Sands and Riviera Hotel convention centers as well, boasting 1.6 million square feet of exhibits.

In 1997, the National Tire Dealers and Retreaders (NTDRA) Show was combined with SEMA, highlighted by a Goodyear-sponsored Racers Night Out at nearby Las Vegas Motor Speedway.

In 1998, the SEMA Show broke records with 502,912 square feet of rented booth space. In 2002, the Las Vegas Convention Center completed construction of an additional 1 million square feet with the new twin-level south hall that was immediately filled.

In 2003, a vehicle proving ground was added on the upper level between the north and south halls where showgoers could experience exhibitor's products in action.

In 2014, the new event SEMA Ignited (the Friday-evening SEMA Show after party) was established where consumers were allowed to get up close and be part of the action.

The year 2016 heralded the 50th anniversary of the SEMA Show with 140,000 industry professionals from all over the world in attendance. The event was marked by an 11x143-foot mural in the Grand Lobby of the Las Vegas Convention Center that featured a pictorial timeline of the show's evolution and milestones. Entertainment at the 2016 SEMA banquet was none other than Larry the Cable Guy.

Dave McClelland, who retired as the show's 40-year master of ceremonies that night

Dave McClelland.
(Photo Courtesy SEMA)

CarTech Books based in Forest Lake, Minnesota, is the publisher of the hobby's most-popular subjects and book titles and routinely displays its wares at SEMA. This 2017 photo shows the publisher keeping good company with one of Bob Tasca III's fuel-burning Mustang Funny Cars in the foreground.

Each year, member companies vie for honors in various categories. Shown is the Glassworks corporate display that features an early 1950s gas station theme.

said, "When I did the 1976 SEMA Show, a couple of hundred people in attendance would have been a generous estimate. Forty years have gone by, and the growth of the audience and the expansion and development of the program itself went hand in hand; the larger the crowd, the more complex, entertaining, and thought-provoking the overall show."

The last SEMA Show as of this writing was the 2019 event, where it hosted more than 160,000 individuals, including 71,000 buyers, 2,400 exhibitors and 3,300 journalists. One can only expect that the 2020-edition SEMA Show and ensuing SEMA events in the future will do nothing but get bigger and better.

Great emphasis has been placed on the new Chrysler Corporation's aftermarket arts programs at SEMA events. For example, take this thoroughly modernized mid-1930s Dodge pickup.

This beautiful mild custom, candy-red Lincoln Mark II with modern high-tech powertrain and suspension is another example of the top-notch iron at SEMA.

Outrageous! That's an apt description for this White-manufactured early-1930s 4x4.

"Back in the day, we would actually sit down at SEMA and go through the new catalog and write orders on the spot," said Wayne Wolfe, a former sales representative for Holley. "Holley Sales Rep. Terry Fowler and I actually wrote a $1 million order with Bellweather Automotive at one show. I also remember having written an order with Motor State Distributing for having bought a trailerload of Holley intake manifolds."

SEMA movers and shakers Linda Vaughn, also known as Miss Hurst Golden Shifter, then–SEMA President Lou Baney, and Hot Rod Industry News Editor and SEMA Washington Representative Don Prieto pose during one of the many cocktail party mixers during SEMA Week.

Mr. Prieto Goes to Washington

Author's note: Louisiana native Don Prieto is one of the most-respected figures in the hot rod industry. Prieto is one of those guys who has been there and done that, ranging from his early days working in a speed shop to running a Top Fuel dragster, editing Hot Rod Industry News, *and meeting with then-President Gerald Ford at the White House as a SEMA representative. Don was happy to share a few thoughts regarding the latter:*

"After running a Top Fuel car, I ended up working at *Drag Racing* magazine," Don said. "This led to the editor-

One of the articles Don Prieto wrote during his tenure at **Hot Rod Industry News** *was titled "Is the Speed Shop Dead?" Don, who is also an accomplished photographer, took this photo using Petersen Publishing Company staffers John Dianna, Al Hall, Don Evans, Alex Xydias, and Ralph Vendilou, who served as models for the opening photo used in the article. (Photo Courtesy Don Prieto)*

While at **Hot Rod Industry News**, *Don Prieto penned a number of poignant articles with their primary focus on the collector-car hobby. The article "Clean Air Engine" was undoubtedly one of the most well received. (Photo Courtesy Don Prieto)*

ship of *Hot Rod Industry News*. I was hired by Publisher Alex Xydias on the rationale that I had experience in retail sales, having worked for Jake's Speed Shop in New Orleans prior to my move to the West Coast, and I had magazine experience, having previously worked at *Drag Racing* magazine. That lasted for three or four years.

"When I was appointed director of communications at SEMA, it was virgin territory. I was faced with lobbying state governments on subjects like engine modifications, suspension modifications, noisy muffler systems, and loud race tracks. And while I knew the subjects (having been in the high-performance business most of my life), I had never faced a group of government types.

"Fortunately, Robert E. Petersen funded a great lawyer [Dale Hogue] from Washington, D.C., on behalf of SEMA and put him at my disposal. Dale trained me to explain to those officials in plain English that what they were trying to do would run into antitrust laws. He guided my explanations such that the officials could accomplish the desired effect without running afoul of existing law. In other words, we would help them write regulations that would accomplish the desired outcome and not put any member companies out of business in doing so. It worked like magic.

"We met with a group of highway patrol administrators and outlined how this would be accomplished. They, all 50 state administrator types, bought our story in its entirety. They saw how relatively easy it would be to get everybody on board. Dale and I, with the help of some heavyweight industry types, assembled the documents and laid them out for the compact. With that simple act, we saved the entire high-performance industry in one fell swoop.

"The series of success convinced Dale Hogue to lure me to Washington, D.C., to work with him on establishing federal regulations favorable to the industry. He recommended that I go to work for APAA and do the same thing I was doing at SEMA only on the national level.

"The idea sounded good, and the money was even better. I was introduced to the United States House and Senate and became an official card-carrying industry lobbyist . . . even got to meet with Presidents Richard Nixon and Gerald Ford. It was interesting and exciting at first, but I was quick to learn that nothing gets done in Washington, D.C. I spent the next three years working on Title II of the Clean Air Act and hated it. I finished the document on the day I left to return to California. That was 1977. It has yet to be implemented even though it is required by law.

"It was a hell of a maneuver for a kid from New Orleans who didn't have much by the way of a formal education, and I wouldn't have traded the experience for all the world."

MASS MARKETING

In the opening section of this chapter, we touch upon the pioneering efforts of some of the speed equipment industry's earliest mass marketers, such as Almquist Engineering, Honest Charley Speed Shop, and Speedway Motors. These companies established themselves as key players in the retail sector of the speed equipment aftermarket through the printing of fully illustrated yearly catalogs and early car-enthusiast magazine mail-order advertisement campaigns.

Had it not been for these early pioneers, it's highly doubtful that today's speed equipment industry moguls (the modern-day giants, the game changers, and the architects of a more-efficient and more-profitable way of doing business) would have existed or become as successful. Today's moguls owe a huge debt of gratitude to these groundbreaking pioneers.

Almquist Engineering
Milford, Pennsylvania

It would be safe to call the late Ed Almquist, who lived from 1921 to 2015, *Mr. Everything*.

Born in Zim, Minnesota, Almquist was inspired by the soap box derby craze that was sweeping the nation and built an improved version using a Maytag washing machine motor. By age 14, Ed was working on Model T Fords in the Almquist family backyard. Due to family finances (the Great Depression was in full swing), Ed did double duty as a celery farmer and a railroad brakeman. Almquist never went to college; everything he learned was self-taught.

In 1946, Ed served in the US Maritime Service and met young US Naval Officer Henry Ford II, and they became lifelong friends. While in the service, Ed wrote his first of many books, which was titled *Speed & Mileage Manual*, and ultimately sold 10,000 copies at $1.98 per copy after purchasing a $12 *Popular Mechanics* magazine classified ad.

With the war's end, Ed moved to Milford, Pennsylvania, where he remained until his death. In 1946, Ed founded Almquist Engineering and began manufacturing Ford flathead intake manifolds and cylinder heads. With

In 1946, US Maritime serviceman Ed Almquist wrote, published, and advertised his first book titled Speed & Mileage Manual, *which retailed for $1.98 per copy and ultimately sold 10,000 copies. This initial success launched the Almquist Engineering Company empire.*

marketing being a bit of a dicey proposition for anyone other than the fat cats with huge corporate advertising budgets, Ed took to the streets with a traveling showroom (essentially a traveling speed shop) and sold his wares. Almquist's marketing genius was also manifested in car-enthusiast magazines, such as *Hop Up*, *Honk*, *Hot Rod*, *Car Craft*, and others. He took out full-page advertisements not only selling his products but also many other well-known brands, which qualified Almquist

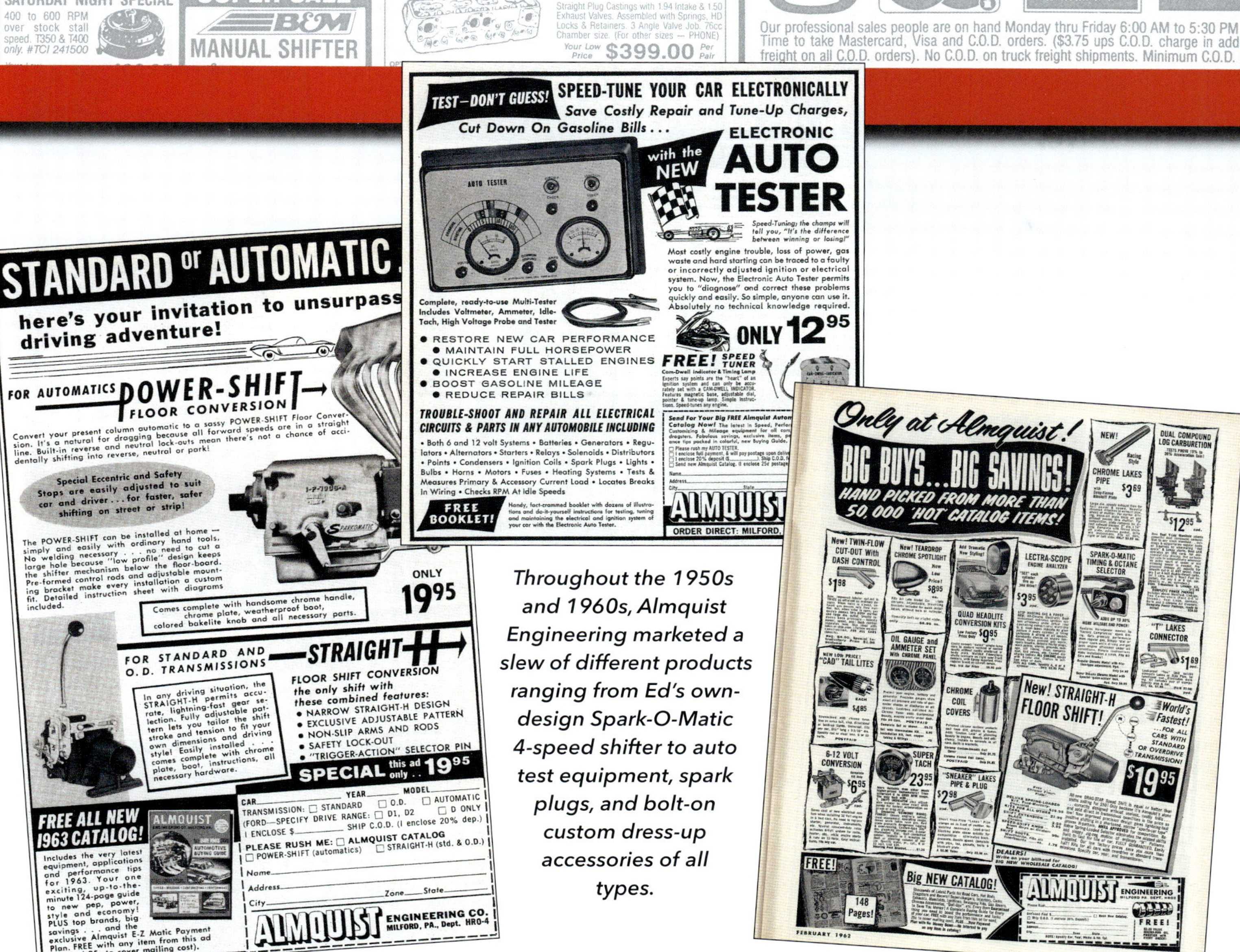

Throughout the 1950s and 1960s, Almquist Engineering marketed a slew of different products ranging from Ed's own-design Spark-O-Matic 4-speed shifter to auto test equipment, spark plugs, and bolt-on custom dress-up accessories of all types.

Engineering as being one of the first, if not *the* first mass marketer in the speed equipment industry.

In 1959, Ed teamed up with George Hurst and Jim Campbell on the Hurst shifter design project. All three submitted floor-shifter designs, and George's was the one that was accepted. An extension of that project was Almquist's patented Universal Shift Kit, which was marketed through Montgomery Ward, Sears Roebuck, Firestone, JC Whitney, and Western Auto stores and sold like hot cakes.

Later, Ed founded Spark-O-Matic Corporation, which was based on the Spark-O-Matic multiple-electrode spark plugs. Although a mild success, Spark-O-Matic also branded Ed's triple-pattern shifter design, which in part drew its inspiration from Almquist's previous involvement with the Hurst shifter program. Almquist's far-sightedness was also manifested in the super lubricant facet of the oil modifier/oil additive industry with his introduction of Presto-Moly, which was brought to market a decade or more before Slick 50, Lubri-Lon, Duration, Ultra-Lon, and other Teflon-based oil modifiers that hit the shelves.

All told, Ed Almquist held seven US patents and four foreign patents and wrote a number of best-selling automotive books. His last effort, *Hot Rod Pioneers: The Creators of the Fastest Sport on Wheels*, served as a desk reference book for many of the entries made in this publication.

Honest Charley Speed Shop
Chattanooga, Tennessee

To put it bluntly, the sport of hot rodding is chock full of colorful characters. Charles Edward Card Jr., who lived from 1905 to 1974, was by far the most colorful of them all.

Judging from Card's zany, cartoon-like magazine ads, one might think that Charlie Card never took anything seriously. However, that was far from the truth.

Tennessee-born "Honest Charley" Card was a car enthusiast from the get-go, having attended his first Indianapolis 500 race in mid-1930s. Although not of professional caliber, Card competed in and won the 1953 Daytona Century Race driving a modified 1939 Ford. (Photo Courtesy Greg Sharp Collection)

In 1948, Card opened Honest Charley Speed Shop on a shoestring budget. Card and his daughters hand drew, collated, and stapled the first Honest Charley Speed Shop catalogs. Over the years, the release of each and every edition Honest Charley Speed Shop catalog was treated like a major event.

On the inside, Card was a very serious businessman who managed to change the face of the high-performance mail-order speed equipment industry while gaining a huge loyal following of Honest Charley customers.

Historically, Card received the name *Honest Charley* from the customers at his restaurant in Chattanooga, Tennessee, that he operated on Chestnut Street. He allowed his clientele to figure out how much they owed for their meals and leave their money in a small cash box by the front door, thereby prompting the remark, "You sure are honest, Charley." The nickname just stuck, and Card added the moniker "hisself" behind it just to keep things folksy.

Card began going to the local races in the early 1930s and attended every Indianapolis 500 race from mid-1930 to mid-1970. In the post-war years, Card began selling speed equipment out of the trunk of his car. Then, in 1948, Card opened a small speed shop at 200 McCalle Ave. in Chattanooga, which by 1964 had grown from the initial 260 square feet to 30,000 square feet.

However, Card's corporate clout with the manufacturers came through catalog sales from his mail-order speed equipment business. Charlie and his two daughters, Martha and Ann, hand drew, collated, and stapled together Card's first Honest Charley Speed Shop catalogs (all eight pages) on Card's kitchen table. Over the years, those catalogs grew to a total of 200 pages. Moreover, the release of each and every Honest Charley Speed Shop catalog had all the trappings of a Hollywood movie debut with little snippets about its impending release being printed in all the trade publications. These and other zany promotions allowed Card to sell name-brand speed equipment by mail order at a sizeable discount.

In later years, due to volume purchasing and his close friendships with Vic Edelbrock Sr. and Jr., Paul Schiefer, George Hurst, Fred Offenhauser, Els Lohn, Phil Weiand, and others, Card dropped prices even lower. Honest Charley was also the first in the industry to use punch cards to track parts sales and customers, and in the process, he became the first coast-to-coast mail-order distributor of high-performance aftermarket components.

Honest Charley Inc. also sponsored a number of race cars, including "TV Tommy" Ivo and "Jungle Jim" Liberman. "Hisself" even raced in and won the 1953 Daytona Century Race with a Mercury flathead-engine 1939 Ford at 139 mph.

Honest Charley Card died in 1974 at age 69. With ever-increasing pressure from the big-box stores, the business slogged along until 1990 before closing its doors. Today, Honest Charley Inc. is owned by Corky Coker of Coker Tire Company fame, who acquired the brand rights to use the Honest Charley name in 1998. The company's website is honestcharley.com.

Here's an example of an early Honest Charley Speed Shop advertisement selling Ford flathead cylinder heads.

Over the years, Honest Charley Speed Shops sponsored some pretty impressive talent, such as "TV Tommy" Ivo and his Top Fuel dragsters. (Photo Courtesy Tommy Ivo)

The name Honest Charley also rode into battle on the fender flanks of the late "Jungle Jim" Liberman's Chevrolet Camaro and Vega Funny Cars.

Today, Honest Charley is a property of Coker Tire Company founder Corky Coker, who has an Honest Charley/ Coker Tire Museum and gift shop at 1309 Chestnut St., Chattanooga, Tennessee. (Photos Courtesy Tommy Lee Byrd).

The Super Shops Automotive Performance Centers
San Bernardino, California

The Super Shops Automotive Performance Centers based in San Bernardino, California, used the chain-store approach as opposed to mass marketing product that was generated through a single location, print media, or a combination of both.

Founded on July 1, 1963, by ex–US Air Force veteran Harry Eberlin, who previously sold speed equipment at swap meets and local street races out of the trunk of his car, the parent company was originally known as San Bernardino Racing Equipment at 25824 E. Baseline Rd. Eberlin invested untold hours into the operation, negotiating long deals with name-brand speed equipment manufacturers such as Holley, BFGoodrich, Sig Erson Cams, Black Jack Headers, Hedman, Mallory Ignitions, etc., and passed the savings on to his customers. This seemingly endless process earned Eberlin the necessary customer loyalty and return business that allowed him to pursue even loftier plans—namely expansion.

In June 1972, Harry Eberlin opened up his second Super Shops Performance Center at 3893 7th St., Riverside, California. The third Super Shops Performance Center opened in Ontario, California, on March 30, 1973. On March 22, 1974, Eberlin opened store No. 4 at 4550 University Ave., San Diego, California. This was followed in 1975 with the opening of store No. 5 in Garden Grove, California, store No. 6 in Long Beach, California, stores No. 7 and 8 in Covina and Van Nuys, California in 1977, and store No. 9 in Sacramento, California in 1978.

Eberlin's first out-of-state Super Shops Performance Centers set up shop in Tucson, Arizona, and Lakewood, Colorado, in 1978. Then, one was established in San Jose, California, making it a total of 15 stores. However, we may be getting ahead of ourselves here.

Win This Car!

In 1975, San Bernardino, California AA/Fuel Altered movers and shakers Dave and Lynn Hough were building a new *Nanook* AA/FA, having just sold their previous car, and they were looking for a sponsor.

What the Houghs did next was unique unto the class and groundbreaking to the sport of drag racing as a whole, which at that time had very few corporate sponsorship entities. The Houghs had the first and only AA/Fuel Altered to ever enjoy national sponsorship.

Dave and Lynn were happy to share their thoughts with author Bob McClurg.

Author: How did it all begin, Dave?

Dave: In the spring of 1975, we heard through the grapevine that San Bernardino, California's Super Shops Inc. was about to do something unique. It was going to give away a race car as its grand prize to promote its business through a year-long contest. We had heard through a couple of its store managers that it was originally going to give away a Pro Stock car that it would sponsor and campaign on a national level throughout the year. I had known Harry [Eberlin] for a number of years, so we kind of stormed down to San Bernardino Racing Equipment at just about the time the company was changing its name to Super Shops and said, "We hear you're going to be giving away a race car. Why don't you do something really crazy and give away a Fuel Altered?"

I said anybody can give away a Pro Stock car, but it takes a little creative genius and some real ingenuity to give away an AA/Fuel Altered. Harry's second in command was a guy named Mike Cunningham, who was his promotional director, and he's going, "God, I really like it."

I told them that we would run the car for them throughout the year, and we would name the car *Super Nanook*. They asked us to submit a proposal. We came back within a couple of days with the idea that they would build and own the car. They would let us campaign it for the year, and we would race it all over where we normally did as well as display the car at select Super Shops Inc. locations. Then, when the NHRA World Finals came around, I would return the car to them in running condition, and they would give the car away.

Author: How many events did you have booked that year?

Dave: About 30 in all, virtually everywhere west of Denver. We raced the car up in Washington, Oregon, Arizona, Nevada, Colorado, and all over California. We also

The original Super Shops, also known as San Bernardino Racing Equipment, was at 25824 E. Baseline Rd., San Bernardino, California. From this humble beginning, the company went on to become the nation's largest chain of speed equipment retailers in the country (and the world for that matter) with 165 Super Shops Performance Centers and counting. (Photo Courtesy Nanook Racing)

In 1975, Dave and Linda Hough's Super Nanook *AA/Fuel Altered roadster hooked up with the Super Shops (which started in the Hough's hometown of San Bernardino, California) on a unique Fuel Altered giveaway program, where some lucky contestant would win Super Nanook and a Chevrolet LUV mini truck at year's end. It was the breakout publicity program of the era and it vaulted the Super Shops into the national limelight.*

did a number of personal appearances. Super Shops was a big radio sponsor on KLOS FM radio in LA, in fact, one of the largest, so we also had KLOS advertising on the car as well.

Author: You also did high school appearances?

Dave: Yes. We took the car around to about 10 to 12 high schools with the "Don't Race on the Street; Race on the Track" theme. We also covered vehicle safety and touched on some of the negative things that can happen to you when you race on the street. We did that for one full year.

Author: How did the actual giveaway promotion go?

Dave: It really went well. Super Shops had hundreds of thousands of entries, and Harry played it smart. He made sure that they had the winner sitting there at the NHRA World Finals when they drew his name. During the giveaway, [Super Shops] also included a fully decked-out Chevy LUV mini truck in the contest as well, and it gave one of those away once a month. The idea was that [Super Shops] would have all 12 of those winners sitting in the stands, and they would pull one of the original 12 out of a box, and he or she would be the winner of *Super Nanook.* I did about a half-track burnout with the car, backed up, shut the car off, and they did the drawing right there on the starting line. Winner Jim Perkins came running out of the stands whooping and hollering and came down and took possession of the car!

Author: But that wasn't the end of the story, was it?

Dave: Unfortunately, the car would never be run as an AA/Fuel Altered again. The guy sold the blown Fuel Hemi out of *Super Nanook* to a Top Fuel blown hydro racer, and they installed a carbureted motor in the car and ran it as a bracket racer for the rest of its life.

Author: Does the car still exist?

The Super Nanook *and the Houghs spread the word about performance, drag racing safety, and the Super Shops. This photo was taken at a high school assembly in San Bernardino, California. (Photo Courtesy Nanook Racing)*

The sign says it plainly enough: "Win a Race Car." When it was all said and done, a gentleman named Jim Perkins was the big winner. (Photo Courtesy Nanook Racing)

90 Chapter Six

Dave: Yes, it still exists today. About five years ago, a guy from Monrovia, California, called, told me that he had the car, and asked if I would be interested in buying it. I told him that yes, I would be interested for a reasonable price, but the guy wanted $25,000 for the car. I said, "Pass," and had original builder, Norm Porter, who still had the original blueprints for *Super Nanook*, recreate the car, and we have that car now. We run it every other year along with the restored green and orange *Nanook* No. 3.

Author: You guys also ran a Super Shops Funny Car, right?

Dave: Right. Actually, we built our Plymouth Arrow late in the season before giving the *Super Nanook* AA/FA away. After the drawing was over, I got out of the Altered, walked over to the Funny Car and got strapped in. After they rolled the Altered off the line, they made the announcement that if you thought giving the *Super Nanook* AA/FA away was wild, we [Super Shops Performance Centers Inc.] are now giving away a $100,000 nitro Funny Car. As soon as they said that, Lynn and our son Rick fired up the car and lowered the body, and I made a half-track pass. The better thing about the Funny Car over the Altered is that we only had one Altered and we had to do a lot of traveling with *Super Nanook* to honor our commitments.

With the Funny Car, we actually built two of them and used one as a touring display car and hauled that one all over the United States. Rather than giving a mini truck away that year [in 1978], they had a Dodge mini-van all decked out in Super Shops colors, and they gave one of those away every month!

Author: Was the second Funny Car the one Pat Foster built?

The following year, the Super Shops followed up with a Plymouth Arrow Funny Car giveaway. Two cars were built. One was shown, while the other was campaigned by Dave Hough, Pat Foster, and lastly Ed "Ace" McCullouch, who won Funny Car at the 1980 US Nationals. (Photo Courtesy Nanook Racing)

Dave: Yes. Pat built the second car, but the original Arrow was built by Norm Porter. My deal ended with them when they decided to start opening stores from the Midwest all the way to the East Coast. Harry came to me and said, "I need for you to quit your job and tour this car full time." At the time, I had two kids in high school and a mortgage to pay, and I was a little uncomfortable quitting my job of 18 years and going out on tour. I went to Harry and told him that I needed X-amount of money to go out on tour and wanted a 5-year employment agreement to cover myself after the program ended. He kind of took it personal and was offended that I wanted something in writing. After all, it would have become a full-time job.

When I was racing *Super Nanook*, the car was maintained in my garage, and I did all the maintenance on it myself. When we moved over to the Funny Car, Harry wanted it moved 65 miles away to Ed Pink's shop [in Van Nuys, California] and maintained there. It all got to be a bit too much. Finally, Harry came to me one day and said, "Since you're unwilling to tour the car nationally, we don't need your services anymore." Then, he gave the car to Pat Foster to drive. Pat drove the car for about six to eight months, and then they gave the car to Ed McCullouch, and Ed won Indy with it in 1980.

Author: Any parting comments about the Super Shops drag racing program?

Dave: Well, the only bad thing I think was nobody ever liked the brown and tan paint job. Our cars had always been green, green and white, or green and orange. I had to kind of give up the family colors to go corporate. They gave us $120,000 to run the car that year, which in 1975 dollars represented a lot of money. After that, Harry gave $250,000 to Eddie Hill to put the Super Shops name on his car, and after that, he gave Garlits $400,000. So, at the time, we were kind of a bargain, but with all the work we put into the project, I often feel like I sold my soul for the money.

Author: Lynn, what are your thoughts about the *Super Nanook* sponsorship program?

Lynn: The Super Shops program started out great. They were there when we needed them. They put together a nice program for David, and it kept the Nanook name (and his) out in front of the crowd. David was able to do things he had only dreamed about for a long time because he didn't have to worry about where his next dime was coming from. So, from those standpoints, it was a great deal.

Creative Financing

Campaigning a Fuel car isn't cheap by any means, and sponsoring one requires some pretty deep pockets. In

1975, Super Shops Performance Centers Inc. CEO Harry Eberlin took a different tack when it came to the subject of corporate sponsorship, and it worked like a charm. Dave Hough was happy to detail Harry's thought process.

"The greatest thing that Eberlin ever did was going to every Super Shops vendor to say that he wanted a check for $10,000 each," Dave said. "In exchange, he would put their names [corporate logos] on the car all in equal size. At the end of the year, if any of them felt that they didn't get their money's worth in promotional value, he would return their money. All told, he got $110,000 worth of sponsorship start-up monies, and nobody asked for their money back. This, of course, was for the original *Nanook* AA/FA sponsorship. No doubt the sponsorship monies commanded for the Eddie Hill and Don Garlits sponsorships were much larger."

Epilogue

Eberlin continued to expand the Super Shops Performance Centers Inc. brand throughout the 1970s and 1980s with phenomenal success. By 1980, he had 143 stores up and down the West Coast as well as locations in Arizona, Nevada, New Mexico, and Colorado. By 1992, Eberlin had 165 retail locations serviced by a series of three warehouses located in San Bernardino, California; Grand Prairie, Texas; and Jacksonville, Florida, and was making plans to expand nationwide.

At the height of operations, Super Shops Performance Centers Inc. employed in excess of 1,300 full-time employees, and some claim 1,500. However, the Super Shops Performance Centers Inc. runaway success also produced negative side effects. A chief customer complaint was that the company often hired minimum-wage employees who were poorly prepared and didn't know the product lines being sold, which resulted in the unfair nickname *Stupid Shops*. This wasn't always the rule, of course, but in some cases, there was a mentionable exception.

However, the real Harbinger of Doom for Super Shops Performance Centers Inc. came with the coming of the Organization of the Petroleum Exporting Countries (OPEC) and the lingering effects it had on the automotive aftermarket as a whole. Rather than buying performance cars, people were buying import cars and vans. What matters more was how speed equipment manufacturers failed to adapt to the oncoming black-box technology, which was taking over the automotive industry as a whole, and for the most part, kept on producing product based on 1960s-speed equipment technology.

Sadly, many speed shops faded into obscurity. However, in spite of how the financially laden Super Shops Performance Centers Inc. filed bankruptcy in 1998, the company is fondly remembered. In fact, the Super Shops trademark and corporate name were both obtained in 2013 by a nostalgia group of former Super Shops employees and customers who started their own Super Shops website. Go to supershopsracing.com for further details.

Performance Automotive Wholesale
Van Nuys, California

On January 22, 1982, Performance Automotive Wholesale Inc. (PAW), headquartered in Chatsworth, California, filed articles of incorporation with the state of California. The company's slogan was "the Home Mechanics Warehouse," and it came like a bolt of lightning out of the blue and changed the mail-order speed equipment industry practically overnight.

The company hit the ground running with a fully Illustrated 1,000-page catalog, listing practically every thing automotive component under the sun from engine bearings and stroker kits to complete crate engines. Moreover, PAW's advertising schedules in publications like *Street Rodder*, *Hot Rod*, *Car Craft*, *Popular Hot Rodding*, *Super Chevy*, and other front-line car-enthusiast magazines matched with a pricing structure that was "to die for." It endeared the company to mail-order customers who ordered parts from across the United States and Canada, particularly to those who were slaving away on that special project car out in the nation's hinterlands.

However, for those who still preferred the traditional one-on-one experience, PAW offered a well-stocked Speed Shop Super Mart at 8966 Mason Ave., Chatsworth, California, 91311. Visiting PAW's showroom was a visual experience. Not only did the speed equipment mega retailer carry all the leading name-brand speed parts at the ready but it also had Kenny Bernstein's *Budweiser King* Top Fuel dragster and *Budweiser King* Buick AA/Fuel Funny Car perched upon the walls along with one of Don "the Snake" Prudhomme's *Skoal Bandit* AA/FD's!

Speaking of Top Fuel dragsters, PAW sponsored none other than three-time NHRA Winston Top Fuel World Champion Shirley Muldowney on her 1986 comeback tour after she experienced a near-fatal top-end crash in 1984 in Montreal, Canada.

"In the winter of 1985, Performance Automotive Wholesale CEO Keith Harvie heard that I was planning my comeback tour and that I was looking for a major sponsorship," Muldowney said. "Keith called me up, and we agreed to meet out in California that winter. Four weeks later, I drove from Michigan to California to not only meet with Keith but also to finish up my rehab out there, as I was still pretty badly hurt.

"Anyhow, we came to terms, and PAW became my

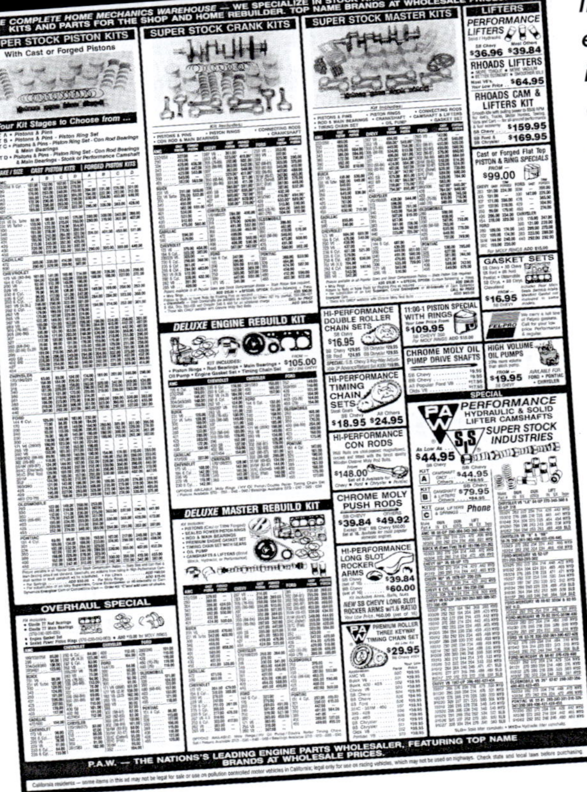

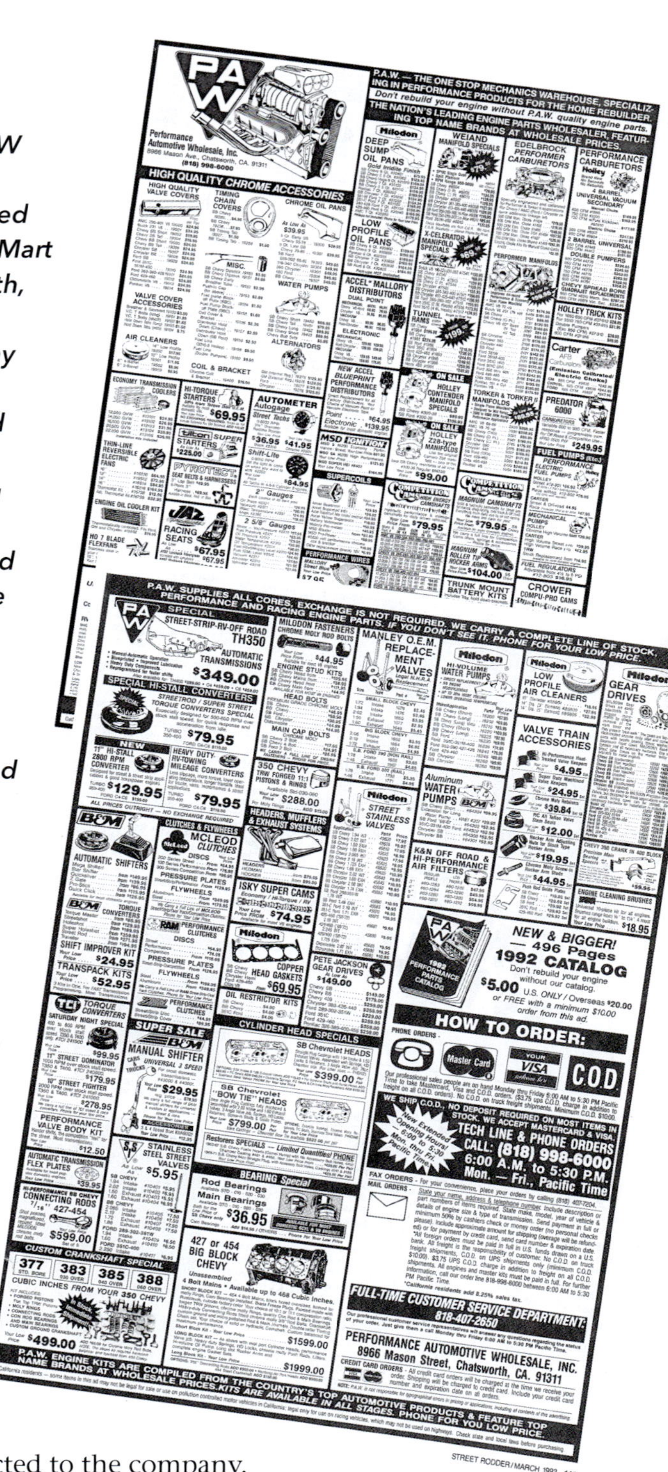

Although PAW had a well-stocked Speed Shop Super Mart in Chatsworth, California, the company counted on catalog and magazine advertising like this three-page example that appeared in the April 1992 issue of Street Rodder magazine as its main source for revenue. From 1986 through 1989, PAW sponsored three-time (1977, 1980, and 1982) NHRA Top Fuel World Champion Shirley Muldowney, who rewarded the company with a Top Fuel Eliminator win at the 1989 Arizona Nationals and ran a best of 4.97 at 284 mph.

official sponsor from the 1986 to 1989 seasons. That's how it happened. There wasn't anything special about it. Keith simply heard that we were looking for a sponsorship deal, and the two of us put one together!"

During her three-year PAW sponsorship, Muldowney ran as quickly as a 4.97, as fast as 284 mph, and won Top Fuel Eliminator at the 1989 NHRA Arizona Nationals. Clearly, the Muldowney sponsorship cemented PAW as a major player in the retail facet of the speed equipment industry.

However, by the dawn of the new millennium, PAW was struggling. By 2010, the company was a former image of itself and fading fast. What exactly happened at PAW to cause such a staggering reversal of fortune? Opinions vary, and unfortunately, in spite of numerous attempts, we were not able to make contact with anyone officially connected to the company.

Members from our nation's blogosphere site under the heading "Performance Automotive Warehouse, R.I.P" provide takes on the subject, and you can decide for yourself.

"I just found a copy of my 2004 PAW catalog that I used to spend hours poring over. They used to have some crazy prices compared to what you have to pay today! Complete Pontiac 455 short-block kits were like $1,800! Supercharged big-block Chevrolet kits sold for like $6,000, block, heads, rods, pistons, cam, 6.71 supercharger belt, pretty much everything except the carbs and distributor. Too bad PAW waited too long to make the move to the net. They would have probably ruled the [high-performance] industry had they applied the same business model they used for their catalog!

"When I was in the United States Air Force, I had a roommate who had just gotten back from an overseas tour. He sold all of his stereo equipment and bought a 1969 Chevelle. He then broke out the PAW catalog and ordered a complete big-block for it and it worked out well for him!"

"I used to use PAW for [ordering] some of my stock car stuff when I did circle track racing in the mid-1990s. They weren't a bad company to deal with. Sorry they went to the early Hemi stuff only in 2010. I thought that was a major downfall for them. Before too long, they will not even be a blip on the radar."

"Used to order from PAW on occasion several years ago based on magazine advertising; a classic example of failing to update your business model to move with the times. Summit Racing Equipment does a pretty good job, and what a lot of people probably don't realize is that Summit also sells their shipping and handling expertise, and other companies use Summit to handle and distribute their products; smart business sense to use your own network to add value to your own business by supplying service to others."

"I remember trying to find PAW on the internet in the 1990s with little luck. When they finally made a website, it was horrible. You basically had to look up the part number in their paper catalog and then order it from there. I think they just refused to make the internet transition in a timely fashion and ended up getting killed by Summit, JEGS, eBay, and all the other specialty shops. I also don't think they adjusted their business model for the import and late-model performance car craze that Summit and JEGS did very well!"

"I'd almost forgotten about PAW. That just goes to show how much we use the internet. Those companies that didn't successfully make the transition are now extinct!"

Summit Racing Equipment
Tallmadge, Ohio

These days, Summit Racing Equipment is known as the *World's Speed Shop*, but, like most businesses, it came from humble beginnings.

In 1968, Summit Racing Equipment was founded in the basement of a doughnut shop in Stow, Ohio, as a part-time business by drag racer Paul D. Sergi Sr., who was frustrated by the lack of speed shops available in northeastern Ohio. As word of the company's great prices and friendly technical help spread, the little business grew rapidly. To meet the demands of local drag racers and muscle car enthusiasts, Summit Racing opened its first retail store located in Akron, Ohio. Product lines included Accel, Holley, Mallory, Hurst, and Mickey Thompson.

In 1972, Summit Racing expanded into the mail-order business by placing small ads selling Mickey Thompson tires and E.T. Wheels in *Hot Rod* and *Car Craft* magazines. In no time at all, the company was processing orders from all across the continental United States. In fact, those magazine ads were so successful that Summit Racing created its first mail-order catalog in 1976 and added a full-time sales and customer-service staff to handle the volume, and the rest is history.

In 1978, Summit Racing moved to a larger four-building complex in Akron that boasted enough warehouse space to accommodate an increase in inventory and much-needed sales and personnel offices.

In 1987, the Summit Racing catalog expanded from a yearly catalog to a bi-monthly publication full of the hottest new products, up-to-date pricing, and more parts than ever. In 1988, Bill Kuhlman became the first Summit Racing–sponsored professional drag racer. Kuhlman's Corvette was the first doorslammer to break the magical 200-mph barrier, and he was one of the founding fathers of Pro Mod.

In 1990, Summit Racing added 24/7 customer service and order lines so that customers could order parts day or night. That same year, Summit Racing became the corpo-

A virtual city unto itself, Summit Racing Equipment's national headquarters is located right off of Interstate 76 at 1200 Southeast Ave., Tallmadge, Ohio, 44278. You can't miss it.

The would-be Summit Racing Equipment customer is greeted as he or she walks through the door by a jam-packed showroom that practically defies description. You'll find brand-name speed equipment everywhere, and the walls are decorated with numerous successful Summit Racing–sponsored race cars.

Looking for custom wheels? Summit Racing Equipment stocks virtually every name brand of wheel in most popular bolt patterns, offsets, and sizes.

How about aluminum-alloy aftermarket cylinder heads? Summit Racing Equipment stocks virtually every name brand and application.

rate sponsor for NHRA Pro Stock star Joe Lepone Jr. The sponsorship lasted for three years. Summit Racing also added a centerfold car feature to the pages of its catalogs. Garage walls would rejoice.

In 1992, Summit racing moved into its new home at 1200 Southeast Ave., Tallmadge, Ohio. The new building boasted 30,000 square feet of space with plenty of room for the sales and customer staff, plus a sizeable retail store for walk-in customers. Also included was a new high-tech distribution center with more room and equipment to ship orders out more quickly, which enabled local customers (Ohio and surrounding states) to receive orders in just 1 to 2 days with regular ground shipping.

In 1993, Summit Racing celebrated its 25th anniversary with the first Super Summit Car Show, which became an annual event. Summit also entered into the 12-year sponsorship of NHRA Pro Stock driver Mark Pawuk and his Chevrolet Camaro Pro Stock car. In 1994, Summit Racing became a major contingency sponsor for NHRA Sportsman class racing and remains one to this day.

In 1995, Summit Racing installed its first toll-free order number, 1-800-230-3030, and started its website, summitracing.com. The site expanded rapidly from a simple landing page that featured a few product offerings into the speed equipment industry's go-to website that featured a huge online catalog, tech articles, frequently asked questions, feature vehicle stories, motorsports updates, etc. Summit Racing also debuted the *Quadra-Deuce*, the world's first all-wheel-drive 1932 Ford roadster that year to rave revues.

In 1996, the first TruckFest all-truck show was at Summit Racing's megastore in Tallmadge, Ohio. In 1998, Summit Racing opened a second distribution center and retail store at 960 E. Glendale Ave., Sparks, Nevada, 89431, to better serve its customer base in the Western United States and allow customers to receive their orders in one or two days with ground shipping. In 2000, Summit Racing doubled the size of its operation in Tallmadge, Ohio, to keep up with the ever-growing customer demand. With more than a million parts in inventory and more than 100 brand-name manufacturers listed in its catalog, the upgrade was absolutely necessary. *Muscle Mustangs & Fast Fords* magazine debuted Summit Racing's 1,000-hp *QuikStang* to the delight of Ford fans all across the nation. That same year, the company also became the official mail-order sponsor of the NHRA and IHRA.

In 2002, Summit Racing opened its new 25,000-square-foot super store at its Tallmadge, Ohio, location. In 2004, Summit Racing sponsored the Ken Black Racing NHRA Pro Stock Camaro driven by professional racer Greg Anderson, who won his first NHRA Pro Stock World Championship under Summit sponsorship. The company also became an associate sponsor on Tim Wilkerson's Mustang AA/FC.

Summit Racing also became a sponsor/parts supplier for the popular cable TV show *Overhaulin'*.

In 2005, Summit Racing's foray into the wide world of automotive cable television continued with its sponsorship of the cable TV shows *HorsePower TV*, *Detroit Muscle*, *Truck Tech*, and *Xtreme 4x4*.

In 2006, Summit Racing opened its third distribution center and second 25,000-square-foot retail super store, which was at 20 King Mill Rd., McDonough, Georgia. It allowed the World's Speed Shop to deliver parts to customers in the Southern United States within 1 to 2 days with ground shipping. That same year, the speed equipment mega retailer introduced its new tools and garage accessories catalog, which featured hundreds of hand and power tools, shop equipment, paint and bodywork supplies, and much more.

In 2007, Summit Racing acquired the naming rights for Summit Racing Equipment Motorsports Park in Norwalk, Ohio. Summit Racing also acquired Genuine Hot Rod Hardware, a company that specialized in hot rod lifestyle products, such as die-cast collectibles, retro automotive signs, pedal cars, and auto apparel. Last but certainly not the least, Summit-sponsored racer Jason Line won his first NHRA Pro Stock World Championship while driving Ken Black's KB Racing/Summit Racing Equipment Chevrolet Camaro.

Summit Racing celebrated its 40th anniversary in 2008. Founder Paul D. Sergi Sr.'s 1967 LT1 427 big-block Corvette, the car that started it all (sporting a 496-ci big-block with 590 hp) was restored to commemorate the occasion.

In 2009, Summit Racing launched its new and improved website, summitracing.com. It featured enhanced search tools for easier shopping, savings central (pages of sales prices, retailers, and exclusive Summit Bucks offers), a giant library with anytime access to product installation instructions and much more.

In 2010, Summit expanded its lineup of Summit-branded products, including paint and bodywork products, carburetors, intake manifolds, ignition systems, and Pro Packs, which provide matched parts combinations to save customers time and hassle. The company also expanded its line of 4x4 offerings (specifically Jeep) and offered more products for the circle track, restoration, and late-model performance markets.

Summit Racing also launched Operation Appreciation, which was an annual trip by Summit Racing Equipment–sponsored racers to visit American troops deployed overseas. Summit Racing also assumed title sponsorship of the ISCA Summit Racing Equipment Show Car Series.

In 2011, Summit Racing added a large selection of OEM replacement parts for the everyday motorist, including OEM items manufactured by ACDelco, Standard Motor Products, Delphi, Dorman, Bosch, and others. Also, new to Summit Racing was its landed cost delivery service for international customers, which was used to deliver parts right to the customers' door with no additional charges or fees to pay.

Summit Racing's 2012 business year saw the parts ordering process made easier with the implementation of the shared cart, which allows customers to order anything from summitracing.com, genuinehotrod.com, and powersportsplace.com using a single shopping cart and paying just one inexpensive handling charge. Once again, Jason Line won the NHRA Pro Stock World Championship driving a Ken Black–owned Chevrolet Camaro.

In 2012, Summit Racing partnered with Factory Five Racing to build a replica of a 427 Cobra based on the Factory Five MKIV kit, using parts from the Summit Racing catalog.

In 2013, Summit Racing expanded its television presence by becoming parts supplier to several cable reality TV programs, including *Overhaulin'* (2012), *All Girls Garage* (2013), *Fat N' Furious: Rolling Thunder* (2014), and *Lost in Transmission* (2015). The company also teamed up with *NASCAR Trackside* and *Top Gear USA* star Rutledge Wood to build a 1949 Chevy Kurbmaster step van that was featured on many national automotive cable TV shows.

In 2014, Summit Racing again teamed up with Factory Five Racing to sponsor an all-girls build of a Factory Five 427 Cobra replica, which was shown on *PowerNation* and *Detroit Muscle*.

Summit Racing had a busy year in 2015. It joined forces with Rutledge Wood to build a 1953 Plymouth Suburban, which was presented to Wood by famed NASCAR racing legend Richard Petty. The company also became an associate sponsor of nine-time European FIA World Pro Stock Champion Jimmy Alund. The same year, Summit Racing became a major series sponsor for the Australian National Drag Racing Association (ANDRA) racing series. Then, Summit Racing expanded its presence in overseas markets by running ads and airing TV commercials in Sweden, Australia, New Zealand, Great Britain, Mexico, and the Middle East.

The construction of Summit Racing's fourth order-fulfillment center, retail store, and customer fulfillment center was completed in 2016 in Arlington, Texas. Out on the race track, Jason Line won his third NHRA Pro

Stock Championship driving the Ken Black–owned, Summit Racing–sponsored Chevrolet Pro Stock Camaro.

In 2017, Summit Racing's Arlington, Texas, facility officially opened for business. The new facility allowed one-day delivery on orders for in-stock parts to customers in most of Texas and adjacent states. Summit Racing expanded its product line to more than 1,500 manufacturers, which was the most ever. New motorsports sponsorships were announced for the United States Modified Touring Series (USMTS), Sports Car Club of America (SCCA) road racing program, and European Drag Racing Series (EDRS). Summit Racing acquired the naming rights to the Good Guys annual Summit Racing Lone Star Nationals in Fort Worth, Texas.

Summit Racing celebrated its 50th anniversary in 2018 by expanding its motorsports programs to include Formula Drift, the Mid-West Drag Racing (Pro Mod) Series, and the Midwest Junior (Dragster) Super Series.

In 2019, Summit Racing unveiled its first corporate display at the 2019 SEMA Show in Las Vegas, Nevada, where 160,000 individuals, 74,000 buyers, and 3,300 members of the automotive press came to see Summit Racing's new Pro LS product line for General Motors LS-Series small-block engines. That included camshafts, rotating assemblies, pistons, engine-swap radiators and oil pans, and assembly tools.

Following on the heels of SEMA, Summit Racing had its first official corporate display at the 2020 Barrett-Jackson Collector Car Auction in Scottsdale, Arizona. Summit Racing's redesigned 2020 website and mobile app were also launched to make it even easier for customers to find the parts they need as well as learn about special offers and sales. Also launched in 2020 was Summit Racing's Truck catalog, which features products for late-model trucks.

It's no small wonder that Summit Racing Equipment is known as the World's Speed Shop.

JEGS
Columbus, Ohio

JEGS is the second-largest speed equipment retailer in the United States—and the world for that matter. Historically, JEGS has been around since 1960, when Gas coupe and sedan racer Jeg Coughlin Sr., who came from a family deeply steeped in retail sales, set up shop at 751 E. 11th Ave. in Columbus, Ohio. Word of Columbus having its first *real* speed shop grew, and by 1968, Coughlin expanded the 11th Avenue location to 12,000 square feet.

In the meantime, Coughlin was gaining quite an on-track reputation. He raced a Plymouth Barracuda A/Fuel Funny Car that yielded him his first national event win (Competition Eliminator honors at the 1970 NHRA

Springnationals, Dallas, Texas), and he was presented with the NHRA Sportsman Driver of the Year award in the NHRA's Division 3 (North Central Division). Ever the eagle-eye promoter, Coughlin awarded his 1973 Chevrolet Vega Pro Stock car to one lucky winner as part of a huge promotional giveaway during the National Trail Raceway Divisional Championships.

In 1988, sons John, Troy, Mike, and Jeg Jr. purchased speed shop operations with the support of their father and big ideas in the works. One year later, JEGS debuted its first issue of the JEGS mail-order catalogue to rave revues.

JEGS founder Jeg Coughlin Sr. comes from a strong family background in retail business. JEGS High Performance (speed shop) was founded in 1960.

Known as The Captain, *Coughlin first burst upon the national stage when he won Competition Eliminator driving his 1970 Plymouth Barracuda A/FC to victory at the NHRA Springnationals in Dallas, Texas.*

In 1992, Jeg Coughlin Jr. was crowned NHRA Super Gas Champion, his first of many NHRA Championship crowns. In 1994, following in his brother's footsteps, Troy Coughlin fielded his first entry in NHRA Pro Stock Eliminator. In 1998, high-speed cameras rode along with Jeg Jr. as he shifted gears in the JEGS Chevrolet Pro Stocker. That same year, Jeg Jr. was also crowned NHRA Rookie of the Year.

Team JEGS opened its state-of-the-art mail-order facility in Delaware, Ohio, and big things happened trackside for the Coughlin family. Troy Coughlin won the NHRA's All-Star event at Bristol, Tennessee, and was one of only five Pro Stock drivers to qualify for every event. Even bigger news, Jeg Coughlin Jr. won his first NHRA Pro Stock World Championship. On the business side of

In 1973 and 1974, Coughlin stepped out of the driver's seat to devote more time to growing JEGS but wisely retained Dale Emery, Dee Gant, and Fred Miller to run his Camaro Funny Car. He was rewarded with three national event wins, including winning FC Eliminator at the 1974 NHRA Winternationals.

In 1998, jegs.com launched its huge warehouse facility in Delaware, Ohio, which is home to JEGS corporate offices as well as the mail order, tech, shipping, and warehousing facilities. It's a city unto itself.

The reception area features a number of past JEGS performers and many trophies, a JEGS timeline, movie history, and more. Check out the unique trophy staircase.

Everything has a purpose at JEGS mail order. Those huge pallet racks also serve as uprights for the roof.

The heart of the beast is the JEGS mail order center, which operates 24/7. The JEGS technical department also operates at full throttle.

The JEGS warehouse is one of the most proactive shipping departments in the business, where orders are received, pulled, shipped, and gone in 24 hours or less.

the coil, JEGS celebrated the 40th anniversary of JEGS mail order along with the dedication of a new research and development facility on the Delaware, Ohio campus.

The year 2002 was a banner year for the Delaware, Ohio–headquartered speed equipment retailer. JEGS donated the championship vehicle from the 2000 season to the Center of Science and Industry (COSI) speed exhibit, which was a traveling exhibit that focused on the science and technology of achieving record-breaking speed. The exhibit traveled for five to seven years. Even bigger news was that Jeg Coughlin Jr. was selected as a U.S. Olympics torch bearer. Jeg Sr. was named Central Ohio's Entrepreneur of the Year in the Master Entrepreneur category by Ernst & Young. Jeg Sr. was also presented with *Car Craft* magazine's All-Star Drag Racing Team "Ollie" Award for lifetime achievement in the sport of drag racing. Last, but certainly not least, Jeg Coughlin Jr. was crowned NHRA Pro Stock World Champion.

In 2003, the Coughlin family established the JEGS Foundation. That same year, Jeg Coughlin Jr. appeared in a national ad campaign for Powerade.

In 2004, JEGS mail order shipped more than a million packages to customers.

In 2005, JEGS celebrated its 45th anniversary with the debut of its 1- to 2-day free nationwide shipping. NHRA Pro Stock fans were happy to see Jeg Coughlin Jr. return to NHRA Pro Stock after a brief layoff.

In 2006, JEGS debuted same-day shipping for orders placed by 9 a.m.

In 2007, Jeg Coughlin Jr. eclipsed the 50-win mark and won his third NHRA Pro Stock World Championship, John Coughlin won the Top Dragster Division Championship, and Mike Coughlin won the Top Sportsman Division Championship. In more big news, Jeg Coughlin Sr. was crowned grand marshal of the NHRA Hot Rod Reunion in Bowling Green, Kentucky.

In 2008, Jeg Coughlin Jr. won back-to-back NHRA Pro Stock World Championships. The following year, Cody Coughlin broke ground as the first third-generation champ. Also in 2009, Troy Coughlin Sr. won the NMCA Pro Street Championship and his first national event, while Mike Coughlin won the NHRA Division 3 Top Sportsman

Championship and John Coughlin won the NHRA Division 3 Top Dragster Championship.

In 2010, JEGS celebrated its 50th anniversary. The following year, Cody Coughlin won the Howie Letton Rookie of the Year Award on CRA dirt. In 2012, Troy Coughlin captured the NHRA Pro Mod Championship.

In 2013, Troy Coughlin scored his 100th NHRA national event win. Cody Coughlin won the CRA Championship to become the first Coughlin to win a non–drag racing championship. Jeg Jr. won his fifth NHRA Pro Stock Championship, and Troy Jr. won the NHRA Division 3 Super Gas Championship.

In 2015, Troy won his second NHRA Pro Mod Championship. The following year, Cody Coughlin won the ARCA/CRA Super Series and JEGS/CRA All-Star Tour. In 2017, Troy Coughlin won his third NHRA Pro Mod Championship.

In 2020, Jeg Coughlin Jr. announced that he would retire from Pro Stock driving to more fully concentrate his efforts on overseeing his duties at jegs.com. One of the winningest drivers in NHRA Nationals event history, Coughlin has 82 national event wins (62 in NHRA Pro Stock) and five NHRA Pro Stock World Championships: 2000, 2002, 2007, 2008, and 2017.

All of the Coughlin boys followed in their racing father's footsteps. The most noteworthy was Jeg Coughlin Jr., who virtually dominated NHRA Pro Stock. (Photo Courtesy Bob Johnson)

Warehouse Distribution

By Wayne Wolfe
Former Holley Carburetor Company Sales Representative

As the need and demand for performance equipment grew and with speed equipment manufacturers (Holley, Edelbrock, Clay Smith, Iskenderian, Weiand, Winfield, etc.) practically popping out of the woodwork, the ability for the average speed shop to stock a myriad of brand-name speed parts became increasingly more difficult.

By the mid-1950s and early 1960s, there was a network of nearly 50 warehouse distributors (WDs) in the country, including Buckeye Sales, Detroit High Performance, Jobber's Warehouse, Keystone Automotive Warehouse, Midwest Auto Specialties, Motor State Distributors, Racer's Warehouse, etc. These WDs stocked virtually every name-brand product in the thousands.

Some WDs also had retail outlets, such as AutoSales (Summit Racing), Buckeye Sales (JEGS), Detroit High Performance Warehouse (Gratiot Auto Supply), Ramchargers Detroit (Ramchargers Speed Shops), Rush Sales (Midwest Auto Parts), etc., that were used as avenues to sell retail.

The following is a brief summation of the WD process:

The manufacturer sells product to the warehouse distributor. What profit did the manufacturer make? As much as possible. When a WD sells to a jobber, the profit margin is usually 28 to 35 percent, but that varies throughout the parts sheet. The jobber's profit margin is usually 30 percent. Obviously, there's lots of wheeling and dealing going on.

The WD will tell the jobber, "Give us an order for $3,500 or more, and you get 10 percent off. Also, if you pay on time, you qualify for an extra 2 percent over the normal discount."

In the industry, there is a confidential WD sheet, and there are blue sheets for the jobber and green sheets for retail sales, or the manufacturer's suggested retail price (MSRP).

CHAPTER 7

LOST SPEED SHOPS: PIONEERS IN HIGH PERFORMANCE

Author's note: Listed below is a representative selection of lost speed shops generated from contacting parties involved either by telephone or by email. Unfortunately, not everyone contacted saw the value in being listed herein. Some failed to respond, and others were unable to be located. In cases where there were no photos available of the actual storefront being featured, we (whenever possible) substituted photos of popular race cars that the particular speed shop being queried sponsored and/or campaigned.

Anaheim Speed Engineers
Anaheim, California

The names *Anaheim Speed Engineers* and *Pure Heaven* are synonymous with fire-breathing, guardrail-to-guardrail, 16-car AA/Fuel Altered shows from the mid-1960s shows that used to pack the stands at hallowed palaces of speed up and down the West Coast, such as Carlsbad, Orange County, Lions, Irwindale, and Fremont raceways.

Ironically, the Anaheim Speed Engineers saga actually began one city over in Fullerton, California, around 1962 when aspiring Fuel Altered star Leon Fitzgerald opened a modest speed shop (also known as Fitzgerald's Racing Equipment) on the front part of the lot where the late Jess Tyree's header building shop was located. It was there that Fitzgerald and friend Jack Eskelson built a steel-bodied 1948 Fiat Topolino Altered that was ultimately powered by a blown and injected nitro-burning small-block Chevy capable of propelling the car into the mid-9-second zone.

The year 1965 proved to be a banner year when Fitzgerald and former racing buddy Glenn McMullok opened Anaheim Speed Engineers at 266 Manchester Blvd. in Anaheim, California. One of their first projects in conjunction with Jack Eskelson was building the Reed, Rockman, & Fitzgerald *Pure Heaven* 1932 Austin Bantam AA/FA roadster, which was powered by the same small-block

This photo of Frank "Hawk" Harris's big-block Chevrolet A/Gas dragster was taken in front of Anaheim Speed Engineers at 266 Manchester Blvd. in Anaheim, California.

Chevy nitro gulper that had powered the Fiat.

However, as good as *Pure Heaven* was (high 7s at 168 mph), it paled in comparison to Reed, Rockman, & Fitzgerald's patriotically hued, big-block 427-Chevrolet-engine *Pure Heaven II* that was built in early 1967 and dominated local Fuel Altered racing up and down the West Coast. More importantly, in 1968, *Pure Heaven II* participated in the very first AA/Fuel Altered National Tour along with Marcellus & Borsch and the famed *Winged Express*, Leroy Chadderton and the *Magnificent 7*, and Henry Harrison driving Nolan Pritchard's *Beaver Hunter* AA/FAs.

Fitzgerald continued to tour *Pure Heaven II, III,* and *IV* well into the early 1970s. However, unfortunately, Anaheim Speed Engineers (which also listed Richard and Joe Campos's *Lo Blow* and *Low Blow II* and Frank "Hawk" Harris's A/Gas dragster as works cars) only survived until 1968. That was the year when partner Glenn McMullok, who was feeling the strain of trying to eke out a living by

Leon Fitzgerald (sharing the trophy with Miss Irwindale Raceway) and partner Glenn McMullok are all smiles in the Irwindale Raceway winner's circle after capturing one of many AA/Fuel Altered weekend features with **Pure Heaven II** at the famed palace of speed circa 1968.

Anaheim Speed Engineers' official corporate logo was reminiscent of Hanna Barbera's *Flintstones* cartoon series, which was high in network TV ratings and all the rage at the time.

and yes, there was even a *Pure Heaven* sand rail at one point accompanying the original *Pure Heaven II* race car that was restored in the mid-1980s by current owner and caretaker Bob Nylander. *Pure Heaven II* is permanently on display at the Wally Parks NHRA Motorsports Museum in San Dimas, California, and makes cameo appearances at select vintage drag racing events, such as the Southern California Auto Club–sponsored California Hot Rod Reunion. Once a Fuel Altered driver, always a Fuel Altered driver, as Fitzgerald and son-in-law Jeff Bennett and grandson Chris Bennett race an all new *Pure Heaven* AA/FA nostalgia racer, which has run a best of 6.59 at 240 mph.

Driver Tom Ferraro lights up the M&Hs in Joe and Richard Campos' *Lo Blow* AA/FA off of the Orange County International Raceway starting line circa 1968. The Campos brothers' T-bucket was powered by a Glenn McMullok/Anaheim Speed Engineers blown nitro Chevrolet small-block.

running the shop all by himself while Leon was out on tour, took a job elsewhere.

With the closing of Anaheim Speed Engineers, Fitzgerald took a job at Chrysler's New Car Prep Department in nearby Santa Fe Springs, California, and remained there throughout the 1970s. The building that housed Anaheim Speed Engineers was leveled in the name of progress in the mid-1970s to make room for a new California Interstate 5 freeway offramp.

Today, Leon and his wife, Darlene, own a sand rail component manufacturing company called Billet Pro,

Big Ed's Speed Shop
Alexandria, Virginia

"Big Ed" Sloper was one of those guys who lived up to his namesake. Sloper was (as it has been frequently said) larger than life. A long-standing member of the Accelerators Car Club, the former United States Postal Service (USPS) mail carrier sold used speed equipment as a side business out of his home garage and the trunk of his car at NHRA Northeast Division 1 "land of Ned" tracks, such as Acquasco Speedway; Capitol Raceway; Cecil County Raceway; Suffolk, Virginia; York US-30 Dragway; and Manassas, Virginia.

Big Ed's Speed Shop published one of the first catalogs on the Eastern Seaboard and shipped many of them free of charge to US troops fighting in Vietnam.

Well-known East Coast Fuel Funny Car Circuit (ECFFCC) racer Gene Altizer was sponsored by Big Ed's Speed Shop while running a series of Pure Chevrolet-powered fuel injected nitro-burning Funny Cars.

"It seemed as though the Roadway Express truck would always be dropping off or picking up parts at our house," Sloper's widow Sandy said.

Ed Sloper opened the first Big Ed's Speed Shop on King Street in Alexandria, Virginia, in early 1960 and remained at that location for four years. Big Ed's Speed Shop was a major proponent of mail order and was an early advertiser in the *Eastern Drag News* and *Super Stock and Drag Illustrated* magazines, which were both owned by Eastern Publishing Company in Alexandria, Virginia. It also advertised in later-1960s *Drag Times*, which was a reformation of the old *Eastern Drag News* group under different ownership. Moreover, Big Ed was a firm believer in catalog sales and was the first speed shop on the Eastern Seaboard to publish one.

"Ed would publish a new catalog every year," said T. P. "Jack" Redd, former *Drag Times* editor and drag racing historian. "I remember he ran a picture of the original Miss Hurst Golden Shifter girl, Pat Flannery, on the cover. You would have thought that it was a copy of *Playboy* magazine the way those things flew out the door."

Above all Big Ed Sloper was a patriot.

"Ed would send mail-order catalogs to our soldiers serving in Vietnam," said Sandy Sloper. "Those guys would write him letters requesting catalogs, and he would send them free of charge. Then, when they ordered parts, he would give them a military discount. He was a very generous man."

Big Ed's Speed Shop was also known for its huge George Washington's Birthday Sales as well as staging other major holiday sale events, and tons of people would come pouring in. By late 1964 or early 1965, Big Ed had outgrown his original location and moved to a much larger facility in the Powhatten Shopping Center by the Monroe Avenue bridge in Alexandria, Virginia. Big Ed's Speed Shop also sponsored a number of up-and-coming racers around the tri-state area, including gasser pilot-turned-injected-fuel Funny Car racer Gene Altizer.

"I first met with Big Ed in 1968 to talk to him about sponsorship after I bought Malcolm Durham's old Corvair Funny Car to run on the East Coast Fuel Funny Car Circuit [ECFFCC]," Altizer said. "We sat down for a while and talked. Then, he called me a couple of days later, and we talked some more. He asked me what I needed from him, as he had never sponsored a Fuel Funny Car before. We went ahead with the sponsorship, and that's when he took a picture of the Corvair and put it on the cover of his latest catalog.

"Then, he ran a picture of my 1970 Logghe Nova on the cover of his next catalog. After I bought my new Camaro Fuel car from Logghe Stamping, he ran a photo of that car on the cover of his next catalog as well. Big Ed was always good to me. He gave me all the fuel, oil, gaskets, spark plugs, and anything else I needed. He had a deal set up through his suppliers like Mr. Gasket for example. All I had to do was drive

This was the official Big Ed's Speed Shop corporate logo. Ed printed thousands of decals using this logo, and they could be found in the dandiest of places.

down to the shop, get what I needed, sign a ticket, and that was it. We had a really great relationship."

All told, there were four Big Ed's Speed Shops, including a couple of satellite operations. However, after losing his lease to McDonald's Corporation at the main store and citing a major downturn in sales during the dismal 1970s, Big Ed's Speed Shop reluctantly closed its doors.

With a growing family to support, Sloper took a job at Zayre's department store as a buyer prior to obtaining a more permanent position with the US Navy that better suited to his talents. He worked as an inventory manager at the US Navy's Potomac Gateway Crystal City complex, where he assigned naval landing craft to US ships among other duties. He rose to a Spec 13 rating prior to his retirement.

Bing's Speed Shop
Santa Rosa, California

Ed Binggeli and his brother Walter learned how to wrench on farm equipment at an early age while living on the family farm in Windsor, California. During that time period, the boys bought a Model T Ford tracklayer and rebuilt it into a functioning farm tractor and put it to good use. At the same time, Ed's father had a blossoming side business selling used cars and put the boys to work maintaining a 1922 Dort, a 1926 and 1931 Dodge Brothers vehicle, and a 1941 Chrysler. However, none of those old relics were what you would exactly call hot rods.

Ed eventually purchased a channeled 1931 Model A Ford roaster to which he added a 1937 DeSoto grille and hood. Powering this conglomeration of discarded sheet metal on wheels was a Ford Model B 4-banger engine equipped with a Cragar OHV cylinder head and three Winfield carburetors. For a short time, Binggeli drove his A-Bone to Heraldsburg High School before the local constable suspended his driver's license for six months for buzzing the school grounds and doing broadies.

In 1941, Ed graduated from Heraldsburg High, and he and his roadster were off to Sacramento Junior College, where he studied aircraft mechanics. Within a year, he was employed by the US Air Force as a flight line mechanic servicing BT-13 and AT-6 trainers at Gardner Field in Taft, California. When not wrenching on airplanes, Binggeli and other like-minded locals street raced on the back roads of Tulare County.

With the advent of World War II, Binggeli was inducted into the service and sent to Bozeman, Montana, for aviation training and pilot's school. Then, he went to Santa Ana, California, to attend bombardier school. Ed spent the remainder of the war practicing bombing missions in Big Springs, Texas. Simultaneously, brother Walter Binggeli served in the US Army Corps. of Engineers

This photo was taken circa 1950 in front of Bing's Speed Shop in Santa Rosa, California. (Photo Courtesy David Fetherston)

building the Alaska-Canadian Highway and was present at the D-Day invasion in Normandy, France.

Prior to entering the service, the brothers aspired to own their own automotive repair business. It became a reality when their father purchased an old gas station on Windsor's River Road for them while they were away serving their country. Walter Binggeli arrived home first in 1945 and began running the business. In the spring of 1946, Ed Binggeli boarded a Greyhound bus with discharge papers hot in hand and headed to California. With the two brothers working full time Bing's Garage & Gas grew and flourished.

Ed Binggeli's first postwar hot rod was a rolled 1937 Ford coupe that he whacked the top off of and installed a Hall's Upholstery–built Carson top in its place. Ed's '37 had fender skirts, spinner hubcaps, and Appleton spot-

Ed Binggeli's first drag car was a flathead-engine 1937 Ford coupe that competed in C/Gas seen here outrunning an unidentified 1939 Ford gasser on a converted air strip somewhere in Santa Maria, California. (Photo Courtesy David Fetherston)

Binggeli also sponsored a lot of dirt track cars, or jalopies, as they were known. If it had wheels, the Binggelis were into it. (Photo Courtesy David Fetherston)

lights and was powered by a fairly healthy V-8 60 Ford flathead engine. However, the '37 wasn't fast enough, so a new 1931 Model A roadster was soon underway. Then, the dry lakes bug bit him. Binggeli took a 1932 Ford frame and installed a 1927 Model T roadster body. The car featured drop-link steering and modified Ford suspension with 1937 Ford Kelsey-Hayes wire wheels. Power was in the form of a twin-carbureted Cragar OHV Model A 4-banger that ran 106 mph at El Mirage Dry Lakes. As a member of the Russian River Roadster Club, Binggeli also raced at White Lake just outside of Reno.

In due time, Binggeli's 4-banger gave way to a bored-and-stroked 1941 Ford flathead equipped with an Edelbrock intake and a set of Offenhauser cylinder heads. At the 1949 Cal Neva Meet, Ed's roadster recorded the fastest quarter-mile time at 119.8 mph. Once home, Ed installed a Harmon & Collins cam, a Weber aluminum flywheel, a Schiefer clutch, and Kong ignition and proceeded to clock the fastest time of the day at 127.6 mph.

Although Binggeli enjoyed the publicity, Bing's garage became the direct beneficiary with a marked increase in business as local flathead racers got wind of the fact that there was a flathead expert living among them. As business grew, it began to overtake the space allotted for regular service work, and the Binggeli brothers decided that it was time to split the business into two separate entities.

In 1953, Ed opened Bing's Speed Shop in Santa Rosa about five miles south of Bing's Garage & Gas. Five years later, Bing's moved to its new location on Barham Avenue in Santa Rosa and became a major supplier of parts to the dry lakes racers and local hot rod genre.

Bing's Speed Shop also worked on a number of higher-profile SCCA sports car programs, including cars for the La Carrera Pan America program of racer Peter Culkin. Binggeli changed things a bit by becoming

involved in racing Modified Hardtops at local dirt tracks throughout the area, and he won a string of Modified events.

However, by the mid-1950s, drag racing was seriously taking hold, and Binggeli became involved as a car and engine builder and sponsor. One of the customer cars was Bob Consani's nitro-burning flathead roadster, which became a consistent winner turning speeds in the 128-mph bracket. Binggeli's first drag car was a flathead-engine 1937 Ford coupe that ran in C/Gas. Next was a 1934 Ford that ran in D/Gas and then a '57 Chevy that also competed in D/Gas.

In 1960, Ed built his most famous race car, a flathead-engine 1940 Willys coupe. On the track, the Willys was a solid competitor, running (and beating) Buick Nailheads, Oldsmobiles, and Chrysler Hemis with a best of 12.87 at 104.21 mph in the process. Running in F/Gas, the Binggellis' best effort was a 12.82, which prompted Dick Wells, editor of the NHRA's house organ *National Dragster* to comment.

"To me, this man shows more sportsmanship, perseverance, and spirit of competition than all the Hayden Proffitts and "Big Daddy" Don Garlits in the business. Give this man some credit!"

To that end, *Hot Rod* magazine ran a four-page spread on Binggeli's Willys in its November 1962 issue. Binggeli continued to race the Bing's Speed Shop Willys until 1973, when he retired from racing. In the meantime, Ed continued selling hard parts and building engines, but by then, he was building record-setting Chevys and other OHVs.

In 1976, Ed sold the speed shop and worked at Windsor's Chris Zootis Racing Engines. Today, Bing's Speed Shop is a fond but distant memory.

When speaking of the Binggeli's flathead-engine 1940 Willys F/Gasser, former Hot Rod magazine staffer the late Dick Wells wrote that Binggeli deserved as much credit as anyone in the business. (Photo Courtesy David Fetherston)

Brockman's Speed Shop
Dayton, Ohio

The name *Brockman* carries a lot of weight in business circles around the Buckeye and Hoosier states.

According to 34-year William Brockman & Sons Heating and Cooling Company employee Fred Metz, "Dick Brockman founded the company [speed shop] in the late 1950s as a spin off from the parent company Brockman's Heating and Cooling, which was located at 114 Valley St. at the intersection of Troy and Valley streets in Dayton, Ohio. Dick saw a niche market in selling custom mufflers out of the back of the heating and air-conditioning shop [Cherry Bomb mufflers were one of Brockman's best sellers], and things sort of grew from there."

Former NHRA Division 3 Pro Stock champion Bobby Yowell of Yowell Movers Inc. was one of those who traded at Brockman's Speed Shop.

"It was just a small place," Yowell said. "In fact, you wouldn't hardly notice it if you weren't looking for it, but it was a genuine, for-real, honest-to-gosh speed shop. They built engines, they built transmissions, they built rear ends, and above all, they sold a ton of hot rod parts."

Brockman's was known as *the* place to go in the tri-state area (Ohio, Indiana, and Illinois) if you had a Hilborn fuel injection system that needed tuning or an ignition system in need of ironing out. Veteran drag race driver and master mechanic Paul Frost worked at Brockman's machine shop for several years working on engine blocks, crankshafts, etc.

"During that time [1966], I built an A/Gas Supercharged 1940 Willys coupe that I ran through 1967 with Brockman's sponsorship," Frost said. "In 1968, I built a lightweight 1933 AA/GS Willys that I mostly match raced again under Brockman's sponsorship, but it got to the point to where I spent more time on the road racing than I did working in the machine shop, so Jim Mullen and I came to a mutual agreement that I had to fire myself [laughs]."

Other than being a sponsor at nearby Kil Kare Speedway, Brockman's Speed Shop did little advertising. Actually, it didn't have to; it was all walk-in trade.

In 1985, Brockman's Speed Shop reluctantly closed its doors. At the time, all the mom-and-pop speed shops within the Central Ohio area were starting to feel the pressure from big chain stores like the Nationwise Rod Shop and others.

Today, the actual Brockman's Speed Shop showroom is now a warehouse space for the heating and air-conditioning business, while the machine shop and engine-building area was converted to administrative offices for William Brockman & Sons Heating and Cooling employees.

Douglas Speed Sport Center
Silver Spring, Maryland

Formerly located at 8207 Fenton St. between Ripley and Silver Spring avenues, Silver Spring, Maryland's Douglas Speed Sport Center was another one of those mom-and-pop speed shops within the Washington, D.C./Baltimore, Maryland, Beltway.

Original employee and future owner Steve Novik remembered it fondly.

"I was there when Douglas Speed Sport Center opened its doors for the first time in July 1965," Novik said. "Doug Fleharty was the owner. It wasn't really a big

The Rod Shop: Confessions of a Speed Shop Counterman
By Dave Wallace Jr.
Photos by Pete Le Barberaa

I saw the shotgun barrel first, coming through the glass front door. It was just before 9 p.m. closing time on a winter weeknight when the unfamiliar pickup pulled up. The Rod Shop in Beltsville, Maryland, was one of the few retail operations open late in the Washington, D.C., region, certainly the only cash business teasing potential thieves at that time of night with brightly lit speed equipment in the glass storefront and the money collected during a typical 12-hour workday.

By the time it registered that I—a 22-year-old who'd recently survived 14 months in Vietnam with nothing worse than a knocked-out front tooth (a basketball casualty)—was about to be robbed in a peaceful suburb and potentially bleed out against a pegboard of bubble-wrapped Mr. Gasket parts, I was frozen to my stool. My final words were something like, "Uh, can I help you, sir?"

The stranger scanned the shop, as if searching for other employees, and said nothing. The muzzle was still aimed upward but in my general direction.

Finally, he said, "Oh, this isn't a gun store? I saw the Rod Shop sign from the road. Well, goodnight."

Other 1972 through 1973 evenings were less memorable but much more fun. As likely as not, some customer or pal would hang around while I closed up, maybe even follow my truck to the bank where I'd deposit the proceeds nightly. The Rod Shop was a reliable evening hangout,

Shown is the Austin Bantam Altered chassis that the Rod Shop team was working on. In the background is Gary Manley's satin, striped, and flamed 1939 Ford.

particularly for lonely guys and 16- to 20-year-olds barred from the bars.

Founding manager Pete La Barbera—who created a local following as a wise-cracking counterman at Creative Speed & Cycle in College Park, Maryland, before launching this store in 1971—created a vibe more akin to a neighborhood bar than a parts store. Potted plants and music from radio station WHFS welcomed an extraordinary eclectic clientele of little-guy racers, baby boomers driving muscle cars, and slightly older guys with hot rods. Government workers and others showed up like clockwork on Saturdays to pick up the week's *Drag News* and *Drag Times* newspapers, sticking around to enjoy bench racing and ball breaking with local legends.

A General Motors retiree named John Kennedy and his drag-racer son, Robbie, opened the original Rod Shop in Philadelphia in the late 1960s. The continued success of that store and Pete's prodding inspired a second Maryland location opening in 1972. Accordingly, I was recruited from LA to manage Beltsville, while Pete put together a beautiful shop in a Rockville strip mall.

Our little chain wasn't large enough to qualify for direct discounts with most manufacturers, but competitive pricing from the régime's multiple warehouse distributors ensured margins of around 30 percentage points on most items. That is unheard of since the advent of mail-order discounters and, later, online sellers. The main exception was ACDelco, whose air shocks and electrical components were priced lower than anyone due to the senior Kennedy's previous career in GM management.

One time his 454-powered Chevrolet station wagon came down from Philly with a full load of vintage, tach-drive Corvette distributors discovered somewhere in GM's vast parts system. Kennedy's corporate connections also paid off with Carter Products. Almost nobody wanted a spread-bore 4-barrel, but electric Carter fuel pumps sold well at approximately half the cost of Holley's blue model.

Pete was expert at reading and predicting local markets. After the van craze broke out in California, he flew west and lined up a manufacturer that shipped hundreds of portholes to The Rod Shop. For months, vanners came from throughout the Northeast to buy the only non-performance part displayed in our otherwise hard-core parts store. We stocked the ever-popular 780-cfm 3310 and 650-cfm vacuum-secondary Holleys, plus double pumpers in every size, even Dominators.

Other mainstay lines included Zoom, Lakewood, Flex-A-Lite, and VHT. We sold everything needed to create custom carburetor linkage and a complete fuel and exhaust system. For hard-core race parts, the Coleman Brothers warehouse was just a half-hour dash north on Route 1. David and Bill Coleman also patiently answered advanced technical questions beyond the considerable expertise collectively available in-house from part-time countermen Gary Manley, Jimmy Noll, and Frank Porto, all of whom were wrench-turning hot rodders unlike our boss.

Pete was at once the best boss and the worst mechanic I'd experienced. Nevertheless, he was regarded as a peer by Mid-Atlantic engine and chassis builders, customizers, painters, upholsterers, racers, and rodders. Nobody knew more about East Coast hot rodding and drag racing history. What Pete lacked in mechanical ability, he made up for in genuine respect and admiration for anyone possessing such skills. He spoke of being humbled, and downright humiliated, as a teenager by cruel countermen at "cliquey" speed shops catering to racers. He taught his employees by example. Upselling to a higher-margin brand or product was forbidden, as was pushing anything that did not help the customer achieve his or her stated goal. Each visitor was treated as if he or she knew more about individual parts and combinations than Pete or me (and usually did.) He was often seen out in the parking lot, looking under someone's hood or rear bumper, saying something complimentary about even the most disastrous project.

All three Rod Shops appeared prosperous in 1973, when an irresistible job offer from C. J. and Hazel Hart from Orange County International Raceway (OCIR) pulled me

The Eastern Seaboard–based Rod Shop corporate logo is pictured.

back West. In fact, the high-rent Rockville location was not delivering desired results and was shuttered soon after I left, bringing Pete La Barbera back to Beltsville temporarily. Without notice or explanation, the owners reclaimed the Beltsville inventory and walked away from the lease that Pete had signed on their behalf. He was able to replace only a small percentage of the missing merchandise with parts fronted by sympathetic distributors, which was not nearly enough to prevent impatient customers from defecting to well-stocked area stores while he attempted to rebuild inventory. The father of five soon ran out of savings, closed up, and reluctantly went to work for a series of former competitors.

The Rod Shop was certainly special, though hardly unique. Every town seemed to have at least one such business in the 1960s and 1970s before national chains used their superior purchasing and promotional power to undercut retail prices and before mega warehouses started advertising and shipping hard-core parts directly to consumers, cutting out the counterman entirely. Independent speed shops served as community halls for a semi-underground culture of dirt track rednecks, hippie vanners, street racers, class-legal and bracket racers, criminals, blacks and whites, wives and girlfriends. Whenever one faded away, much more than a small business was lost. That's why old racers and rodders around D.C. can still be heard reminiscing about the little Beltsville, Maryland, store that was booming a half century ago. None of us working that busy counter could've imagined that such a magical start to the 1970s marked the beginning of the end of a uniquely American institution.

The Rod Shop mentioned has no affiliation with the Rod Shop started by Gil Kirk and Jim Thompson in the late 1960s based in Columbus, Ohio.

place—maybe about 2,000 square feet. We actually took two small stores and opened the wall in the front, built a counter to do business on, and used the back for inventory and storage. I worked at Douglas Speed Sport from 1965 to 1968. Then, I bounced back and forth from 1970 to 1971.

"In 1966, Doug was on the verge of being drafted, so he joined the US Navy and was shipped overseas. I ran the store for a while until I found another business opportunity that was too good to pass up and some other people came in and ran the place. About that time, Doug was starting to get a little discouraged, so, in 1976, a dear friend of mine named Tony De Carlo and I made Doug an offer and bought the business the following year [1977].

"A year after that, my partner opened his own automotive repair shop, so he left, and I took on another partner named Steve Kantor. Those were the days when the feds [the Environmental Protection Agency (EPA)] were starting to place restrictions on engine modifications to cars, and we were starting to get a little nervous. So, in 1980, I sold out to Kantor and left the business. Eventually Steve sold out to another fellow in the early 2000s, and he had the business for maybe two to three years and

Douglas Speed Sport Center opened its doors in July 1965. The Doug Fleharty–owned business carried all the top lines and moved a lot of product—all from a 2,000-square-foot building. After 39 years in business, Douglas Speed Sport Center closed its doors in 2004. (Photo Courtesy Bruce Wheeler)

Bruce Wheeler's Wheeler Dealer *AA/FD driven by the late Al Friedman was one of many cars in the Washington, D.C., Beltway area to enjoy sponsorship from Douglas Speed Sport Center. (Photo Courtesy Bruce Wheeler)*

finally closed the doors around 2004.

"When we had that place, it was packed to the rafters with speed equipment. To give you a little insight, we were the first speed shop on the Eastern Seaboard to do business with Mr. Gasket. When we signed on with them, founder Joe Hrudka was still working out of his garage. We were on their Warehouse Distributor pricing list, and we dealt directly with them. Ed Cholokian was another one of our earliest clients; in fact, he came and visited the shop one day. We also carried Edelbrock, Crane Cams, Holley, Doug's Headers, Stewart Warner and Sun instruments, and Iskenderian Cams—we did all the major stuff.

"We never published a catalog, but we did advertise in *Drag Times*, which was published locally. We also sponsored a number of our own race cars, including a 1965 big-block Chevelle and a 409-engine 1961 Chevy Impala, but with the speed shop taking up most of our time, we didn't campaign those cars for very long. Probably our highest-profile sponsorship was Bruce Wheeler's *Wheeler Dealer* Top Fuel car driven by the late Al Friedman and later on by Bub Reese."

Former Top Fuel racer Bruce "Wheeler Dealer" Wheeler also remembers Douglas Speed Sport Center fondly.

"Initially, Doug and his mother ran the store," Wheeler said. "He ran the parts counter, and she did the bookkeeping. I went to work there right out of the US Air Force in September 1966 as Steve Novik's assistant parts manager. I worked there until June 1967, when I decided that I needed to attend to my running the *Wheeler Dealer* AA/FD full time. Douglas Speed Sport Center was a good place to work. Doug was a very generous man almost to a fault, and he always gave us parts at cost."

Novik said his time at Douglas Speed Sport Center was fulfilling and helped prepare him for the future.

"Working at Douglas Speed Sport Center gave me the opportunity to meet new people and impart some of the knowledge I knew about cars and picking the right speed equipment to make a particular car go fast," Novik said. "It was a very satisfying experience. Plus, I was able to apply much of the business experience I had gained through running and owning Douglas Speed Sport Center in future business ventures. Today, I just feel like I'm a better person from it."

Goodies Speed Shop
San Jose, Salinas, San Carlos, and Walnut Creek, California

Founded in 1962 by speed equipment entrepreneur Rich Guess, Goodies Speed Shop was one of the most recognized speed shop chains hailing from the Western region of the continental United States.

The parent company, located at 342 Lincoln Ave., in San Jose, California, quickly endeared itself to the racing community through affordable prices and good old-fashioned hands-on service. The company's mantra of "Quality Speed Equipment at Discount Prices" was no joke, and Goodies practiced what it preached, actively sponsoring local racers, including Nunez & Dillon's 1941 Willys B/Gasser; Rich Corbari, AA/FA; Don Servanti, A/FD; and Jim Liberman and his *Hemi Hercules* A/MP Chevy II. Goodies was also a presenting sponsor at nearby Fremont Drag Strip (later known as Baylands Raceway) and Vacaville Drag Strip and sponsored numerous local events and car shows throughout the San Francisco Bay Area.

However, the program, which reaped the most benefits on the national level was Goodies sponsorship of Lew Arrington's hemi-powered *Brutus* 1965 Pontiac GTO match racer driven by Jim Liberman. Liberman fielded a series of Jungle Jim Chevrolet Nova and Camaro Funny Cars of his own, touring along with Arrington from one end of the nation to the other with the Goodies Speed Shop banner emblazoned along their side flanks. Other nitro Funny Cars (such as the Goodies-sponsored *Hairy Canary* Plymouth Valiant of Hammons and Williamson and the *Samson* Dodge Dart of Rich Abate) followed suit. It prompted Guess, who by then had stores in San Jose, Salinas, San Carlos, and Walnut Creek, California, to boast that Goodies Speed Shop sponsored a Funny Car at every location!

Unfortunately, all good things must come to an end. After moving the business across the street to a purpose-built modern facility in 1969, Guess sold the

The name Goodies first appeared on the national stage gracing the rear quarter panels of Lew Arrington's original Brutus 1965 Pontiac GTO Funny Car.

For nine years, San Jose, California's Goodies Speed Shop (1962 to 1971) was sort of an American institution in the San Francisco Bay area. The top photo shows the Goodies San Jose location complete with the company's 360-ci Dodge delivery van that was known to smoke the tires at will. (Photos Courtesy Steve Reyes)

The late great "Jungle Jim" Liberman was another member of the Goodies Speed Shop entourage with his nitro-burning Chevy Novas and later Camaro AA/FCs. (Photo Courtesy G. K. Callaway)

business in 1971, citing a drop in sales at all four Goodies Speed Shop locations due to escalating insurance prices, OPEC, and a dramatic shift from high-performance to economy cars.

Soon after the sale, all four Goodies Speed Shops were closed, and California Speed Merchants took over the San Jose building. California Speed Merchants remained at that same location servicing the high-performance community until it was sold in 2007. When new owner Tracy Edmunds learned that the Goodies name was available, a reboot of the classic Goodies Speed Shop (in all of its 1970s glory) opened in 2007 and remained in business until 2013, when Goodies Speed Shop closed its doors for good.

Goodies Speed Shop was a high-profile sponsor at nearby Fremont Drag Strip. Pictured is another Goodies-sponsored flopper, the Chrysler-powered Samson Dodge Dart Funny Car that was campaigned by Rich Abate. (Photo Courtesy Steve Reyes)

The last Funny Car in the Goodies Speed Shop fleet was the Hammons and Williamson *Hairy Canary* Chrysler-engine Plymouth Valiant. (Photo Courtesy G. K. Callaway)

Jim Green's Performance Center
Monroe, Washington

The late Jim C. "Cricket" (a childhood nickname given him by his mother) Green got his start in the business working for B-Boys Auto Supply, which was established in 1950 in Lake City, Washington.

The following is a conversation with Jim and author Bob McClurg in 2018.

Jim: I started working at B-Boys around 1956 or 1957. In 1966, B-Boys built a new building, and I took over the old one and renamed the business B-Boys Speed Center. Within two years, I had outgrown that facility, closed it, and started up another store in Lynnwood, Washington. Around 1970, I renamed the business Jim Green's Performance Center. The name was more fitting for business, as we not only had the speed shop going but we also had a machine shop and an installation center to work on cars. We also started doing a lot of fabrication work and even launched a traction bar product line called Traction by Cricket.

Author: Jim Green's Performance Center also built engines?

Jim: The engine-building operation turned out to be approximately 70 percent of our business. We built Stock class motors that won class at the NHRA Winternationals. We built boat motors for 7.0-liter hydroplanes. We built all kinds of motors for street rods, street machines, and bracket cars—pretty much everything under the sun.

Author: And, of course, blown Fuel Chrysler Hemis?

Jim: Yes! That's where the *Green Elephant* name came from. When we were building our first Vega Funny Car, we were trying to figure out a name for it. One of my employees said that I didn't have a hair on my . . . if I didn't name the car the *Green Elephant*. After all, there

In the mid-1950s, Jim Green worked behind the counter at B-Boys Auto Parts in Lake City, Washington. When B-Boys expanded operations in 1966, Green took over the lease on the old building and launched B-Boys Speed Center, the forerunner of Jim Green's Performance Center. Check out that snazzy custom Plymouth! (Photo Courtesy Jim Green)

were black elephants and there were pink elephants. So, why not a green elephant?

Author: When did you start drag racing?

Jim: That was during the B-Boys Auto Parts era. I had this 1938 Chevrolet sedan sitting around, so I pulled a 283 small-block out of a wrecked 1958 Chevrolet and added a set of four Stromberg 97 carburetors on it and ran it for a while. Then, I put that engine in a dragster during the B-Boys Speed Shop era and ran it in the B/Dragster class. [Jim's granddaughter Nicky is now taking that car to car shows and doing exhibition start-ups as a tribute to her late grandfather.]

After that came the yellow C/Dragster, which was called *Engines by Cricket*. Since I was too busy running my business, Ray Hadford drove that car for me and won the 1968 NHRA Competition Eliminator World Championship.

In 1970, Ray and I put together a blown Chrysler Top Gas dragster, but the class was short lived. Two years later, I decided to build an injected aluminum-block 427-Chevy-engine Vega Funny Car on alcohol. I bought one of Joe Pisano's old Vega Funny Car chassis and bodies minus the engine and transmission and planned to drive the car myself. However, Ray Hadford and racing buddy

Green raced a number of dragsters, including this blown small-block Chevy digger that Ray Hadford drove to the 1968 NHRA Competition Eliminator World Championship. (Photo Courtesy Jim Green)

From 1972 to 1977, driver Frank Hall piloted Jim's Green Elephant *series of Chevrolet Vega AA/Fuel Funny Cars to many national event wins, including clinching the 1973 NHRA Winston Funny Car World Championship and finishing in the runner-up spot in FC Eliminator at the 1977 NHRA US Nationals.*

Ray Maxwell talked me into converting the car back to a Top Fuel Funny Car instead. Frank Hall and I raced that car for a year and sold it in late 1972. In 1973, we built a new Don Long Vega AA/FC and Frank and I won the NHRA Funny Car World Championship with it!"

Author note: Jim Green continued racing Funny Cars until the end of 1977 and was runner-up in Funny Car

Jim and staff proudly pose in front of Jim's speed shop in Lynnwood, Washington, where they celebrated the 35th anniversary of Jim Green's Performance Center. (Photo Courtesy Jim Green)

Eliminator at the NHRA US Nationals that year. In 1982, Green became engrossed in truck and tractor pulling, which lasted into 1997. In fact, his widow, Betty, still has his last tractor, a tri-engine blown 426 Hemi monster that she occasionally fires up just because, well, she can! Now let's trace the growth of Jim Green's Performance Center.

Jim: We switched the name from B-Boys Speed Shop to Jim Green's Speed Shop, and lastly, Jim Green's Performance Center in 1968. Over the years, we've sold virtually every name-brand part, at least 40 product lines at last count, and we became a warehouse distributor in the mid-1970s. On January 1, 2010, we moved from Lynnwood to our new 37,000-square-foot facility at 17520 147th St. SE, Monroe, Washington. We have an even-larger speed shop than we've ever had before, we have three times the machine-shop space, we have nine hoists—everything's just bigger and better.

Author note: While the speed shop occupied about 20 percent of the interior space, and the machine shop occupied another 30 percent of the space, the remainder of the building housed Jim Green's expansive museum.

Jim: It's a complete town. Inside, we have the restored *Assassin* 427 Ford front-engine Top Fuel dragster [once driven by Bob Muravez] on display along with Betty's super radical supercharged 427 SOHC flip-top 1934 Ford touring car and my 427 SOHC engine flip-top Ford F-100 pickup. Also sitting in repose is my 427 SOHC engine 1957 Ford Ranchero push car.

In 2010, Green moved into this humongous 37,00-square-foot facility at 15720 147th St. SE in Monroe, Washington. With 30 percent of the building devoted to the actual speed shop, the lineup of name-brand speed parts was absolutely awe inspiring. (Photo Courtesy Jim Green)

Jim's museum had a little bit of everything in it: a mock 1950s gas station, speed shop, etc., which was all gathered over a lifetime of involvement with fast cars. (Photo Courtesy Jim Green)

Author note: You think this guy likes 427 Ford Cammers or what? Green invented a belt-drive system for the 427 Ford Cammer that replaced that fidgety OEM chain drive, and he sold a ton of them. Also waiting in the wings for restoration is Jim's yellow A/Dragster and his NHRA Championship–winning Don Long Vega AA/FC.

Declining health forced Jim Green to close the Jim Green Performance Center on June 1, 2017. Sadly, James C. Green passed away from non-alcoholic liver failure on June 11, 2019. The legacy he left behind him is nothing short of immense.

Of particular interest is Jim's 427 SOHC flip-top body Ford F-100 that was formerly featured in Street Trucks *magazine.*

Harry's Hot Rod, Auto & Truck Parts
Grand Prairie, Texas

Back in 1968 when Harry Green opened his speed shop, it was simply known as Harry's Hot Rod or Harry's Hot Rod Shop, which was located at 105 NW 13th St., Grand Prairie, Texas, 78050.

In those days, the phrase *Race on Sunday [Saturday too], sell parts on Monday* was quite accurate, as there were a number of drag strips (Dallas International, Green Valley, Kennedale, and Yellow Belly) located around the Greater Dallas/Fort Worth area. However, times change, and Harry's changed with them.

In the mid-1980s, Harry's expanded the original 1,500-square-foot building to at least three times the size, and the name was changed to Harry's Hot Rod, Auto & Truck Parts to better serve the needs of the hot rodding community in its many forms: drag racing, circle track, street rod and muscle car, restoration, custom street truck and 4x4, and straight auto mechanics.

Over the years, Harry's also held and/or sponsored a number of car and truck shows in the Greater Dallas/ Forth Worth area, beginning with his most noteworthy event held in the early 1970s at the Dallas Convention Center. Harry's guest of honor was John Travolta, whose breakout role as Vinnie Barbarino on the TV series *Welcome Back, Kotter* soon vaulted the young actor to super stardom.

Harry Green also got into the warehouse distributing business first with the launch of TLM Performance Warehouse and later Motorsports Warehouse. As one blogger put it, "Times change, but good service (and even better speed equipment) is alive and well at Hot Rod Harry's, where Central Texas comes to buy their parts!"

After 50 years in the business, Harry's Hot Rod, Auto & Truck Parts closed its doors in 2018 due to an illness in the family, and, with the passing of yet another Texas institution, hot rodders from all across the Lone Star state observed a moment of silence.

Not the first, but certainly one of the best, founder Harry Green brought top-quality speed equipment to the Dallas/Fort Worth, Texas, metroplex and continued to grow the business during the next 50 years.

Harry's remained at the same address for 50 years, constantly expanding the business and changing with the times. Sorry to see you go, Harry.

Harry's Hot Rod Shop was established in 1968 in a little 1,500-square-foot building in Grand Prairie, Texas. Shown is Carl T. Stone's Hot Rod Harry's–sponsored Rollin Stone Racing Team, which consisted of a blown-Chrysler-engine AA/A roadster, an injected Chevrolet-engine A/A roadster, a blown-Chrysler-engine Chevrolet Monza BB/FC, and a custom Ford van.

Jerauld's
National City, California

The following is a conversation with former Jerauld's employee Jacob Bagnell and author Bob McClurg.

Author: Where was Jerauld's speed shop located, and when was it founded?

Jacob: Jerauld's was located at 2020 National Ave., National City, California, and was founded by Al Jerauld right after World War II. I practically grew up there as a kid.

The two people who ran the place were Al Jerauld and George Barber; they had raced together for years. After World War II, Al's mother bought the old Chrysler dealership in town, and Al bought a vacant lot at 2020 National Ave. Then, they moved the building there. Now, George Barber owned a back-alley shop called Barber Brothers that did machine work and fabrication after the war. However, it ran into financial trouble, Al kind of bailed them out, and George came along as one of the assets of the business. Al and George built quite a few cars together. In fact, their belly tank still holds the Class Q record for 90-ci engines.

Author: Who drove the belly tank?

Jacob: George drove it for a few years; then, Lou "Uncle Louie" Kaiser drove it for a year. It was quite a piece of engineering. Joaquin Arnett from the Bean Bandits once said that George and Al were the smartest people he had ever met. Aside from being powered by that de-stroked Ford V-8 60, they also built their own fuel injection system, [which was] quite a feat in those days.

Author: Did Jerauld's manufacture its own line of speed equipment?

Jacob: I wouldn't exactly call it a line, but Jerauld's did build Y intake manifolds for the Ford flathead long before Tommy Thickstun or Vic Edelbrock Sr. ever did. They also built custom flywheels long before Paul Schiefer [also from National City] got into the business.

Author: Obviously, a lot of famous people hung out at Jerauld's?

Jacob: You wouldn't believe all the people who used to come in there and ask Al and George for technical information. Billy Vuckovich from Indianapolis 500 fame would hang out there. Phil Weiand would come in quite often. In fact, I worked on his wheelchair once. Vic Edelbrock Sr. and Jr. used to pay us visits, and we would have M80 and Cherry Bomb fights. Clay Smith came in there, Bruce Crower, Alex Xydias, Eddy Ottinger, Emery Cook, Danny Ongais, and Jimmy Phillips all used to hang out at Jerauld's. It was so much fun growing up there.

Author: How many years was Jerauld's in business?

Jacob: In 1980, they sold the business. By then, it was going by the name *Jerauld's Muffler Shop*. That was shortly

Jerauld's Speed Shop was at 2020 National Ave., National City, California. A one-time hangout for some of the greatest names in hot rodding, the business was founded by Al Jerauld shortly after World War II.

before Al passed away. The building is still there with Jerauld's Muffler Shop in the back where the custom engine shop used to be. Jerauld's Paint Supply is now located in the former speed shop area, but the Jerauld's family has nothing to do with the business.

Author: Did any other famous cars run out of Jerauld's Speed Shop?

Jacob: Oh my God, there were so many. Almost anyone who was anybody either raced at Jerauld's or hung out there. To name a few: Eddy Ottinger, Emery Cook, Jimmy Phillips, and Cal Rayburn. Jerauld's worked on every type of race car and motorcycle that you could imagine. In those days, we had Balboa Stadium here in San Diego, where midgets, quarter midgets, and sprint cars raced. Another name that comes to mind is Jim Culvert from Culvert Automotive Engineering.

Author: Any other comments?

Jacob: Growing up as a kid around Jerauld's, I never realized what I was exposed to and was experiencing. Much of Lou Kaiser's sheet metal engine prototype

Jerauld's belly tank held a ton of records at Bonneville using various-displacement Ford engines. In fact, old 45 still holds the class Q record for 90-ci powerplants.

project was designed at Jerauld's and built at Tice Engineering in Chula Vista, California, where Uncle Louie was one of the head machinists.

Uncle Louie held patents for Harley-Davidson and Triumph engine components until the day he died. This included the Andrews Harley-Davidson twin-carbureted cylinder heads and Triumph Bonneville cylinder head. He built all the Triumph factory-sponsored racing bikes for Johnson Motors in Los Angeles and Triumph of Detroit. He also built all of Cal Rayburn's bikes, every bike Cal ever rode except the one he got killed on in New Zealand.

I remember that Alex Xydias, who held the record in the So-Cal Speed Shop belly tank, also used to come in there. In later years, the guys from Schneider Cams, Chuck from San Diego Steel Products [later renamed Auto Power] and many others used to hang out at Jerauld's.

Author: In your opinion, what was the main factor in Jerauld's closing aside from Al Jerauld's passing?

Jacob: When the Super Shops came along, they took away a lot of your everyday bread-and-butter speed-parts business. Jerauld's still sold quite a bit of product, but it wasn't anything like it was before. The Super Shops got the price down so low that places like Jerauld's just couldn't compete. Al decided that there was more money to be made in the exhaust system business. However, one thing that the Super Shops couldn't provide was the same degree of technical support to their customers that Al and George were able to provide. When you went into Jerauld's, Al would school you on how to build a complete engine. He would give you the part numbers, "If you buy this, this, and this, this is how fast you're going to go."

Author: How did hanging out at Jerauld's shape you as a person?

Jacob: I based my whole automotive teaching curriculum at Santee, California's Santana High School, where I taught for almost 40 years, on what I learned at Jerauld's. I have a former student who became an assistant manager at the Bellagio Hotel in Las Vegas, Nevada. Another one of my students became a top engineer at Boeing Aircraft and designed winged profiles. Other former students became successful in starting their own businesses ranging from automotive repair to building construction, while others became technicians in the US Armed Forces.

I started at Jerauld's as a little kid in the late 1950s, probably 8 or 9 years old, polishing their belly tank. I had been running with the wrong crowd and got into so much trouble that my mother, Madelon, asked Al if he could give me a menial job to help keep me off the street. It was awesome working there. I progressed from cleaning the shop in my junior-high-school years [the early 1960s] to installing exhaust systems and ulti-

mately building engines after hours when I was in high school.

I worked at Jerauld's until I graduated from college. Al and George were like fathers to me (my real father left us) and loved me and cared about me and were highly instrumental in turning my life around. Al and George not only taught me all about mechanics but they also taught me how to be a productive person, and their examples contributed to everything I've done in my life.

Steve Kanuika Speed Shops

East Coast speed shop icon Steve Kanuika was born in Philadelphia, Pennsylvania, to parents William and Mary Kanuika. During his formative years, Steve lived a normal life—that is, the normal life of a budding gearhead.

As word of 17-year-old Steve's mechanical prowess spread among the local street racing fraternity in the late 1950s, he and his older brother Bill felt confident enough to open up a small speed shop in the basement of their parent's home. Bill acted as the official mouthpiece for the newly minted Kanuika Brothers Speed Shop, while Steve was totally hands-on, building complete engines along with performing other mechanical work.

With each and every Steve Kanuika Racing Engine completed, the brothers used their father's tractor to

This sticker could be found on everything from blown nitro Chevrolet big-blocks to tractor pullers—even under the hoods of a few Saudi limousines.

hoist them out of the basement one by one while performing on-the-spot engine installations in their mother's driveway! Well, it didn't take very long before Mary Kanuika grew tired of the smell of gasoline and oil and the sounds of wise-cracking teens coming and going at all hours of the day and night. So, she gave the brothers their walking papers.

Steve and Bill opened up their first legitimate speed shop in an old Upper Darby, Pennsylvania, gas station and appropriately named it Kanuika Brothers Automotive. At this juncture, it should be noted that Kanuika's first legitimate race car, a 283-engine 1954 Chevrolet

In 1969, "Jungle Clare" Sanders piloted Jim Liberman's No. 2 Chevrolet Nova AA/FC to defeat Ray "Engine Masters" Alley's Barracuda to annex the first Funny Car Eliminator title in NHRA Winternationals history and Steve Kanuika Speed Shops rode along with them.

3100 Series half-ton pickup, also served as the company parts chaser while holding D/Gas records at the Vineland, New Jersey, and the Langhorne and York, Pennsylvania, drag strips.

Business was booming throughout the 1960s, and at one time, Kanuika had four speed shops. Kanuika and K&G Speed Associates pretty much controlled all the speed shop business in the area. It was during this time that he struck up a friendship with "Jungle Jim" Liberman, who called nearby Westchester, Pennsylvania, his summer home.

In 1969, Liberman was one of the first drag racers to field a two-car Funny Car team by re-bodying his 1968 Logghe Nova (also known as the East Coast car) and giving it to Clare Sanders to drive, while he ordered an all-new 1969 Logghe Nova (also known as the West Coast car) for himself. Longtime sponsor, San Jose, California's Goodies Speed Shop was already signed up with Liberman to sponsor Jungle's car, but he needed a sponsor for Sanders' Nova, and Kanuika and the staff at his Concord Township, Pennsylvania, speed shop were more than willing to oblige.

When Clare Sanders won the very first Funny Car Eliminator title in NHRA history at the 1969 NHRA Winternationals (defeating Ray Alley and his Engine Masters Plymouth Barracuda on the final), the Kanuika name became a household word in drag racing circles. That same year, Kanuika also debuted a 1969 ZL1 Camaro match race stocker as part of the Jungle Jim/Steve Kanuika alliance.

After 38 years in the business, Steve Kanuika retired in the late 1990s, although he occasionally still built engines by appointment. With the coming of the drag racing nostalgia craze, the soft-spoken Philadelphia native delighted in the notoriety. Steve Kanuika passed away at age 69 on September 20, 2009, due to complications from heart surgery at the University of Pennsylvania Medical Center in Philadelphia. To this day, those who knew Steve Kanuika speak of him with reverence and respect.

"Steve was a terrific guy," Clare Sanders said. "He was well liked. He was smart. He knew how to make things go fast. Steve Kanuika accomplished a lot of things in his lifetime, some of which nobody ever even heard about. For example, he was known to have built several high-performance V-8 engines for the Saudis. Those engines were used to power their limousines that were so weighted down with armament that with the stock engines they [originally] had could hardly move them under their own power."

Manhattan Speed
New York, New York

Manhattan Speed was an outgrowth of Manhattan, New York's Worth Auto Parts, which was founded in 1936 by brothers Sal and Vito Doto.

The company was originally at 194 Worth St. in Manhattan, but it expanded operations to a second store at 232 W. Broadway Ave., which is where Manhattan Speed founder Joe Doto comes in.

"I started working at Worth Auto Parts at 16 years old, running errands and learning the ropes," Doto said. "When I was 20, I started Manhattan Speed Shop out of Worth Auto, but the building was too small, so we left the W. Broadway location intact and moved to 5th Street and 3rd Avenue. That's where Manhattan Speed grew and flourished.

"Little by little, we started to handle more [product] lines direct. We warehoused GK Cams, Crane, Comp Cams, Sun Gauges, S&W Gauges, Speed Products, Mr. Gasket, Moroso, Grand, EMPI, Schiefer, Weber, Zoom, Hays, Vertex, Lakewood, Mallory, Accel, Henry Axles, Doug's Headers, Kustom Headers, Thrush, etc., and distributed parts to other shops in the Bronx and the other boroughs as well as Upstate New York, New Jersey, and other places."

This early 1960s photo shows Joe and his 1929 Model A roadster pickup parked in front of Worth Auto Parts store at 194 Worth St., Manhattan, New York. "My lifestyle has always been cars," said Doto. (Photo Courtesy Joe Doto)

*Manhattan Speed sponsored a number of different race cars, including employee Nick Pizzillo and the **Nasty Nick** 1968 A/MP Hemi 'Cuda. (Photo Courtesy Joe Doto)*

Manhattan Speed also carried a magazine advertising schedule with the late Pat "Seymour Balls" Cunningham from Engeldrum Publishing Company, which published *Hot Cars Magazine*, *Chevy Power*, *Vans & Trucks Magazine*, and other titles. In the early 1970s, Manhattan Speed also opened a speed shop in Salinas, Puerto Rico.

"My father owned part interest in Salinas Speedway in Puerto Rico, so opening up the speed shop just made good business sense," Doto said.

Due to a rapidly changing business climate, Manhattan Speed closed in 2000, but that's not the end of the story. Today, Joe Doto operates Bronx Automotive at 124 Atlantic Ave., Garden City Park, New York, which specializes in antique Ford restoration and street rod parts, Buick Gran National parts, etc.

Maryland Hi-Performance Sales
Wheaton, Maryland

Sam Auxier Jr.'s long and colorful career as a racer, speed shop owner, automotive radio talk show host, and TV commentator (*The Sam Auxier Jr. Show, Interviewing the Greatest Names in Racing*) is renown.

In the late 1960s, Sam and racing partner Chick DeNinno raced heads-up on the NASCAR Ultra Stock circuit, running a big-block Mustang and Mopar, respectively, prior to the boys transcending to NHRA Pro Stock in the early 1970s. Simultaneously, Sam and company opened Maryland Hi-Performance Sales (MHP) in Wheaton, Maryland. Sam provided his perspective.

"Back in the day, there were very few true speed shops around the Washington, D.C. Beltway, other than Coleman Brothers, which was a WD for just about everything in the world at that time—kind of a local JEGS in the area," he said. "I mean, there were a lot of goody shops and stuff like that, but not much of anything for serious racers. I knew Dave and Bill real well, and we had bought many parts for our race cars through them.

"For some reason, we—my dad [Sam Auxier Sr.], Chick, and I—decided that we should go into the speed equipment retail business for ourselves. Around 1971, we found a 3,000-square-foot storefront located on Redie Drive in Wheaton, Maryland. At the time, the primary speed equipment lines we carried were Goodyear racing tires, Holley Carburetor, Hurst Performance, Mickey Thompson, Mr. Gasket, Competition Products, Strange Engineering (we were actually one of Bob Strange's first customers), and Doug Nash."

"Speaking of Doug Nash, this is one of the really big stories from that era that has never been told. We had been doing big business with Doug Nash ordering gears and transmission products, and Jim Kerr [Kerr & Associates] came in one day and he said, 'You know, Doug is a great engineer, and he has this concept for a full-race, 5-speed manual transmission. He's gone to every bank, he's gone to the Big Three, he's tried to get investors any way he could, and it's been a real problem. The only collateral he has to put up are his train sets (he had an enormous collection of vintage train sets), and he's in need of money to build these transmissions.'

"So, we said, 'Well, how much does he need?' He said, '$72,000.'

Well, that was a lot of money in 1972 dollars. Anyhow, the next day, my father and I were on a plane to Detroit. Doug had his shop spit-shined by the time we got there. We looked over Doug's blueprints and everything and asked him how long it would take to build an engineering prototype. Doug gave us a production time estimate of 6 to 8 months for the prototype, and my dad

This photo was taken of MHP's original storefront located on Redie Drive in Wheaton, Maryland. (Photo Courtesy Sam Auxier Jr.)

Sam Auxier Jr. and partner Chick DeNinno pose behind the counter of Maryland Hi-Performance's well-stocked showroom while the cardboard cutout likeness of Linda "Miss Hurst Golden Shifter" Vaughn approvingly looks on. (Photo Courtesy Sam Auxier Jr.)

said, 'We'll do it!' I looked at my dad and said, 'You got $72,000 somewhere I don't know about?' So, then Doug said, 'The only things I've got for collateral are these train sets.' My dad said, 'Well, I don't want any toy trains, but this looks like one heck of an opportunity.'

"The next thing you know, he shook hands with Doug, and they had a deal. Within a week or so, they had a contract written up with the only stipulation being that we be one of the ones to field test the prototype as well as being one of the first aftermarket distributors on the Eastern Seaboard to stock and service those transmissions.

"Of course, it's an American success story. Eventually, the Doug Nash DN5 went into the Corvette among other

uses. Unfortunately, the downside to that is that some thieves broke into MHP and stole that transmission. Fortunately, they couldn't keep their mouths shut, and five or six months later, the police recovered it."

Other than servicing the DN5s and the Goodyear racing tire line (MHP worked closely in conjunction with Huggins Tires in North Carolina), MHP was pretty much in walk-in retail sales.

"Occasionally we would do on-spot service," Sam said. "If we sold you a Holley carburetor and you couldn't get the thing running right, we would jump under the hood and help you get it running smoothly. If you were to buy a Doug Nash gearset, we would build a transmission for you for a nominal fee. We were also a Doug Thorley Headers distributor, and it wasn't above us to do the occasional header installation. One of the things we prided ourselves in was pointing our customers in the right direction. If you were to come in and say, 'I want this, this, and this,' we would ask you to give us the specific use application, and after due consideration, we would say, 'No. You need this, this, and that, instead and this, and here is the reason why."

All told, Maryland Hi-Performance Sales was in business for 12 years.

"Chick only lasted for 8 to 10 months before he got a lucrative job offer with Sox & Martin, so then it was just dad and I," Sam said. "Back then, the mail-order business boom was still probably 5 to 6 years off. For the most part, we were solely reliant on walk-in trade, and that sometimes made things kind of tough. During that timeframe, we moved four times, first to Silver Spring, Maryland, after my dad bought a boat business there,

Both Sam Auxier Jr. and Chick DeNinno were involved in NASCAR Ultra Stock and later NHRA Pro Stock racing running Ford and Chrysler products, respectively. This picture was taken of Sammy and his 1971 Pro Stock Mustang doing its thing at Cecil County Drag-O-Way.

and twice to Rockville, Maryland. Unfortunately, we had hired a guy to run the speed shop who seemed savvy enough, but after discovering some irregularities on our inventory sheets, we discovered that this guy had in a short time stolen $60,000 in cash sales. Obviously, that was a big blow to the business. We also had another guy working there who was building engines on the side at home in his garage at night and buying parts through us at cost paying no markup whatsoever. We also put a stop to that."

Mom's Speed Shop
Redwood City, California

Mom's Speed Shop was established in 1967, according to former owner Rich Welch.

"It's been a long time, so I'm probably not going to be clear on a lot of stuff," Welch said. "In the early 1960s, I had worked over at Cow Palace Shell with Jessie Perkins, who ran the Cow Palace Shell Top Fuel dragster, and from that I became interested in the performance-parts aspect of the whole thing. If you recall, my twin brother, Les, and I used to take pictures out at Fremont Raceway. After that, I went to work at Cash Auto Parts in South San Francisco. At that time, Cash was the only speed shop in the Bay Area. While at Cash, another counterguy there named John Schamali and I got together and decided that we could do a better job at this by ourselves. We started looking for a retail location, and that's the beginning of it.

"Mom's Speed Shop was officially opened in mid-1967 at 1034 and 1036 El Camino Real in Redwood City. We had two storefronts side by side. One side was a retail front with a large glass window, and the other side was an installation shop with an overhead door, where we

This night shot looks almost like a Christmas card, doesn't it? Mom's Speed Shop was chock full of toys for big boys. (Photo Courtesy Les Welch)

(John and I) did complete engines, engine swaps, equipment installations, and things like that. The shop was big enough for six cars, but we also maintained Derry O'Donovan's A/Fuel dragster there.

Later on, as the business grew, we actually hired a couple of kids to work for us. We worked ourselves up to the point where we became a WD for three or four lines or brands in our [protected] area, such as Savage Clutches and Jardine Headers. We would do some wholesaling, shipping out product to other stores, and continued doing that until 1974, when the bottom sort of dropped out of the business. Here's a story for you.

"A California Highway Patrol buddy of mine who actually worked with me on Derry's crew came to me one day and said, 'I've got a duty where we have to provide security for a shipment of gasoline rationing coupons going north out of the Bay Area.'

"I said, 'What?'

"He said, 'This might affect you if gasoline goes into rationing.'

"If you remember, those were the years of the gasoline crisis. Well, I got right on it. At that time, I had bought out my partner, and I'm thinking 'Wow! I'm precariously perched here.'

"So, I started calling around, and finally, I called Leo J. Ryan, who was our congressman at the time. It took me about four tries to get through to him, and I said, 'I hear you guys are doing this, this, and this.'

"And he said, 'I can't tell you anything.'

The Mom's Speed Shop '55 Chevrolet sedan delivery was a fixture at the Fremont Drag Strip, which was near the GM Assembly Plant off of Interstate 17 in Fremont, California. (Photo Courtesy Les Welch)

"Finally, I asked him, 'If you had all your money in the world invested in a speed shop whose customers required cheap [inexpensive] gas to operate their cars, what would you do?'

"There was a long pause on the telephone, and he said, 'I guess I would be closing my business and find myself another line of work.'

"After that, I just kind of let the business wind down and played with a couple of different ideas. I went to school and became a cop for a while, but that wasn't my cup of tea, so I wound up in retail. In later years, I became involved in property management, and today I'm retired."

Rick Voeglin is the former editor of *Car Craft* magazine, co-owner of the Voeglin/Mayerson Super Gas Camaro, and CEO High Performance Communications Marketing and Advertising Inc., retired. He shared his memories of Mom's Speed Shop.

"When I was a struggling student at Stanford [University], I had a 1957 Chevy Junior Stock car that lived in the car port below the studio apartment I had while going to school," Voeglin said. "I used to go over to Mom's Speed Shop and just hang out there. Living on just $343 per month, I couldn't afford to do much of anything else, but yeah, I could dream!"

Motion Performance
Baldwin, Long Island, New York

Webster's New World Dictionary defines the word *motion* as "moving from one place to another," or "a moving of a part of a body specific." Perhaps beneath *motion*, Webster's should have listed "see performance" and under that "see Joel Rosen."

There's no denying the fact that Joel Rosen's Islip, Long Island, New York, muscle car building empire was one of the key motivators and driving influences in the late 1960s and early 1970s General Motors muscle car movement. Out West, there was Bill Thomas Race Cars and Dana Chevrolet; in the Midwest, there was Nickey Chevrolet and later Dick Harrell–Fred Gibb Chevrolet; in the Southeast, there was Anderson Chevrolet; and in the East, there was Yenko Chevrolet and Baldwin-Motion.

Joel Rosen was a Brooklyn, New York, kid who had honed his mechanical skills in the US Air Force working on World War II radial-piston engines. In the early 1960s, Rosen used his muster-out pay to open a 20x200-square-foot automotive repair shop in Brooklyn while racing a series of Corvettes in both local hill-climb competition and at the local drag strip. With the opening of New York National Speedway on March 20, 1966, Rosen relocated his business to the more geographically suited town of Baldwin, Long Island, New York, which proved to be a wise decision.

This is the car that started it all. Motion Performance founder Joel Rosen poses with his trophy-winning 1965 396-ci, 425-hp L78 Corvette. (Photo Courtesy Martyn L. Schorr)

Rosen convinced Baldwin, Long Island, New York, Chevrolet dealership owner Ed Simonin that with Baldwin sponsorship, Hi-Performance Cars *magazine promotional prowess, 427 power under the hood, and driver Mike Fons behind the wheel that he could successfully assault the A & B/Modified Production class records, which he did. (Photo Courtesy Martyn L. Schorr)*

Simultaneously, Bronx-born Martyn "Marty" L. Schorr was working his way through the car magazine publishing chain of command in the early 1960s at New York's Magnum-Royal Publications as editor of the magazines *Custom Rodder* and *Car Speed and Style*. After a brief hiatus in Uncle Sam's service, Schorr returned to Magnum-Royal in late 1963, where he became the editor of *Hi-Performance Cars*, which was followed by his appointment as Magnum-Royal's editorial director.

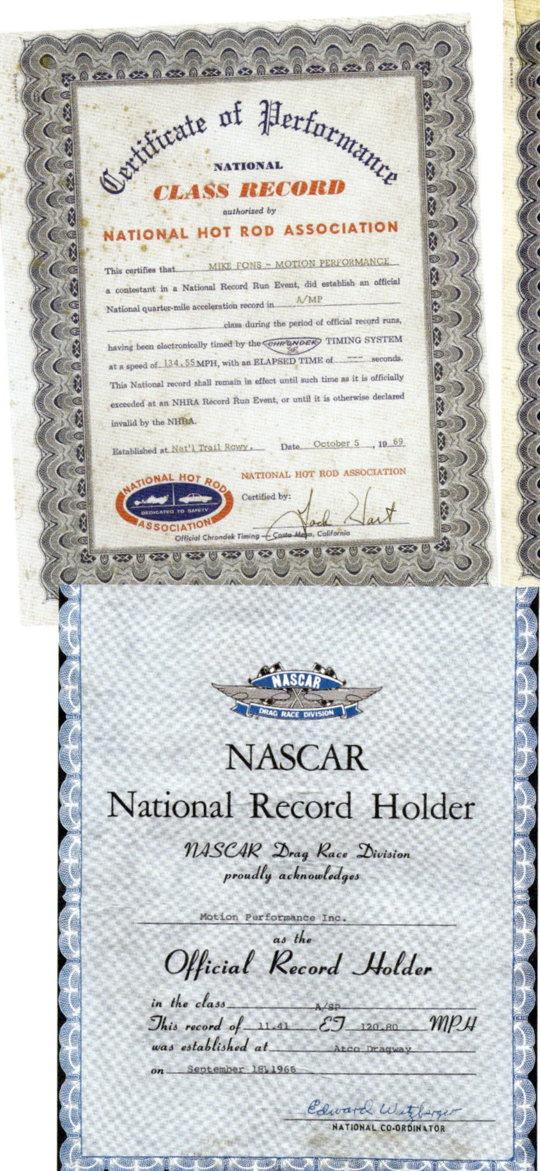

Here's a sampling of the records that Baldwin-Motion-Fons set in NHRA, AHRA, and NASCAR drag racing competition. (Photos Courtesy Martyn L. Schorr)

With the installation of a new Clayton dyno, Motion Performance's business picked up exponentially. (Photo Courtesy Martyn L. Schorr)

With the Clayton dynamometer in full song, Rosen and company didn't discriminate. Not only did the Baldwin, Long Island, tuner shop specialize in Chevrolet muscle, it also dabbled in dyno tuning other brands with wanton abandon. (Photo Courtesy Martyn L. Schorr)

With Baldwin-Motion's on-track successes, Joel Rosen launched his SS 427 Camaro Super Car program. (Photo Courtesy Martyn L. Schorr)

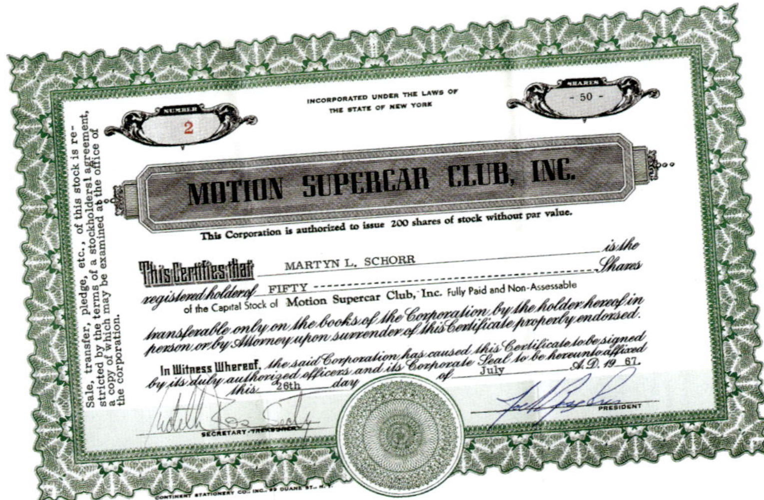

Ever the selfless promoters, Rosen and Schorr launched the Motion Super Car Club, which included a monthly newsletter, parts discounts, a jacket patch, mylar sticker, and free catalog. (Photo Courtesy Martyn L. Schorr)

Rosen (center) strikes a pose with Baldwin Chevrolet General Manager Dave Bean (left) and CEO Ed Simonin (right) directly in front of Baldwin Chevrolet's showroom advertising the Fantastic Five circa 1968. (Photo Courtesy Martyn L. Schorr)

This publicity shot was taken in front Baldwin Chevrolet in 1969 when Rosen and Schorr publicized the arrival of the Motionized 427 COPO Chevrolets. (Photo Courtesy Martyn L. Schorr)

A popular month-to-month feature in *Cars* was its muscle car drive tests (largely conducted at New York National in later years). Wanting to achieve maximum test results, Schorr sent his test cars over to Rosen's shop, where they were expertly tuned prior to testing using Motion's Clayton dynamometer to achieve maximum performance. Before long, Motion Performance and *Cars* magazine were deep into building project cars, with Rosen and his staff spinning the wrenches and Schorr providing the outside connections, inspiration, and ink.

Things gained momentum with GM's fall 1966 release of its new Camaro. It was available in 302-ci small-block Z28 or 375-hp SS 396 trim. The big-block version was the closest thing to the 1965 396 425-hp L78 Corvette that Rosen was currently racing. Joel reasoned that a 427 version of the new Camaro would be a total killer in NHRA A/Modified Production class. He and business partner Jack Geiselman persuaded Baldwin Chevrolet Parts Manager John Mahler to set up a meeting with Baldwin Chevrolet's owner, Ed Simonin, to convince Simonin that a successful racing program (with *Cars* magazine promotional sponsorship) would sell more product. The result was the Baldwin Chevrolet and *Cars* magazine–sponsored Motion Performance A/MP 1967 Camaro.

As the program began to gather (ahem) *motion*, Rosen's business went from the occasional customer tune-up or engine build to requests for turn-key cars. Much like Nickey, Dana, and others, the idea of a turn-key Motion Super Camaro (with publicity from Schorr and *Cars* magazine) seemed feasible enough with Baldwin Chevrolet supplying the cars, Rosen doing the builds, and John Mahler making sure that the L88 engines and support

hardware were available through GM. The result was the Baldwin-Motion SS 427 Camaro super car available with—get this—a GM factory warranty and GMAC financing. Wow!

A Baldwin-Motion Phase III SS 427 Camaro came with F41 (heavy-duty SS suspension), American mag wheels with Goodyear Polyglas Blue Streak tires, a 427/425-hp L78 big-block engine equipped with Holley carburetor and Edelbrock high-rise aluminum intake, cast-iron headers, and a set of high-performance mufflers. Super Bite traction bars, a 1967 Corvette Stinger fiberglass hood, and SS 427 badges were also on the bill of lading.

Unlike the Yenko or Fred Gibb–Dick Harrell product offerings, the sky was the limit when it came to accessorizing these cars. For starters, the customer chose the

Motion Performance continued its romp through the A/MP record books with this 1971 Motion Super Camaro driven by Dennis Ferrara.

Here's one of those Motion Performance catalogs you would receive with your Motion Super Car Club membership. (Photo Courtesy Martyn L. Schorr)

body color, interior color and trim, and had the option to order every factory gee-gaw listed in the book. Also, every Baldwin-Motion Phase III 427 Camaro came with Joel Rosen's personal guarantee that the car would run 11.50 seconds at 120 mph in the standing quarter-mile straight out of the box. Schorr's first print ad didn't mince any words: "The quickest and fastest super car! (Baldwin-Motion) SS-427 Camaro. Dyno tuned and ready to wail. $3,650.00!"

Once Rosen and Schorr were satisfied with their Baldwin-Motion SS 427 Camaro performance package, they expanded the line the following year (1968) to include Baldwin-Motion SS 427 Chevelles, SS 427 Novas, SS 427 Impalas/Biscaynes, and SS 427 Corvettes, all being marketed under the *Fantastic Five* moniker. When it came to bowtie muscle, this across-the-board thinking effectively covered all the bases.

As the years rolled on, Baldwin-Motion's Fantastic Five product lineup changed with the times, including the release of a Motion Super Vega small-block V-8 package in the early 1970s. Moreover, the development and refinement of the Baldwin-Motion Fantastic Five allowed Rosen to think outside the box and push the boundaries with his first love, the Corvette, to the outer limits, producing the Motion Phase III SS 427 Corvette, the Motion Phase III GT Corvette, the Motion Maco Shark and Manta Ray Corvettes, the Motion Moray Eel Corvette, and lastly the Motion Can-Am Spyder.

However, Rosen's creative genes were not solely aligned with GM. He also worked his magic on a pair of Motion-ized Shelby 289 and 427 Cobras and co-founded Motion Mini Car, which focused on VW and dune buggy high performance with Schorr and future World Products founder Billy Mitchell as copartners. This diversification enabled Motion to survive throughout the dismal 1970s, but as it grew harder and harder to turn a profit in this anemic marketplace, Rosen decided to close Motion Performance Inc., retire to Florida, and pursue military models, which are his other passion. Visit Motionmodels.com.

For more information about Motion Performance Inc., its products, and its history, pick up a copy of Martyn L. Schorr's book *Motion Performance: Tales of a Muscle Car Builder*, which is available on Amazon.

National Speed Shop
Canoga Park, California

In 1967, John Guedel and Bill Holland formed National Automotive Specialties and manufactured several items for drag racers. One item was the Drag A Log, which was believed to be the first mass-produced dedicated log book for recording on-track performance

Motown (Speed Shop) Memories
By Ted Spehar of Motown Missile *fame*

Around 1956, a friend of mine, the late Dee Nichols and I, used to hitchhike down to the Highland Park Hot Rod Shop in Highland Park, Michigan, but [now] it's long gone. That was my first recollection of a Detroit-area speed shop.

My oldest brother, Pete, who got me interested in cars, also used to go there. We would either have to take the bus or, like I said, hitchhike. The who's who of Detroit racing came in (Top Fuel driver Setto Postoian was one of the bigger names), and that's how you learned. Gratiot Auto Supply was also around, but they were a really, really long way away on the east side of Detroit, and I only think I went there a couple times.

In 1961, Dee and I built a flathead-engine Chassis Research dragster together. Then, we sold that and bought the third Logghe dragster chassis that Ron and Gene built and ran that car with a flathead. During that period, I also worked at Custom Speed Enterprises which was over in East Detroit.

By 1963, I bought my first Texaco gas station, and after that, there was no reason to hang around a speed shop anymore because I could buy all those parts WD. Of course, that was the beginning of the muscle car era, and things were really starting to get interesting. Meanwhile, Dee decided that he was going to open up a speed shop of his own called M&S Automotive, which was on Normandy [Road] and Woodward Avenue in Royal Oak, Michigan. I would frequent that place more than anywhere else because it was local, and why not give your friend the business?

Around that time [1966], I was running my second gas station [Gulf Oil] and was running a Super Stock car and

Ted Spehar's Motown Missile *1970 and 1971 Dodge Challenger Pro Stocker was (next to Sox & Martin's Hemi 'Cuda) the most-feared Mopar in NHRA Pro Stock. Driven by the late Don Carlton, the* Missile *could always be counted on to set either top speed or low ET at NHRA National events.*

became involved with Chrysler doing magazine prep cars. M&S was a happening place. Everybody that was anybody had their machine work done at M&S. That was before Midwest Auto Parts was around. I mean, they were around, but they weren't involved in high-performance work until at least 1966.

Around 1968, I purchased a Sunoco station, ran that and continued to do work with the Chrysler Corporation Special Vehicle Development Group. Of course, that led to my involvement with the *Motown Missile* Pro Stock cars. That was a long time ago. I wish I could remember more, but those are the memories I have about Detroit-area speed shops.

information, and another was the squeeze-bulb hydrometer for checking the percentage mixture of nitro methane and alcohol fuels.

Around 1968, safety equipment mogul Jim Deist indicated that he would like to sell the speed shop that he operated next door to his safety-equipment emporium on Victory Boulevard in Burbank, California, on the Glendale/Burbank border. Guedel and Holland bought the business and after a while opted to move it to the West San Fernando Valley. The two found a location on Sherman Way in Canoga Park, California, just down the street from a thriving Bob's Big Boy drive-in restaurant, which seemed perfect for entertaining out-of-town customers, Holland said.

"Since we had some identity with the *National* name, we called it National Speed Shop," he said. "Our long-term goal was to establish multiple locations nationally. Nice

In the mid-1960s, future National Dragster *Editor Bill Holland and TV producer John Guedel campaigned the Art Linkletter's House Party All American* AA/Fuel Dragster *in NHRA Division 7. (Photo Courtesy Leslie Lovett)*

The *Art Linkletter's House Party All American* AA/FD was sponsored by National Speed Shop located at 21214 Sherman Way, Canoga Park, California, just down the street from a thriving Bob's Big Boy drive-in. Sadly, both enterprises are gone now. (Photo Courtesy Leslie Lovett)

thinking, but unfortunately, a guy from Dallas, Texas, by the name of Chuck Tanko had the same idea and opened National Speed Centers. There was more than a bit of confusion in the marketplace.

"The front of our 2,500-square-foot store was retail, and we had a shop area in the back where we kept our *Art Linkletter's House Party All American* Top Fuel Dragster. Customers could stroll down a walkway on their way out to the parking lot in the rear and see everything.

"In addition to campaigning our own Top Fuel car, National sponsored the short-lived Pro Stock Camaro of Ed "Schnarpezel" Sigmon, but the car perished in a garage fire. We also provided limited sponsorship to a few oval track racers who competed at nearby Saugus Speedway. Our customers included noted intake-manifold guru Tim Hogan and big-block Chevrolet cylinder head expert Larry Olsen."

Unfortunately, National Speed Shop was short-lived. John Guedel was involved in his father's television production business (where the *Art Linkletter's House Party All American* sponsorship came from), and Bill Holland, who had formerly worked as a journalist at the *Valley Times* newspaper, accepted the job as editor of the NHRA's in-house organ, *National Dragster*.

Holland and Guedel hired Jim Watson, formerly of the Hot Rod Shop in Milwaukee, Wisconsin, as manager, but he got pirated away to Rocket Racing Products in the early 1970s. Since neither Bill nor John had the time to run the place, the two sold the business to Top Fuel racer Mike Greth (Fitt and Greth), and it soldiered along for a few more years.

Bill Holland drives the National Speed Shop Dodge van as it tows John Guedel and John Mulligan down Hollywood Boulevard during Santa Claus Lane Parade festivities. (Photo Courtesy Leslie Lovett)

Art Linkletter and his niece make a cameo appearance with the team during downtime at Hollywood, California's Santa Clause Lane Parade. John Guedel is in the cockpit, and Bill Holland is on the right. (Photo Courtesy Leslie Lovett)

Nickey Chevrolet Speed Shop
Chicago, Illinois

Nickey Performance CEO Stefano Bimbi said the following:

"In regard to the Nickey Chevrolet Speed Shop, before there ever was a Nickey super car, there was the Nickey Chevrolet Speed Shop," he said. "The way that came about was that Don Selig was the vice president of Nickey Chevrolet [4501 W. Irving Park Rd., Chicago, Illinois] and in charge of fixed operations. What that

This is a copy of a Nickey Chevrolet Speed Shop catalog with the late Dick Harrell, a Nickey-sponsored Funny Car match race star, on its cover. (Photo Courtesy Nickey Performance)

meant was that while the agency owners, the Stephani brothers [Edward and John], pretty much ran both the sales and financial aspects of the dealership [established in 1925], Don ran parts and services.

"Selig had an energetic young guy working for him in the late 1950s named Don Swiatek. Don was a local Chicago boy, and had graduated from Lane Tech High School and went straight to work for Nickey right out of school. The story goes that the Stefani brothers were recruiting people to become future Nickey Chevrolet technicians and offered Don a job at a high school job fair and he accepted.

"Nickey Chevrolet was a pretty big operation. In the 1960s, it had hundreds of people on the payroll. It had about 30 to 40 technicians and about 50 salespeople—a big, big operation. Anyhow, when Swiatek reported for work the first day, Selig handed him a push broom and said, 'You start at one end of the shop and work your way to the other end of the shop. When you're done, come see me.'

"Anyhow, Don had a long and colorful career at Nickey Chevrolet. He was the one and only high-performance parts manager that the dealership ever had. One of the first things he did was organize an in-house speed shop under the Nickey Chevrolet brand. Nickey had a body shop that, according to Don, was not very profitable.

"[In 1965], Don and the dealership were into different forms of racing (circle track, Can-Am, drags, etc.), and they saw what was happening with the kids who were buying performance cars and the speed equipment that was being developed and installed on those cars. Nickey decided to close the body shop, appoint Don as high-performance manager, and make a go of having a speed shop inside the dealership. Up to that point, no one had ever done that. Now, this was not the regular parts department where you could order a high-performance part and they would install it for you. This was an honest-to-gosh legitimate speed shop. In fact, it was one of Vic Edelbrock Jr.'s first rep accounts, and that is where the Nickey Chicago brand began.

"At the time, Vince Piggins was the performance czar at General Motors. Even though he wasn't supposed to push GM Performance products, he was keeping his eye on the people and dealers who had the ability to move the products that Zora Arkus-Duntov had already developed up to that point, including Duntov cams. Piggins had visited Nickey Chevrolet and talked to the company about selling those kinds of products, so it was kind of a culmination of events.

"Nickey Chevrolet did some neat marketing to make everything work. For example, at that time there were blue laws that prevented the dealership from being open

Nickey Chevrolet also enlisted the services of the late Dan Blocker, who played Hoss Cartwright in the TV series Bonanza. Blocker owned a Nickey-sponsored Can-Am race car. Shown in this photo is Blocker and Nickey's Jack Stephani. (Photo Courtesy Nickey Performance)

In 1967, the Nickey Chevrolet Speed Shop and Anaheim, California's Bill Thomas Race Cars jointly ran this double truck advertisement in Hot Rod *magazine. Check out all those toys.*

and selling cars on Sunday. However, they didn't apply to the speed shop, which was open until midnight every day of the week. The important thing to remember is that back then there were a lot of guys who were street racing and building hot rods—not to mention the fact that the Greater Chicago area had at least four drag strips in operation. So, there was a readily available market there to justify those long hours.

"Of course, it was a double-edged sword when speed shop customers saw all the cool Chevrolet muscle cars that Nickey had on the floor of its well-lit 20,000-square-foot showroom and it stimulated new car sales. In retrospect, the Nickey Chevrolet Speed Shop was a very novel idea and a fairly successful one.

When it came to promotion, Nickey was extremely proactive. Check out the agency's Chevrolet Apache parts runner. (Photo Courtesy Nickey Performance)

"They also published their own catalog and retained Dan Blocker, who starred in the TV series *Bonanza*, ran a Nickey-sponsored Can-Am car of his own, and was a spokesperson. Nickey's Speed Shop stayed open from 1965 until the dealership was sold in 1973 and became Keystone Chevrolet. During that time frame, Nickey sponsored Chevrolet match racers Dick Harrell and Hayden Proffitt. In addition (at Vince Piggins's request), the dealership became associated with Anaheim, California's Bill Thomas Race Cars, which was unofficially Chevrolet Division's backdoor engineering department on the West Coast.

Nickey exhibited at early editions of the SEMA Show. (Photo Courtesy Nickey Performance)

Thanks to Stefano Bimbi, the Nickey Super Camaro legend lives on. In 2003, Bimbi acquired the rights to the Nickey name and is carrying on the Nickey Super Camaro super car program.

"After Nickey Chevrolet's closure, Don Selig, Don Swiatek, and the Stephani brothers opened up the Nickey Performance Speed Shop on Milwaukee Avenue, where they not only sold parts but also continued to build customer-order cars. In retrospect, the opening of the Milwaukee Avenue shop may have been poorly timed, as escalating insurance rates (which brought about the demise of the American muscle car) and OPEC pretty much killed off (if only momentarily) the high-performance aftermarket. The whole thing came to a screeching halt when Nickey shuttered the doors in 1977."

In 2003, Stefano Bimbi acquired the licensing rights to the Nickey name and opened Nickey Performance Inc. at 6927 N. Alpine Rd., Loves Park, Illinois.

Parr Automotive
Oklahoma City, Oklahoma

In the early 1940s, auto mechanic Don Parr moved from Hollis, Oklahoma, to Oklahoma City and worked at a number of gas stations around town. Around 1947, Parr decided that it was high time that he struck out on his own. He purchased property at 4933 NW 10th St. and built a two-bay concrete-block building that was dedicated in 1949. Parr Automotive initially catered to the man on the street and specialized in general automotive repair, and the company's fortunes went straight up from there.

"In those days [the 1950s], dirt track racing was about the only thing that was going on in this part of Oklahoma, so naturally we got into building and repairing dirt track cars," said Don's son Cody in the summer of 2018. "When it came to the racing, I tried my hand at it for a while, but I wasn't any good and left the driving to someone else.

"Then, when drag racing became popular in this area in 1953, Dad and I started doing a whole bunch of high-performance stuff, tune-ups, drivetrain, engine and transmission work, etc. Then, around 1955, we began phasing out the general automotive repair trade."

Around the same time, the younger Parr put together a Cadillac-engine 1923 Model T roadster pickup for the street, but with all that power on tap, the car quickly morphed into a drag car complete with a GMC supercharger. *Hot Rod* magazine was so impressed with it that it ran a photo of Cody competing in 1956 at the second-annual NHRA US Nationals in Oklahoma City.

"We raced that thing four or five years and hardly ever lost a race," Cody said. "When it came to the business, we started specializing in custom cars and drag cars and became particularly involved in chassis preparation work.

"On the retail side, we became involved with Dean Moon as a distributor. Vic Edelbrock Jr. came by, and we

In the early 1960s, Oklahoma City, Oklahoma, resident Cody Parr and his father, Don, built built a Cadillac-engine 1923 Model T roadster running out of their shop, Parr Automotive. The car quickly graduated from street rod to race car with the addition of a GMC supercharger, winning class at the 1956 NHRA Nationals in Oklahoma City. (Photo Courtesy Cody Parr)

got signed up with him. By the late 1950s, we carried most of the top name brands. It all just kind of evolved.

"Then, some of the local guys wanted some parts built. I had an old lathe in the back of the shop, and I built front spoke wheels for dragsters, tubular front axles, etc. One of the things I am most proud of is that I built a Hilborn fuel pump extension for the front of a blown small-block Chevrolet engine, and Dean [Moon] bought quite a few of those."

Parr Automotive kept growing throughout the 1960s. Business was so good that Don and Cody tore down the original concrete-block building and built the current metal building (with five times the space), which housed Parr Automotive for its remaining years.

"When it came to drag racing, I stayed with the blown Gas Altereds," Cody said. "We built a new chassis with a blown Chevrolet small-block engine and held the NHRA and AHRA national record for the class. I was also the NHRA Division 4 points champion and wound up with the No. 1 spot for two years on the *Drag News Standard 1320* Junior Gas list. We ran that thing all over the Southeastern US. We ran Beeline in Phoenix and ran Pomona a couple of times. The car became sort of a rolling advertisement for the company, and in 1968, *Popular Hot Rodding* magazine published a four-page article

The original roadster was replaced by this more-modern 1923 T-bucket complete with a gasoline-burning blown small-block Chevrolet engine. The car won the NHRA Division 4 title, held both NHRA and AHRA national records and held a spot on the Drag News *Standard 1320 Junior Gas list. (Photo Courtesy Cody Parr)*

[with photographs by the late Dan Wadley] on the car. We got pretty good at building drag race chassis (mainly altereds), but I did put together a few dragsters."

When asked if he ever aspired to driving dragsters, Cody said, "I did a few times. Guys wanted me to sort out their chassis, but the long cars didn't give me the same thrills that the Altereds did. You know well enough from all those years of taking pictures of Fuel Altereds that they never go where you want them to, so there was always that element of surprise. Those were the days when all of the old guys who are still with us got it in their minds that we ran faster than we really did."

In the early 1970s, the street rod movement took hold, and people started coming into Parr Automotive asking for street rod parts.

"We outsourced parts from select suppliers and even set up a special section in our showroom," Cody said. "We started advertising in *Street Rodder* magazine, printed our first catalog around 1975 or 1976, put together a little trailer and pickup truck, and started going to all the rod runs. That was kind of the standard deal. The 1980s were pretty much the same thing. We increased the size of our show trailer a couple of times during that period and put on another addition to the building and kept the magazine advertising going. It was pretty much business as usual!"

The following is a conversation with Cody Parr and author Bob McClurg.

Author: When did you quit drag racing?

Cody: I quit driving in 1970, but I would occasionally tinker with them [Altereds] and take 'em out and test 'em. After I went to the second California Hot Rod

In the mid-1960s, the Parrs tore down the original two-bay concrete block building and erected this new metal building at the same address. Parr Automotive's spacious showroom was brightly lit and well stocked. (Photos Courtesy Cody Parr)

The Oklahoma, City, Oklahoma–based company also had a traveling truck and trailer that went to all the rod runs, and the company was inducted into the National Street Rod Association Hall of Fame.

Reunion at Bakersfield, I got the bug all over again and made the mistake of cloning my old race car. I took it out to the third-annual NHRA Hot Rod Reunion at Bowling Green, Kentucky, and ran it. I still run it occasionally at tracks around here. It keeps my heart pumping and keeps me young.

Author: Did Parr Automotive experience the same problem that the other mom-and-pop speed shops experienced when the PAWs, Summits and JEGS of the world started coming in? Did that take a big bite out of your business?

Cody: It affected the performance end of our business somewhat, but as far as the street rod side of the business goes, I didn't notice any discernible problem to speak of. Now, had we not closed the doors in 2016 and remained in business, it quite possibly may have."

Author: Please tell us the reason why you closed the doors of one of the best-known speed shops in the Southwest?

Cody: Well, my age was one thing. I was in my early 80s, and here I am still working 10- to 12-hour days—out of habit, I guess. My wife, Liz, and I talked about that for several years, but the main reason why I closed up was that she died of pancreatic cancer in 2014, and that just kind of took the wind out of my sails. [The couple was married for 57 years.] I dealt with it until 2016, but I wasn't having any fun anymore, and instead of going crazy, I just decided to sell it. I didn't really have anyone to leave it to. I have a son, but he's not into hot rods; he's into other stuff.

I had originally looked for a buyer, but nobody I knew had enough money to pay the price I was asking, so we closed the doors, got ahold of an auction company late last year, and in two days time auctioned everything off."

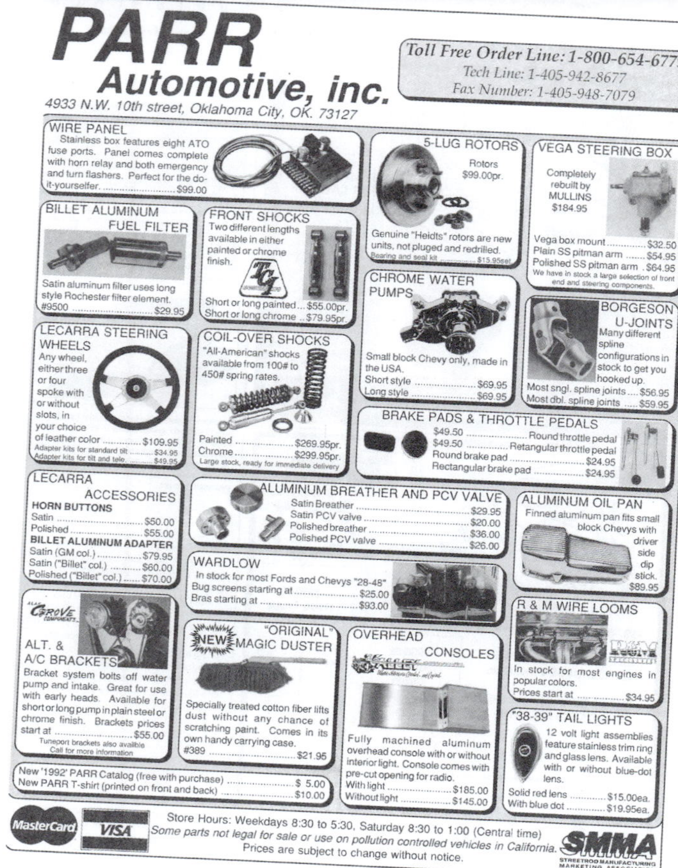

This Parr Automotive advertisement was printed in the April 1992 issue of Street Rodder magazine.

Author: What are you doing now?

Cody: Of course, this retirement thing just didn't happen. We finally finished all the paperwork on closing the shop last November, and now I'm just trying to get my feet pointed in the right direction. I've still got the properties, the buildings. I've also still got the race car and this and that. I plan on going to more of the drag racing nostalgia events and all that stuff but not openly competing. I just want to have a little fun."

Author: So, maybe we'll see you at the NHRA Hot Rod Reunion this summer at Bowling Green, Kentucky. In closing, what has being involved in the speed equipment and street rod industry meant to you?

Cody: I don't know if I can actually express it in words. Like a lot of folks, I started out in the business quite young and got hooked on it at an early age. As things progressed, the racing became one of the biggest parts of our lives.

When it came to the business, I enjoyed going to the SEMA Shows. I went to the seventh one held across the street from Disneyland at the Anaheim Convention Center and have been going to them ever since. I've enjoyed meeting new customers and building lasting friendships with the older ones. Gosh, we've had some great employees working for us. They were a big part of our lives.

After visiting the second-annual California Hot Rod Reunion at Old Famoso Drag Strip in Bakersfield, California, Cody was bitten by the drag racing nostalgia bug and built an updated replica of his blown small-block Chevrolet Altered, which he runs at events like the Holley National Hot Rod Reunion, in Bowling Green, Kentucky.

I really appreciated the awards we got. I think the National Street Rod Association (NSRA) Hall of Fame award was one of the biggest. Another was the lifetime achievement award my wife, Liz, and I got at one of the later SEMA Shows. Things like that stand out in my mind the most, but when you get right down to it, having a wife and family that enjoyed what I did, well, you really can't say much more than that except I've had a great time all these years and I wouldn't have traded it for anything!"

Ramchargers Speed Shop
Taylor, Michigan

The Ramchargers Speed Shops were an outgrowth of the Ramchargers Racing Engines operation, which was an outgrowth of the original Ramchargers Drag Racing Team. Dave Rockwell provided his perspective as a former partner, original Ramchargers Racing Team member, and author of the book *We Were the Ramchargers: Inside Drag Racing's Legendary Team.*

"There had always been a fair amount of interest in Ramcharger motors because we had been fairly successful with our race cars," Rockwell said. "In 1964, we ran the first 426 Hemi Super Stock car, and that same year, we developed the first 426 Hemi engine to compete in Top Fuel Eliminator.

Goldstein smokes the hides at the 1st-annual Professional Dragster Association (PDA) Championships at Lions Associated Drag Strip, Wilmington, California. (Photo Courtesy G. K. Callaway)

"In 1967, we had gone out to the PDA race in Long Beach where we were the No. 3 qualifier. On the way home, we ran into the *Wheeler Dealer* Top Fuel team from Maryland, which qualified No. 1 at PDA with an Ed Pink–customer engine, and that got us to thinking. At the time, our motors were probably the most powerful in the sport, so we started thinking seriously about the proposition of going into the engine-building business. At the end of 1967, the majority of the original Ramchargers Racing Team (which were mostly all Chrysler engineers) decided to retire from actively campaigning the Funny Car, so myself, Dick Skoglund, Phil Goulet, and Dan Knapp

Leroy Goldstein launches the Ramchargers Dodge-bodied mini Challenger off the starting line at the 1972 NHRA US Nationals at Indianapolis Raceway Park. The original Ramchargers campaigned some of the hottest Funny Cars in the sport.

The last Ramchargers door cars weren't even Dodges. This SS/DA 1970 Plymouth Hemi 'Cuda was piloted by Dean Nicopolis (seen in action at the 1974 NHRA Gatornationals) and was one of the last Mopars to carry that illustrious name into battle.

decided to re-form the Ramchargers Maximum Performance Corporation into Ramchargers Racing Engines.

"We moved into a shop down by Tiger Stadium on Trumbull Avenue and began to build motors. The demand was pretty strong right off the bat. In the process of developing the late-model Chrysler Hemi into a blown Fuel motor, we had come up with some products of our own. One of them was an increased [high] volume oil pump that everybody who was running a late-model Chrysler Hemi started using. That, and running our new Woody Gilmore Race Car Engineering–chassis Top Fuel car pretty much kept us occupied all throughout 1968. Then, in 1969, we moved to a much larger retail attractive building in Allen Park. After taking on a number of racer-friendly product lines, we officially opened up the first Ramchargers Speed Shop in conjunction with our engine-building and racing operations."

Within the next two years, the Ramchargers expanded its speed shop operation to include five stores around the Greater Detroit area, each run by one of the partners. In 1974, the Ramchargers Racing Team ceased Funny Car operations, which allowed Phil Goulet to come back into the business and become more hands on.

"One of the things that was really cool about that place was that back in the mid-1970s when Detroit Dragway was going strong, all the traveling pros who ran Ramcharger Racing Engines would hang out at the shop and work on their cars," Rockwell said. "Sometimes the parking lot would have a dozen race car haulers in there, and that attracted even more business."

The Ramchargers chain closed in 2005 in the wake of the September 11 tragedy, which negatively impacted

business decisions made just prior to then. One could say the business was caught in the downdraft of September 11. It was sad but true.

Another Ramchargers project was the codevelopment of the 16–spark plug Hemi cylinder head that was used in Pro Stock with "Dandy Dick" Landy and in the Ramchargers AA/Fuel Funny Car driven by Leroy Goldstein.

Rocco & Cheater's Speed Shop
Birmingham, Alabama

You may have seen the segment that co-hosts Mike Wolfe and Frank Fritz from the History Channel's *American Pickers* TV show did during the 2018 season on Rocco & Cheater's Speed Shop. During one of their excursions through Alabama's Jefferson County, the boys stumbled upon the landmark speed shop at 300 1st Ave. in Birmingham, Alabama. Talk about a blast into the past.

The Rocco & Cheater's Speed Shop saga began in 1946 and went on to become one of the most well-known speed shops in the South. Started as a general automotive repair garage in 1944, the brothers Rocco and Cheater Sanfillippo incorporated the business in 1946 and renamed it Rocco & Cheater's Speed Shop.

Upon his discharge from the US Navy in 1954, younger brother Dominic "Mimi" Sanfillippo joined the operation. Dominic's wife, Jean, and his daughter Angi also worked there and were instrumental in helping grow the business.

Rocco & Cheater's specialized in all types of racing and were friends with some of the NHRA and NASCAR's earliest rising stars. The company was also renowned for stocking some of the best parts in the business including those from Accel, Ansen, Appliance, Champion, Cragar, Edelbrock, Fel-Pro, Grant, Hedman, Holley, Hooker, Hurst, Iskenderian, M&H, Offenhauser, Schiefer, Trans-Dapt, Radar, and Weiand just to name a few. The

Rocco & Cheater's Speed Shop was open for business from 1946 to 2007. Note the company's bright yellow two-ton GMC van. Back in the day, it could be seen at racetracks all over the South.

Road King Recollections

Nationally prominent drag racers Bob Muravez (known by his pseudonym Floyd Lippencott Jr.) and "TV Tommy" Ivo both grew up in Burbank, California, and are charter members of the Road Kings Car Club, which was established 1953.

Bob Muravez

These are Muravez's memories of the local speed shop scene in the 1950s and 1960s Burbank/Glendale area.

"When I was old enough to get serious about racing [Muravez's first hot rod was the ex-Betty Grable 1953 Chevrolet Corvette], I hung out at a number of speed shops located in the Greater Burbank/Glendale area," Muravez said. "Alex Xydias opened the original So-Cal Speed Shop on Victory Boulevard near Magnolia Avenue in Burbank. The original building is still there, but today it's a custom paint shop.

"Famed customizer Gene Winfield would often come in from the desert to buy hot rod parts for his lakes cars that he ran at Edwards Air Force Base. Of course, when it came to dry lakes racing, Alex was no slouch himself when running either the Pierson Brothers So-Cal Speed Shop 1934 Ford coupe or later the So-Cal Speed Shop belly tank.

"I also used to hang out at a place called Accessories Limited, which was located on the corner of Sonora Avenue and Victory Boulevard in Glendale. The shop was owned by a guy named Jerry Moffett. Congressional Medal of Honor recipient US Naval Admiral William Adger Moffett was his uncle. Accessories Limited was basically a muffler shop.

"Back in the old days, most speed shops started out as muffler shops because changing out your car's stock exhaust system to something like a set of Smitty's or Hollywood Muffler glasspacks was an easy and inexpensive thing to do. Then, as more products came to market, they would start handling headers, manifolds, carburetor kits, and other items, such as Moon discs, spinner hubcaps, and other stuff. I still have an Accessories Limited T-shirt somewhere. They used the Fred Flintstone character on their logo. Then, after they went out of business, Glendale Speed Center used it.

"When safety icon Jim Deist started his safety equipment company [Deist Safety], it was at 911 S. Victory Blvd. in Burbank. Jim's place was never a speed shop per se; it was a safety-equipment company that sold parachutes, safety harnesses, fire suits, gloves, face masks, and things like that for your race car. Jim and I tested the first Deist parachute on my BB/Gas dragster [the Janke and Muravez BB/GD] at San Fernando Drag Strip.

"Rich Cholakian opened Glendale Speed Center on South Brand Boulevard in Glendale. Later on, he purchased some property on Brand Boulevard and Los Feliz and ran

Road Kings Car Club of Burbank charter member AA/GD pilot Bob Muravez, also known as Floyd Lippencott Jr., fondly remembers his days hanging out at local Burbank/ Glendale, California, speed shops, such as So-Cal Speed Shop, Accessories Limited, Glendale Speed Center, and other hot rodding haunts.

the business from that location for many, many years. After he closed up, Chet Knox opened Western Performance at that address, and it's still in business. When I ran my first dragster, I was fortunate enough to have Paul Schiefer [Schiefer Clutches and Flywheels] sponsor me with clutches, and Phil Weiand [Weiand Equipment Co.] on S. San Fernando Boulevard sponsored me with manifolds.

"Those are my recollections of early speed shops in the Burbank/Glendale/San Fernando area!"

"TV Tommy" Ivo

Tommy Ivo also has positive memories of the local speed shop scene in the 1950s and 1960s Burbank/Glendale area.

"Undoubtedly, my fondest remembrances of a speed shop in the Burbank/Glendale area was Alex Xydias's So-Cal Speed Shop, which was about 10 blocks from my house on Victory Boulevard near Alameda Avenue," Ivo said. "There really wasn't much to it. It was just a small speed shop. While attending a Road Kings meeting, Alex once laughingly said he always made a nice, tidy little profit out of the place—that is until I showed up and wanted the long deal on everything [laughs].

"There was another speed shop down the street at the corner of Sonora and Victory Boulevard called Accessories Limited. It was a nice little place, and they were my first sponsor on my four-motor car. There was no sponsorship money involved. They just allowed me to buy parts at cost.

"I also remember Valley Custom, but they really weren't a speed shop per se. Barnett Buick in Burbank, California, was another one of my earliest sponsors. They were on the back of my single-engine car, and they were also with me when *Hot Rod* magazine did a center spread on my twin-engine car. That was quite a feather in my cap to have that magazine spread, so when I was getting ready to build my four-engine *Showboat*, I walked right into Buick Motor Division in Detroit with the magazine center spread hot in hand and told them I needed some motors. You should have seen the look on the face of Barnett Buick's service manager when all those engines started showing up!"

Tommy Ivo's infamous Showboat *four-engine Buick dragster does what it did best. One of the car's first sponsors was Burbank, California's Accessories Unlimited. (Jim Kelly Photo Courtesy Tommy Ivo)*

Rocco & Cheater's Speed Shop used to pass out these water decals at the races, and they were very popular with the kids.

brothers Sanfillippo were celebrated for their onsite service with their fully stocked, bright yellow 1955 GMC van making weekly appearances at racetracks all across the South.

In the late 1970s, Dominic's son Sam Sanfillippo assumed control of the company and eventually was joined by his son Andrew. In its heyday, Rocco & Cheater's was known as a full-service, or *real*, speed shop, meaning that it not only sold speed equipment from its well-stocked showroom but it also had a fabrication and modest machine shop in the back of its 100x100-square-foot facility to service its customers' needs.

Rocco & Cheater's was truly a memorable place. As one blogger wrote, "Rocco & Cheater's was to Birmingham, Alabama, what Honest Charley's Speed Shop was to Chattanooga, Tennessee!"

The Alabama Auto Racing Pioneers seconded that motion when Rocco, Cheater, and Dominic were respectively inducted into its 1999 and 2012 hall of fame. Sadly, Rocco & Cheater's Speed Shop became yet another victim of modern-day mass marketing. After 69½ years in business, Rocco & Cheater's Speed Shop closed in December 2007.

However, the building remains intact, and for those fortunate enough to receive an invitation to come and visit, it will feel like they've stepped back through time with rows upon rows of 1940s through 1970s NOS speed equipment piled to the rafters. Oh, if those hallowed walls could only talk.

Santa Ana Speed Center
Santa Ana, California

Santa Ana Speed Center was established in the late 1960s and was located at 110 to 120 S. Broadway Ave. in the Central Historic District of the Heninger Park neighborhood of Santa Ana, California. Owned by Larry Rowehorst and managed by Rudy Martinez, its parent company was United Auto Parts Inc.

Santa Ana Speed Center was considered a full-service facility. It was 4,000 square feet, was engaged in retail sales, and had its own machine shop, installation shop, and warehouse. Not surprisingly, Santa Ana Speed Center's motto was "A Real Hot Rod Shop with Parts for Real Hot Rods." And they had the clientele to prove it.

However, as the years rolled on, the neighborhood surrounding Santa Ana Speed Center lapsed into decline, and rising crime rates seriously affected the overall business climate. To add insult to injury, customer ratings on various blogger sites ranged from less than kind to downright accusatory.

After 36 years in business, it all came to a screeching halt on March 22, 2013, when the US Food and Drug

Santa Ana Speed Center was at 110 to 120 S. Broadway Ave. in Santa Ana, California.

Back in the day, in fact, way back in the day, former Car Craft *magazine Editor Rick Voeglin campaigned a 1955 Chevy shoebox with sponsorship from Santa Ana Speed Center. (Photo Courtesy John Shanks)*

Administration (FDA), the Health Hazardous Materials Division (HHMD), and Los Angeles County Sherriff's Department in cooperation with the City of Santa Ana Police Department cited Santa Ana Speed Center for illegal and improper use, storage, and sales of nitrous oxide. Also listed on that same complaint were 16 other speed shops and/or automotive performance shops located in the LA/Orange County area.

For a short time, Santa Ana Speed Center also owned a satellite operation in Costa Mesa, California, called Costa Mesa Speed Center located on Newport Boulevard.

Otie's Automotive
Akron, Ohio

Born March 6, 1920, in Cookeville, Tennessee, Otis "Otie" Smith was raised with his two brothers and one sister on a dirt farm in the Tennessee Valley.

When the Tennessee Valley Authority (TVA) confiscated the Smith family farm along with everyone else's in the valley, it effectively ended a multi-generational lifestyle that started when Otis's great grandfather settled the area in the early 1800s. Otis's father, Ray, felt that there had to be something better out there for his family and packed all their worldly possessions into an old Ford coupe and headed to Akron, Ohio, where jobs could be readily had in the booming tire and rubber manufacturing business.

"My grandfather got a job working at the Firestone Tire & Rubber Company, and my grandmother got a job working at BFGoodrich," Otis's son Bill said. "So, instead of talking about planting crops at night around the dinner table, the subject of conversation changed to how tires were made."

When World War II came along, Smith's father received a service deferment and continued making tires for the war effort and so did his mother. In the meantime (1938), Otis graduated from Coventry High School in Manchester, Ohio, and got a job at Firestone as a machinist building gun mounts for the Bow Fur Machine Gun. At the close of the war in 1946, Firestone shut down that plant, and Smith accepted a job working as a machinist for the French manufacturing firm Marchant, which built mechanical calculators.

In the 1950s, Smith bought a 1936 Ford Tudor sedan. Like everyone else in those days, the car had a modified flathead V-8 engine that he built himself. However, being that the old Ford was his daily driver, the engine couldn't be too radical.

As a member of the Akron Cam Jammers car club, Smith raced the 1936 Ford at the Akron Airport track and did pretty well with the car but found the old Ford to be too heavy, so he built up a full-fender 1932 Ford road-

Southern Speed Shop Remembrances

These days, transplanted Louisiana native Don Prieto is best known as the driving force behind Torrance, California's Prietive Group, which services a select group of high-end car manufacturers in the area with vehicle loans, public relations, promotions, advertising, and events.

With seven decades of industry service and dedication under his belt, Don is considered one of the premier drag racing historians in the sport and we were fortunate enough to button him down long enough to talk about hanging out at some of the State of Louisiana's most memorable speed shops.

"It's been a lot of years, but I'm glad that I still remember those early days well enough to be able to shed some light on a few of the places where I hung out at as a kid," Prieto said. "There were many speed shops in NHRA's Division 4, but I distinctly remember these: Jake's Speed Shop in New Orleans, Louisiana; Shreve Automotive in Shreveport, Louisiana; and the Car Shop Inc. in Houma, Louisiana."

Jake's Speed Shop
By Don Prieto

Out of those, I remember Jake's Speed Shop the best. I worked for Jake Howard for a short time. His shop was located on 2323 Iberville St. in New Orleans, and I usually worked there in the summers answering the telephones and taking stuff to the Greyhound bus station. Jake started his business in 1945 and lasted for 45 years. He started as an engine builder, tuner, and supplier of parts to the rum runners all over the South.

Then, as drag racing came along, he became much more prosperous because drag racing was [semi] legit, and

Jake's well-lit showroom was well stocked, and if you didn't see it there, it was hanging on the wall in the parts department. (Photos Courtesy Don Prieto)

Established in 1945, the likeable Jake Howard was the proprietor of Jake's Speed Shop, which was located at 2323 Iberville St. in New Orleans, Louisiana, and boasted clients like Ronnie Martin, Paul Candies, Leonard Hughes, and many others as customers. (Photos Courtesy Don Prieto)

This 1939–1941 Ford Sedan Delivery served as a parts runner for Jake's Speed Shop. Initially flathead powered, the old Ford eventually was upgraded to a small-block Chevrolet. Nice looking delivery, eh? (Photo Courtesy Don Prieto)

Jake's Speed Shop sponsored the 1965 altered-wheelbase Plymouth match racer of Paul Candies and Leonard Hughes. This car has since been restored and is owned by Kenosha, Wisconsin, muscle car collector Jim Paulsen.

there was a much higher level of participation. Jake also did a lot of oval track stuff. Not so much the Stock cars, but he was strong in Modified Racing [1939 Fords, etc.], which ran flatheads and that kind of stuff.

Albert Waites was a Chevy dragster racer who was sponsored by Jake's Speed Shop and won a lot of races at La Place, Opelousas, and tracks like that in the 1950s and 1960s. Jake also sponsored a guy named Joe "Q-Ball" Wales, who raced a Top Fuel car sponsored by Paul "Tugboat" Candies. Later, of course, Candies teamed up with Leonard Hughes on the Jake's Speed Shop–sponsored *Moon Shot* altered-wheelbase 1965 Plymouth, its first of many drag cars."

Shreve Automotive

Ray Harris opened up Shreve Automotive in Shreveport, Louisiana, primarily as a hot rod shop in the 1950s

One of Shreve's more famous sponsored race cars when the company was still in Shreveport was this blown Oldsmobile 32 highboy driven by Don Eiland. (Photo Courtesy Don Prieto)

with partners Russell Wooley and the late Bud Hargrove. Hargrove was the original driver of the Shreve Automotive-sponsored *Tank* altered 1929 Model A roadster and 1929 Model A Tudor sedan as well as the *Tuna Tank* 1948 Fiat Topolino AA/Altered race cars.

The shop (not to be confused with the now-defunct Shreve Automotive in Austin, Texas) moved to New Orleans in the late 1960s and was responsible for several top-flite cars, the most worthy being the Shreve Automotive-sponsored AA/FD driven by Dave Chenevert, who won the inaugural NHRA Gatornationals. Other well-known racers who ran out of Shreve Automotive were Jerry Grice, Ray Russell, and Ronnie Martin.

Shreve Automotive was founded in the early 1950s by partners Russell Wooley and Bud Hargrove. However, in the 1960s, the company moved to New Orleans in search of a better business climate. (Photo Courtesy Don Prieto)

Car Shop Inc.

The Car Shop Inc. worked on everything from Funny Cars (Henry Garcia drove the Car Shop Camaro FC) to customer cars.

Shreveport, Louisiana's Car Shop, Inc. had all the markings of a successful speed shop business. It raced a Funny Car and had a high-tech, modern shop stocked to the rafters with name-brand speed parts. Its only problem was cash flow. More was going out than what was coming in. (Photo Courtesy Don Prieto)

It was a going concern and even imported Californians Don Ratican and Gene Mooneyham as employees, but it didn't make any money. That was the problem. The owner had a propensity for giving away stuff and/or selling stuff at cost because he liked the racers, and his generosity eventually got the best of him!"

Howard Auto Parts
Shreveport, Louisiana

Howard Auto Parts (no relation to Jake Howard) was another speed shop in town, but it mostly sold trash and trinkets, spinner hubcaps, dual exhaust tips, and that type of stuff—not much of anything by way of hard parts.

Vanderley Automotive
Biloxi, Mississippi

Paul Vanderley had a place in Biloxi, Mississippi, called Vanderley Automotive, which raced Top Fuel with Garlits's old *Swamp Rat III* car. Garlits sold it to a guy named Jimmy Duet, and Connie Swingle went along with the package. Connie drove the car for a while. Then, Boogie Scott drove it under Vanderley sponsorship. I think Garlits may have gotten the car back and restored it for his museum, but I'm not sure.

Paul Vanderley also raced a 1964 427 Mercury Comet in the A/FX class and won the NASCAR Winternationals event at Daytona Beach, Florida. In later years, he teamed up with the late Dick Moroso on a Modified Production Corvette and won the NHRA Division 4 Modified Eliminator point's championship and the eliminator title at the 1976 NHRA Cajun Nationals.

However, Vanderley wasn't solely preoccupied with drag racing. He also enjoyed a reasonably successful Super Modified career, and in later years, he built engines with John Callies at Pontiac Motorsports for IMSA's highly popular GTU and GTP classes, winning the 24 Hours of Daytona. Vanderley also raced a 1934 Ford roadster at Bonneville with partner Jack Mendenhall where he became a member of the Bonneville Nationals highly coveted 200 MPH Club.

ster instead. Otie raced the 1932 Ford for a total of three years. His son Bill said that depending on how many cars were in a particular class on a given weekend, his father would either race the 1932 Ford in the roadster class with fenders on or he would unbolt and remove the fenders and run the car in the Altered class.

In 1955, Smith built a flathead-engine 1923 T-Bucket to compete in the B/Hot Rod class and set a record at the first NHRA Nationals in Great Bend, Kansas. In 1956, Smith built a lighter chassis and installed a steel 1927 T roadster body and a 265-ci Chevrolet small-block (his first OHV) that he bought out of a totaled vehicle and ran the car in B/Roadster. Smith raced his 1927 T for two years. In that time, the 265 gave way to a 354 Chrysler Hemi, which was Otie's signature engine for the remainder of his racing career.

Otie Smith went on to campaign a series of incredibly fast Model T- and Fiat-bodied AA/Altereds and captured numerous NHRA and AHRA records and class wins. He was featured as part of the 1960 NHRA Winternationals coverage on the cover of *Hot Rod* magazine.

In 1964, Smith rebodied Bill's old Fiat chassis into a Model T roadster and ran in the 1964 Fuel and Gas Championships, where he suffered an engine explosion that locked up the drivetrain and sent him sliding backward through the lights at 165 mph.

In 1965, Otie Smith's last car was a Chrysler-powered Drag Master–chassis AA/A roadster that won the Best Engineered Award at the NHRA Springnationals in Bristol, Tennessee. However, after being on the road for six weeks, Smith came back home to Akron and told his wife Betty that enough was enough. However, that wasn't the end of the Smith family racing dynasty.

Otie's son Bill told the following story about his upbringing.

In 1955, Otie Smith opened Otie's Automotive Specialties as a part-time business to offset his racing expenses while still employed as a machinist at Marchant. In 1959, Smith abruptly quit Marchant and concentrated all of his efforts on growing the business. (Photo Courtesy Bill Smith)

Otis "Otie" Smith's breakout car was this 265 Chevrolet-engine 1927 Model T that he raced in the B/Roadster class. (Photo Courtesy Bill Smith)

"I didn't go to the shop on weeknights until I became a junior in high school," Bill said. "It was about a 10-minute walk from school, and dad stayed open until 9 p.m. as a convenience to the guys who raced but held regular jobs.

"When I was about 14, I spent my summers working there 12 hours a day, 6 days a week. I told my father that I didn't want a paycheck; I wanted him to save the money, and when I turned 16, I wanted him to buy me a street car. Well, when I turned 16, he didn't buy me the street car that I was expecting. But, when I came home from school one day, there was a B/Altered Fiat coupe sitting on a trailer in the driveway with a note stuck in the window. It said, 'This is your car. Get it in the garage and tear it apart.' It was a West Coast Altered that had been owned and campaigned by Waldo Hirschfield, who had won class at Indy with it and was runner-up in the Eliminator the year before.

"It had a B&M Hydro and a small-block Chevy in it and ran consistent 11s all day long. I never got the street car that I was expecting, and when I went out on a date, I borrowed the shop truck and never gave it a second thought."

Around 1966, Bill graduated up to a Top Gas dragster and ran the car with moderate success right up to the day that the NHRA eliminated the class. By then, he could see the way things were going in the sport and

Even lighter and quicker race cars would follow, such as this blown Chrysler-powered 1923 T that won the 1959 NHRA Nationals at Detroit Dragway. Presenting the trophy is Glynanna Hamm, wife of NHRA Division 4 Director Dale Hamm, while Otie's son Bill looks on. (Photo Courtesy Bill Smith)

Smith gives the camera his best Ipana smile (Photo Courtesy Bill Smith)

Smith's last speed shop was at 2020 Kenmore Rd. in Akron, Ohio. The business closed in 1988. (Photo Courtesy Bill Smith)

This is a Precision Engine Balancing advertisement from Otie's Manchester Avenue store, which was the first store that Smith operated.

Otie Smith's last race car (1965) was this Dragmaster-chassis Chrysler engine 1923 T, which ran in AA/A. The car won Best Engineered Car at the NHRA Springnationals in Bristol, Tennessee. One day, Odie and another old racer named Smiley were talking about racing fast cars. Odie finally tired of the conversation and said, "Look, don't tell me about how fast you were—I've gone through the quarter-mile lights faster than you backwards!"

decided to concentrate on helping grow the family business instead.

Bill has theorized that Otie's Automotive was opened in 1955 as a part-time business venture to help fund his father's racing operation. Smith had rented a small building at 1950 Manchester Rd. in Akron. However, being that he still worked at Marchant, it became necessary for him to hire some part-time helpers to keep things moving in the right direction.

Akron native and former Holley sales representative Wayne Wolfe shared his memories about Otie's Automotive.

"The place was kind of small, but every square inch of that place was parts on peg boards, display counters with a couple of guys behind the counter, and always three or four race cars in the shop," he said. "Otie's Automotive was a genuine, for real speed shop."

In 1959, Otie Smith left Marchant to go racing at the US Nationals in Detroit and never returned. Instead, he concentrated on running Otie's Automotive full time. Under his leadership, Otie's Automotive grew and flourished throughout the late 1950s and early 1960s. Bill estimated that approximately 30 percent of the business was selling parts (with lines including Jahns Pistons, Weber Clutches & Flywheels, Fenton Exhaust Systems, D-A Speed Sport Oil, Iskenderian Cams, Forge True, Howard's Cams, Mickey Thompson, and other name brands),

Bill Smith followed in his father's footsteps, driving this Chrysler-engine AA/Gas dragster that he raced until the bitter end, when NHRA killed the class in 1970. (Photo Courtesy Bill Smith)

Here's one of Otie's later ads that touts, "We Don't Put A Price On Good Advice!" (Photo Courtesy Bill Smith)

while the remainder of the building housed the machine shop and fabrication departments.

Otie's Automotive moved for the last time to a 20,000-square-foot facility at 2020 Kenmore Blvd. in Akron. In the process, Otie's also got into the WD end of the business and also dabbled in mail order but not on a huge scale.

While many assume that Otie's Automotive strictly catered to drag racers (Virgil Cates, Bob Riggle, Ron Hassel, and the Hrudka Brothers, etc.) that couldn't be further from the truth. With three dirt tracks (Sharon, Ohio; Oroville, Ohio; and Sandusky, Ohio) and one asphalt track (Cleveland, Ohio) less than an hour's drive away, Otie's also serviced the needs of sprint car and round track racers.

In 1988, Smith closed Otie's Automotive and retired. Otis Smith passed away at age 94 on May 22, 2014. However, that's not the end of the story. A few years ago, a local historical society erected a plaque in front of the Akron Airport air dock (near where the drag strip used to be), commemorating Akron, Ohio, racing legends Walt and Art Arfons, Otis "Otie" Smith, and "Akron Arlen" Vanke.

The Rod Shop/Nationwise Rod Shop
Columbus, Ohio

The following is a conversation with Rod Shop co-founder Gil Kirk and author Bob McClurg.

Author: What can you tell us about your background?

Gil: I was born in 1941 and went to Duke University. In 1957, I was 16 years old and immersed into classic 1950s Americana. It was a great time to be living in America. Dwight D. Eisenhower was president. I was in a rock-and-roll band, and we did Elvis [Presley] songs.

From day one, I was hopelessly hooked on cars. I ran my parents Hydra-matic Cadillac out at Northway Drag Strip out on Main Street for the first time and won C/Stock against a guy who had won all these races—and that was it, I wanted to be a drag racer.

In those days, the '57 Chevys were outrunning almost everything. There were also two 1957 Pontiac Bonnevilles out there, white with blue stripes. One had Tri-Power, and the other one was [Rochester] fuel injected—absolutely beautiful cars. They were running 103 mph and beating everybody. Then, Ray Christian showed up with his 1958 Plymouth Fury and annihilated everyone, which was pretty amazing to me. He was way ahead of the curve for a long, long time.

Author: So, what was your first car?

Gil: I bought a 1965 Plymouth Fury 383. It wasn't particularly fast. At the time, I was selling real estate,

Here's the Rod Shop lineup for 1971, when Dodge came on board as corporate sponsor. In the front row (left to right) are Dave Boertman, Stock; Bob Riffle, Modified Production; and Mike Fons, Pro Stock. In the back row (left to right) are Ray Noltmeyer, Altered; and Gil Kirk and Jim Thompson, Gas. (Photo Courtesy Gil Kirk)

"In those days [the early 1970s], Dave Boertman could make pass after pass, and you would hear the name Rod Shop *being called out on the microphone all day long," said Gil Kirk. Here's a shot of old Dave putting his SS/JA Dodge Challenger through its paces at the IHRA Springnationals in Bristol, Tennessee.*

using it to haul customers around, and doing quite well selling these big houses. One of my customers worked for Citi Bank, and when he got out of the car, he told me, "Sell this car," which meant "Wake up. You can't do business like this." However, I didn't.

Instead, I found Bob Riffle and had him take one hundred thousandths off the heads and install a bigger cam and bigger street tires on the back (Gil's Plymouth already had a set of Cragar S/S wheels), and the car seemed to run a lot better. The car was good up to 65, 70 mph.

Then, this guy pulled up beside me in a black 409 Chevy and off we went. I was out in front by about a third of a car, but then *whoosh*; he blew by me. As he went by me, I saw the words *Black Beauty* painted on the back. Well, I had to find out who the guy was. As it turned out, it was Billy McGraw. We became great friends and partners in a 1965 Corvette I bought and raced at all the local tracks—and I was winning.

Then, I went out to National Trail Raceway, and there was an identical Corvette running out there like mine owned by a guy named Bob Pigg, who raced Gas class cars later. We raced three times, and he beat me by three car lengths. That was it for me. I decided to turn the Corvette into a full-on race car. I found Bob Riffle and a guy named Wally Rush who prepared the car and I named it *My Ass Is Draggin'*. I raced the Corvette a lot at Kil Kare Drag Strip, and that's where I met Billy "the Kid" Stepp and *Little Red Riding Hood*.

Anyhow, I was hooked big time. Billy [McGraw] and

I switched roles. When I was driving the car, I was breaking parts, and Billy was having to fix it, which got kind of old.

I raced Fred Hurst a couple of times for the money with that big A/Gas Hemi of his chasing me down. He went shooting by me on the top end, and there's almost no light down at the end of the track at night. Anyhow, I won $500 a couple of times, and we would go down to the truck stop at about 2 a.m. and hang out with all the other racers. A few times, I would see Woody Hayes [the Ohio State football coach] in there with a great big offensive lineman type, one of the country boys he was recruiting.

Anyhow, I was caught between worlds. Selling real estate or going drag racing. I thought that drag racing wasn't something that I could do and do well, but I loved it. I was driven so hard that way.

I started the Rod Shop in 1968 with Jim Thompson, who is a big-time talent. Jim could build anything. He was the fastest learner I've ever seen. Jim had been in the Army, and his nickname was *Sarge*. He had a lot of attitude, funny characteristics, and he didn't suffer fools at all. He was way smarter than everyone else, and he knew what he was doing. Jim had a little company up in Marion, Ohio, called the Rod Shop. It was his name to start with, but then he closed the place and went to work down at JEGS.

I raced Ray Scott Gilo's Corvette fastback that Jim had worked on, and it ran damned well. We raced each other at the US Nationals, and at that point in time, I decided I wanted to meet Jim because I was really fascinated by his talent. I went down to JEGS and said, "Let's do our own speed shop." My idea at the time was somewhat immature, really. I thought, "Well, I'll have a business, and then I can write off my racing expenses," which was totally crazy, but that's what we did.

We formed the Rod Shop. I bought a bunch of shop equipment. I found an old bakery on Livingston Avenue in Columbus. It had four garages in the back. It had a tile floor, and when you polished it up, the place looked really nice. Basically, Jim and I set up that company. We finished an A/MP Camaro that I was racing at the US Nationals. It had this fancy lace paint job and the words *Rod Shop* painted on its fenders.

I was going to the races now on a full-time basis, and I was seeing all these super-fast Gas class and Modified cars and these terrific drivers, but there was no identity or commonality between them. So, I started to sponsor cars. What I mean by that is that we [the Rod Shop] would build their motors for them and give them money off parts and services or whatever. We had a Ford—Tommy Schumacher's 1967 Fairlane was just a rip-snortin' fast car. We built small-block Chevy motors for Dick Shroyer and Bob Riffle's Anglias, and we were starting to make a name for ourselves. However, we limited who could put our name on their cars to certain people who had work done that would effectively allow them to run well.

That program took us up to 1969, when I decided that we were going to build a racing team. Now, Dick Padar was the only guy around here who had a Top Fueler. It wasn't like a Saturday night at Lions, where you had 68 cars show up. Nobody around here had a Top Fuel car except him, and when he fired his car up, we all ran down to the fence to see if he made it down the track, and I don't think he ever did. He was like the "Wild Willie" Borsch of Midwestern Top Fuel racing. It was so exciting to reach out and try to do these things in those days. Anyway, I decided that I wanted to have a racing team, and the best way to do that was paint all the cars the same colors, and red, white, and blue was a big deal.

We had Short Round and Dauber do the paint jobs. They were probably the best custom painters in the world. Larry Morgan once told me that the first time he took his car to them to paint it, the car weighed 400 pounds more. I never really thought of the weight; I just wanted the cars to look good. But in the process of winning Best Appearing Crew, Best Appearing Car, and Best Engine, I tried to upgrade the sport a little bit by my standards. I noticed that one car that would get my attention at all these national meets: Barrie Poole driving Sandy Elliot's car. When he would turn around on the drag strip, you could always spot him because he had those black and white stripes. I decided that you had to have a car that was visible from both ends of the drag strip, so that led to the development of the Rod Shop striped paint schemes. We basically wanted everything to be show and go.

We lost a lot of races by inches, but we made a huge impact at the 1968 US Nationals, and they were talking about us quite a bit. Then Dick Shroyer gave the Rod Shop its first national event win at the 1970 NHRA Summernationals; it was a thrilling time.

So now, I have this winning race team, but I had this machine shop that I had just opened, and from inception, that's all it was ever intended to be. Then, I came on the idea that the best thing to do was try to create a sales operation. So, I did. We had a retail store and a warehouse, but I had trouble getting any of the name brands like Hurst and Holley because JEGS was fighting hard to keep us from getting anything.

I thought that being a WD was the most important thing, but I was so naive that I didn't know that when you take on a major product line, such as Holley for example, they make you take on all their stuff, and you end up with about three carburetors that are worth selling. So, the inventory idea was no good, and believe me, I was a total rookie. I would say I was in the idiot zone really. All I'm thinking about is promotion. I'm all promotion and thinking about public relations. I knew all about that, and I was a natural. However, the rest of it I didn't know anything about at all.

The Rod Shop's reemergence into NHRA Championship Drag Racing began with this lone Ron Butler-built Trans Am Pontiac Firebird that Leal later claimed to be one of his all-time-favorite race cars.

So, here I am. I have one store. I have two stores. I have three stores. I knew we were running out of parts, and we weren't getting the parts we needed to sell. So, then the winters came, and I was having cash-flow problems that were unbelievable, and I couldn't figure out why I was having them as I walked by my $90,000 worth of inventory every day that was piling up and not selling.

My bookkeeping wasn't running the way it should. So, the first thing I did was go to the SEMA Show dressed up in a pinstriped suit and a vest, and all I wanted to do was talk to the manufacturers about starting a drag racing team. Well, nobody wanted to talk to me about sponsoring a drag racing team, but I was hell-bent. I come from Columbus, Ohio, where the words *All American* mean something.

I noticed that there was a guy walking in front of me with a different colored badge on, and people would run out to him to shake hands, so I asked, "Why are they doing that?" Someone said, "Well, he's a warehouse distributor, and you're only a jobber. You buy from him."

I said, "Really?

So, I hightailed it back out front and changed my badge to warehouse distributor. So, these guys would come out to talk to me, and I would get in there. After about 20 minutes of talking to a manufacturer, I would show them these pictures that Getty had drawn for me, and I'd say, "This is my racing team. Would you like to sponsor it?"

Then, they would get really upset. So, I would say, "Look, are you selling Hays clutches in Columbus, Ohio? Are you selling that stuff here? No, because Schiefer is

what Jeg sells. I mean, right now, your stuff is just sitting on a shelf in your warehouse. I'll take your product, and I'll make your product famous in this area (which we did), and I'll make him buy your product."

So, whenever I couldn't get a cash sponsorship, which was most of the time, I said would take $10,000 worth of parts at warehouse distributor prices. I would say something like, "We're not Sox & Martin, but . . ." And they would say, "Who is Sox & Martin?"

Well, after about the second or third guy asking who Sox & Martin was, I thought, "If they don't know the difference between me [Rod Shop] and Sox & Martin, then I'm going to start calling us the Rod Shop All American Drag Racing Team." And that's what I did.

In three days time, I must have walked 45 or 50 miles just on fire and came back with enough money to build the cars. I ran into Mickey Thompson one time, and he was yelling at the sponsor. He was telling them, "I'm Mickey Thompson, and this is what you have to do. You've got to sponsor me."

I thought to myself, "Well, hell, if that's the way Mickey sells, I can do better than that." That was the basis of how I did it. I got these parts, and we sold them through our speed shop and managed to build both a drag racing team and save the business.

Author: The year 1970 was your banner year wasn't it?

Gil: In 1970, we had a hell of a run. We only won one race, but we were all over the place. So, then I was getting more serious about this and trying to figure out the next step. I thought, "How can I compete with Don "the Snake" Prudhomme with these cars? Nobody even knows we're out there, so by putting different cars in different classes, the Rod Shop name was being repeated all the time.

I even took that a step further after Dave Koeffel from Chrysler Corporation contacted Jim as a sponsor. Jim built a Plymouth Barracuda to run in C/Gas and set the national record. I just leaped for joy, and Dave Koeffel just couldn't believe that we had done that. The result was that in 1971, we went straight across the board with Chrysler sponsorship, we had the Rod Shop Dodge All American Drag Racing Team, and we ended up hiring Mike Fons. We put together sort of a *Motown Missile*–type Pro Stock program with him as the driver. Actually, we had the clone car to the *Missile*, and we were very fast.

Author: So how did you determine who got what as far as sponsorship money?

Gil: I hadn't determined how the sponsorship should work with people. What should I be getting for my money? So, I ran into this whole clash of egos. We were building a motor for this guy, and without that, he can't do anything. At the same time, he thinks his name is bigger than our name [the Rod Shop], and it created sparks. We had never thought it through. I finally started telling people, "This is the way it's going to be if we're going to put the Rod Shop name on the door."

I got into a three-year scrape with Dick Shroyer, and that's where the whole problem started, and that problem ran consistently throughout the whole era. So, I knew that I had to create the idea of the Rod Shop as the corporate umbrella, and these guys could come and go, and we would both get the publicity.

Around 1972, I had my three stores (Grove City, Morse Road, and Livingston Avenue) and I was doing about as well as I was going to do, and I was getting the whole picture of what it was like to be a wholesaler and retailer. And boy, did I not like that business, but I was making it in spite of tough times. Pretty soon, I was in *get me the hell out of this business* mode, so I closed the stores and became a full-time racing operation. That happened in 1973 or 1974. But being a retail speed shop made us. We were the biggest around. The rest of them were not even close.

Something that I failed to mention was how we came up with the distinctive Rod Shop/Miss America flag paint scheme. Like I mentioned before, when it comes to drag racing, seeing and being seen is an all-important factor. So, in 1971, I decided that we would paint the Pro Stockers white with red stripes and a blue top, we'd paint the Modified cars red with white stripes and a blue top, and we'd make the Super Stocks and Stockers blue with white stripes. So, that was another innovation that came from our racing team program.

In those days, Boertman (whose wife, Judy, won Stock Eliminator at the 1972 NHRA Winternationals driving the Rod Shop Dodge station wagon) could make pass after pass, and you could hear the name *Rod Shop* being called out on the microphone all day long. The achievement was to try and figure out how to take and make the Rod Shop a national name and compete in all classes, including Top Fuel and Funny Car, which we ultimately did with "TV Tommy" Ivo.

Essentially, we raced through 1977, when Donnie Carlton was killed and Chrysler said that they were through. At that time, we just pulled in our horns and basically survived as one speed shop and a warehouse.

Nationwise Rod Shop Phase II

Gil: Anyhow, from 1978 on, we were really subdued, and we were going from hand-to-mouth primarily with the machine shop. We had blown through 10 years of just kicking ass, and now everything had quieted down.

I had one car, which was a 1964 Dodge A990 Coronet that Carroll Fink had raced at one time. Well, one of our engine builders named Bruce Meals came to me and

asked "Can I race this car?

I said, "Okay, you can race the car, but if the Rod Shop name is diminished by one iota, it's over." Well, every Monday I would come to work, and he'd say, "We [Meals and his driver] won this weekend."

I'd say, "Really?"

Suddenly, my whole body felt better. It was drag racing again, and I thought that was fantastic. That's how I met driver Larry Morgan.

Author: Then you switched to Pontiac?

Gil: In 1983, Butch Leal came to me and said, "Let's go do this!"

He pushed me and pushed me and pushed me, and I said, "Ah, I really can't."

Well, he finally convinced me to go racing again, and we had Ron Butler build this stealth-looking black and gold Pro Stock Pontiac Firebird. It cost me $357,000 to do that. I had no sponsorship or anything. We took the car to the SEMA Show, and Pontiac put the car on a turnstile. I'm standing there, and there's a great big tall guy, as tall

In the early 1970s, Bob Riffle was the absolute king of Modified class racing with the Rod Shop Dodge Demon. No doubt the rest of the Modified class cars drew a huge sigh of relief when Bob switched over to Pro Stock Eliminator.

as I was, standing there looking at the car and he goes, "Phew! How much did this cost us?" Turns out that he was the president of Pontiac Motor Division who later became the president of Chevrolet.

Author: Did Pontiac approach you, or did you approach Pontiac?

Gil: It was like this. It was a really desperate thing. I called up my buddy John Warner, and he was running the Advanced Engineering staff at General Motors. I said to him, "Let's do this car, but I need some help."

He and I went over to the racing department, which was a couple of cubicles away from his desk, and there was a bunch of NASCAR stuff in it. The guy who was running it, who is well-known and shall remain nameless, made us wait for 30 minutes!

Finally, John said, "That's it!"

The next thing I knew, the guy was fired! John put a guy in there named John Callies. Now, John Callies didn't know anything about drag racing, but he had been working on Pontiac's Indy 500 Pace Car program.

Well, the GM Division of Pontiac had never raced in Pro Stock before, so John said, "Let's go down and see Callies, and we'll see what we can do."

That was such a stressful time. My dad had an aneurism and had to have emergency surgery. I went to the hospital and said, "Dad, I've got to go do this. This is a one-shot deal."

He said, "Go on, son!"

I went to meet John and ended up getting the deal with Pontiac. They agreed to go racing in Pro Stock, so now I had a car and a deal with Pontiac but no money as of yet.

Author: So, when did the Nationwise deal come about?

Gil: I had been working on Nationwise for what seemed like my whole life. Larry Skulnik was running it, and he became so frustrated. Every time they went to the SEMA Show or any place else like that with this 222-store chain—about the biggest in the country, I think—people would say, "You're from Columbus, Ohio, home of the Rod Shop?" Every time, I swear to God!

I had one sales pitch to get Larry to sponsor me, and I knew that he wanted to. I was up all night, and this was a make-or-break situation.

My hands started sweating on the way to go over to meet him, and I remembered my dad telling me about when he would give verbal medical exams when you're trying to become a doctor. He would shake hands with these guys, and their palms would always sweat. I was thinking that I was having a nervous breakdown. I was supposed to be there at 10 a.m., so I went and got some powder and put it on my hands. Then, I go into Larry's office at 10 a.m. and started talking. I was damn near over the edge and almost started crying. By the time I got done, Larry said okay. Within a few weeks, I had signed a contract for a million and some dollars.

So, then I put together the deal with Castrol motor oil. We put Nationwise and Castrol on the car, and down the road we went. We started racing for Nationwise in 1983 with four cars. We had Butch, Boertman, Larry Morgan, and David Nickens. We raced for Nationwise, Castrol, and Pontiac until 1989. One year, Butch was runner-up

Leal's Trans Am was recently cloned (the original car had been destroyed) by Mike Roppo and was and on hand at the 2020 NHRA Winternationals, where Butch was part of the 50th-anniversary celebration of NHRA Pro Stock. (Photo Courtesy Andy Willsheer)

in the NHRA Pro Stock Eliminator World Championship.

Author: In the meantime, Nationwise made the best of the situation, didn't it?

Gil: I went to Nationwise and said, "Look, you need a special Rod Shop section in your stores."

So, they put a Rod Shop section in every store, and we cherry picked the best high-priced stuff, so they were doing what we couldn't do back in 1968. Of course, that put some pressure on across the street [JEGS] because they [Nationwise] were actually selling some of the best top-end speed parts. Plus, we would take the cars and do shows and all sorts of things. It was a tough sponsorship.

You asked how it ended? Our contract had run out, and by that time, they [Nationwise] had gone into NASCAR with the sponsorship of driver Lake Speed. So, after he was runner-up at the Daytona 500, I knew what I was up against.

Basically, Nationwise started splintering off in different directions, but we held on as long as we could. Butch talked me into building a Chevrolet Pro Stock Beretta toward the end of our sponsorship. We ran that car for two years, but without the prevailing Chevrolet big-block technology available to us, it was a loss of tons and tons of money. Finally, the deal was over, and I was out on the street.

Author: What did the Rod Shop meant to you?

Gil: I had my family, the real estate business, and the Rod Shop, so every place I went, I was thinking about the other side of it. Going racing was a fulfillment of my ego driven to have the world's fastest car, which we essentially did in 1971.

When speaking of the Nationwise Rod Shop Pontiac All American Drag Racing Team, owner/manager Gil Kirk said, "It was like managing a rock band, and Butch [Leal] was the lead singer."

Leal received the Lucas Oil/NHRA 50th Anniversary Pro Stock Honoree trophy during 2020 NHRA Winternationals festivities. (Photo Courtesy Andy Willsheer)

Then, after it was all over, I thought that I needed to get out there and become a team owner in NASCAR and all that stuff, but that would have been the end of my family life. That was an issue, and I had stretched that out as far as I could. I was under so much pressure the whole time and running around like a maniac. I must have run 40 miles at a race going up and down the track telling all the sponsors everything that happened: "Hey, Boertman did this, and Riffle did this."

Philosophically, I attributed my burning desire to go racing to that great culture of which I'm a part, as are you. The only thing I know after thinking about it long enough is that it was a great time to be growing up in America. Between rock and roll and cars, I was living the dream. With the exception of my wife and family, I've never had that much passion for anything since.

Van Iderstine Speed Shop
East Hanover, New Jersey

The following is a conversation with Van Iderstine Speed Shop founder Peter Van Iderstine and author Bob McClurg.

Author: What can you tell us about your background?

Peter: I grew up in a white-collar town in suburban New Jersey. Most everybody's father commuted to New York on the train, and you were expected to follow in their footsteps. You go to college, then you get on the train, ride into the city, work all day, then come back home again at night. But I wasn't much of a student. Hot rods were my thing.

I remember when the first copy of *Hot Rod* magazine hit town. It was the May 1950 issue. Joe Nitti's 1932 Ford was on the cover. I saw that, and I've been a 1932 Ford nut ever since. In fact, I've got four of them. One's a barn find that came out of New Jersey, and I personally built the other three.

When I was I attending Chatham High School in my home town of Chatham, New Jersey [graduating in 1954], I wasn't much of a student. It was girls and cars. My first car was a channeled 1932 Ford roadster. No hood. No fenders. No top. I just liked driving that thing around town rain or shine. Anyhow, I got accepted of all things to Lehigh University, which is now known as Monmouth University. I don't know how, but I did. Anyhow, I went to school four days a week and worked two. I also got married before I got out of college, so it took me a while to graduate, but I had decided that since no one else in my family had graduated from college up to that point, I would be the first one.

As I was getting toward my senior year, I started thinking seriously about what I was going to do for a living. There were companies coming to the school and approaching seniors about the possibilities of a job and all that, but something told me not to make any appointments. By the time I got out of college [1962], I didn't have any children and was draft eligible, so I went into the Navy Reserve for six months as an antisubmarine warfare aircraft radar operator, which wasn't such a bad deal.

In November 1962, Tony Feil and I decided to rent a building together. I was going to sell parts, and he was going to do engines. It was a little two-car-garage kind of a building on Route 10 in East Hanover, New Jersey. The competition at that time was Don's Speed Shop in Metuchen, New Jersey, and California Speed and Sport in New Brunswick. Fortunately, I was located far enough away to not really bother Don too much, and I didn't pose any real threat to California Speed and Sport because they mostly specialized in circle track racing.

I remember going to a building supply place, and they would let us go behind the building where they had broken 2x4s and let us raid their scrap pile. That's how we made our counters. Once people knew that we were there, sales reps who handled all the West Coast brands would stop in and see us. Once they realized that we weren't some backyard type of an operation, things grew. We spent many-a-day working all day long only to go home long enough at night to grab dinner and then go right back to work again. It was nothing for us to work six days a week and stay open until 9 or 9:30 p.m. We just kept plugging away and created a demand for stuff.

I stayed in that building for two years and got to the point where I was able to go out on my own. In 1964, I rented a building right around the corner from where I had been, and in another two years I outgrew that location. I think that both Don Raleigh and I were there when drag racing, whether it was street or quarter-mile, was in its growth period. Tri-Five Chevrolets, Camaros, and Corvettes were household words with a lot of people. Now, Don and I used to talk a lot about this. I felt that not everybody in one town is your customer. Every house has a box of Kleenex in it, but not everybody knows what a Hurst shifter is or is going to buy one, so you had to have a business location that was relatively easy to find. If you were located on some back street, no one would bother. We had guys who would drive two hours just to come to our store.

I remember that there were certain lines that I had a hard time buying. Sun tachometers was one of them. They just weren't going to sell to me directly. I understood that but kept working on them anyway. Dixco was another brand of tachometer I could sell, but everybody wanted a Sun tach. Edelbrock wouldn't sell directly to me either, so I had Weiand. I didn't sell Schiefer because they didn't have a balanced assembly, but I sold Weber. You could buy one of those, take it home, bolt it right up, and away you went.

In 1964, the first big-block Chevrolet came out. We were connected with a Chevrolet dealer (Star Chevrolet in East Orange, New Jersey), so we ordered a brand-new 396 Chevrolet crate motor. I had it sitting on the floor in the shop, and oh boy, everybody wanted to come in and see that. Now, obviously things were great with Chevrolet. Everything with Chevrolet interchanged, but I never could quite figure out Ford. To this day, I never could understand them.

For example, Chevrolet had one 163-tooth flywheel that you could bolt up to practically any engine. With Ford, there was an external balance and an internal balance. There were different tooth counts. It was just crazy. I distinctly remember when the Cobra Jet came out, one bolt hole on the flywheel was an eighth of an inch off. They had different exhaust flanges; everything was off. Chrysler was another one that was hard to deal with. I remember guys pulling street Hemis apart only to find out that they had 10 under bearings on the crankshaft. What the hell? This was nuts.

Chevrolet was the king because they made it easier for a guy with a limited budget to afford to have something. I did a little research on this. To my knowledge, all 283 Chevys had a 2-barrel carburetor. If a guy bolted a 4-barrel carburetor on one, you would have thought that he had a rocket ship. I found out that a 300-hp cast-iron Corvette intake manifold would bolt right onto a 283. A guy could make the swap at home in his garage.

We were selling a lot of Carter carburetors in those days. I remember I would buy a 300-hp 4V cast-iron Chevrolet intake manifold in a box a half dozen at a time. I would take a 3721 Carter 4-barrel carburetor with a manual choke and take four tap screws and bolt that carburetor up to that manifold and put it on the shelf. We used to get $59.95 for one of those, and we sold a ton of them. If a guy had a 283 and he bolted one on, he was king, especially if he had a standard shift transmission. There were times I would get guys with Rochester fuel injection cars that were so pissed off at their fuel injection systems that they would trade them in for one of those intakes. I would allow a guy $30 off toward one of those 4-barrel intakes. Now, one of those Rochester fuel injection systems is worth $5,000 if you can find one.

Author: When did you start sponsoring race cars?

Peter: Island Dragway in New Jersey opened in 1959, so it was right away. But that got to be a problem, and it bit you in the ass. There was a Roger's Speed Shop at the time, and he would give them (customer cars) money, but I would never give them money. I would give a guy parts at a discount, and he would put our name on his car. Then, another guy would come along, and he would want you to do the same thing. You can only do that so many times and stay in business.

So, when you turn the next guy down, he gets all pissed off at you. It caused customer relations problems more than anything else. I tried to stay away from that, but the problem I also had was I had good friends who were customers, and they would put my name on their cars out of loyalty and respect and wouldn't even ask. I couldn't go to these guys and ask them to take my name off their car. It just turned out to be a delicate situation.

Author: Surely you sponsored someone, right?

Peter: We sponsored Ken Poffenberger and his *Poff's Puffer* Corvair Funny Car. There was a guy working for us named Bob Bradshaw who had a '55 Chevy gasser, and we also sponsored him. We also ran our own Top Fuel car for quite a few years and had our name gold leafed on the front bodywork.

Author: When did you start publishing catalogs?

Peter: I never did. I never needed to. Our business was mostly local. I did a little mail order. I would put ads in *Car Craft*, *Hot Rod* and other books. For example, I would advertise a Weiand 2x4 intake manifold with two Carter WAFBs on it, and we would ship those things all over the place. I also found out that there was a Cyclone sprint car header kit that worked really well on T-Buckets, and we would ship 3 or 4 of those out a month. They made a nice sale.

I worked hard at buying as a WD. Now, some competitors had a problem with that, but I worked hard at it and wanted to get the best price you could get. I often had to buy a quantity of stuff to get a decent price, but that was fine. I also paid my bills right on time. When it came to paying my bills, I never screwed speed equipment manufacturers around because they're your life's blood. We finally got Edelbrock as a WD, and Hurst wasn't located too far away, so we never had a problem with them. Harry Weber was the champion of flywheels and clutches, and we sold a lot of his stuff.

Then, the custom wheel craze came along, and wheels were a big deal. Mickey Thompson came along with his Rader wheels, and we sold a bunch of them. The first Rader wheels I bought would have been around 1964. I think Don Raleigh [Don's Speed Shop] was the first person to sell an aftermarket wheel in the state of New Jersey, and I was the second. I would order 12 sets at a time, as freight was cheap back in those days. I remember I bought a 1963 Ford 390 Country Squire wagon to use as a tow car, and I installed a set of Rader wheels on it. Man, it looked great.

Then, along came other wheels, such as the Hurst Performance wheel, and they came in a can. I also became good friends with Louie Senter at Ansen and sold a lot of Ansen Sprint wheels. We also did a lot of business with Appliance. The custom wheels thing became a big part of our business.

Author: How many Van Iderstine Speed Shop locations did you have?

Peter: I opened my second store down the street on Route 10 East in Springfield, New Jersey. Then, I went around the corner on Route 10 East and opened a third store in an old Sunoco gas station that had a huge showroom and repair bay. It was 3,400 square feet, and I ended up putting a second level on the building for the warehouse. Then, I bought some property on 10 East and built a brand-new 15,000-square-foot building. That was my fourth location. We also started getting into wholesaling at that location, but delivery was a problem, so I ended up buying four or five delivery trucks to handle the volume. From there, I just kept expanding the business.

I never did any installation work, and neither did Don. You were asking for problems when you did installations. I remember Cragar S/S wheels. A guy would go to mount a tire, and if he cinched the wheel down on the tire machine too tight, he would end up breaking the center out of the wheel.

Installing headers was the worst thing in the world. Chrysler products used to drive us nuts. Everyone used to blame the header manufacturer, but it wasn't their fault. I remember one time we had two identical 1965 Plymouth 426 Max Wedge cars parked at my second store. We lifted the hoods, and from the driver's side valve cover to the firewall, there was a 1-inch difference between the two cars. There was no way in hell you're going to install headers on the one car without banging on them!

As time went on, the business was still drag racing oriented or for wannabe drag racers fixing up their cars, jacked-up suspensions, air bags, and big wheels and tires. Again, it was mostly Chevrolet. I was a TRW warehouse, which was a blessing in disguise. We sold a lot of TRW engine parts, especially for Chevrolets. I don't know why those guys got out of the high-performance parts business, but they did. We also had Engle Cams, Crane, Holley, and other lines. We talked the language and things went along pretty well.

Author: What was the high point of Van Iderstine Speed Shop?

Peter: There never was a high point. Back in those days, I don't think there was anybody making money hand over fist in the speed shop business. The problem is it's just like the guy selling washing machines. You go to 20 places and price one, and there's very little difference. It was like the car magazines. I never sold car magazines because the ads from the competition like Honest Charley for example was like selling someone else's catalog.

I didn't gouge anybody, but I had to make a certain profit. What would happen is that I would sell a Sun tach or a Hurst shifter for my price, and a guy sees an ad and realizes that he paid $8 more than what he could have bought it for from an ad in a magazine, and he's pissed off at you not taking into consideration of course product availability, your overhead, employee salaries, and everything else under the sun. So, to answer your question, there was never a time we were making money hand over fist, but with the exception of some winter months, it was steady. Once spring came and the drag strips opened, sales would go up again.

Author: You mentioned employee salaries. At the height of Van Iderstine Speed Shop, how many people did you have working for you?

Peter: I had 43 employees covering 10 stores, and I liked every one of them. I was very fortunate. I hired people who would increase my sales and not hurt them. Unlike an auto parts store that hires a grunt to work behind the counter because he's dealing with a customer who's not happy to be there in the first place because he had an alternator crap out, my customers came in because they wanted to make their cars run faster or look different. It was a hobby business.

I used to tell my employees that you've got to think of this place like it's a sporting goods store. Nobody really needs anything that we have. They come in here because they want what we have, so you have to hire people who are happy to be working there in the first place and speak the language.

Author: What would you say being in the speed shop business and the racing industry as a whole has done for you as a person?

Peter: Working for someone else, especially now is really tough. You don't know from one moment to the next whether you're going to have a job or not. I've had a memorable career doing something that I've always liked doing. Had I to do it over again, would I do things differently? Maybe a few things but not many. I liked what I was doing, and thank God I was successful at it. In the final analysis, some of it was luck and some of it was timing.

Van Senus Auto Parts
Hammond, Indiana

Van Senus Auto Parts was located at 6920 Kennedy Ave. in Hammond, Indiana, and was founded in 1946 by Fred Van Senus Sr. In 1953, Fred Van Senus Jr. began working in the store after school hours. After attending Indiana University and doing a short stint in Uncle Sam's National Guard, Fred Jr. returned to work with his father at the shop with renewed resolve.

"In those days [the mid-1950s], drag racing was just starting to take hold in the state of Indiana," Van Senus Jr. said. "I wasn't all that interested in your run-of-the-mill auto parts business as much as I was in selling racing parts. That was more of an exclusive market. It had a good profit margin, and it was a great way to grow the business."

However, that didn't mean that Van Senus Auto Parts was going to phase out the bread-and-butter auto parts trade by any means.

"My brother Don was also involved with the business, and he elected to stay with the traditional parts trade," Van Senus Jr. said.

Van Senus also had a pretty busy machine shop business.

"My foreman's name was Gene Crow, who later went to work for the late actor/racer Paul Newman as his crew chief," Van Senus Jr. said. "Gene was a Saturday night racer at a local round track called Blue Island. He started bringing in circle track customer work, and with his help, we successfully built up that segment of the business."

But Fred Jr. wasn't all that happy with the prices he was paying for speed equipment through the local WDs.

"I hated going through a second party," Van Senus Jr. said. "Whenever I was at a national event, I would go to the manufacturers and work out deals to sell their product through the business. I also started going to the SEMA Show, which at that time was in Los Angeles, California, at Dodger Stadium. The more speed equipment we sold, the better the deals we got. I ended up buying direct through Ed Iskenderian and Vic Edelbrock Sr."

When it was all said and done, Van Senus Auto Parts negotiated deals with some of the biggest names in the speed equipment industry and stocked 1,600 product lines and about 60,000 part numbers. Top sellers included Magna Flow, Hooker, Hedman, Crane, Holley, MSD, and other major performance brands. Throughout the 1960s, 1970s, and 1980s, Van Senus Auto Parts was all about growth.

"In 1961 we had about 15 employees," Van Senus Jr. said. "By 2011, we added another store and had our own 11,000-square-foot warehouse distribution center with about 180 employees."

Still, the company kept it local.

"For 15 years, I made my own cable TV commercials through Prime Time Cable Advertising, and they were very well-known in the Northeastern Indiana region," Van Senus Jr. said. "They were down to earth,

This poster pays tribute to Fred Van Senus Jr., who grew a humble Hammond, Indiana, auto parts store into one of the biggest speed shops in the Midwest.

Van Senus Auto Parts sponsored a number of cars and teams, but it was NHRA/IHRA/UDRA Pro Stock racer Joe Satmary and his We-Haul Camaros (shown at Great Lakes Dragaway in Union Grove, Wisconsin) that vaulted the Van Senus Auto Parts name onto the national stage.

sincere ads—nothing off the wall. Quite often, we would co-op our advertising with one of our top accounts like Edelbrock Equipment Company, for example. We also printed our own catalogs and advertised sales through direct mail."

When asked if Van Senus sponsored any of the local racers, the answer was a definitive yes.

"We sponsored about 20 local customer cars," Van Senus Jr. said. "If they bought their parts from us, I would give them some money whenever they won a race."

One of the best-known racers out of that group was NHRA Pro Stock racer Joe Satmary, who campaigned his Van Senus Auto Parts–sponsored *We-Haul* Camaros nationally.

"Everyone who worked for me behind the counter at the Hammond store had their own race car," Van Senus

Jr. said. "Technically we had an extreme advantage, and the company grew from practically nothing to a multimillion-dollar business."

In 1998, Fred Van Senus won the SEMA Warehouser of the Year award, and he was also awarded the 2002 Pioneer of the Industry award by the Performance Warehouse Association (PWA). He proudly displays both awards on the wall in his man cave at home.

In 2014, Van Senus Auto Parts was bought out by auto parts chain Auto Wares which has 56 locations throughout the Midwest. It was the end of an era.

Von Fritch Automotive
Garden Grove, California

Von Fritch Automotive was founded in the early 1960s by Southern California hot rodder Ronnie Roseberry. In its earliest days, the shop, which was located on Anabell Avenue in Garden Grove, California, was engaged in race car fabrication and piece work. However, Ronnie wanted more.

In 1967, Roseberry merged the business with Thweatt's Automotive, which was formerly located in downtown Los Angeles. Once the merger with Thweatt's was completed, Roseberry moved lock, stock, and barrel into

Radici and Wise *driver Paul "Wrong Way" Radici lights them up at Southern California's Irwindale Raceway driving the Vega-bodied Funny Car that carried the Wise Speed Shop banner into battle.*

the former Garden Grove US Post Office building on Garden Grove Boulevard. Aside from the benefits of having a speed shop, the merger with Thweatt's also brought with it a nitro-burning Hemi-engine 1965 Dodge A990 sedan that was quickly repainted and relettered with the name *Von Fritch Automotive* on its side flanks.

Roseberry also built a jet-engine 1957 Plymouth sedan that was quite popular with the fans.

Unfortunately, due to limited finances and a huge monthly rent bill, Von Fritch Automotive closed in the late 1960s. However, Ronnie (who later owned a really primo, 100-percent original 1932 Ford Tudor sedan) kept his hand in hot rodding until his passing in the early 2000s.

Wise Speed Shop
St. Louis, Missouri

For the 45 or so years that it was in business, Wise Speed Shop, a division of Wise Distributing Company, called 5817 Hampton Ave., St. Louis, Missouri home.

Founded in 1963 by Vic Wise as a traditional retail auto parts store, the company ultimately evolved into a speed shop when son Dave Wise joined the business. Dave was one half of the Radici & Wise Funny Car team that rose to stardom in the late 1960s. First, it was with a flip-top Pontiac Firebird, then a nitro-burning Chevrolet Camaro, which was followed by a pair of early 1970s Chevrolet Vegas and, lastly, a Chevrolet Monza flopper, all driven by the late Paul "Wrong Way" Radici.

Although Radici & Wise never won a national Funny Car title, the team held the NHRA eighth-mile elapsed time record for a brief time (4.52 at 176 mph) and participated in the famed Coca-Cola Funny Car Cavalcade of Stars, or Coke Circuit, as it was also known. Unlike many of its competitors, Wise Speed Shop wasn't a huge mega store, but within its well-stocked walls, you could find practically every name brand under the sun to improve your vehicle's performance.

As blogger Jack Harley wrote, "The place even *smelled* like race parts!"

Clearly, Wise Speed Shop had a strong following, but like many of your mom-and-pop speed shops, it just couldn't compete with the mass marketers and ultimately fell by the wayside.

CHAPTER 8

SPEED SHOP SURVIVORS

In this dog-eat-dog world, regardless of what type of business, only the strongest survive. With the emergence of the speed equipment industry's big-box stores, that's especially true.

The spirit of competition and free enterprise still reigns. Listed below is a grouping of some (not all) independently-run speed shops that currently do business in the USA.

Don's Hot Rod Shop
Tucson, Arizona

Address: 2811 N. Stone Ave., Tucson, AZ 85705
Phone: 520-884-8892

Don's Hot Rod Shop at 2811 N. Stone Ave., Tucson, Arizona, 85705, was founded in 1962 by Don Toia, the nephew of Bill Toia, who originally founded Gratiot Auto Supply in Detroit, Michigan.

The following is a conversation with Don's Hot Rod Shop founder Don Toia and author Bob McClurg.

Author: What can you tell us about your background?

Don: The speed shop business is kind of in our blood. Our family moved to Tucson in 1947, and my father, Leo, bought a Shell gas station at 2823 Stone Ave. Dad sold gas for a few years and then converted it to an auto parts store. In 1962, I opened up a hot rod shop in the back section of his store. The place really wasn't that big. It was 32 feet wide x 40 feet deep, but it had a tall ceiling, so we built an upstairs for storage and inventory.

Author note: In 1976, Toia and company built a new building just south of the original site, and they have been doing business there ever since.

Author: Does Don's Hot Rod Shop publish a catalog?

Don: No. We send out flyers to our customers, and we occasionally list special items for sale on eBay. We also have a website: donshotrodshop.net.

Author: What is Don's biggest seller?

Don: As far as brand names go, I would say that the Holley Performance Products line (Holley, Earls, Hooker, Weiand, Mr. Gasket, Accel, Super Chips, Lakewood, Quick

Don's Hot Rod Shop, established in 1962, has been calling 2811 N. Stone Avenue, Tucson, Arizona, home since 1976. Three generations of Toia family have guided and grown the business that founder Don Toia Sr. refers to as a family legacy. (Photo Courtesy Jim Kelso)

The well-lit and well-stocked showroom inside Don's Hot Rod Shop is staffed by six, including Don's wife, Madonna, and son Donny II. "Hopefully, someday my grandchildren will be running the business," Don said. (Photo Courtesy Jim Kelso)

The folks at Don's Hot Rod Shop practice what they preach. Founder Don Toia raced a Chrysler-powered 1941 Willys coupe, then this Chrysler-engine BB/GS 1970 Ford Maverick named Incognito, *and lastly, a Chrysler-engine 1923 T that Don ran in the AA/A class.*

Fuel, Hurst, B&M, NOS, etc.), pretty much covers everything under the sun. We also sell quite a bit of Edelbrock Performance Products and buy direct from 50 to 60 other companies.

Author note: Don's Hot Rod Shop employs a staff of six, including Toia's wife, Madonna, and son Don Toia II.

Don: We call him Donny II, and we also have a Donny III, who plays major league soccer for Real Salt Lake. We also employ two other countermen and a bookkeeper.

Author: With the mass marketers out there, has it been hard to remain solvent?

Don: Yes. I think the main reason why we remain competitive is because my son Donny and employee Jay Axtell know their subject matter so well. When it comes to drag racing, they're both experts. They know exactly what these guys need to go out to the track and be competitive, and they [Don's Hot Rod Shop customers] come in for help and useful information all the time.

As far as pricing goes, we basically try and match the mass marketers' prices or at least try to get the price as close as possible. Sometimes, that's hard. One thing that has really helped is the minimum advertised pricing (MAP) that most of the manufacturers are coming out with.

Author: So, you're here to stay?

Don: Don's Hot Rod Shop is a third-generation business, and we just want to keep going. It all started with my dad, and hopefully one day my grandchildren will be running the business. You might say it's our family legacy.

Author note: MAP is the lowest price that a retailer can advertise a product for sale. This does not refer to the

lowest price that a retailer can list it in their store. The MAP price is established by the manufacturer and regulated by the Federal Trade Commission (FTC).

Don's Speed Shop
Newington, Connecticut

Address: 2193 Berlin Turnpike, Newington, CT 06111
Phone: 860-666-9156

The following is a conversation with Paul Gallant of Don's Speed Shop and author Bob McClurg.

Author: Don's Speed Shop in Newington, Connecticut, has a rich and colorful history on the Eastern Seaboard. When was the company founded?

Paul: Originally, it was known as Don's Automotive Specialties and was operated out of an old Atlantic gas station that my father, Don Gallant, ran on the Berlin Turnpike in Wethersfield, Connecticut. At the time [1953], the speed and hot rod industry was just starting to come alive.

My father was already souping up his own cars and saw an opportunity to open his own business selling speed parts through the gas station. Back then, the traveling sales reps would come around and sell him parts out of the trunks of their cars. In turn, he would sell them to his customers, and the business just kind of grew from there.

Author: Did he race as well?

Paul: Yes. Dad was involved in just about every kind of racing there was in New England.

In the early 1950s, he started going to the Charleston, Rhode Island, air strip, where they set up one of the East Coast's first drag strips. He also used to race a dirt track car at Safford Springs Speedway, and he drag raced a Chevy 6-cylinder-powered 1927 Ford roadster known as the *Gold Rush*, which was originally an early hot rod turned into a drag car. It was a very famous car around here in New England and ran a number of different classes and different sizes of engines.

In the 1960s, he campaigned a '55 Chevy called the *Golden Gasser*. He and a guy named Dick Rupp would quite often run the two cars together, and they would take home a bunch of trophies.

Author: Did your father hold any NHRA, AHRA, or NASCAR Drag Racing Division class records?

Paul: I'm not sure if he did or not. I know that the first Don's Speed Shop Chevrolet Top Fuel dragster campaigned by Al Riccio and Joe Simone set some kind of a record at Indy. In 1964, they set both Top Speed and Low ET for the meet. M&H Tire had just come out with its new directional slicks, and they had a set of those on

Don's Speed Shop, which was established in 1953, is at 2193 Berlin Turnpike, Newington, Connecticut. Founder Don Gallant started the business out of on an old Atlantic gas station. Today, the company is housed in this 2,400-square-foot facility, which includes a speed shop and two service bays, along with an adjacent 3,000-square-foot warehouse.

the car. Unfortunately, on their backup run, they got the slicks reversed, and the car went sideways and crashed on the top end of the track. They also had a coupe body for the car so that they could also run it in the Competition Coupe class.

Riccio, Simone, and Gallant raced a number of dragsters out of Don's Speed Shop well into the 1970s with great success. After a while, I believe Joe Simone didn't want to drive anymore, so a guy named Richard Couch took over the driving duties. In 1972, they also raced a Chevy Nova in Pro Stock called *Stage Coach* that ran in the 9s. That car was eventually sold to a guy in Puerto Rico who ended up crashing it.

Author: Tell us a little about the first Don's Speed Shop.

Paul: In 1958, dad moved to 2191 Berlin Turnpike, which is the same piece of property we're on now. He bought an old gas station and held a total of three mortgages on it. The pumps were still in operation, but he didn't buy the place to pump gas. He wanted to open it as a speed shop and named it Don's Automotive Specialties. We always wondered why dad called it that instead of Don's Speed Shop. He said that with hot rodding being somewhat outlaw in nature and carrying with it a bit of a stigma, the words *Automotive Specialties* looked better on paper to the citizenry and was more acceptable to his insurance company. Who could argue with that?

The building itself was about 2,400 square feet and had a two-car bay. It also had a showroom off to the side and no real insulation to speak of; it was just a concrete-block building. That's where a lot of stuff happened. In the early days, Berlin Turnpike was the main road between New York and Boston, so he did a lot of service work, such as fixing flats, rebuilding generators, and that kind of stuff. People would be traveling between the cities, and that initially proved to be dad's bread and butter.

However, once they opened up the new interstate, this road became more of a cruising route and the ideal location for a speed shop because there was a lot of street racing going on. And when I say a lot, I mean *a lot*! At the time, there were probably about 10 or 15 other speed shops on this road, but they all came to Don's to get their parts.

Author: And that would include a few touring pros?

Paul: Yes, Roland Leong was a friend of Dad's, and he used to service his *Hawaiian* dragsters and Funny Cars there when he was touring the East Coast. He and Dad met when Dad was running the dragster, and they raced each other several times.

One day Roland called and said, "Hey, Don. I need some help. We got into a towing accident, and I need a place to fix the car."

I guess the car was pretty badly damaged. Anyhow, Dad said to bring it on over. Roland and his crew took over one of the bays and pulled the car completely apart. Basically, a bunch of different shops in the area got together with Dad and donated their time and resources and came up with the parts they needed to fix the car. Of course, Leong and Snively went on to win the NHRA Top Fuel Points Championship in 1966. I still have a copy of the ad they took out in *National Dragster* thanking us.

Author: You said that you are one of six? What are the names of your other siblings?

Paul: Donald is my oldest brother. He's 18 years older than me. He saw all the cool stuff happen. He was a parts guy and worked the counter. Later, he staged a cruise night here on Berlin Turnpike that helped legitimize cruising in this part of the state and put us on the map.

At Don's, it's multigenerational. Seated is founder Don Gallant with his wife, Claire, behind him. On the right is youngest son and general manager Paul Gallant.

I also had a brother named Raymond who has since passed away. He was two years younger than Donald, and he had a real mechanical mind and was particularly good at rebuilding 4-speeds. He could take them apart and put them back together with his eyes closed. He often helped my father out in the shop, but he was real hard on cars. He would beat the heck out of them, which is how he learned to fix them.

The next youngest was my sister Andrea. She used to accompany Dad to the car shows and help him out.

Below her was my brother Adrianne. He was the super mechanic in the family and graduated top in his class from the Harley-Davidson Mechanics School, which is probably why Roland wanted him to pit on his cars whenever he raced locally. He was also in the US Air Force Reserves and worked on the A-10 Tank Busters. Mechanic-wise, he was probably the closest to Dad in mechanical ability. I remember when I was 8 or 9, Dad took me to a race at Lebanon Valley, New York. Adrianne was there working on Roland Leong's *King's Hawaiian Bread* Dodge Charger Funny Car. It was a night race, and the lights were all glowing and kind of surreal.

I also have one sister above me named Renee, who also used to work the car shows with Dad, and then there's me.

Author: Did you guys always have the newest and trickest in street machines?

Paul: Actually, never. We always built what we drove. Believe it or not, that black Chevrolet dually sitting out there in the parking lot is the first vehicle I've ever made payments on.

"Parts is parts," and Don's Speed Shop has all the good stuff in stock.

Author: We're sitting here in this beautiful metal building on the back lot at 2193 Berlin Turnpike. How many years did the original Don's Automotive Specialties building survive?

Paul: From 1958 to 2003. The only reason we moved back here was we had a fire gut the original building in 2003. My dad had a wood stove in the shop to supplement the old 1950s-style furnace. Well, that old furnace smoldered all weekend, and when Dad went to open the doors on Monday, it created a back-draft effect, and the place went up like an inferno.

Author: That pretty much destroyed the business?

Paul: Yeah, we lost a good third of our inventory, maybe more. A lot of it was stuff that you just couldn't salvage. A friend of mine and I took one shovelful at a time and sifted through the rubble. We probably had about $110,000 worth of Hurst shifters and Hurst motor mount kits, some stuff they don't even make anymore, old air cleaners like vintage Cal Custom stuff, a lot of NOS factory performance parts, rods, pistons, cranks,

Paul holds up a vintage Pontiac Tri-Power intake that could be yours for the right price. Don's Speed Shop founder Don Gallant has always traded in used parts. Make no mistake, he'll be happy to sell you something new if you want it, but he's also happy to do a little horse trading.

When looking around Don's showroom, the phrase well stocked **comes to mind.**

etc. We salvaged some of it, but it was merely a fraction of the stuff that was lost in the fire. Thankfully, the fire department responded quickly, as many of the firemen had bought parts from Dad and knew right where the place was.

Author: So, is that when you built the new building?

Paul: I'll get around to that.

But first, having grown up in the Depression, Dad never threw anything away. At one point, when he was still in the front station [the early 1980s], things were starting to evolve quickly on this road, and the town was getting after him to clean up the place because the back lot was beginning to look like a small junkyard.

I remember when I was a kid, I helped clean up the backyard, and there was a pile behind the back door that was about 15 feet in diameter and about 5 feet high. It was nothing but factory exhaust manifolds that had been cast aside with the installation of a set of headers: 426 Hemi exhaust manifolds, big-block Chevrolet and Pontiac exhaust manifolds, 426 Max Wedge exhaust manifolds, some so heavy I almost couldn't lift them. Had we saved all that stuff, it would have been worth a fortune today. However, we didn't throw out everything.

Author: When did you break ground on the new building?

Paul: Originally this was a 2,400-square-foot building that we built as a warehouse, and we had all kinds of trouble with the city. They city zoning inspector definitely didn't want us here. Luckily, the city building inspector was a car guy. He said, "Why don't you put plumbing in the floor so if you ever want to activate the building, you can?"

I said, "You can really do that?"

He said, "Yes."

So, we put pipes in the ground, and thank God we did because in 2003 when the fire happened, the plumbing was there, and we were able to go to the town and temporarily set up business in this building. The city didn't make it easy, but we dug in and rebuilt. We also put up a 3,000-square-foot, two-story building in the back that functions strictly as storage. Believe it or not, we have four 40-foot containers worth of parts stored back there.

Author: Who was your first name dealer?

Paul: It might have been Edelbrock, Giovanni Cams, or Grant Piston Rings. Or, it might have been Nixon, or Harmon & Collins. We're talking about as far back as 1953, so I think only my dad would be able to tell you!

Author: What are your main product lines today?

Paul: We sell a lot of Edelbrock, Moroso, ARP, Manley, Hurst, All-Star, RPC, and Mr. Gasket. Dad used to be a WD for a bunch of other companies. The 1980s and 1990s were really tough. As Summit and JEGS got bigger, some manufacturers dropped many of the smaller WDs. But, God bless 'em, due to our reputation and company history, we're still able to buy direct from the majority of the manufacturers that I just mentioned.

Another thing we've always done is sell used parts. My dad was always allowing his customers to do trade-ins. One of Dad's mottos has been and always will be "More Go for Less Dough."

East Coast Speed
Cranston, Rhode Island

Address: 1528 Elmwood Ave. Cranston, RI 02910
Phone: 401-467-3507
Website: andyseastcoastspeed.com

East Coast Speed is unofficially the oldest speed shop in Rhode Island.

Ralph Papa founded the business in 1962 and operated it until he passed away in 1980. East Coast Speed is currently owned and operated by Andy Anderson. The epitome of your mom-and-pop speed shop, East Coast Speed operates out of an old two-bay gas station and not only sells speed parts but also services what it sells.

"Outside of bodywork and major electrical, we pretty much service anything having to do with a car's drivetrain: camshafts, carburetor work, intake and exhaust, clutches, transmissions, suspension, brakes, and tires," Andy said.

Over the years, East Coast Speed has worked on quite a few well-known cars in the New England area, with the most noteworthy being the restoration of Tony Nancy's injected Buick-engine *22 Jr.*

"We finished that car according to a *Hot Rod* magazine article circa 1960, where the car appeared on the cover," Andy said. "We've also done marine stuff. We worked on a boat for a customer who owned the 42-foot Chris-Craft that was used on the TV show *Miami Vice*. We rebuilt the original big-block Chevrolet engines and then built him a couple of bigger-displacement big-blocks. That was a fun project. When it comes to working on customer cars. We've tried to self-limit ourselves to early American cars up to the year 2000. We're old school. We don't take on jobs that we can't handle and don't service anything having to do with modern electronic engine management systems."

When Andy was asked if it was hard for a little guy like him to stay afloat with the rise of the big-box stores, his answer was a definitive yes.

"It's been very difficult and has been for years," Andy said. "The mail-order companies will undercut us on price every time. Unless we look at their mail-order catalogs, we don't know how badly we're being beaten up.

"I have walk-in customers who insult me when I tell them what my price is. I have customers who walk in, pick my brain, and then order the same part from Summit or JEGS. Then, they have the nerve to walk back in and want me to install it for them. I'll do it for a nominal installation fee, but I won't warranty the job if something goes wrong. I tell the customer, 'Listen, you didn't buy it here. You brought it in for me to install. I'll do the same quality work that I would for a customer who ordered the part through me. However, if it breaks or something else goes wrong, it's on you, not me.'"

Being involved as a retailer in the speed equipment industry has its pros and cons, Andy said.

"At times, it's no fun being a one-man band," he said. "There's a lot of hard work involved. Obviously, I'm never going to get rich at it, but it put three kids through school, so if I didn't enjoy it, I wouldn't still be doing it. It's certainly been an enlightening experience—that much I can tell you."

George's Speed Shop
Dayton, Ohio

Address: 716 Brantley Ave., Dayton, OH 45404
Phone: 937-233-0353
Website: georgespeedshop.com

He was called "Ohio George" at the drag strip, but when you walk through the doors at 716 Brantley Ave., in Dayton, Ohio, you're speaking with Mr. George Montgomery, the proprietor of George's Speed Shop. Although, he simply answers the telephone, "George's." After 70 years in the speed shop business, and at the same location no less, that's really all he has to do.

The following is a conversation with George's Speed Shop founder George Montgomery and author Bob McClurg.

Author: Exactly when did you open George's Speed Shop?

George: It was 1950 to the best of my recollection. At that time, it was just a small thing where I was installing cams in the afternoons after I got home from working my job at ACDelco. I charged $20 to install a cam and $5 extra to grind the valves. That was a biggie, and I installed a lot of them.

In the early days, I didn't have any room to park the cars, so I would do it outside. Sometimes I would do one a night and would stay up until I got the job done. Back in those days, that was good money.

In the beginning, I had a deal with Brockman's Speed Shop. They would do parts sales, and I would do the installations. In other words, I wouldn't sell parts, and they wouldn't sell service. Well, that went on for a few

In the late 1950s, George Montgomery raced this blown-Cadillac-engine, powder blue 1933 Willys coupe that won the 1959 NHRA Nationals. Montgomery's Willys changed with the times, next running a blown small-block Chevrolet in 1963, and lastly a factory-sponsored blown 427 SOHC Ford in 1965. (Photo Courtesy Greg Sharp Collection)

years. Evidentially, someone down there thought that I was doing quite well, so they decided to build their own installation shop and came to me and said, "We're going to start selling service."

I responded, "Well, then I'm going to start selling parts!"

That was around 1952, so I guess that's really when George's Speed Shop actually became George's Speed Shop.

Author: What were your first product lines?

George: I bought a lot of product from Wolverine.

Since I met and knew most of the sales reps through drag racing, it was a pretty easy thing to do to take on all the other major product lines, which we eventually did.

Author: When was the speed shop hitting on all eight cylinders?

George: I was extremely busy throughout the course of my entire racing career. You're at the races, you're winning. Remember, this was before we had the JEGSs and the Summits of the world. I remember times when customers would be lined up outside the door. That went on for many years until the bigness of the internet and the other shops that now do mail-order stuff took over the market.

Today, the speed shop is practically non-existent. We still do a little bit of business in parts sales, but we [still] have a strong machine shop business. A lot of the good machine shops aren't around anymore. It's kind of hard for a guy who has a nice numbers-matching engine that he doesn't want anybody to screw up and wants it done right; they come here from all over. We probably do more out-of-town work than we do in town.

Right now, we're probably one of the premier places for doing Boss 429s. We do them for customers from all across the country. If you'll remember, I raced that engine with Ford for many years. I understand them greatly, and I make some unique parts for them. I'm not saying that's our strongest-selling engine line, but we do a lot of them. In fact, we had nine of them going together at one time.

Author: When did you decide to get serious about your drag racing career?

George: I don't think there was just any day that I started drag racing. I was mechanically inclined from the early days. The first engine I overhauled was an old

At Ford's urging in 1967, George parked the Willys, built this supercharged 427 SOHC 1967 Mustang known as the Malco Gasser, and forever changed the face of supercharged Gas coupe and sedan racing as we know it.

Fordson tractor. I was in the fourth grade at the time, so I had to be about 10 years old. I just like mechanical stuff.

In 1941, my folks built the place next door, and since they didn't have a high school nearby, I had to go to Weber High in Dayton. Would you believe at 14 years old, the State of Ohio granted me a driver's license so that I could go to school? Although that's somewhat unusual, I kept my nose clean, and I was allowed to drive to and from school and to and from work.

Then, one thing led to another, and I started building a street rod, raced them, and things kind of went from there.

Author: Where did you work?

George: I was an apprentice tool maker at Patterson Co-op School. Those were the days when you had to think and make. There was no such thing as going to your local speed shop. I those days, your parts supplier was the local salvage yard. You'd pick up what you needed and modify it to do whatever you wanted it to do.

Author: Was your first car your 1934 Ford?

George: No. My first car was a 1921 Chevrolet, but that was just to get around. Then, I got a 1937 Chevy and then a 1939 Chevy. The '39 was the one I started playing around with and modifying a little bit. When I graduated from high school, my grandmother gave me a thousand dollars, which was a lot of money way back then. In 1950, that was half the price of a brand-new Ford convertible. My father reluctantly signed for me, and with paying half down, I agreed to make payments for 12 months.

Author: So, did you leave the 1950 Ford stock, or did you start modifying it to suit your tastes?

George: My dad was quite conservative, and he couldn't understand why I would put on these big exhaust pipes. He couldn't understand why I would do that to a new car. Well, I'd be out street racing with it. On Main Street, we had this big monument, and we would race up one side of the street and swing it [the car] around and race back down the other.

Author: I bet you got in a lot of trouble with the Dayton Police Department for doing that?

George: No. Would you believe these street races were broadcast on WING AM? They had a studio located inside the theater downtown, and they would broadcast them on the radio. Of course, you didn't do that too often, but the police were a lot easier to get along with than they would be today. You didn't have the traffic, and the cars weren't as fast. We also used to gather out on some of the more-desolate roads, and we would have informal get-togethers. Then, when there got to be too many cars, the police would come out and say, "You boys have to break it up now and go home."

And that would be the end if it. Things were much more relaxed then they are today.

George's Speed Shop was founded in 1952 and was built on what was then the Montgomery family farm. However, today the business sits in the middle of a rural Dayton, Ohio, neighborhood.

George and his son Greg greet us as we walk through the front door. George's Speed Shop showroom is like a museum with all of his many awards, trophies, and 22 national record certificates that are proudly displayed for friends and would-be customers to see.

Author: What high school was it that you graduated from?

George: I went to Kaiser High School in Dayton for two years. Then, I went to Patterson Co-Op School for the last two years of my schooling. I would work two weeks and go to school for two weeks. My Co-op job was at Dayton Lawnmower Company, where I rebuilt single-cylinder lawnmower engines. So, it's always been one type of engine or another all of my life.

Author: When did you build your 1934 Ford coupe?

George: It had to have been in the early 1950s. I can't

really remember where I got the car or how much I paid for it. But I made it into a street rod. It had a flathead in it of course. I took the car to Bonneville in 1952 and ran 117 mph, and that car today is in "Big Daddy" Don Garlits's Museum of Drag Racing in Ocala, Florida, and Don absolutely loves it.

Author: What records did you set with the '34?

George: Oh, just about everything that you could. That was actually a B/Gas car, and there were days when it would win Top Eliminator.

Author: You were a wizard with blowers?

George: When I started playing around with superchargers, that was the big breakthrough. I got a couple of McCullough superchargers in the [speed] shop and learned how to make them put out a lot more boost than they would normally make. I had to change a lot of internal parts to make them withstand the extra RPM and the extra wear.

Then, I went to GMC blowers. Pete Robinson and I had become good friends, and we collaborated on our own version of an early GMC blower but better. I did all the machine work, and we went halfsies on the patterns. Money was tight in those days. I made my own end plates. I even made the intake manifold to mount the 6.71 blower onto my Cadillac V-8. I made a lot of unique parts. For example, take the Le Salle 3-speed transmission: I made a motor plate for it out of aluminum. Anything I could do to make things lighter and stronger, I did. I just put more thought into what I was doing, and I surrounded myself with some good people.

Author: What year did you acquire your 1933 Willys coupe, and what did you pay for it?

George: In October 1958, I paid $100 for it. Remember, at that time, it was only a 25-year-old car. I mainly bought that car because of the shorter wheelbase. Our tires were kind of pitiful, and so were a lot of the tracks. The car had better weight transfer than the '34. That was the idea behind that.

Author: A year later, you won US Nationals in Detroit with it?

George: Yes, that was the following September. That was the maiden outing for that car, and it's remarkable that it did as well as it did. That's where I took that 250-pound concrete spare tire that I had and mounted it in the back where the traditional 1933 Willys spare tire went. That cut my ET by half a second because we couldn't use the power that we had with the tires that were available at the time and the track conditions. Well, the NHRA quickly outlawed that. I mean, it wasn't hidden. It just went on right where the stock spare tire went. From that point on, I made a lot of unique improvements throughout my entire career.

Here's the business end of George's Speed Shop. Technician John Gumbert bolts a set of Air Flow Research (AFR) cylinder heads onto an in-progress big-block Chevrolet engine.

Author: And you won the Ford Falcon Ranchero at the NHRA Nationals in 1960?

George: Yes, that was 1960, and I still have it. That was the last year they held the NHRA Nationals in Detroit?

Author: Let's talk about the chronology behind the development of the Willys.

George: Well, I started out with the Cadillac engine because it had a lot of torque and made a lot of power. But in some instances, that wasn't necessarily a good thing with the lousy tires we had and sometimes lousy track conditions.

Then, I went to the small-block Chevrolet in 1963. The NHRA made a rules change where you could run a certain weight per cubic inch, so I was better off with the smaller-displacement engine and much less weight.

Then, when I went with the 427 SOHC Ford, I had to add weight again to stay legal!

Author: How many years did you run the Willys in AA/GS?

George: That would have been up to the spring of 1967. That's when I came out with the *Malco Gasser* [Mustang]. That car was a game changer. By that time, the power was up there, and the tires were better—so much so that aerodynamics were becoming a factor. The Willys was probably one of the first drag cars (Connie Kalitta's *Bounty Hunter* AA/FD was the very first) to be tested in the Ford wind tunnel, and we found out that without the benefit of a few well-placed spoilers (the NHRA wouldn't allow that), the car would fly at approximately 168 mph.

At that time, I'm with Ford, and I've got some of the best engineers around me. When you're surrounded with people like that, you've got to be smart enough to ask the right questions and understand what to do. And it

George's Speed Shop was the Buick V-6 spec engine builder for the Indy Lights Racing Series that ran from 1986 to 2002. How would you like to get your hands on one of these engines and slap one in your street rod?

wasn't just one or two engineers, they had engineers from IndyCar, NASCAR, and all different facets of Ford's motorsports programs. So, we could kind of share some of the information that we learned from all of them.

The biggest thing I learned was that the Willys's days were numbered. That's when I went back to Dayton and built the *Malco Gasser*. That was a genuine race car. It had a lot of trick suspension pieces that you could adjust, and the car had a lot of Ford engineering input.

Author: Let's shift gears for a moment and talk about your Buick Indy Lights engine program.

George: In about 1986, I had become fed up with drag racing. When I was doing some of the development work on my twin turbocharged Boss 429 engine project, it was done in Indianapolis because of the Switzer turbocharger people. I used Sonny Meyer's shop [Patrick Racing] in Indianapolis to do some of the dyno development work. Then, when the Indy Lights program formed (Mr. Patrick was putting that program together), I called Sonny one day and said, "Sonny, how are you going to do all these Buicks?"

He said, "I can't, would you like that job?"

One thing led to another. Of course, I had to be approved by Buick's Joe Negri, and we ended up doing that for 16 years. That was a big, big job taking care of 100 engines for 30 teams. Being spec engines, they were sealed, and nobody was allowed to work on them. Either myself or my son Greg was required to be at every race, and we guaranteed each and every one of those engines for three races or a thousand miles with practically zero engine failures.

Of course, Buick was behind that program 100 percent. In fact, Buick gave me an award (a gold-plated

torque wrench) for having 100 races all trouble-free. To do that, we had two dynos going all week long.

Author: Getting back to the speed shop for a moment, who would you say is your customer today? Who comes in to George's and buys stuff?

George: It isn't like what it used to be. It seems to me the popular thing anymore is when they get some oddball thing they can't find someplace else, so they come here. I don't need to work anymore anyhow, but I'm still around here to help my son do the machine work. I'm probably more at peace doing that than I am doing anything else.

And Son . . .

The following is a conversation with George's Speed Shop founder George Montgomery's son Greg and author Bob McClurg. Greg is chief engine builder and a jack of all trades at the family business.

Author: How old were you when you first started off in the speed shop business?

Greg: Actually, I was 4-and-a-half to 5 years old. Like my father, I'm an only child, and I really wanted to help Dad out. I originally started sweeping floors, but things kind of accelerated from there. After Dad won the 1959 NHRA Nationals, we really started getting busy. In 1961 or 1962, when Dad and Pete Robinson were doing the blowers, we had hundreds of blower plates stacked up, and I was drilling all the holes out at age five. They were made out of magnesium, and Dad told me not to mess any up because they were valuable. There were magnesium chips flying everywhere.

Author: Did you ever have any aspirations to race?

Greg: I never drove, but I was always Dad's helper. Believe me, when we pulled into the drags, we were always feared. I mean, nobody wanted to race Ohio George!

Author: You said you were chief engine builder here at George's Speed Shop?

Greg: In 1986, we got the contract to build all the Buick spec engines for the Indy Lights Series. That was a huge job taking care of all those motors here at the shop. I was part of the program from start to finish, I would help build them, dyno them, and tune them. Then, after that, we started doing a lot of different engine projects, including tractor-puller engines and muscle car engines. In fact, we just took a Boss 429 off the dyno last night.

Author: Never a dull moment, eh?

Greg: We have a really good name here.

Author: What does it mean to you to be working here in the family business rather than having to deal with some crummy job that you hate going to everyday?

Greg: Well, it's job security for one. I was at the mall about two months ago at the local bookstore buying some books, and the clerk at the checkout counter and I got to talking. He was a college-age guy, and he asked me what I did for a living?

I said, "I work at a speed shop."

He looked at me with a crazy look on his face and said, "What's a speed shop?"

Now, any young man from the 1950s, 1960s, or 1970s knew what a speed shop was, but this guy didn't have a clue.

Author: Is there a third-generation Montgomery waiting the wings?

Greg: I have a son named Christopher. He went to college due to my father's generosity and got his degree in automotive engineering. He was hired by Honda Motor Company of America, and he's moved right up to the ladder. For his age (30 years old), he's already been to Tokyo a number of times.

Christopher works out of the Marysville, Ohio, plant where the Honda Accords are made, and they had a big

upper-level management meeting because the president from Honda of Tokyo had flown over. They gathered all the white-collar workers in one room, and Chris was standing there with all his fellow workers. The president was giving his speech in broken English, and he looked over at Chris about halfway through his speech and said, "How is Ohio George?"

Chris was overwhelmed that the president of Honda Automobiles was actually an Ohio George fan! So, Chris stepped forward, bowed, and told the president that his grandfather was fine and doing well. So, I guess the president of Honda Motor Company seriously follows motorsports, and he knew Christopher was on his team.

Glasgo & Company
Akron, Ohio

Address: 2098 S. Main St., Akron, OH 44301
Phone: 330-773-4004
Website: glasgoperformance.com

Glasgo & Company was founded by Tom Glasgo, who grew up working at the family Sohio gas station.

"Back then [when Glasgo & Company was founded], Akron was a big rubber town, and if you were working in the tire manufacturing business, it meant you were making good money," said Tom's son John Glasgo. "It seemed like everybody had a performance car back then, and they would take them to my dad, and he would tune them up. Anything that was cool, he worked on."

Tom Glasgo was particularly *attuned* (if you'll excuse the pun) to high-performance Pontiacs and was known as one of the best Tin Indian tuners in the tri-state area.

"The 1960s Pontiacs originally came with vacuum linkage, and Dad would convert them over to mechanical. He would also rework the distributors and re-jet and super tune the carburetors to perfection. Tom Glasgo was also pretty adept at making L88 Corvettes and big-block Chevelle's run. When a car left his shop, it was perfect."

Speaking of fast Pontiacs, Tom Glasgo campaigned several back in the day, as Paul fondly recalled.

"Dad campaigned a pretty mean 1964 GTO, and he followed that with an equally strong running 1967 GTO. Later in the 1970s, he and a buddy

Ohio George raced Fords throughout the remainder of his driving career. One of his most successful cars was this 1969 twin-turbocharged Boss 429 Mustang. It set the drag racing world on its ear (and won Best Engineered at the NHRA Springnationals) when it bombed the NHRA record so much so that the NHRA threatened to handicap the metal-flake red Mach 1 Mustang if he didn't slow the car down.

Glasgo & Company (formerly Glasgo & Sons) is just a stone's throw away from the original Firestone Tire & Rubber Company factory in Akron, Ohio.

For being roughly only 1,200 square feet in size, there's a lot going on at Glasgo & Company. In the foreground is the roofline of a 1970 Chevelle SS 454 big-block, a 1958 Corvette occupies a different area of the shop, and an under-restoration Pontiac GTO occupies another.

named John Heagle campaigned a 1970 Ram Air IV GTO and did quite well with that car."

It seemed that everyone loved Tom Glasgo and respected him for what he did.

"Dad had a great personality," Paul said. "It seemed like the local car guys just couldn't get enough of him. Even after business hours, it was nonstop cars at our house, and there was always something cool sitting in the driveway. He was a wealth of information and taught us everything we know. Working with him was better than going to any mechanics trade school. He was good at showing us what to do and what not to do."

In 1988, Tom and the boys moved to their current location and continued to grow the business. Sadly, Tom Glasgo passed away, but that same passion that made him famous around Akron area car circles was passed down to his sons John and Paul.

"My first car was a 1966 Pontiac GTO that Dad talked me into buying," Paul said. "We took the car completely apart, and he showed me how to put everything back together again the right way. I went from showing that car to racing it, and that aspect of the business just kept getting bigger and bigger to where it's become an addition that you just can't get away from."

These days, the Glasgo brothers run a series of potent Pontiacs and compete in events such as the Pure Stock Drags, Muscle Car Drags, National Street Car Association (NSCA) Super Car Showdown, or any event that focuses on muscle cars. In the process, Glasgo and Company has become *the* premier muscle car tuner shop in Ohio and specializes in everything from performance tune-ups to complete engine builds. Stop on by, say hello to John and Paul, and see for yourself.

Greg's Speed Shop
Waupaca, Wisconsin

Address: 4259 E. Gate Dr., Waupaca, WI 54981
Phone: 920-867-2939
Website: gregsspeedshopllc.com
Email: gregsspeedshop@gmail.com

Traveling east on Highway 10 from Appleton, Wisconsin, into the sleepy little town of Waupaca, a huge billboard on the left side of the highway just before exit 254 proudly proclaims, "Greg's Speed Shop, LLC: Full Restorations, Custom Fabrication, All Mechanical Needs, Pin Up and Vintage Clothing!"

Dedicated in March 2012, Greg Stelse's massive 20,000-square-foot facility is rapidly becoming one of the state's premier hot rod shops.

"I was just 16 years old when the high-performance bug bit me," Greg said. "You might say that when it comes to fast cars, street rods, and custom cars, I'm definitely addicted."

Greg's father, Larry Stelse, and stepfather, Gary Sands, were his two greatest influences.

"Dad [Larry Stelse] was a drag racer most of his life and ran a number of hot cars, including a 1962 Impala SS 409 with dual quads and 4-speed and a 1962 Corvette 327 Fuelie," Greg said. "I learned the mechanical aspects of the hobby from him. When I was a student at New London Senior High School, I was the guy that everybody turned to when they needed to have their car worked on. I was always changing cams, building engines, installing blowers, rebuilding transmissions, and that kind of stuff. I'm one of those people who just can't leave well enough

Exit 254 of Wisconsin Highway 10 South marks the home of Greg's Speed Shop, while the actual physical address is 4259 E. Gate Dr., Waupaca, Wisconsin. Owners Greg and Leah Stelse and staff pose for our cameras. Pictured (from left to right) are Tom Stelse, Bill Peters, Jason Starks, Leah and Greg Stelse, Rebecca Livermore, Dustin Stelse, and Bart Kuhnke.

Street rod enthusiasts and custom car geeks are in for a real treat when they walk into Greg's showroom. It's like stepping back in time.

Greg couldn't find a vintage Texaco gas station that would fit inside his showroom, so he built one. Parked inside the service bay is an in-progress 1962 Cadillac restoration.

Just in case you were wondering, that chassis, complete with the blown 351 Windsor Ford engine will ultimately be mated to 1940 Ford sheet metal.

alone. If you were to hand me a brand-new carburetor, I would immediately start fiddling with it until the engine it's installed on ran absolutely perfect."

When it came to paint and bodywork, Greg's stepfather, Gary Sands, was his greatest influence.

"After graduating from high school, I started doing body work and became a full-time painter," Greg said. "That lasted for a number of years, and I even got caught up in the customizing craze chopping tops and all that kind of crazy stuff. Unfortunately, I couldn't make enough money to support my family, and at age 20, I was becoming quite frustrated. My father drove a truck his whole life and said, "You need to get into truck driving and start making yourself some serious money."

So, that's what I did for the next 27 years."

Greg and his wife, Leah, started New London, Wisconsin's GS Trucking LLC with just one truck but ultimately expanded the operation to include a total of 18.

"It was quite a grind, but the rewards were obvious," Greg said. "One of the side benefits of driving a truck is that you get to drive around the country, checking out all the cool cars that are lying around. By 2009, I had four full-time guys in my shop restoring cars, and I knew that was the direction I wanted to take. It was just something I ultimately had to do. That's where my heart lies."

However, the real motivation came from when Greg and Leah visited the Henry Ford Museum, also known as the Edison Institute, at Greenfield Village in Dearborn, Michigan.

"It was such a powerful feeling," Greg said. "The minute I walked in there, I instantly knew what I was going to do to the rest of my life."

The actual work area inside Greg's Speed Shop is clean, well-lit, and large enough to accommodate a couple dozen cars at once.

When you exit the showroom, the speed shop itself is located on the right. Greg and Leah Stelse stand behind the counter. Greg's Speed Shop carries a wide variety of name-brand hot rod parts, including the full line of Edelbrock and Holley components, Aeroquip, American Racing, Centerforce, Towel City, Motor State Distributing, Schoenfeld Headers, Hooker, and others.

Greg Stelse's high-tech PPG paint room allows technicians the option to computer match virtually any color under the rainbow.

Greg's Speed Shop employs 11 full-time employees, and when you walk through the front door, it's more like walking into a museum. The main building is jam-packed with oil, gas, and hot rod memorabilia. It's absolutely mind-boggling. Furthermore, Greg also has a 4,800-square-foot satellite shop (in a manner of speaking) in Iola, Wisconsin, which is the site of the annual Iola Car Show and Swap Meet. Of particular interest is that he and customizing great Gene Winfield chopped a 1951 Chevrolet live at the 2018 event, and they're slated to perform even more radical surgery on the old Stovebolt at the 2020 event.

"Greg's Speed Shop is about the average person," Greg said. "That's who we really focus on. Right now, working on the cars [Stelse estimated that his shop turns out between 35 and 40 cars per year] far surpasses parts sales. However, after finally getting hooked up with all the right WDs—Motor States Distributors, which carries and sells all the right kinds of parts (Moroso, Schoenfeld Headers, Centerforce, Holley, Hooker, Doug Nash, Edelbrock, Air Equip, NOS, etc.)—I'm confident that particular segment of the business is going to grow and flourish.

"We particularly excel in service. In the last year, we've sold and installed a minimum of 75 carburetors on cars. We also do a lot of intake, alternator, starter, header/exhaust system, and clutch and transmission installations, and we build turn-key engines too. At the present, we're booked two months ahead, which I believe is a good problem to have."

Greg's Speed Shop technicians Tony Stelse and Jason Shanks smooth out the exterior of this work-in-progress Chevelle street machine.

JBA Speed Shop Inc.
San Diego, California

Address: 5675 Kearny Villa Rd., San Diego, CA 92123
Phone: 858-495-3395
Website: jbaspeedshop.com

San Diego, California, gearhead J. Bittle holds a Bachelor of Science degree in sociology from Texas A&M University, which happens to boast the oldest and most active student body–run sports car clubs in the country.

"The experience that I received from college covered the gauntlet of racing disciplines," said Bittle. "On that campus, you were exposed to domestic [cars] and imports, drag racing and autocrossing, on- and off-road, and then there was Texas World Speedway (TWS) just 6 miles from the A&M campus. When I wasn't studying, I spent most of my time there. You might say I grew up racing the high-banked ovals."

During his senior year at Texas A&M, Bittle ascended to the presidency of the Texas A&M Sports Car Club and built a huge membership. In the process, Bittle also became actively involved in the local chapter of the SCCA and was a charter member and the Texas Regional Representative of an exciting new car enthusiast club. This club was dedicated to the cars that Carroll Shelby created for the Ford Motor Company in the mid-1960s (namely the 289 and 427 Cobra and the Shelby GT350 and Shelby GT500 Mustangs) and was officially known as the Shelby American Automobile Club (SAAC).

After graduating from college, Bittle opened his first speed shop in College Station, Texas, called Total Performance. It was devoted to both general and high-performance automotive repair work. Many late nights of race prep occurred in those service bays. However, Bittle longed to return to his native California. So, in 1982, he and his newly minted bride, Vickie, relocated to suburban San Diego.

"I got a job working at Drew Ford as a performance specialist," Bittle said. "Ford Motor Company was just getting back into high performance again. The 5.0L Mustang V-8 had just been reintroduced as the GT along with a totally new turbocharged Mustang inline 4-cylinder package known as the SVO. At Ford, big things in marketing performance were really starting to happen."

Bittle's involvement with Drew Ford's blossoming Ford SVO and Ford Motorsport parts program put him in direct contact with J. Walter Thompson and mentor Austin C. Craig, the boys in the Big Glass House in Dearborn, and set the stage for even bigger and better things. Part of Bittle's one-on-one relationship with Ford led to the creation of a Ford SVO training film that showed Ford dealers how to effectively sell performance cars on the local level.

In 1985, Bittle left Drew Ford to open J. Bittle American (JBA). The new enterprise quickly became one of the largest Ford SVO/Ford Motorsport warehouses in the country from 1988 to 1992 and made SVO's prestigious top-10 dealer list. In the process, J. Bittle American gained national attention with performance enthusiast magazines, including *Road & Track*, *Car Craft*, *Autoweek*, *MotorTrend*, *Popular Hot Rodding*, and *Fabulous Mustangs*.

"We were one of the original West Coast warehouses (along with Ford Power Parts' Ron Miler, Kaufmann Products' Chris Kaufmann, and Maier Racing's Bill Maier) to get into the national mail-order of Ford Performance parts," Bittle said.

Along the way, Bittle helped another would-be Ford great named Steve Saleen. In 1986, Steve wanted to establish Saleen Performance Parts in conjunction with La Habra, California's Burch Ford, and from 1986 to 1988, JBA also functioned as a Saleen Performance Parts warehouse and parts division.

In the later 1980s, exhaust-header manufacturing became a new priority at JBA.

"Early on, we realized that you can't build performance without a free-flowing exhaust," Bittle said. "In 1986, Bittle introduced his first header, a 1¾-inch-diameter big-tube, full-length race header for the Shelby GT350 Mustang. At the time, there were a number of small-block Ford cylinder head applications available, and we made our headers to fit those popular cylinder heads (TFS, Root/SVO, J302 etc.)."

Directly on the heels of the JBA Shelby GT350 1¾-diameter big-tube, full-length header was the 1987 release of the JBA 5.0L 1⅝-inch-diameter, big-tube shorty

JBA Speed Center calls San Diego, California, home. The 25,000-square-foot facility is staffed by 20 highly trained and dedicated JBA technicians.

As this photo illustrates, when it comes to high performance, JBA doesn't discriminate.

header manufactured and distributed throughout the country. It was the first of many innovations that JBA was responsible for within the fast-growing 5.0L late-model Mustang marketplace.

Next, JBA developed a full line of chassis and suspension components for the Fox-platform Mustangs that became extremely popular. In fact, JBA won *Road & Track* and *MotorTrend*'s Super Car Shootout, which included handling, braking, and top-speed competitions that JBA Speed Shop participated in with its JBA Dominator GTA and GTB wide body (25th-anniversary Mustang project car) Mustangs.

In 1990, Bittle took his company in yet another direction with the acquisition of John Hamilton's engine-building shop, which was moved from San Antonio, Texas, to San Diego, California, and renamed JBA Racing Engines.

By 1993, JBA's header operation had grown to a point that the company was split into three separate divisions: JBA Headers, JBA Service Center (later renamed JBA Speed Shop), and JBA Racing Engines. Simultaneously, the entire JBA operation moved to a new 15,000-square-foot facility at 7149 Mission Rd., San Diego, California, 92140. As the Mustang aftermarket was becoming more and more saturated in 1994 with new entrepreneurial entities, Bittle diversified.

"Initially we branched into the General Motors' product line using our header division to open the door," Bittle said.

In 1994, JBA released California Air Resources Board (CARB)–compliant shorty headers for 350-ci small-block Chevrolet Camaros and Firebirds. However, JBA's best-selling GM part number turned out to be for the 305/350 small-block engine 1988 to 1995 Chevrolet pickup.

"We built the business up to the point where we now have 450 part numbers in our JBA header product lineup," Bittle said. "We cover all Ford, GM, and Chrysler V-8 applications for big-block and small-block engines as well as many V-6 applications and select 4-cylinder applications like the Ford Focus.

"Basically, we make headers for all sport-utility applications, S-10s, Dakotas, Durangos, Explorers, Mountaineers, Rangers, and F-150s. We've found that in the header marketplace there was an opportunity for a quality smog-legal header product, and we've addressed that."

Bittle's patented Fire Cone collector was a directional-flow device in a header system that helped make a large majority of JBA header products (particularly space-restrictive shorty, cat-forward-design headers) comparable in power to full-length headers. They were EPA compliant and emissions legal in all 50 states. In the early 2000s, JBA Headers became the official header supplier for Carroll Shelby Automobiles, Roush Racing, Steeda Autosport, and Scott Drake Mustang Parts.

By 2001, the company once again experienced growing pains and expanded to maintain a second facility located at 7149 Convoy St., San Diego, California, 92123, for the speed shop.

In 2008, JBA underwent a refocusing and restructuring, including the sale of the JBA Headers division, which had built a 36,000-square-foot manufacturing plant in Tijuana, Mexico, to Pertronix Company in San Dimas, California.

"You can still buy any JBA header system through JBA Speed Shop and have it installed as well," Bittle said. "The exhaust fabrication department includes the same team that developed the JBA exhaust product line."

In 2009, Bittle launched GreenSpeedCo, a division of JBA solely dedicated to merging old-school cool with

JBA's Engine Building division is led by Chief Engine Builder John Elderhorst, who checks the deck height of a big-block Chevrolet engine.

J. Bittle's dyno technician Bruce Tucker flexes the muscles of this late-model 5.0L Mustang using (quite appropriately) JBA's Mustang chassis dynamometer.

JBA technician Gary Wilkey performs a three-angle-cut valve job on a set of Ford cylinder heads.

modern, emissions-legal, high-performance electronic engine management and powertrain technology.

"Since 1992, J. Bittle companies have been leaders in optimizing performance cars with innovative and patented JBA technologies and products," Bittle said. "With more than 50 CARB Executive Order D-216–approved applications (beginning with the first aftermarket CARB–approved small-block Ford cylinder head, high-lift rocker arms, and Fire Cone–patented JBA shorty headers), this continuing effort to combine EPA/CARB compliance with fuel efficiency and performance while supporting the industries' growing emissions protocols has kept JBA relevant. GreenSpeedCo is our commitment to distributing environmentally friendly products and technologies while maximizing drivetrain efficiencies."

An example of GreenSpeedCo technology is JBA's new 2015 to 2021 Shelby GT350 supercharger kit, which is currently under CARB application testing for the 5.2L Voodoo. This system joins JBA 2012 to 2013 Boss 302 JBA/

The Baer cross-drilled and slotted front disc brake rotor kit is installed on a 2019 Shelby GT500 Mustang.

Vortech supercharger kit as further evidence of JBA Speed Shop's ongoing effort to push the high-performance envelope. Other examples of GreenSpeedCo technology in action include Kyle Madsen's 1969 Chevelle with LS7 power, a '57 Chevy Bel Air convertible with LS3 power, a 1964 Ford Ranchero with Coyote 5.0L power, a 1968 Mustang GT/CS with 5.4L DOHC Boss 302 power, and a 1968 Dodge Charger R/T with Viper V-10 power.

"At JBA, lean is mean . . . and green," Bittle said.

The JBA Speed Shop showroom is chock full of name-brand speed equipment.

"We're using technology driven from decades of experience in tuning performance vehicles for maximum efficiency."

In 2010, Bittle again moved to an even-larger 25,000-square-foot facility (two buildings) at 5675 Kearny Villa Rd., San Diego, California, 92123. The company is concentrated on growing the GreenSpeedCo, JBA Speed Shop, and JBA Engine Building divisions.

JBA's well-stocked speed shop, which is managed by Bittle's son, Austin "Secret Sauce" Bittle, is chock full of brand-name speed equipment, including Holley, Edelbrock, Moroso, NOS, Wilwood, Vortech, Hotchkiss Suspension, ARP, Classic Restoration & Performance Parts, Earls, Fel-Pro, Ford Racing, Lunati Cams, MagnaFlow, Mickey Thompson tires, Mr. Gasket, NOS, Pertronix-JBA Headers, Roush, Vortech, Paxton, VP Racing Fuels, and countless others.

"South of Los Angeles, we consider ourselves to be the premier performance and installation center for Chevrolet, Ford, and Chrysler performance cars, trucks, and SUVs," Bittle said. "We specialize in everything from dyno tuning to complete engine and powertrain builds. With a staff of 20 dedicated technicians, our services are practically all inclusive."

JBA technicians pose for this 2019 photo. Standing fifth from the right is CFO Vickie Bittle with her husband CEO J. Bittle standing behind her. The man in the red shirt is JBA Service and Parts Director Austin Bittle.

When it comes to high performance, Bittle is totally hands on. Case in point: Jay races the former Hinchcliff & Ross 302 Ford tunnel-port Mustang coupe at select SAAC and SCCA vintage racing events with great success.

However, Bittle isn't always content with going around in circles. The San Diego, California, speed merchant also campaigns this 500-plus-ci 1966 Mustang fastback at NMCA events.

J&M Speed Center
Riverside, California

Address: 3230 Motor Cir., Riverside, CA 02504
Phone: 1-800-350-7110
Website: jmspeedcenter.com

J&M Speed Center originally began in 1957 as Phil's Muffler Shop and was located on North Main Street in Riverside, California. Founder Phil Braybrooks, a hot rodder from the get-go, was friends with Dean Moon, Vic Edelbrock Sr., and Harvey Crane, and Braybrooks started selling their wares to racers around the Inland Empire as sort of a side hustle.

However, after a few years, the speed equipment business surpassed the muffler shop business, so Braybrooks

J&M Speed Center was an extension of Riverside, California's Phil's Muffler Shop, which was founded in 1957 by the late Phil Braybrooks. Braybrooks was a jack of all trades and an accomplished master at just about anything automotive. At one point, he had aspirations of competing in the Daytona 500 and even built a 1962 409-ci Chevy Impala to do so. (Photo Courtesy J&M Speed Center)

rented a building on new-car row at 2726 N. Main St. in Riverside and opened J&M Speed Center.

"Phil started selling speed equipment, but it was mostly all on consignment, and it just sort of grew from there," said Phil's widow, Pat.

In the mid-1960s, all the new car dealers relocated to Auto Center Drive right off of Interstate 91, and Phil went right along with them.

The following is a conversation with Pat Braybrooks (Phil's widow), Lisa Somody (Phil's daughter and J&M Speed Shop general manager), Mike Braybrooks (Phil's son), and author Bob McClurg.

Author: Who are the *J* and *M* in J&M Speed Center?

Lisa: When Dad had the muffler shop, people used to come in all the time and ask for Phil, which at times made getting a day's work done near impossible. When he started J&M Speed Center, he didn't want to have people coming in asking for Phil all the time, so that's why he chose J&M. He had some friends who owned J&S Speed Center in Westminster. Another one had Glendale Speed Center in Glendale. And the first Super Shops was in San Bernardino, so that's why he chose J&M."

Author: What were Phil Braybrooks's racing aspirations?

Mike: Dad started out with motorcycles. In 1962, he built a 409 Chevrolet to run on the NASCAR circuit, and he even had aspirations of taking the car to Daytona. Then, he met his future wife, Pat (Bunker), who worked out at Norton Air Force Base, and everything changed. Two weeks before the race, he had to decide whether he was going to run Daytona or marry my mother.

Author note: Eventually the newly minted Mrs. Braybrooks quit her job at Norton Air Force Base and went to work full time at the J&M Speed Center.

Pat: By then [1967], Phil was deeply involved in drag racing. He bought Doug Thorley's *Chevy 2 Much*, and we went racing with that car. Back then, it was a lot easier going drag racing on the weekends, and you could have a good time doing it. Then, all of a sudden, they started showing up with these big tractor-trailer rigs and big-time sponsors. Just a regular little-guy speed shop like us couldn't compete with that, so we just went back to selling the parts.

Author: J&M sponsored a lot of racers back in the day. Can you name a few?

Mike: There were Walt and Jim Marshall. They ran a '56 Chevy gasser, then a 1941 Willys, and later they bought Bill Bagshaw's Hemi Dart. All three cars ran under the J&M banner. Fuel Altered racer the late Leroy Chadderton was also J&M sponsored. In fact, our name was on his car when he ran the first 6-second run clocked by an AA/Fuel Altered at 6.77, 201.34 mph at Lions Drag Strip. It seemed J&M sponsored all the local guys around here.

Author: Can you tell us about the growth cycle of J&M from muffler shop to where you are today?

Lisa: It's been a steady climb all the way through the 1960s, and into the 1970s. The early smog laws kind of slowed us down a little bit in the late 1970s but not that much. When the Super Shops closed down [in the late 1970s], we experienced a huge surge in business. We also had a store in San Bernardino, and we were going to expand out to Orange County, but Dad changed his mind. He liked the one on one with the customers and didn't want to lose that.

Author: Lisa, how is it that you became the general manager of J&M Speed Center?

Lisa: As a 16-year-old girl, having a dad who owned the local hot rod shop made me pretty popular with the boys. I was sort of a prodigy. I was the one who would hang out in the garage with Dad. I was his little tomboy who loved racing and loved going to the drags. When I was 16, I started running parts for my dad between the two stores. At the time, I was also racing go-karts, and my dad, my mom, and I would run the local circuits.

Author: Did you win any big races?

Lisa: I won a few.

The father and son team of Walt and Jim Marshall have been loyal J&M customers for years and have campaigned a number of J&M-sponsored race cars with their hard-charging 1941 Willys B/Gas coupe being one of the more memorable ones.

Out of all the J&M-sponsored hot rods, the late Leroy Chadderton's late-model Hemi-engine AA/Fuel Altered Model T roadster was the one that vaulted to the national stage when it clocked a 6.77 at 201.34 mph at Lions Drag Strip at a time when the Awful Awfuls were still clocking low 7s. (Photo Courtesy J&M Speed Center)

Mike: She's way too modest. Let me tell you the whole story. When Lisa was a little girl, they put her in a pool, and she learned to swim within a week and was swimming national-event lap times. When she was 13, they put her on a horse, and a month later, she had offers to compete in the girls' division of Pro Rodeo. They put her in a go-kart, and two years later [1988] she's the multi-class Interstate Kart Series (IKS) national champion. She raced around the world and set records at every track she ran for like a year straight.

Lisa: I was very fortunate. I think it was a combination of my driving ability and my dad making sure that my karts ran strong and stayed together. I was one of three Americans to be invited over to Australia and New Zealand to represent the US in their karting series.

Author: And you worked at the store?

Lisa: Cars have always been in my heart all these years, and I love being around them and car people. Dad started me out in the shipping department. I took out trash, swept the floors, filled the Coke machine, and all the usual stuff.

Then, I went to work for a sporting goods store for 10 years and learned a lot about retail sales and marketing. When I returned 24 years ago, Dad ended up giving me one of our product lines (Doug Thorley Headers) to learn, advertise, market, and sell it online. That first year, we stocked about 10 to 15 sets or part numbers. After about a year of my taking on that line, we were stocking about 300 sets and selling over $1 million a year just from selling Doug Thorley Headers.

It's kind of nice running the family business. I was born and raised in Riverside. I live about 2 miles away from my parents. My dad was my best friend and taught me the business from the ground up. Over the years, I've done everything in the business. I do the accounting. I do the purchasing. I do the hiring. I negotiate all the deals with the manufacturers, and I attend the Performance Warehouse Association (PWA) and SEMA Shows. Over the years, I've met all the key players and key manufacturers in the speed equipment industry.

Author: Do you publish a catalog? If so, when was your first one?

Lisa: We published our first catalog about 16 to 20 years ago. We're also online at jmspeedcenter.com.

Author: Do you know the ratio of walk-in sales to online sales?

Lisa: We're definitely still the brick-and-mortar, or walk-in, trade. We do wholesale and retail. Right now, our retail's a lot higher than our wholesale as far as percentage is, but that can change. I credit our still being here to our father. Every time we got ahead, he put the money back into the business.

Pat: We also have another daughter named Jenni. She's in the fashion industry and not into cars. In fact, one month, Jenni was on the front cover of *Teen* magazine and Lisa was on the cover of *Crash & Burn* magazine.

Author: *Crash & Burn*? Really? That's great!

Lisa: I'll have to send a copy of that to you. It's a go-kart magazine, and there's this guy in the first corner of a race, and we're all crashing, and this guy is still going upside down. You don't lift. We were helmet to helmet.

Author: At one time, J&M did speed equipment

The Braybrooks built a speed shop dynasty, which at one time had two shops with a third in the works. However, with a growing family and a real desire to be one on one with his customers, Phil decided to dial it back and concentrate on one shop at 3230 Motor Cir. in Riverside, California.

J&M Speed Center celebrates "Fifty Years of Speed." (Art Courtesy J&M Speed Center)

installations. When did that phase out?

Lisa: I think it was with the Phil's Muffler Shop. We also built engines, but Dad decided to stop that while he was out drag racing some of our customers because there's a bit of conflict there. He backed off and just wanted to service the customers.

Pat: He also rebuilt Chevrolet distributors and Muncie 4-speeds. He used to go out to the Pomona Swap Meet, pick up transmissions and distributors, bring them back here, and rebuild them.

J&M's well-stocked showroom is filled to the rafters with eye candy for hot rodders. Yes, it's all for sale.

Author: How does J&M feel positioned in this modern marketplace? Is it tough sledding going up against the mass marketers?

Lisa: A few years ago, we were having a real problem with those guys chopping down the prices. It's definitely gotten a lot better, and I think it has to do with SEMA working with the manufacturers.

You know, I don't think people realize that we're all pretty much on the same playing field as far as selling price. Manufacturers have been working with all of us to where we're all equal. We're all selling at the same price. People have that perception that they can get it cheaper online. Well, that's not always true. We keep a huge stock of inventory. I have the same prices if not sometimes better prices on certain things, and you can come in and talk to an experienced person. My guys drag race. My guys have hot cars, and you can have that conversation with them about what you need and then come back in and get it.

Author: Tell us about the J&M Speed Center Memorial Car Show.

Lisa: When Dad died, a lot of people drove their hot rods to the cemetery out of respect for our father. I myself even drove my hot rod instead of jumping into the limo. We buried Dad in a custom-painted, gold-flamed, candy-apple-red casket painted by Gormo and McPeak.

The cemetery suggested that with that many cars in attendance, maybe we should have a memorial car show the following year. I decided that if I'm going to have a car show, we're going to do it here at the shop. That first year, we made up some flyers and handed them out, expecting to get only 50 people. People began preregistering, and suddenly it was up to 50. Then, it was up to 75. Then, suddenly I'm up to 300 cars!

Fortunately, the dealerships around us started clearing off their lots and making room. It turned out to be a great day and a great event. We had 325 cars that first year. Then, we had 415 cars the second year. We've been doing this for 9 years now. Next year will be our 10th anniversary, and all the proceeds are donated to the Southern California Hospice Foundation (SCHF). Since that first show, we've given the SCHF over $90,000.

Editor's note: J&M Speed Center operates California High Performance Warehouse, which is part of the US Performance Buying Group that consists of about 15 different warehouses in the contiguous United States, Hawaii, and Canada.

Loper's Performance Center
Phoenix, Arizona

Address: 916 E. Indian School Rd., Phoenix, AZ 85014
Phone: 602-264-5288
Website: lopersperformancecenter.com

In 1967, Gas coupe and sedan racer Johnny Loper from Phoenix, Arizona, founded Loper's Performance Center, which originally started as a speed shop and a small installation department.

As the business became more and more successful, Loper built it up to become one of Arizona's premier speed

Loper's Performance Center has been in business for 53 years.

shops/performance centers in the state. In fact, at one time, Loper's boasted four shops in the Greater Phoenix area.

When Johnny passed away in 2006, the business was left to his son John Loper Jr., who carried on until 2013, when he sold Loper's Performance Center to Mike Kelly. Kelley, together with a staff of three sales associates (Logan Loper, Neil Briss, and J. C. Henderson), continued on in the Loper's Performance Center tradition of selling brand-name performance parts with fair prices and offering fast and knowledgeable service.

Loper's 5,000-square-foot showroom is jam-packed with Edelbrock, Holley, Comp Cams, Moroso ARP, RPC, Hooker, Doug's Headers, Pro Form, JBA Headers, Fel-Pro, Patriot, Mr. Gasket, NOS, Lokar ZEX Nitrous, Sunoco Race Fuels, and other name brands.

With the exception of machine work, Loper's Service Center can do pretty much everything having to do with performance tune-ups from speed equipment installations to engine builds and complete cars.

In the early 1960s, Johnny Loper burst onto the national stage driving Little Hoss, *an immaculately prepared big-block Chevrolet-engine Anglia that set the record in A/Gas.*

As Loper's business grew, so did the class of cars that Loper campaigned. Although no longer a driver, Johnny raced a Chevrolet Monza, and lastly a Plymouth Arrow in AA/Fuel Funny Car with Eddie Pauling and Tripp Shumake as respective drivers.

In addition to a fully equipped showroom, Loper's also services what it sells. It can also build compete engines and turn-key race cars. (Photos Courtesy Jim Kelso)

So-Cal Speed Shop
Pomona, California

Address: 1357 E. Grand Ave., Pomona, CA 91766
Phone: 909-469-6171
Website: est1946.com

In late 1997, hot rod industry mover and shaker the late Pete Chapouris (from Pete & Jake's fame) got together with Alex Xydias and resurrected the So-Cal Speed Shop brand in Pomona, California.

A genuine California kid, Chapouris's car-building exploits earned him spots on the Route 66, SEMA, and SRMA Hall of Fame award lists. In the mid-1990s, Chapouris teamed up with GM Performance and built four highly publicized LSR cars based on contemporary GM models.

The relaunched and greatly improved So-Cal Speed Shop (now managed by Pete Chapouris IV) offers full builds, chassis fabrication and repairs, steel roadster and coupe bodies, So-Cal front-end kits and components, early Ford front disc brake kits and components, So-Cal custom wheels, Vintique Inc. Ford reproduction parts, lifestyle items from the Alex Xydias Collection, and So-Cal Speed Shop collectibles and gift certificates.

So-Cal Speed Shop stocks virtually every brand-name street rod component and (at the customer's bidding,) is capable of building complete turn-key cars.

So-Cal Speed Shop of Arizona
Phoenix, Arizona

Address: 3427 E. McDowell Rd., Phoenix, AZ 85008
Phone: 602-275-7990
Website: so-cal-az.com

The Phoenix-based So-Cal Speed Shop of Arizona traces its roots back to 1974 as a part-time hobby shop when Frank Streff, Frank Pittenger, and Wally Lassila opened Vintage Ford and Chevrolet Parts of Arizona.

Over the years, Streff and his wife, Mary, bought out the partners, and in 1992, they became the sole proprietors. That same year in October, Brian Benzing was hired to organize the yard and keep the store in running order.

In 2017, Brian and his wife, Angie, purchased the company from its former owners. Digressing somewhat, in 1998, the company obtained licensing rights with So-Cal Speed Shop and reincorporated under the name So-Cal Speed Shop of Arizona.

Inventory includes American Auto Wire, Baer Brakes, Borgeson Universal, Classic Instruments, Dakota Digital, Dennis Carpenter, Dirty Dingo, ididit, Lokar Performance, Ridetech Suspension, Vintage Air, Scott Drake Mustang Parts, and other name brands. As Benzing said, "We're just one big, happy, car-crazy family living under the same roof."

So-Cal Speed Shop is in Pomona, California, across the freeway from Pomona Raceway, home of the NHRA Winternationals and World Finals. Peter Chapouris IV is chief cook and bottle washer. (Photo Courtesy Ansell Aperature)

So-Cal Speed Shop of Arizona and its parent company, Vintage Ford and Chevrolet Parts of Arizona, stocks a complete line of So-Cal Speed Shop street rod components and top name brands in the street rod parts and vintage Ford and Chevrolet restoration business. (Photo Courtesy SCSSOA)

This photo taken with a wide-angle lens shows numerous top name brands in both the street rod and restoration business in stock and ready for shipment. (Photo Courtesy SCSSOA).

Wallace Engine Company
Essex, Maryland

Address: 1801 Eastern Blvd., Essex, MD 21221
Phone: 410-686-9242
Email: wallaceengineco@hotmail.com

Wallace Engine Company is located in Essex, Maryland. Former British Airways aircraft mechanic Robert L. "Bob" Wallace worked at Harbor Field on the flying boats (China Clippers) during World War II and started the business after British Airways closed its terminal in 1948.

Bob leased a bay in Stevens Sunoco Station on Eastern Boulevard in Middle River, Maryland, and called the budding enterprise Bob Wallace Speed.

About three years later (1951), Bob moved into a larger building about a half mile up the road that accommodated more cars. Bob Wallace Speed mainly specialized in hot rods, but the business eventually branched out into stock car racing and worked with several other people to build Dorsey Speedway. With the speedway's completion in late 1950, Wallace was appointed presi-

dent of the Free State Stock Car Association.

The following is a conversation with Wallace Engine Company CEO Brad Wallace (Bob Wallace's son) and author Bob McClurg.

Brad: As a kid, I remember my father would take my brother and I at 5 and 6 years old to the track while it was still under construction, and we would come home with "gifts" for my mother: snakes, turtles, and frogs. Dad stayed involved with the speedway in some function or another for about five or six years until it switched to NASCAR sanctioning.

Author: Did Wallace Machine sponsor any race cars?

Brad: That's was something my dad didn't necessarily do as sponsor. He would generally partner with the owners. In the 1950s and the 1960s, he had an early engine-rental program, or what is known as a commission program. He would supply an engine (generally a Ford or small-block Chevrolet) to either a reputable owner or a talented driver on a commission basis. At any given time, he would have 25 or 30 engines racing at various tracks that he was drawing an income from.

Nowadays, people think that engine leasing programs are a novelty. Well, my dad did that way back in the 1950s and 1960s.

Author: Can you name some of the teams Wallace Engine Company supplied commission engines to?

Brad: The person my dad worked with and had the most success was Melvin Joseph from Georgetown, Delaware. Melvin was a very successful contractor, and he was the builder of Georgetown Speedway and Dover International Speedway.

Melvin had a lot of different drivers. He had one car that ran one of my dad's Ford engines win the beach race at Daytona in 1955 and 1958. Then, he had a car that won the first Sportsman Modified race at Daytona International Speedway with Banjo Matthews driving the car in 1959. Other than being a contractor, Melvin also became a partner in a Ford dealership in Georgetown, Delaware, in 1949, and most all his Sportsman and Modified car numbers were either *49* or *49 Jr.*

My dad also worked close with a local team here in Maryland owned by local garage owner George Hefner. His car numbers were *88* and *88 Jr.* They won the Sportsman Modified National Championships in 1960 and 1961 with Johnny Roberts as driver. Some of the people in this area that used my dad's engines were Roy Slaten, who was pretty well-known on the Eastern Seaboard, Johnny Roberts, Ralph Smith, Ken Marriot, Reg Cagle, and Ralph Moody of Holman & Moody fame.

Moody drove cars for Melvin running Dad's engines. Then, when Melvin went to what is known as the cup cars, he hired my dad as crew chief, but Dad was a little too independent and wanted to stay local and have a broader horizon so to speak.

Author: So, you were brought up in the business?

Brad: During high school, I had one brother, DeWayne, and two sisters, Pam and Dawn, who all worked in some capacity in the business either cleaning parts or learning machine work. After our homework was done and dinner was over, we spent a couple of hours with the business.

Actually, when Dawn was in high school, she ran the cam grinder! She happened to be very popular with the boys because her daddy had a speed shop and she ground the cams. Dad just wanted to give everybody in the family an understanding of a work ethic.

Author: So, you were saying when it came to running Wallace Engine Company that your dad kind of flew solo?

Brad: For a number of years, my dad did all the machining and engine work in the basement of the house. Then, in 1962, he built a new shop on the property that my parents bought in 1951, which is located at 1801 Eastern Blvd. in Essex.

Author: Are you still into mostly circle track stuff?

Brad: Right now, most of what we're doing is muscle car engine restoration and Sportsman racing. [We're also doing] circle track, drags, street rods, street machines, boats, and an occasional aircraft engine. My dad's love and passion was airplanes. Over the years, he would do aircraft engines for a select few. He carried a current inspection ticket so that he could inspect and certify aircraft. He used his airplanes to fly to different tracks. He would fly to certain drag strips and land on the strip. He would buzz the strip first so that the owners would know that it was him. Then, he would land on the strip, get out, grab his toolbox, and go to work.

Author: Did you ever race?

Brad: My dad bought an old stock car for my brother and I when we were still in high school. He gave us a retired race engine to put in it and connived, bribed, or threatened someone to drive the car. My brother and I quickly realized that dirt track racing was a contact sport. As an owner, I didn't like it. All we were doing after school was repairing or replacing a lot of bent sheet metal.

My brother and I were more into drag racing. Dad bought us a 1937 Ford coupe that had been abandoned in a junkyard, and he took the flathead engine out of the dirt track car and put it in the '37. Dad would flat tow the car out to the track (and we're talking about the days when they still had flag starters), he would unhitch the '37, and my brother and sisters would go drag racing.

My parents had to sign a waiver because we were only 13 or 14 years old at the time. We're talking about the early 1960s. My mom would pack a picnic lunch, and we would spend the whole afternoon playing with the drag car. Looking back now, I realize that it gave us an appreciation of learning how to tune a car, learning how to make adjustments, and learning that if you break something, you've got to fix it.

Author: What product lines do you mostly carry at Wallace Engine Company?

Brad: Our premier lines that I carry and use includes Comp Cams products, Edelbrock products, Eagle products, DART, Total Seal Piston Rings, Wiseco pistons, ARP—more or less premium brands of parts.

Author: How badly has your business been affected by the big-box stores?

Brad: Well, there's no denying that it's become a dog-eat-dog world in the speed equipment business. I blame it on the manufacturers for not supporting the people that helped them grow. I mentioned that to Vic Edelbrock a number of years ago. He asked, "How you doing with my products?

I said, "To be honest with you, Vic, I like the product but hate the corporation. The way you've got it set up now doesn't help the people that got you there. In other words, you're not dancing with the people that brought you."

He said, "Oh, we're trying to fix that."

I said, "Well, it's too late."

Back in the day, my dad personally knew and met (at Daytona, Indianapolis, or some other place) Vic's father and Ed Iskenderian. He worked with Cliff Collins from Harmon & Collins Cams to help develop the first roller cam for the Y-block Ford. Back in those days, there wasn't any big network. You just picked up the phone and called them. It's a given that things become global and things grow. You might say the speed equipment business is like a marriage. A lot of them work, but unfortunately, some of them don't, and the marriage between the manufacturers and mail order is still up in the air. I mean, they're married, but they don't get along. The speed shops are the children of the manufacturers, and the children have been hurt.

Author: How big is Wallace Engine Company?

Brad: Right now, our shop measures 1,800 square feet. However, we have three buildings, which includes machining and storage measuring a total of 6,000 square feet.

Author: What would you say is Wallace Engine Company's crowning achievement?

Brad: One of the highlights came near the end of my dad's life. In the year 2000, we did an antique aircraft engine for the people of Thailand. The airplane was called *Miss Siam*, and it was a reproduction/restoration of the first civilian airplane owned in Thailand. It had as much significance to the people of Thailand as the Wright Brothers airplane had to us. We took a vintage World War I Curtis OX-5 engine and overhauled and upgraded it to flying condition. They were going to do a re-creation of a famous early flight in Thailand, and we were invited, but because of security reasons stemming from 9/11, we didn't go. However, we have a copy of a magazine article that was published about the flight.

Author: Any parting comments?

Brad: Whenever I'm asked what kind of work we do, I tell people we do work for people from kitties to kings.

White's Pit Stop
Schererville, Indiana

Address: 330 E. US-30, Schererville, IN 46375
Phone: 708-846-0439 or 888-856-7223
Website: wpsracing.com

The following is a conversation from 2018 with White's Pit Stop Store Manager David White and author Bob McClurg.

Author: How did your father, Jim White, come to open White's Pit Stop?

David: Back in the mid-1960s, my father was a tool and die maker by trade, and my mother, Carol White, who worked at A Member Owned Cooperative Union (AMOCO), had the idea to open their own speed shop.

The original idea was to start it out as a part-time business because they both had good jobs. I remember my father went to tell my grandfather John that he was going to open a speed shop, and my grandfather asked, "What is a speed shop?"

Then, he said, "If you quit your job, I'll never speak to you again."

In 1967, my parents borrowed $2,000 from my mother's credit union at AMOCO and started the business. Within a month, my father lost his job when things slowed down in the tool and die–making industry, and that's how White's Pit Stop turned into a full-time business.

Author: A full-time family business?

David: A full-time family business. That's what it's always been. Dad was always into cars. He always had hot rods back in the 1950s and 1960s, and that was his dream to start his own speed shop.

Author: Where was the first White's Pit Stop located?

David: It was located at 132 E. Sibley Blvd. in Dalton, Illinois, and was probably about 700 square feet in total. Within a month of opening, business was absolutely booming. It was a dream come true for my parents, so much so that my mother quit her job at AMOCO, came to work full time at the speed shop, and brought another AMOCO worker along with her.

We filled the place with speed equipment rather quickly and were bursting at the seams. There was a small vacuum cleaner repair shop next door to us, and we ended up taking over their spot as well.

The following year [1968], we got the village to approve an aluminum addition to the backside of the building that actually went right up to the alleyway behind us, and we used that building for storage."

Author: How long were you at the original location?

David: Actually, we had two locations. We had the Sibley Boulevard building and we opened a speed shop–only store in Tinley Park, Illinois, on South Dalton Avenue. By 1970, my mother and father decided that we needed a larger building, and they bought a car dealership in South Holland, Illinois, that had just gone out of business. That was quite a jump going from 1,200 square feet to 30,000 square feet (complete with outer buildings and much, much more).

The South Holland location was absolutely beautiful. It had a great big showroom, where we had a race car on a turntable inside the showroom. We had custom motorcycles inside the showroom. Vans were becoming popular, so we had a Van Alley, where we had a custom van on display, and we had Street Rod Alley with a street rod on a turntable; all of this was inside one building. Once we made our move to the South Holland facility, with it being so large, people were willing to travel. So, we closed the Tinley Park store. We always said that South Holland was a one-stop

For 53 years, Jim and Carol White and their family have carried on the Midwest tradition of fair prices and knowledgeable service at White's Pit Stop.

shop location. At the time, we pretty much had it all.

Author: How long were you at the South Holland location?

David: We stayed at that location until 1990, a total of 20 years. We had our ups and downs, but we always had something to fall back on because of our diversity. There were times in the 1980s when race car parts sales were way down. Tracks were closing; it just wasn't the same action out there as it was in the 1960s and 1970s. But then the chopper thing began to grow. When that tailed off, parts for custom vans became the big thing. Then, race cars came back again, so we were always busy at some point, but not in all departments.

Author: Did you have your own installation department?

David: We didn't have an installation department on the premises, but we were always close to custom shops where we could refer customers to do the work. In fact, many of those installation shops became great clients of ours, and some of them would return the favor and send us new customers.

Author: When and why did you move from the South Holland location?

David: In 1990 we moved to Lansing, Illinois, into an 11,000-square-foot facility there. It was located right on the Illinois-Indiana border. We did downsize a little bit but continued to carry car and motorcycle accessories—not as much street rod products anymore, and vans had totally tapered off. We had our grand opening on Fourth of July weekend, and business began booming again.

We were located directly off Interstate 80, and we had seven expressways coming in within a 5-mile radius, which was probably the busiest expressway access point in the entire county. You virtually had access to any state in the country right from our doorstep. I remember Linda "Miss Hurst Golden Shifter" Vaughn was at our grand opening. She was out there in the parking lot on the Hurst Olds greeting the crowd, and when I go to the SEMA or PRI Shows, she remembers me to this very day!

Author: How many employees did White's Pit Shop have?

David: At that point, we had approximately 30 employees working for us, most of them being salespeo-

White's Pit Stop is divided into two departments: the speed shop and custom motorcycle parts. It's your one-stop shopping location for serious gearheads

ple in the car and motorcycle departments.

Author: And your entire family works here?

David: All of my immediate family has worked here: my father, Jim; my mother, Carol; my younger brother, Steve; and my younger sister, Cathy. We've also had aunts, uncles, and cousins working here, so it's pretty much been a wide array of the family. No third-generation employees yet. My brother, Steve, has one son, but the rest of the third generation of the White's Pit Stop family are all girls, so we'll just have to wait and see.

Author: Is White's Pit Stop a WD on any product lines?

David: Within months of our grand opening, I believe we had every manufacturer knocking on our door to be a WD. We didn't have the internet then, but we were the biggest thing going. Our name was on the *Chi-Town Hustler* Funny Car. Our name was on Jack Ditmar's *The Mini Brute* Opel Altered. We were on the *Shake, Rattle, and Run* '57 Chevy gasser. To my recollection, we sponsored close to 50 cars. You couldn't go to a drag strip in the Midwest and not see our name. I think that was a key to our success.

White's Pit Stop's sponsorship of Farkonas, Coil, & Minnick's 1969–1971 Chi-Town Hustler Dodge Charger and Challenger AA/FCs vaulted the company's name to the national stage.

Author: How about catalogs and the internet?

David: We did do catalogs in the 1970s and 1980s, but now we have an internet base, wpsracing.com. It's not a huge website, but we do offer around 60,000 to 70,000 items, which seems like a lot, but when you're fighting against the giants out there that have somewhere along the way bypassed us, that has made things more difficult in these times.

Author: Let's talk about how White's Pit Stop got into the custom motorcycle parts business.

David: In 1969, we decided to also start selling custom motorcycle parts. When we started our motorcycle business, every manufacturer in the world was knocking on our door, begging us to put in their line. I remember we would have two or three semi-trucks full of parts pull up on a Friday night, and by Saturday morning at 9 a.m., we would have customers from 10 or 12 states there waiting for us to open the doors of those trailers to buy both motorcycle and custom car parts. By the end of the day, all three trailers would be empty.

Author: David, you had mentioned "fighting against the giants." Would you care to further elaborate on the subject?

David: Any of the big-name speed equipment or motorcycle parts manufacturers were in the parts business in the 1960s, 1970s, or 1980s, and we bought parts directly from them. As I said before, every manufacturer in the world came knocking on our door begging us to put in their line. Nowadays, you have these giant internet businesses that do hundreds of millions of dollars in business online, and all of a sudden, they [the internet businesses] become their [the manufacturers'] babies.

The smaller walk-in businesses that still exists today don't get the same treatment that we got back in the old days. Sometimes I feel like the manufacturers need to remember where their roots are, how they got started, where the customers go whenever they have a problem, and where they go to when they need something on a given weekend and they need it right now. We've always tried to be that place throughout all the years that was able to service the customer with quality products, great pricing, and knowledgeable salespeople. We've had some of the same customers coming here or calling us for information for the last 50 years and want to deal with someone who's not only knowledgeable but also personable.

Author: Do you get many customers who pick your brain about a certain part, leave, and walk back through the door with the same product that they bought through one of the mass marketers and say, "I can't figure out how this goes on correctly"?

David: We get more of that now than we did in the old days. I can certainly understand the ease of online shopping. I do it myself with some personal items, but we'll match any price that's out there, and we also offer ease of shipping to other states. So, to answer your question, we try to offer just as much value and service as we can. But again, it's not always easy competing with the giants.

Author: What's the farthest destination you've ever shipped product to?

David: We've shipped all around the world. In the 1980s, prior to the internet, we would run three full-page ads in *Hot Rod, Street Rodder, Easyriders,* and *Street Chopper* magazines so that our ads would be seen worldwide. I remember nights getting out of school and coming into work because we got a shipment of 150 tires that we had to put away because we were getting another load of 150 sets of headers coming in the very next day.

Author: Tell us about your car shows.

David: My father started the car show thing back in the 1960s. At the time, we only had parking for about eight cars. We would choose eight race cars and street rods and put them out in front of our store on Sibley Avenue in Dalton. When we moved to South Holland, we had a huge parking lot, and we would have everybody come out for those shows. We would have 50 to 60 race cars on display that we sponsored. Now, and this is the truth, people would walk two miles to get to that show. We would give away things. I remember Big Willie Robinson came to one of our shows. Linda Vaughn was there at another. Austin Coil would come out. All kinds of people would come to our shows.

Now that we're located in this mall, we have our shows when most of the surrounding businesses are closed. Every Wednesday, we have big cruise nights and attract 250 cars weather permitting. We have parking for close to 700 cars, and the businesses that are located next to us, the restaurants and the bars, just love us. Last year, when we put on our US-30 Drag Strip show, we had over 5,000 people in attendance.

Author: Do you do charity work with these shows?

David: We have done charity work in the past. We've donated quite a bit of money to local foundations in the motorcycle industry. We've made donations to the American Diabetes Association, the Northwestern (Heart) Transplant program, the Cancer Society of America, and others.

Author: What has being in this business done for you as far as making you a better person or shaping your life?

David: I was born in 1963, so I was there when the business opened in 1967. I remember being a small child, and my mother, father, and a couple of family members would make our own gaskets before there were actually gaskets being commercially made for all the vehicles. We had a setup in the basement of our house where we custom made gaskets for all the racers.

I also remember going to the drive-in with my mom and dad. My father, Jim, is a member of Vintage Tin Street Rods and had a variety of cars. One I fondly remember was a mid-1950s Studebaker that had a parachute on the back. My mother, Carol, owned both a 1968 Shelby GT500 and a 1972 Corvette, so my whole life has basically revolved around cars, motorcycles, and boats—just speed in general.

Being in this business, I've met so many great people, whether its manufacturers or just going to SEMA and seeing all the people that knew my mother and father from the early days and recognized the name. Spending time with them was fun. Back in the old days, hot rodders and motorcyclists didn't always have the best reputation. However, when you work with them on a daily basis, well, there's nobody else in the world I would rather spend my time with, and I think my entire family would say the same thing.

Winner's Circle Speed Shop
Joliet, Illinois

Address: 207 N. Scott St. Joliet, IL 60432
Phone: 815-727-6631
Website: winnerscircle.com

The following is a conversation with Winner's Circle Speed Shop Co-founder Jim Bingham and author Bob McClurg.

Author: When was Winners Circle Speed Shop founded?

Jim: Our first day of business was June 1, 1970. My partner, Don Wiley, and I met at Lang Auto Parts, a division of Lang Buick in Kankakee, Illinois. He and I both worked at the parts counter at Lang Auto Parts prior to his taking the job as counterman at the Buick dealership. It was during that time that we started talking about the idea of getting a speed shop started. It was an ideal matchup. Don was into drag racing, and I was more into circle track racing, so we figured we had all the bases covered.

Author: And you shared your ideas with your boss?

Jim: Yes. I met with owner Rollin Lang and told him

Winner's Circle Speed Shop is located in Joliet, Illinois, and as far Midwest speed shops go, Winner's Circle is one of the best.

Winner's Circle CEO Jim Bingham is rightly proud of his business. This place is stocked to the rafters with every brand-name speed part under the sun.

what I thought we [Lang Auto Parts] should do, but he said he wasn't interested. At the time, I was a young stallion and raring to go, so I talked Don into joining me in the partnership.

Author: But things didn't go quite as smoothly as planned?

Jim: Like I said, we opened our first store June 1, 1970. A week later, Rollin changed his mind and opened up a speed shop across the street from us. In less than a week, the town of Kankakee, Illinois, had two speed shops operating. It was like gundown at sundown. Rollin had a lot of money but no real experience at marketing speed equipment. We had the knowledge and a lot of desire but no money. It was a real paradox. What that did was make us work that much harder. We survived and eventually expanded the business.

Author: And they didn't?

Jim: No. They stayed in business for about a year and a half.

Author: What was the address of that first store?

Jim: It was 275 W. Court St., Kankakee, Illinois, but the building is no longer there. They built a CVS Pharmacy on that lot.

Author: When did you open your second location?

Jim: We opened our second store up at 207 N. Scott St. in Joliet, Illinois, on May 1, 1971, which was exactly 11 months from the day we opened the first store, and we've been going strong at that location ever since.

Author: What were your primary product lines at the stores?

Jim: We've had Holley, Hedman, Iskenderian, Mickey Thompson, Crane Cams, and Edelbrock. Those companies were all with us from the start. Then, we added companies such as Earls, Competition Cams, and others as

they came into the marketplace. Offhand, I would say that the header, camshaft, and carburetor lines have been and continue to be our core business.

Winner's Circle stocks virtually every brand name under the sun.

Do you want tires? Winner's Circle Speed Shop has all the name brands from Mickey Thompson to BFG and Hoosier.

Friendly service, good prices, and a knowledgeable and informed staff are the epitome of a top-gear speed shop, and Winner's Circle Speed Shop has all three.

Winner's Circle Speed Shop uses the original brick-and-mortar building next door that once housed the business for warehouse storage, and the place is loaded.

Author: Was Winner's Circle Speed Shop involved at all in the mail-order catalog business?

Jim: We did some mail order, but we were mostly eyeball-to-eyeball and have been for 46 years. We also printed store flyers back in the day, but now with the internet, we don't do that anymore. We have two websites: winnerscircle.com and winnerscircleonline.com.

I guess you could say our No. 1 mission statement would have to be that we pride ourselves in making sure that the customer doesn't waste his money. For example, when a customer comes in and asks for a carburetor, we're going to quiz him or her about what they are going to do with it. We want to make sure that the part number and model they asked for is the right fit for the particular application before they leave the store.

Author: So, is Winner's Circle Speed Shop still a family-run business?

Jim: Yes. In fact, we have three generations working here. There's myself and my wife, Linda, my son Rodney and my two grandsons Noah and David.

Author: Has Winner's Circle Speed Shop sponsored any name race cars over the years?

Jim: At one time, we had our name on several cars. For example, in the later years we sponsored John Lawson's Top Alcohol Funny Car, and there have been others.

Author: Any other honors?

Jim: In 2015 we were inducted into the SEMA Hall of Fame, which we consider to be quite an achievement. But when it comes to the day-to-day business, the bottom line is that we're here to serve our customers and provide them with fair pricing and knowledgeable service.

Author: Any parting comments?

Jim: Yes. Support your local speed shop!

APPENDIX
SPEED SHOPS PAST AND PRESENT

In deciding to undertake a general listing of all the speed shops past and present, I didn't realize what I was getting into. There is no master list to reference, and many of these shops have been gone for a long time or never had much presence to begin with.

For many of the older shops, I referenced the previously mentioned *Popular Mechanics* speed shop guide book. I went through my extensive collection of drag racing photos and recorded all of the speed shops that sponsored cars. I scoured 25 years of magazines for advertising, including *Drag News, National Dragster, Hot Rod, Cars Magazine, Car Craft,* and a boatload of other car magazines. Of course, I googled "speed shop listings by state," and finally, I asked all of my old racing colleagues to mine memories from their brains. The following list is a result of that work.

The space available to feature the shops is limited, but I wanted a list to include the shops that were not included in the previous text. I am fully aware that I will have missed a shop or three. For any shops that I missed, I apologize. Hopefully, I found most of them.

A

Abe's Automotive Service, Chicago, Illinois
Advance Muffler Co., Cambridge, Massachusetts
Advanced Engineering, Los Angeles, California
Advanced Engineering West, Ontario, California
Alamo Speed Shop, Austin, Texas
Alamo Speed Shop, San Antonio, Texas
Al's Speed Shop, Albuquerque, New Mexico
Alec's Auto Parts, West Palm Beach, Florida
Almquist Engineering, Milford, Pennsylvania
Allen Speed Equipment, Hamilton, Ohio
Ak Miller's Garage, Pico Rivera, California
Akron Speed Shop, Akron, Ohio
American Motorsport, Rockford, Illinois
American Speed Enterprises, Moline, Illinois
Anaheim Speed Engineers, Anaheim, California
Andy's Auto Supply, Santa Cruz, California
Ansen Automotive Engineering, Gardena, California
Antelope Valley Speed Center, Antelope Valley, California
Arrow Speed Shop, Pomona, California
Arizona Speed & Sport, Tucson, Arizona
Arndt's Garage, La Fayette, Indiana
Art's Muffler Shop, Idaho Falls, Idaho

Al's Speed Shop, North Aurora, Illinois
Al & Jerry's Speed Shop, Stamford, Connecticut
Albert's Speed Shop, Dayton, Ohio
Atlanta Speed Shop, Atlanta, Georgia
Art's Muffler Shop, Idaho Falls, Idaho
Ashville Speed Equipment, Ashville, North Carolina
Ault & James Speed Shop, Dayton, Ohio
Austin Speed Shop, Austin, Texas
Auto Discount Company, Burbank, California
Auto Equipment Company, Denver, Colorado
Auto Ron's, Davenport, Iowa
Auto Speed Shop, Dover, Delaware
Automotive Engineering, Chicago, Illinois
Automotive Specialties, El Cerrito, California
Automotive Supply Center, Casa Grande, Arizona
Austin Speed Shop, Austin, Texas
A&V Products, Whittier, California

B

Hugh Babb Co., Atlanta, Georgia
Carl Badami Speed Equipment, Kansas City, Kansas
Bailey Brothers Speed Shop, American Canyon, California
Baker Motor Company, Delta, Colorado
Baker's Service, Willits, California
Balboa Radiator & Auto Parts, Los Angeles, California
George A. Barker, Washington, D.C.
H.C. Barnes, Rockford, Illinois
Barbour's Speed Shop, Parma, Nebraska
Baron's Engineering, Los Angeles, California
Barret Automotive Speed Shop/Auto Repair, Lee's Summit, Missouri
Barnett Automotive Performance, Atlanta, Georgia
Battle Creek Hot Rod Shop, Battle Creek, Michigan
Battersby Automotive, Covina, California
Bay View Speed Shop, Milwaukee, Wisconsin
Baxley's Speed Shop, Windham, Maine
Raymond Beadle's Blue Max Performance Center, Dallas, Texas
Bennett Auto Service, Eaton, Illinois
Beattie Motors, Lompoc, California
Belond Exhaust, Los Angeles, California
Bell Auto Parts, Los Angeles, California
Bell & Gaines, Modesto, California
Berlin's Speed Equipment, Nashville, Tennessee
Art Benjamin's, Stockton, California
Betz Speed & Color, Anaheim, California
Big Ed's Speed Shop, Alexandria, Virginia
Bings Speed Shop, Santa Rosa, California
Bill Esser's Mail Order Speed Shop, Chicago, Illinois

Bill's Hollywood Shop, Baltimore, Maryland
Bill's Speed Shop, Jackson, Michigan
Bill's Speed Shop, Rockdale, Illinois
Bing's Garage/Bing's Speed Shop, Santa Rosa, California
Bishop Motors, Hollister, California
Keith Black Racing Engines, South Gate, California
Blair's Speed Shop, Pasadena, California
Blue Max Speed Shop, Midland, Texas
Bob's Speed Shop, Santa Barbara, California
Bob's Speed Shop, Mobile, Alabama
Bob's Speed Shop, Stockton, California
Bob's Speed Shop, Zanesville, Ohio
Bobb's Hot Rod Shop, Abiline, Texas
Jimmy Bou Speed Shop, San Juan, Puerto Rico
Brand-X Racing Ent., San Antonio, Texas
Branford Auto Service, Branford, Connecticut
Brayton's Automotive, St. Helena, California
Brekke & Sons Speed Shop, Albert Lea, Minnesota
Briedgers Speed Shop, Tatamy, Pennsylvania
Broadway Auto Sales, East Chicago, Indiana
Brook's Garage, Decatur, Georgia
Brougher Speed Shop, Pittsburgh, Pennsylvania
Brougher & Sons Speed Shop, Reno, Nevada
Bryant's Speed Shop, Harlingen, Texas
Bud's Race Shop, Pueblo, Colorado
Bud's Speed Shop, Niagara Falls, New York
Budlong Motorsports, Albuquerque, New Mexico
Dick Burns Speed Shop, Carolina Beach, North Carolina
Buttersby Automotive, Covina, California
Bruce's Speed Shop, Rockaway, New Jersey
David Buckmiller Co., Modesto, California
Buddy's Speed Shop, Woodridge, Virginia
Burns Racing Equipment, Bell, California
Burt's Motor Sales, Denver, Colorado
Red Byron Speed Shop, Atlanta, Georgia
B-Boys Auto Parts/B-Boys Speed Shop, Lake City, Washington
B&K Auto Shop, Canaan, Connecticut
B&D Motors, Stockton, California
B&D Speed Shop, Matoon, Illinois
B&H Speed Shop, Erie, Pennsylvania
B-M Speed Shop, Rochester, New York
B&R Garage, Tucson, Arizona
B&R Speed & Custom, Roanoke, Virginia

C

Caesar's Auto Supply, Santa Barbara, California
Cal-Race Speed Equipment & Manufacturing Co., Alhambra, California
California Automotive Parts Co., Los Angeles, California
California Discount Warehouse, Long Beach, California
Calhoun Speed Shop, Alexandria, Virginia
California Speed & Sport, New Brunswick, New Jersey
California Speed Merchants, San Leandro, California
Cal's Racing Parts, Hilo, Hawaii
Cambra Speed Shop, Orange, California
Camp Hill Auto Parts, Camp Hill, Pennsylvania
Don Campbell's Speed Shop, Cincinnati, Ohio
Camp Hill Auto Parts, Camp Hill, Pennsylvania
Cannon Engineering, North Hollywood, California
Capitol Speed Parts, Baltimore, Maryland
Capitol Speed Shop, Sacramento, California
Car & Fleet Racing, Tulsa, Oklahoma

Carl's Hollywood Muffler Shop, Kansas City, Missouri
Car Shop Speed Shop, Moline, Illinois
Car Shoppe, Oklahoma City, Oklahoma
Car Shoppe Inc., Shreveport, Louisiana
Carl Carpenter's, Concord, Massachusetts
Carl's Powerhouse, Pensacola, Florida
Carpenter Equipment Co., Wichita, Kansas
CASH Auto Parts, South San Francisco, California
Central Jersey Speed & Marine, Garwood, New Jersey
Champion Speed Shop, South San Francisco, California
Lee Chapel's Speed Shop/Broken Wheel Auto Salvage, San Fernando, California
Chapman Automotive, Chicago, Illinois
Charlie & Tom's Service, Guadalupe, California
Tom Cherry Automotive Engineering, Muncie, Indiana
Chet Herbert's Speed Shop, Anaheim, California
Chevrolet Brothers, St. Louis, Missouri
Chasco Speed Equipment, Indianapolis, Indiana
Chuck's Muffler Shop, Flagstaff, Arizona
Chittum's Automotive, Miami, Florida
City Cycle & Speed Shop, Salina, Kansas
Clark Headers, Downey, California
Clay Smith Racing Cams, Long Beach, California
Clearlake Speed, Seabrook, Texas
CNC Auto, Manassas, Virginia
Conney's Speed Shop, Cleveland, Ohio
Codner Motor Service, Denver, Colorado
Jimmy Coi, Joliet, Illinois
Competition Specialties, Dallas, Texas
Comstock Speed & Power, Chesapeake, Ohio
Al Cooper Speed Shop, Seattle, Washington
Costa Mesa Speed Center, Costa Mesa, California
Cooper's Auto Supply, Bridgeport, Connecticut
Cooper's Speed Shop, Allentown, Pennsylvania
County Speed Shop, St. Louis, Missouri
Crane Engineering, Hallandale, Florida
Creative Cycle Engineering & Auto Speed, College Park, Maryland
Culver City Speed Shop, Culver City, California
Custom Auto Parts, Marietta, Pennsylvania
Custom Car Supply, Amarillo, Texas
Custom Racing Equipment, San Francisco, California
Custom Speed Enterprises, Livonia, Michigan
Custom Speed Equipment, Chillicothe, Illinois
Custom Speed Equipment Service, Lancaster, Pennsylvania
Custom Auto Parts, Marietta, Pennsylvania
C&C Automotive, Manassas, Virginia
C&T Automotive, Sherman Oaks, California
C&W Auto Parts, Berkley, California
Cole & McCarthy, Oakland, California
Competition Auto, Danbury, Connecticut
Competition Sales, Houston, Texas
Contrell's Garage, Tampa, Florida
County Speed Shop, St. Louis, Missouri
Custom Auto Accessories, Jamestown, New York
Custom Automotive, Dallas, Texas.
Custom Automotive, Washington, D.C.
Custom Equipment Co., Honolulu, Hawaii
Custom Racing Accessories, Detroit, Michigan
The Car Shop, Springville, New York
C.C. Speedway Inc., Corpus Christi, Texas

D

Dahlgreen's Custom Auto, Mesa, Arizona
Dauernham's Speed Shop, Indiana
Danny's Auto Parts, Long Beach, California
Day & Night Speed Center, Tacoma, Washington
Dearborn Speed Shop, Dearborn, Michigan
Jim Deist Speed Shop, Burbank, California
Detroit Racing Equipment, Detroit, Michigan
Frankie Del Roy, Patterson, New Jersey
Don's Speed Shop/Don Garlits High Performance World, Tampa, Florida
Don's Speed Shop, Newington, Connecticut
Don's Speed Shop, Guelph, Ontario, Canada
Don's Hot Rod Shop, Tucson, Arizona
Don's Speed Shop, Southaven, Mississippi
Don's Speed Shop, Memphis, Tennessee
Don's Speed Shop, Edison, New Jersey
Donnie's Speed Shop, Tulare, California
Dos Palmas Machine Shop, San Jose, California
Douglas Automotive Engineering, San Francisco, California
Douglas Speed Sport Center, Silver Spring, Maryland
G.E. Douglas, San Francisco, California
Dick's Automotive Machine & Speed Shop, Hudson, New York
Dick Landy Industries (DLI), Northridge, California
Dino's Speed World, Woodside, New York
Dirty's Speed Shop, Seagoville, Texas
Dragon's Speed Shop, New Lenox, Illinois
Dryer Racing Equipment, Indianapolis, Indiana
Duffie's Speed Shop, Chicago, Illinois
Duffy's Performance Inc., Red Bank, New Jersey
Duke's Speed Spot, Filer, Idaho
Malcolm Durham Racing Enterprises, Washington, D.C.
Dynamic Racing, Alamorgordo, New Mexico
Dynotech, Ridgewood, Queens, New York
D&R Speed Shop, Pittsburgh, Pennsylvania

E

East End Speed Shop, Toronto, Ontario, Canada
Edmunds Equipment Company, Huntington Park, California
East Coast Speed Shop, Cranston, Rhode Island
Eastern Auto Supply Co., Los Angeles, California
Eastern Speed, Pachogue, New York
Eastern Speed Parts, Camden, New Jersey
Eastern Speed Shop, Cockeysville, Maryland
Eastside Speed Shop, Ellenville, New York
Ed's Auto Supply, San Rafael, California
Eddie Meyer Engineering Co., West Hollywood, California
Edelbrock Equipment Co., Torrance, California
Empire Auto Supply, Colorado Springs, Colorado
Ray Erickson Speed Service, Chicago, Illinois
Erie Speed Shop, Erie, Pennsylvania
Esco Auto Supply, Waterloo, Iowa
Bill Esser's Mail Order/Speed Shop, Chicago, Illinois
Elm City Auto Company, New Haven, Connecticut
Ellis Speed Shop, San Angelo, Texas
Evans Speed Equipment, El Monte, California
Everybody Auto Supply, Bell Gardens, California
Excel Automotive, Osceola, Indiana
Excel Automotive Engineering, South Bend, Indiana

F

Fairbanks Speed Shop, Fairbanks, Alaska
Fat Boys Speed Shop, Broken Arrow, Oklahoma
Ed Fell Speed Shop, Holicong, Pennsylvania
Fontana Speed Shop, Fontana, California
Federal Parts, Burlingame, California
Fillip Brothers, San Angelo, California
Fisher Speed Equipment, Louisville, Kentucky
Flash Automotive, Albuquerque, New Mexico
Florida Speed Equipment, Jacksonville, Florida
Forsyth Hot Rod & Auto Supply, Hesperia, California
Bill France's Garage, Daytona Beach, Florida
Frank's High Speed & Power Equipment, Long Island, New York
Frankie Del Roy's Speed Shop, Patterson, New Jersey
Fulmer's Speed Shop, Lake City, Utah
F&F Speed Shop, Brooklyn, New York
F&M (Ford & Mercury) Hot Rod Parts, Denver, Colorado
F&S Equipment Company, Inglewood, California

G

Gaines & Moreno Distributing, Silver Spring, Maryland
Gambardella Racing & Performance, Williamston, New Jersey
Gateway Service, Daytona Beach, Florida
Gem Speed Shop, Warrington, Pennsylvania
Gemler's Performance, Erie, Pennsylvania
Gene's Hobby & Speed Shop, Endwell, New York
Gene's Speed Equipment, Mishawaka, Indiana
Gene's California Accessories, Miamisburg, Ohio
George's Speed Shop, Dayton, Ohio
Bob Gerhard's Speed Shop, East Del Poso Heights, California
Glasgo & Son, Akron, Ohio
GOR DEN Automotive, Buffalo, New York
Gordon's Custom Service, Burlington, Iowa
Gotha Speed Specialists, Harvey, Illinois
Grado Speed Shop, Deming, New Mexico
Grabowski's Speed Shop, Riverside, California
Gramjo Speed Shop, Broken Arrow, Oklahoma
Grand Auto, Chicago, Illinois
Grand Prix Speed Shop, Tulsa, Oklahoma
Grancor Automotive Specialties, Chicago, Illinois
Gratiot Auto Supply, Detroit, Michigan
Jim Green's Performance Center, Monroe, Washington
Greenberg Auto Parts, Birmingham, Alabama
Greg's Speed Shop, Waupaca, Wisconsin
Greenberg Auto Parts, Birmingham, Alabama
Raymond Godman's Speed Shop, Memphis, Tennessee
Gotelli Speed Shop, So San Francisco, California
Goodies Speed Shop, San Jose, California
Goodies Supply Shop, Knox, Indiana
Goody's Speed Shop, Baldwinsville, New York
Gulf Auto Supply, Tampa, Florida
Gunderman Speed Shop, Indianapolis, Indiana
G&D Speed East, Ronkonkoma, New York
G&M Performance Inc., Hyattsville, Maryland

H

Hagen Speed Shop, Akton, Ohio
Halibrand Engineering, Torrance, California
Hall's Speed Shop, Wichita, Kansas
Happy Auto Parts, Madison, Illinois

Don Hardy Race Cars, Floydada, Texas
Hart Automotive, Orange, California
Harper Garage, Chicago, Illinois
Hartman's Hot Rod Shop, Lancaster, New York
Harry's Hot Rod, Auto & Truck Parts, Grand Prairie, Texas
Harry's Rod Shop, Dover, New Jersey
Hashim Automotive, Bakersfield, California
Hawaii Racing, Simi Valley, California
Herb's Hot Rod Shop, St. Louis, Missouri
Jim Herbert's Performance World, Sacramento, California
Chet Herbert (Cams) Speed Shop, Anaheim, California
Heidelberg Speed Shop, San Bernardino, California
Herrick's Speed Equipment, Toledo, Ohio
Hi-Speed Power Equipment, Valley Stream, Long Island, New York
Hi-Speed Service, Toledo, Ohio
High Speed Equipment Co, Latrobe, Pennsylvania
Highland Park Hot Rod Shop, Highland Park, Michigan
Hinch's Speed Shop, Eureka, California
Hines Speed Shop, New Castle, Indiana
Hirschfield Automotive, Los Angeles, California
Hi-Speed Auto Parts, Bell, California
House of Speed, Painesville, Ohio
House of Chrome, La Cruces, New Mexico
House of Chrome, Paterson, New Jersey
Hossie's Speed Shop, Newport Beach, California
Hot Rod Barn, High Point, North Carolina
Hot Rod Shop Inc., Rockford, Illinois
Hot Rod Supply Store, Kenosha, Wisconsin
Hollister Avenue Auto Parts, Bridgeport, Connecticut
Hollywood Auto Accessories, Dayton, Ohio
Hollywood Automotive Accessories, Detroit, Michigan
Hollywood Speed Shop, Dearborn, Michigan
Hollywood Speed Shop, Redding, Pennsylvania
Hop Up Shop, Bellefontaine, Ohio
Howard Auto Parts, Shreveport, Louisiana
Howard's Cams, Los Angeles, California
Howard's Speed Shop, La Farmerville, New York
Vic Hubbard Speed Shop, Hayward, California
Hurlock's Speed Shop, Wilmington, Delaware
Huntington's Automotive, Oroville, California
Honest Charley Speed Shop, Chattanooga, Tennessee
Hot Rod & Racing Equipment, Boston, Massachusetts
Houdek Speed Shop, Madison, South Dakota
Hub Auto Parts, Detroit, Michigan
Hurlock's Speed Shop, Wilmington, Delaware

I

Indianapolis Speed Shop, Indianapolis, Indiana
Jim Inglese Weber Carburetion, Lake City, Florida
Inglewood Speed Shop, Inglewood, California
Inland Automotive, Riverside, California
Island Performance & Off Road Inc., Kona, Hawaii

J

Jack's Muffler & Speed Shop, Richmond, Indiana
Jack's Speed Shop, Boston, Massachusetts
Jack's Speed Shop, Houston, Texas
Jake's Speed Shop, New Orleans, Louisiana
Jay's Motor Service, New Castle, Indiana
JBA Speed Shop, San Diego, California
JEGS, Columbus, Ohio

Jenkin's Competition, Berwyn, Pennsylvania
Jersey Devil Speed Shop, Cherry Hill, New Jersey
Jim Green's Performance Center, Lynwood, Washington
Jim's Speed Supply, Salem, Oregon
Johnnie's Speed Shop, Birmingham, Alabama
Johnnie's Speed & Chrome, Buena Park, California
Wayne Johnston Garage, Sperry, Indiana
Eddie Joyner Speed Equipment, Ashville, North Carolina
J's Speed Shop, San Diego, California
Jerould's Speed Shop, National City, California
Jerry's Speed Shop, Fords, New Jersey
J.C. Whitney, Chicago, Illinois
Jim's World of Speed, Florida
Bob Joenck Speed Shop, Santa Barbara, California
Jones Garage, Tallahassee, Florida
Tommy Johnson's Mail Order Parts, Ottumwa, Iowa
J&J Speed Shop, Granite City, Illinois
J&J Speed Shop, Hyattsville, Maryland
J&L Muffler, Ventura, California
J&M Speed Center, Riverside, California
J&S Speed Center, Westminster, California

K

Kamm Service, Salinas, California
Kar Belt Speed & Custom, Toronto and Montreal, Canada
Karbelt Speed Shop, Lethbridge, Ontario, Canada
Kalman's Automotive, Burbank, California
Kar Shoppe, Oklahoma City, Oklahoma
Ted Kessler Speed Shop, Buffalo, New York
Ken-Russ Speed Equipment, Saginaw, Michigan
Kenz & Leslie, Denver, Colorado
Bob Kell's Speed Shop, Richmond, Virginia
Keystone Automotive, Exeter, Pennsylvania
Kincaid Performance, Albuquerque, New Mexico
King Sales Co, Jacksonville, Florida
Klingman Speed Shop, Mt. Upton, New York
Kustom Speed Enterprises, Livonia, Michigan
K&G Speed Associates, Haverton, Pennsylvania

L

L.A. Speed, Downey, California
Langford Racing & Muffler Co., Wichita Falls, Texas
Lamarr's Speed & Custom, Hurst, Texas
Lane Automotive, Water Volute, Michigan
Langhorne Speed Shop, Langhorne, Pennsylvania
Leader Automotive Inc., Troy, Michigan
Le Blanc's Speed Engineering, Monte Vista, California
Lee's Auto Supply, Tucson, Arizona
Lee's Speed Shop, Oakland, California
Lee's Speed Shop, Richmond, Virgina
Lee's Hot Rod Shop, Tucson, Arizona
Leo's Racing Equipment, Chicago, Illinois
Lelienthal's Speed Shop, East Randolph, New York
Luur's Hot Rod Shop, Romeoville, Illinois
Livernois Auto Parts, Detroit, Michigan
Loper's Speed Shop, Phoenix, Arizona
Lord's Speed Shop, Bakersfield, California
Lou Feger's Speed Shop, Delano, Minnesota
Lynwood Chassis/Lynwood Welding Co., Wilkes Barre, Pennsylvania
L&S Speed Shop, Houston, Texas

M

Mac Racing Equipment, San Jose, California
Mach Engineering, New Orleans, Louisiana
Mac's Roadster Shop, Tampa, Florida
Mac's Speed Shop, Charlotte, North Carolina
Manhattan Speed Shop, Manhattan, New York
Mar-Ken Speed Specialties, Richland, Washington
Marshman Racing Equipment, Yerkes, Pennsylvania
Joe Martin's Speed Shop, Chattanooga, Tennessee
Marvel Auto Stores, Brooklyn, New York
Masters Automotive, Los Angeles, California
Maryland High Performance, Silver Spring, Maryland
Max Speed Nitrous Supply, Carson, California
McCoy's Speed Shop, Canton, Ohio
McGurk Engineering Co., Inglewood, California
Mercury Carburetor Service, Chicago, Illinois
Jack Merkel Automotive, Islip, Long Island, New York
Megger's Roadster Shop, Washington, D.C.
Eddie Meyer Engineering, West Hollywood, California
Miami Speed Shop, Massapequa, New York
Midwest Auto Parts, Berkley, Michigan
Midwest Speed & Power, Milwaukee, Wisconsin
Midwest Racing Equipment, Cleveland, Ohio
Mike's Performance Center, Wall Township, New Jersey
Mike's Speed Shop, Charlotte, North Carolina
Mike's Speed Shop, Warwick, Rhode Island
Mile High Automotive Service, Denver, Colorado
Ken Miles Speed & Custom, Lexington, Kentucky
Millen's Automotive Service, Antioch, California
Miller's Automotive Service, Antioch, California
Miller's Speed Parts, Hartford, Connecticut
Miller's Speed Shop, Los Alamos, New Mexico
Mitchell's Muffler Shop, Pasadena, California
Minnesota Automotive Specialties, St Paul, Minnesota
Moedel's Speed Equipment, Toledo, Ohio
Mo's Speed Shop, Dallas, Georgia
Mom's Speed Shop, Redwood City, California
Frank Morgan Marysville, California
Motor Accessories & Parts, Phoenix, Arizona
Motor City Speed Shop, Detroit, Michigan
Motorpace, Chicago, Illinois
Motion Performance Inc., Baldwin, Long Island, New York
Motiva Performance, Albuquerque, New Mexico
Moon Equipment Co., Santa Fe Springs, California
Mooneyes Inc., Santa Fe Springs, California
Motor Accessories & Parts, Phoenix, Arizona
Murray's Auto Parts, Miami, Florida
The Original Mr. Norm's Performance Inc., Rochester Hills, Michigan
Mr. Speed, Camden, New Jersey
M&T Automotive Service, Ft. Lauderdale, Florida

N

National Speed Center, Canoga Park, California
National Speed, Wilmington, North Carolina
National Speed & Power Equipment Company, Queens, New York
Nationwise Rod Shop, Columbus, Ohio
Navarro Racing Equipment, Glendale, California
Neal's Speed Shop, Austinberg, Ohio
Nelson's Speed Shop, Greenville, Michigan
Netzel's Auto Repair, Chicago, Illinois
Newark Speed Specialties Co., Newark, New Jersey

New England Auto Racing Equipment, Belmont, Massachusetts
New England Speed, Boston, Massachusetts
Newman's Racing & Custom Equipment, Akton, Ohio
New York Speed & Machine, Staten Island, New York
Newhall Speed Center, Newhall, California
Newhouse Automotive, East Los Angeles, California
Nibbett Brothers, Frankford, Delaware
Nicken's Brothers Racing Engines, Conroe, Texas
Nickey Chevrolet Speed Shop, Chicago, Illinois
Nickey Performance, Loves Park, Illinois
Nickle's Speed Shop, Warwick, Rhode Island
Nigrachi Motors, Hillsdale, New York
Norm's Automotive, East Moline, Illinois
North Bay Speed Shop, Santa Rosa, California
North Judson Motor Sales, North Judson, Indiana
Northside Service, Atlanta, Georgia
N&S Automotive, Royal Oak, Michigan

O

Ogden Speed Shop, Ogden, Utah
Okie Speed Shop, Quinton, Oklahoma
Orday Speed, Burbank, California
Olney Speed Parts, Philadelphia, Pennsylvania
Karl Orr Speed Shop, Culver City, California
Bob Oslecki, Atlanta, Georgia
Ohio Speed Center, Akton, Ohio
Ohio Speed Shop, Niles, Ohio
Old Crow Speed Shop, Westlake Village, California
Otie's Automotive, Akron, Ohio

P

Packard's Speed Equipment, Providence, Rhode Island
Paramount Speed Equipment, Paramount, California
Park City Speed Shop, Bridgeport, Connecticut
Parr Automotive, Oklahoma City, Oklahoma
Pacemaker Automotive, Calgary, Alberta, Canada
Performance Automotive Wholesale, Chatsworth, California
Performance Evolution, Smyrna, Delaware
Performance Centers of America, Rahway, New Jersey
Performance Unlimited, Los Angeles, California
Perris Speed Parts, Kalamazoo, Michigan
Perry's Speed Equipment Co., New York, New York
Pfieffer's Speed Shop, Albany, New York
Phil's Speed Shop, Orange, California
Pike's Peak Speed Shop, Colorado Springs, Colorado
Ben Pilla Speed Shop, Philadelphia, Pennsylvania
Ed Pink Racing Engines, Van Nuys, California
Plaza Speed, Burlington, Vermont
Porter Custom Auto Service, Colorado Springs, Colorado
Potvin Automotive Equipment Company, Anaheim, California
Power Engineering, St. Louis, Missouri
Powers Speed Shop, Manhattan, Kansas
Powerhouse Speed Equipment, San Francisco, California
Proformance Speed Shop, Franklin Park, Illinois
Punisher Performance, Albuquerque, New Mexico
P&P Speed Shop, Oxford, North Carolina

Q

Queen City Speed Shop, Toronto, Canada
Quincy Automotive, Santa Monica, California

R

Racing Equipment Company, Alhambra, California
Racing Equipment Company, Hollydale, California
Racing Equipment Company, Marion, Ohio
Raceway Equipment, Cleveland, Ohio
Ralph's Muffler Shop, Indianapolis, Indiana
Ramchargers Racing Engines, Taylor, Michigan
Ralph's Speed Shop, Eatontown, New Jersey
Ralph's Speed Shop, Richmondville, New York
Ramchargers, Speed Shops, Taylor, Michigan
Jim Rathman Inc, Miami, Florida
Raymond Goodman's Speed Shop, Memphis, Tennessee
Red Barn Speed Shop, Ludlow, Massachusetts
Reding Service Center, Loxley, Alabama
Reichenbach Brothers, Chicago, Illinois
Reece's Speed Shop, Kannapolis, North Carolina
Riverside Speed Shop, Oklahoma City, Oklahoma
Roberts Motors, Atlanta, Georgia
Rocco & Cheaters Speed Shop, Birmingham, Alabama
Robison's Speed Shop, Naval Base, South Carolina
Rod Shop, Beltsville, Maryland
Rollin Stone Racing, Dallas, Texas
Ron's Speed Shop, Honolulu, Hawaii
Roger's Motor Service, Bell, California
Rose Haven Speed & Power, Middletown, Connecticut
Roy's Custom Shop, Washington, D.C.
Roy's Custom Hot Rod & Speed Shop, Toronto, Ontario, Canada
Roy's Speed Shop, Hellam, Pennsylvania
R&E Racing, Lancaster, California
R&R Manufacturing, Anderson, Indiana

S

Salem Speed Shop, Salem, Oregon
Salt Point Garage, Carndera, California
San Angelo Auto Supply, San Angelo, California
Santa Ana Speed Center, Santa Ana, California
San Bernardino Racing Equipment, San Bernardino, California
Sachse Rod Shop, Sachse, Texas
Scotty's Muffler, San Bernardino, California
Mike Scorva, Jamaica, New York
Seaboard Speed Shop, Lynn, Massachusetts
Service Center, Van Nuys, California
Art Schedler's Engine Building, Fresno, California
Schleiper's Speed Shop, West Allis, Wisconsin
Segal Automotive Products, Los Angeles, California
Shell Automotive, West Los Angeles, California
Shifty's Speed Shop, Modesto, California
Joe Silnes Service, Indianapolis, Indiana
Six Pack Performance, Albuquerque, New Mexico
Skagg's Racing Equipment, Spokane, Washington
Skippy's Hot Rod Shop, Detroit, Michigan
Sleeper's Speed Shop, Costa Mesa, California
Smart Automotive, San Antonio, Texas
Frank Smith Speed Equipment, Paterson, New Jersey
Smith Auto, Minneapolis, Minnesota
Smith Speed Shop, Cincinnati, Ohio
Smith & Jones Racing Equipment, Long Beach, California
Smith's Speed Shop, Eaton, Ohio
Smitty's Speed Shop, Dayton, Ohio

Smitty's Speed Shop, Terre Haute, Indiana
So-Cal Speed Shop, Burbank, California
Sonic Speed Racing, Queenstown, Maryland
Southern Speed Racing, Tupelo, Mississippi
Southside Automotive, Chicago, Illinois
Sox & Martin Inc., Burlington, North Carolina
Spencer Speed Shop, Belleville, New Jersey
Speed Auto Parts, Pittsburgh, Pennsylvania
Speed-O-Motive, El Monte, California
Speed Barn, Kinderhook, New York
Speed City, Kenosha, Wisconsin
Speed & Custom Supplies, Titonka, Iowa
Speed & Power Equipment, Big Springs, Texas
Speed Engineering, Shelbyville, Indiana
Speed Equipment Co., Andalusia, Pennsylvania
Speed Equipment Company, Euclid, Ohio
Speed Equipment Wholesalers, Renton, Washington
Speed Equipment World, Dallas, Texas
Speed Parts Inc., Paterson, New Jersey
Speed Specialists, Compton, California
Speed & Power Equipment, Buffalo, New York
Speed Sport Power, Lowell, Indiana
Speed Trends, Roland Heights, California
Speed Unlimited, Morningside, Maryland
Speed World Speed Shop, Baldwin, Long Island, New York
Speedway Automotive, Lincoln, Nebraska
Speedway Auto Parts, Waukegan, Illinois
Speedworld Automotive, Elmhurst, New Jersey
Speedway Automotive Parts, Wilmington, California
Speedwin Automotive Power Equipment, Long Island City, New York
Speed's Hobby Shop, Montebello, California
Speed Zone Performance Center, Los Angeles, California
Sports Car Center, Sausalito, California
Standard Motor Parts, North Sacramento, California
Steve's Speed Shop, Pryor, Oklahoma
Steve's Hot Rod Shop, Upper Montclair, New Jersey
Ed Stewart, San Diego, California
Steel City Auto Supply, Pueblo, Colorado
Steel Lizard Performance, Albuquerque, New Mexico
Strode Garage, Mequon, Illinois
Strum Auto Supply, Davenport, Iowa
SRI Performance, Brownsburg, Indiana
Southern Automotive, McDonough, Georgia
The Super Shops Performance Centers Inc., San Bernardino, California
Sunset Auto Supply, Long Beach, California
Stan's Shop, Corona Del Mar, California
Star Automotive, Compton, California
Steve Kanuika Speed Shops, Abington, Pennsylvania
Steve's Speed Shop, Little Rock, Arkansas
Stewart's Speed Automotive, Hillsdale, New York
S-K Speed, Islip, Long Island, New York
Southern Automotive, Collierville, Tennessee
Roy St. Clair's Garage, Sweet Home, Arkansas
Straightaway Speed Shop, Scotia, New York
Shreve Automotive, Shreveport, Louisiana
Strick's Auto, Washington, D.C.
Stiles Performance, York, Pennsylvania
Sumar Enterprises, Terre Haute, Indiana
Summit Racing Equipment, Tallmadge, Ohio
Sutter's Speed Shop & Auto Salvage, Madison, Wisconsin

Supreme Speed Shop, Toronto, Ontario, Canada
S&M Automotive, New Rochelle, New York
S&S Parts Co., Falls Church, Virginia
S&S Racing Equipment, Philadelphia, Pennsylvania
S&S Speed & Customs, Danville, Illinois
S&S Speed Shop, Brooklyn, New York
S&W Race Cars/S&W Speed Shop, Spring City,
   Pennsylvania

T

Talbot Brothers Speed Shop, Nashville, Tennessee
Taylor & Ryan, Whittier, California
Texas Speed & Performance, Georgetown, Texas
Tennessee Speed Sport, Goodlettsville, Tennessee
The Car Shop Inc., Houma, Louisiana
The Car Shop Inc., Moline, Illinois
The Neighborhood Garage, Jersey City, New Jersey
The Hot Rod Shop, Youngstown, Ohio
The Hot Rod Shop, Detroit, Michigan
The Hot Rod Shop, Evansville, Indiana
The Rod Shop, Beltsville, Maryland
The Speed Shop, Flint, Michigan
The Speed Shop, Palmer, Alaska
The Speed Shop, Selbyville, Delaware
The Speed Shop, Wilmington, Delaware
The Speed Spot, Paducah, Kentucky
The Super Shops Inc., San Bernardino, California
Team C Performance, Long Beach, California
Teton Speed, Camden, New Jersey
Tip's Speed Shop, San Antonio, Texas
Toad's Speed Shop, Walls, Mississippi
Tognotti Speed Shop, Sacramento, California
Top Speed Flathead Specialists, Queens, New York
Total Performance, Mt. Clemens, Michigan
Total Performance Inc., Wallingford, Connecticut
Town & Country Speed Shop, Lethbridge, Ontario,
   Canada
Traditional Speed & Custom, Pittsfield, New Hampshire
Trenton Speed Shop, Trenton, New Jersey
Trella's Speed Parts, Meridian, Connecticut
Trojan Automotive, Calgary, Alberta, Canada
Tropical Auto Supply, Miami, Florida
Mickey Thompson Speed Shop, North Long Beach,
   California
Thweatt's Automotive, Los Angeles, California
TPS Automotive, Aurora, Illinois
Wally Taylor's Speed Sport, Birmingham, Alabama

U

Urzi's Drive In Auto Supply, San Jose, California
USA-1 High Performance, Grand Rapids, Michigan
USA Performance Center, Houston, Texas
Up To Speed Auto, Tulsa, Oklahoma

V

Paul Vanderley Automotive, Biloxi, Mississippi
Valley Ford Parts Co, North Hollywood, California
Valley Accessories & Muffler Shop, Glendale, California
Van's Speed Shop, Des Moines, Iowa
Van Senus Auto Parts, Hammond, Indiana
Van Iderstine Speed Shop, Camden, New Jersey
Louis Vermill Speed Shop, Calasrig, California

Red Vogt's Garage, Atlanta, Georgia
Von Essers, Chicago, Illinois
Vic Hubbard's Speed Shop, Hayward, California
Vic's Speed Shop, Girard, Ohio
Von Fritch Automotive, Garden Grove, California
Bill Von Esser, Chicago, Illinois

W

Waltman's Speed Shop, Harrisburg, Pennsylvania
Washington Auto Parts, Indianapolis, Indiana
Warner's Speed Shop, Binghamton, New York
Warshowsky & Co., Chicago, Illinois
Wayne County Speed Shop, Wayne County, Indiana
Wayne Manufacturing Company, Guadalupe, California
Wayne's Speed Shop, Costa Mesa, California
Wayne's Automotive, Water Volute, Michigan
Walden Speed Shop, Pomona, California
Wallace Engine Co., Essex, Maryland
Sid Waterman Racing Engines/Waterman Racing
   Components, Brownsburg, Indiana
West Speed Shop, Rose Hill, Massachusetts
West Coast Racing Equipment, Culver City, California
Western New York Speed Shop, Buffalo, New York
Western Performance, Glendale, California
Westside Performance Speed Shop, Los Angeles,
   California
Wheeler Dealer Speed Shop, Edmonton, Alberta, Canada
Jack Wheeler Speed Shop, Ames, Iowa
White's Pit Stop, Schererville, Indiana
White's Racing Shop, Atlanta, Georgia
Wilcox Brothers Shop, Pueblo, Colorado
Wilkins Speed Equipment, Caldwell, Idaho
Ed Winfield, Glendale, California
Whipp Brothers, Redding, California
Wise Speed Shop, St. Louis, Missouri
Winner's Circle Speed Shop, Joliet, Illinois
World of Speed, Half Day, Illinois
Woods Speed Shop, Pacific Grove, California
Woody & Ken's Speed Shop, San Rafael, California
Wynn Speed Shop, Richland, Mississippi

Y

Yearwood Performance Center, Albuquerque, New
   Mexico
Yearwood Street & Customs, El Paso, Texas
York Speed Shop, Roseville, California
York Speed Shop, St. Elma, New York
Youngstown Speed Shop, Youngstown, Ohio
Yuill Brothers Direct, Reno, Nevada

Z

F.E. Zimmer Co., Encino, California
ZIP Auto Supply, Compton, California

Numeric

555 Auto Parts, Stanton, California
10,000 RPM Speed Equipment, Torrance, California

Additional books that may interest you...

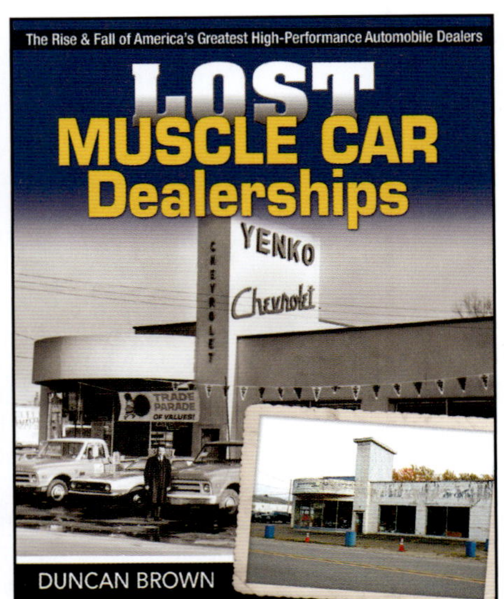

LINDA VAUGHN: The First Lady of Motorsports *by Rob Kinnan and Linda Vaughn* This is the most comprehensive gathering of photography ever assembled on Linda Vaughn. Through her 50-plus years in motorsports, Linda has lived it all, been everywhere, and met everyone. Whether you are simply a fan of Linda or a collector of Linda Vaughn memorabilia, this will be the premier piece in your collection. 8.5 x 11", 224 pgs, 508 photos, Hdbd. ISBN 9781613252321 **Part # CT555**

LOST MUSCLE CAR DEALERSHIPS *by Duncan Brown* Revisit the glorious 1960s and early 1970s, when cars from Reynolds Buick, Yeakel Chrysler-Plymouth, Mel Burns Ford, and others created the lasting muscle car legacy through innovative advertising and over-the-top performance. Detailed text and more than 250 historic photos and illustrations provide the history of those dealerships. 8.5 x 11", 192 pgs, 360 photos, Sftbd. ISBN 9781613254516 **Part # CT644**

ISKY: Ed Iskenderian and the History of Hot Rodding *by Matt Stone* This book tells the whole story of Ed "Isky" Iskenderian, from his pre-war Lake Muroc and car club activities and then his military service, to starting a small business fabricating parts and making cams in the back of a rented shop, and then selling cams to other rodders. 7 x 10", 208 pgs, 253 photos, Hdbd. ISBN 9781613252901 **Part # CT570**

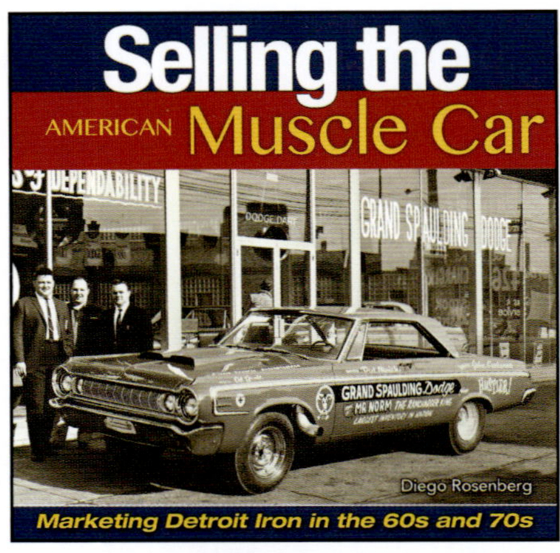

SELLING THE AMERICAN MUSCLE CAR: Marketing Detroit Iron in the 1960s and 1970s *by Diego Rosenberg* Examines the tactics and components used by manufacturers in waging war against one another in the muscle car era. Manufacturers poured millions into racing programs, operating under the principle of "Win on Sunday, Sell on Monday." From racing to commercials to print ads, from dealer showrooms to national auto shows, each manufacturer had its own approach in vying for the buyer's attention, and gimmicks and tactics ranged from comical to dead serious. 10 x 10", 192 pgs, 435 photos, Hdbd. ISBN 9781613252031 **Part # CT542**

✓ **Find our newest books before anyone else**

✓ **Get weekly tech tips from our experts**

✓ **Featuring a new deal each week!**

Exclusive Promotions and Giveaways at www.CarTechBooks.com!

www.cartechbooks.com or 1-800-551-4754

Bud Anderson
UNION SERVICE
7708 BROADWAY

GOOD

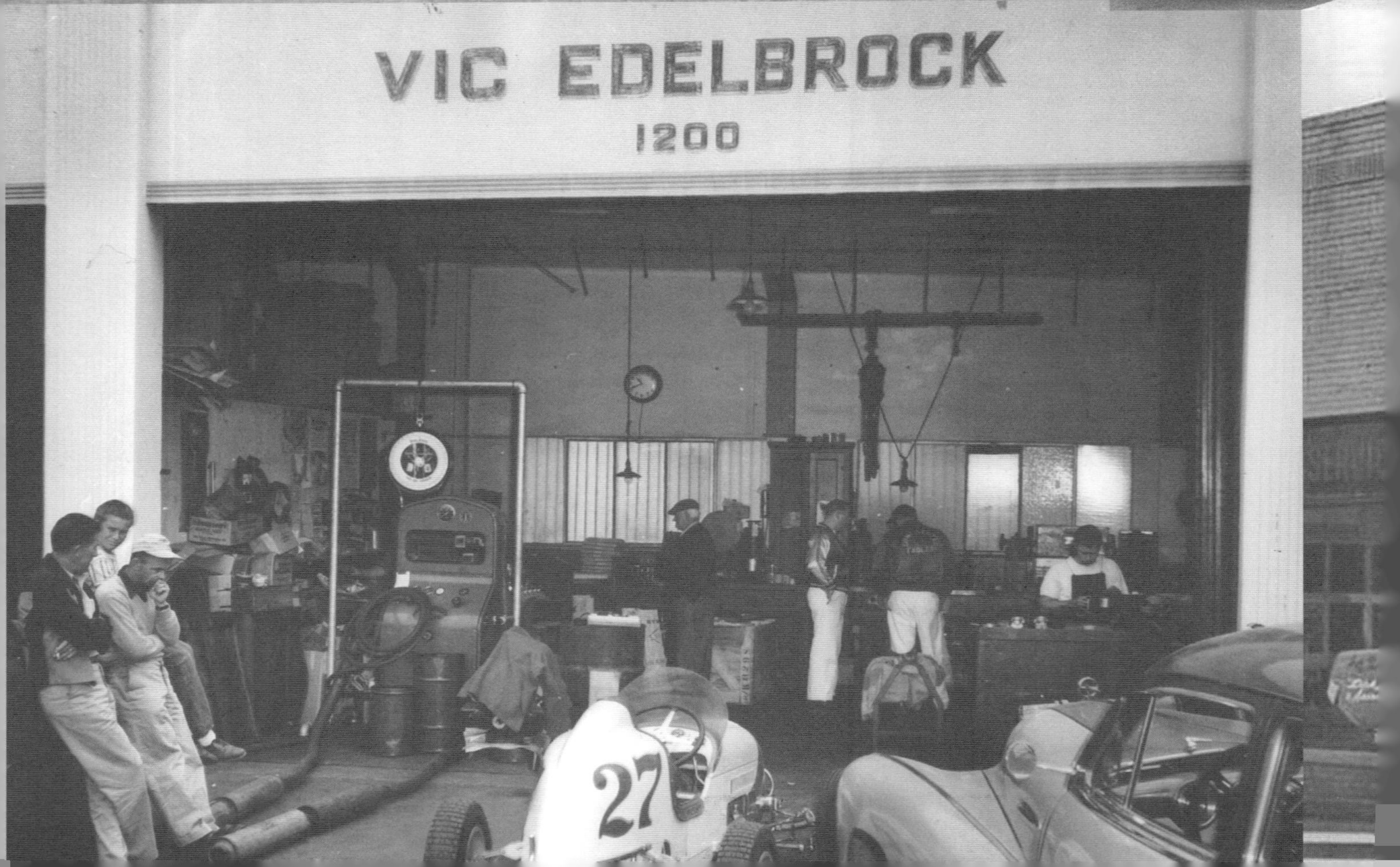

VIC EDELBROCK
1200

27